A Brief History of Pakistan

A Brief History of Pakistan

James Wynbrandt

Foreword by Fawaz A. Gerges

Facts On File
An imprint of Infobase Publishing

A Brief History of Pakistan

Facts On File, Inc.
An imprint of Infobase Publishing
132 West 31st Street
New York NY 10001

Library of Congress Cataloging-in-Publication Data

Wynbrandt, James.
    A brief history of Pakistan / James Wynbrandt; foreword by Fawaz A. Gerges.
        p. cm.—(Brief history)
    Includes bibliographical references and index.
    ISBN-13: 978-0-8160-6184-6
    ISBN-10: 0-8160-6184-X
    1. Pakistan—History. I. Title.
    DS382.W96 2008
    954.91—dc22   2008008921

Facts On File books are available at special discounts when purchased in bulk quantities for businesses, associations, institutions, or sales promotions. Please call our Special Sales Department in New York at (212) 967-8800 or (800) 322-8755.

You can find Facts On File on the World Wide Web at http://www.factsonfile.com

Text design by Joan M. McEvoy
Cover design by Semadar Megged/Jooyoung An
Map design by Sholto Ainslie

Printed in the United States of America

MP Hermitage 10 9 8 7 6 5 4 3 2 1

This book is printed on acid-free paper and contains 30 percent postconsumer recycled content.

CONTENTS

LIST OF ILLUSTRATIONS

LIST OF MAPS

FOREWORD

Since September 11, 2001, Pakistan has emerged as a pivotal front in the U.S. war on terrorism. Its very political destiny is distorted by the unfolding global struggle against al-Qaeda and other militants, such as the Taliban, who have found a home in Pakistan. With the exception of Iraq, the global confrontation against jihadists and their Taliban allies is playing itself out on the streets of Pakistan's crowded urban centers and tribal areas more than in any other country.

From a U.S. perspective, Pakistan's active participation in the fight against terrorism dwarfs everything else in importance, including human rights, socioeconomic equity, and democracy; like its other Arab and Muslim neighbors, Pakistan has become important for the wrong reasons.

A flood of publications and media commentary on Pakistan focuses almost exclusively on Pakistan's commitment to the war on terrorism and the security of its nuclear arsenal. Little is being written or aired on the daily struggle of Pakistan's impoverished population, the endemic corruption of its ruling elite, and the influential role played by the security forces. Little is being said about how America's war on terrorism exacerbates internal tensions and cleavages in the country and deepens and widens the divide between religiously oriented activists and other social and political forces; it also provides the security apparatus with a powerful rationale to suspend constitutional checks and balances and marginalize civil society. America's war on terrorism could easily destabilize the country and turn it into a failed state.

But as James Wynbrandt shows in his incisive history, the Islamic Republic of Pakistan occupies a position of historic and strategic importance as a crossroads of religious and political ideologies that have influenced international events. Although Pakistan is a young nation, born after World War II, Wynbrandt reconstructs the historical continuity of the Indian subcontinent as a cradle of spiritual awakening and intercivilizational fertilization between East and West; Pakistan stands at the center stage of world culture and politics. Before and after achieving independence in 1947, what is now Pakistan was and is a prize and participant in the Great Game of global power politics. More often than not, official Pakistan sided squarely with the Western and U.S. camp against the Soviet Union, communism, and socialism in the developing countries; it has been, on the whole, a faithful ally of the West, though with high costs to state-society relations and institutional consolidation.

A Brief History of Pakistan offers plenty of food for thought about the birth of a nation and the pains and trials accompanying birth pangs and social and political development; it provides a comprehensive, accessible account of the people and events that have shaped Pakistan's character and identity. By doing so, *A Brief History of Pakistan* enables readers to make sense of bewildering news reports about Pakistan's domestic, regional, and international policies.

The author covers all facets of social, political, economic, and cultural life in Pakistan. It is one of the most comprehensive and balanced texts available—an informative introduction to a highly pivotal Muslim country.

Wynbrandt deserves credit for concluding his book with a set of critical questions, not reductionist or simplistic answers. One of the most fundamental challenges facing leaders of Pakistan is their commitment to the rule of law and human rights. Will Pakistan's fragile democracy survive the onslaught of militarism and take deep root in the country's political soil? Or will the repeated bouts of military rule end Pakistan's democratic experiment and plunge it into the permanent throes of authoritarianism? Will Pakistan's myriad communities overcome their ethnic and sectarian differences and coalesce into a greater whole? To what extent will the country's ruling elite address the poverty and lack of education that still afflicts so many of their people? Will they tackle the endemic corruption that has undermined faith in its governmental institutions? Will Pakistan and India find a peaceful way out of their deadly nuclear embrace? Will Pakistan escape politico-economic dependence on its great power patrons and fully integrate into the world economy and society?

Only time will tell if the leaders of Pakistan meet those challenges. Reading Wynbrandt's book helps us to be more informed, as he said, in considering the next chapter of Pakistan's history.

—Fawaz A. Gerges

INTRODUCTION

Situated in the northwest corner of the Indian subcontinent, the Islamic Republic of Pakistan occupies a position of historic importance. Its strategic location, its role in the birth of civilization, and its influence as a crossroads of political and religious ideologies have kept it at the forefront of world events. Geographically, present-day Pakistan has long been a gateway between Eurasia and the subcontinent and between East and West. Its culture and history have been enriched by the countless invaders, traders, and settlers who have been a part of the region's past. Some, like Alexander the Great and his army, merely passed through but left a lasting mark. Others, such as the Arab armies spreading the word of Islam and the British who imposed the ways of the West, became an integral part of the region's culture and character. Some of humankind's greatest works of art and architecture, of verse and word, were created here. Today the region again has taken an outsized role on the world stage: It is a linchpin in the global struggle against terrorism, a cauldron in the heated conflict between secular and theocratic rule, a poster nation for the struggle between autocracy and democracy, and a nuclear power whose relations with its neighbor India have made this one of the most unstable regions in the world.

Most Westerners know little about this region or nation. Though an independent state only since 1947, its homeland has a history unique from the rest of the subcontinent it shares with India. Here the Indus Valley Civilization, one of the world's earliest and greatest, flourished contemporaneously with the Egyptian and Mesopotamian empires. The region has also been a cradle of spiritual awakening. Here Hinduism was born in the aftermath of the Aryan migration into the region that began about 1700–1500 B.C.E. A scant distance away, the Buddha received enlightenment, founding a religion and philosophy that transformed the region. Islam, which would have an even greater impact, gained its foothold in Asia in what is today Pakistan. And the Sikh religion can trace its roots to the region as well.

One of the most fabled dynasties in history, the Mughals, a regime so rich and powerful that today its name is synonymous with those attributes, ruled from here, as over the years have robber princes, religious zealots, and ruthless vagabonds. During the British occupation, what is now Pakistan became a principal theater in the Great Game played by the West against Russia for regional dominance. Pakistan's role as geopolitical fulcrum grew after independence, alternately aligning itself with the East, the West, and as an independent in its foreign policy. It often stood by the United States as an important ally during the cold war. It was from here in 1960 that the U-2 spy plane shot down by the Soviet Union took off. Pakistan also helped turn Afghanistan into the Soviet Union's Vietnam after their occupation in the 1980s. In the new century it has become a major battleground in a new global struggle, pitting terrorism fueled by radical Islam against progressive and secular social forces.

Politically and economically, Pakistan has had a troubled domestic history. Periods of civilian rule marked by corruption and political grid-lock have alternated with years of military dictatorships. Financially stunted at birth, Pakistan has seen improvements in the economy since, which though impressive, have still left the vast majority of its citizens living in poverty. And the dilemma over the role of Islam in government and society continues to stoke contention.

Today these issues have again brought Pakistan to a crossroads. How it resolves these dilemmas will have repercussions far beyond the nation's own borders. The goal in this work is twofold: to provide an accessible account of the people and events that have shaped what is now Pakistan, and to provide a foundation of understanding so readers can be better informed in considering the next chapter of its history.

1

THE LAND AND ITS
EARLY HISTORY

Few nations have as rich or complex a history as the Islamic Republic of Pakistan. Its destiny has been shaped first by its geography. The violent collision of continents that formed this land threw up great mountains that made this corner of the subcontinent a place apart. The sequestered, fertile environment of the Indus Valley nurtured one of the world's first great civilizations. Yet the passes that breached the guarding massifs served as funnels through which invaders both hostile and friendly have poured for millennia. These outsiders have been the second great ingredient in Pakistan's destiny. They brought their traditions, ideas, and ways of life, all of which have become part of the nation's identity. This chapter surveys the nation's physical landscape, its first civilizations, and the provinces that today reflect the historical divisions that have made Pakistan's past and present so vibrant, dynamic, and tumultuous. The chapter also introduces the Aryans, the first of the interloping groups that would shape the history and heritage of what is today Pakistan. The Aryans' experiences here would give rise to the Hindu religion, which continues to be a force with a powerful effect on the region today.

Geology and Geography

Before the continents as we know them came to be, the land that is now Pakistan and India were part of Gondwanaland, an ancient supercontinent. Some 200 million years ago Gondwanaland began to break apart, torn by tectonic forces. Over time the supercontinent's remnants formed landmasses including Africa, South America, Antarctica, Australia, the Arabian Peninsula, and the Deccan Plateau, or the Indian subcontinent. At the time the Eurasian landmass was separated from the disintegrating supercontinent by a long, shallow sea. The streams and rivers that drained what we know now as Asia deposited sandy runoff into this basin while the calcified remains of sea creatures likewise accreted. Over time these deposits became sandstone and limestone. After Gondwanaland splintered, the future Deccan Plateau moved north, toward Eurasia. As the two landmasses drove toward each other, the sandstone and limestone that had carpeted the sea floor between them was thrust upward. At least 45 million years ago the landmasses met.

The submarine deposits ultimately became the fold mountains that now form a ridge across southern Asia from the Mediterranean to the Pacific. The contorted, visible bowing of the sedimentary rocks from which the mountains formed bears evidence of the compression caused by the slow tectonic collision. The peaks reach their highest point at the north end of the subcontinent. These are the Himalayan Mountains. Marine fossils found on Mount Everest, the world's highest peak, attest to its undersea ancestry. The Himalayas and its offshoots, which flank southward on the east and west sides of the subcontinent, have served as a natural barrier to both the elements and humanity, separating the lands that became Pakistan and India from the rest of Asia. By 11 million B.C.E. migration of animals from and to the subcontinent had ended.

Topography

To its south, west, north, and northeast, natural barriers of mountain and sea have sheltered Pakistan. But to the southeast, the land spills out into the Deccan, the vast peninsular homeland of India. The Indus River, historically the lifeblood of what would become Pakistan, and its tributaries drain the plateau. Though its terrain is varied throughout the country, Pakistan can be divided into three basic geographic areas: the northern highlands, the Baluchistan Plateau, and the Indus River plain. These areas can be further segmented into the Salt Mountains and the Potwar Plateau, north of the Indus Plain; the Western Mountain region (composed of the mountains in western Baluchistan); and the Upper and Lower Indus River Plain (roughly corresponding with the present-day provinces of Punjab and Sind, respectively).

The Arabian Sea forms Pakistan's southern border. Its western border is shared with Iran in the south and Afghanistan in the north. Along Pakistan's northern border the slim arm of Afghanistan's Wakhan region separates Pakistan from Tajikistan. China's territories of Xinjiang and Tibet lie on Kashmir's border to the north and east. To Pakistan's east

THE INDUS RIVER

The Indus River is Pakistan's principal waterway. Known as the Sindhu in Sanskrit, the Sinthos in Greek, and the Sindus in Latin, it has been integral to Pakistan's culture and history, yet paradoxically gave its name to India, Pakistan's neighbor and rival. Its headwaters are in the Himalayas in Tibet. It flows northwest through Gilgit-Baltistan in Kashmir before turning south and traversing the length of Pakistan, its total length between 1,800 and 2,000 miles (2,900–3,200 km). The river gave birth to one of the world's first great civilizations, the Indus Valley Civilization. The course of the river has changed since ancient times as a result, it is believed, of earthquakes and other shifts of the land. Today it is damned at Tarbela, at the foothills of the Himalayas between Peshawar and Rawalpindi. Shortly after Pakistan became independent in 1947, India, which was given the region with the river's headwaters by the British, shut the flow of water to the Indus, creating a grave crisis that took more than 15 years to resolve.

The Indus River, Pakistan's principal waterway, has played an integral role in the region's history and culture. (Courtesy Pakistan Tourism Development Corporation)

are the Indian states of Punjab and Rajasthan. The Thar Desert serves as a barrier between these Indian lands and Pakistan. Despite the absence of any other barriers between these two states, historically they developed independently.

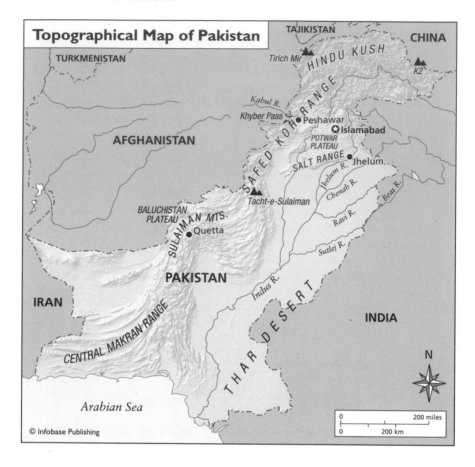

The Himalayas

The Himalayas (meaning "the abode of snow" in Sanskrit) extend in a long bow some 1,500 miles (2,400 km) across the north end of the subcontinent, from the Indus River in the west to the Brahmaputra River (which originates in Tibet and ends in the Bay of Bengal) in the east. Four major ranges comprise the Himalayas: The Outermost, or Sub-Himalayas, are the farthest south. Its low hills, known as the Siwaliks, rise to about 3,000 feet (914 m). To the north lie the Outer, or Lesser Himalayas, whose peaks average 14,000–15,000 feet (4,267–4,572 m). Behind the Pir Panjal Range of the Outer Himalayas rise the Central, or Great Snowy Himalayas. In the Karakoram Range, permanently snow-covered peaks average 20,000 feet (6,096 m) in height and include Mount Everest, the world's loftiest peak (29,028 feet; 8,848 m), and in Pakistan-controlled

4

K2, the world's second-highest peak, is in Pakistan-controlled Kashmir. (Courtesy Pakistan Tourism Development Corporation)

Kashmir, K2, the world's second highest peak (28,251 feet; 8,611 m). North of Pakistan's border is the Ladakh Range, or Inner Himalayas.

In Pakistan's northwest is the Hindu Kush (Hindu Killer) Range, extending from the high plateau of Pamir, sometimes called the Roof of the World, into Afghanistan. Tirich Mir is its highest peak (25,289 ft.; 7,708 m).

The Himalayas have had important historical and climatological effects on Pakistan and the entire subcontinent. They capture moisture-laden winds from the Arabian Sea (and to the east, the Bay of Bengal) and create rain that irrigates the region. In winter they block cold winds from North and Central Asia, keeping the subcontinent's climate mild. Spring melt-offs provide water. Historically the Himalayas and contiguous ranges have also formed a barrier protecting the region from the incursions of outsiders. Several passes along Pakistan's western and northern borders provide routes in and out of the nation and have been key transit points throughout recorded history.

Western Mountains

In Baluchistan, west of the Indus Plain, three minor ranges run parallel south from the Hindu Kush to the Kabul River, their valleys draining the Swat, the Panjikora, and the Chitral-Kunar Rivers.

The Safed Koh Range, which runs east–west, has peaks averaging about 12,000 feet (3,657 m). The Khyber Pass, the most famous of the high-elevation gateways to the subcontinent, cuts through its mountains. About 33 miles (53 km) in length, the pass extends from Jamrud, some 10 miles (16 km) from Peshawar, Pakistan, to Dakka in Afghanistan. South of the range is the Kurram River. The Kurram Pass, which goes through Parachinar, Thal, and Kohat, has long been another favored route to Afghanistan. To the south, the Waziristan Hills lie between the Kurram and Gomal Rivers. The Gomal Pass, named for the Gomal River, which feeds into the Indus, has been an important trade route between Afghanistan and Pakistan for nomadic tribes known as the Powindahs. (Today their entry into Pakistan is restricted.)

South of the Gomal River the Sulaiman Mountains extend for 300 miles (483 km). The main peak, Takht-i-Sulaiman, is 11,100 feet (3,383 m). The Bolan Pass is the most noted transit point of these mountains and the Bolan their main river. The Pakistan city of Quetta guards the northern end of the pass. From here the land descends to the Kirthar Hills, low parallel ranges of some 7,000 feet (2,134 m) in elevation. They get little monsoon rainfall and are barren.

West of the Sulaiman and Kirthar Mountains the land descends to the dry hills of the Baluchistan Plateau, running northeast to southwest at an elevation of about 1,000 feet (305 m). The coastal Makran range borders the south end of Pakistan's western boundary.

The Salt Range and the Potwar Plateau

The Salt Range extends from near Jhelum, on the Jhelum River, northwest to the Indus River and then south into the districts of Bannu and Dera Ismail Khan in the North-West Frontier Province (NWFP). Its peaks average 2,200 feet (671 m) in height, though they reach about 5,000 feet (1,524 m) near Sakesar. In addition to extensive deposits of salt, its steep rock faces in the north contain gypsum, coal, and other minerals. The Salt Range has also attracted the attention of geologists, as it contains one of the world's most complete geological sequences, from the Cambrian to the Pleistocene eras.

The Potwar Plateau extends north of the Salt Range. The elevation ranges from 1,000 to 2,000 feet (305–610 m). The landscape is varied, shaped by glacial erosion. During the last ice ages glaciers that covered Kashmir and much of the northern subcontinent extended over this now semiarid region, creating the plateau's hills and hillocks.

The Indus Plain

South of the Salt Range the vast Indus Plain, drained by the Indus River and its tributaries, stretches to the Arabian Sea. The plain is composed of fertile alluvial deposits left by the overflow of the rivers. Several rivers in addition to the Indus traverse the Himalayan ranges. Their enormous flows in the rainy season often flood the surrounding plains. The northern part is called the Punjab and gives its name to the province that occupies the land. Most of this area is in Pakistan. The elevation here ranges from 600 to 1,000 feet (183–305 m).

The land between two rivers is referred to as a *doab*. The Indus has five major tributaries, and thus Punjab has four *doabs*. The combined waters of these tributaries, before joining the Indus near Mithankot, is called the Panjad (five rivers), thus the name of the province. The Indus and its five major tributaries join in Sind south of Mithankot. Here the land is flat, the river slow and wide, several miles across in the wet season. Silt on its banks forms a natural barrier, but at times the river has broken through and caused vast flooding, and has changed course. Near the coast a delta and flood plain form the mouth of the Indus. A coastal strip five to 25 miles (8–40 km) wide contains scattered mangrove swamps. Canals have been cut through the area, providing access for water traffic and trade. The Thar Desert occupies the southeast portion of the Indus Plain, spanning both Pakistan and India.

Climate

Generally arid, Pakistan lies in a warm temperate zone. The year is popularly regarded as having three seasons: summer, rainy season, and winter. Hot, summery weather lasts from April to September, and cold winters stretch from October to March. Monsoon rains drench the region from July to September. Within its borders the country has four primary climactic regions. The northern and north-western mountains have very cold winters with frequent frosts and heavy snowfalls. Summers are mild. On the plains to the south, the low elevation and absence of sea breezes cause very hot summers. During summer days, dry winds called *loo* blow. In the coastal areas to the south the Arabian Sea provides a moderating influence, and temperature variations are less extreme. The Baluchistan Plateau has a climate similar to that of the northern regions, though warmer in both summer and winter.

7

The Provinces

Today Pakistan is composed of four provinces, Punjab, Sind, the North-West Frontier Province (NWFP), and Baluchistan, and the Federally Administered Tribal Areas (FATA), a region between southwest NWFP and Afghanistan largely outside of government control. The state of Jammu and Kashmir is claimed by both Pakistan and India, and the dispute over the territory has been the defining issue dividing the two nations and inflaming passions on both sides of the border. The portion of Jammu and Kashmir that is administered by the federal government of Pakistan is divided into the Federally Administered Northern Areas, commonly known as the Northern Areas, and Azad Kashmir.

Punjab

Punjab is the most populous and developed of the four provinces. Noted for its arts and crafts, it is considered the cultural capital of Pakistan. Covering an area of 97,192 square miles (205,346 sq. km), Punjab is primarily a plain, though its north is bisected by the Salt Range, composed of the Murree and Kahuta hills on the north side and the Pubbi Hills of Gujrat in the south. The Potwar Plateau (1,000–2,000 feet; 305–610 m) lies north of the Salt Range, between the Jhelum River in the east and the Indus River to the west. It is primarily an agricultural area and boasts one of the largest canal irrigation systems in the world.

Punjab comprises eight administrative divisions. Its capital, Lahore, is linked to most major events and movements in Pakistan's history. Situated on the left bank of the river Ravi, it is bristling with monuments and buildings of great architectural and historical note. These include the Badshahi Mosque, Emperor Jahangir's Mausoleum, and the Shalimar Gardens. Islamabad, the nation's capital, lies some 170 miles (275 km) north of Lahore. Its twin city, Rawalpindi, is a gateway to the hills and mountains of Pakistan's north, which draw hikers, trekkers, and mountain climbers from around the world. Taxila, another of the province's many points of interest, is an ancient city rich in archaeological sites and treasures.

Throughout the province forts, palaces, mosques, and other grand edifices evidence the importance this region has long enjoyed. One of South Asia's earliest existing buildings with enameled tile work, the mausoleum of Shah Yusuf Gardezi in Multan, was built here in 1152 C.E.

A Muslim artistic tradition developed in Punjab early in the Mughal period, influenced by Central Asian and Persian artists. The renown of

8

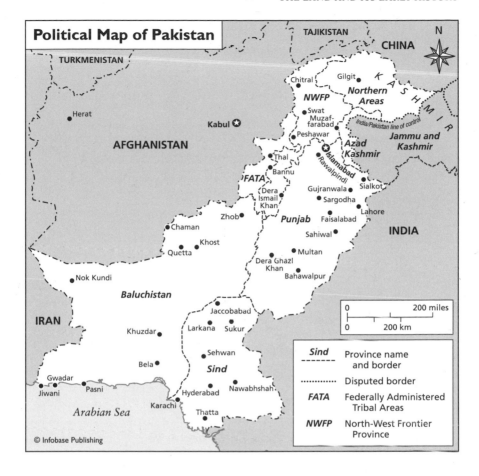

artists such as Abdur Rahman Chughtai (1899–1975) and miniaturist Haji Mohammad Sharif (1889–1978) remains undimmed today, and their legacy remains alive in contemporary artists who continue in their tradition.

Carpet making and pottery, which have a rich history here, are also widely practiced today. The pottery of Multan, where the Muslims first established a foothold in the region, was famed for its blue glazed pottery as early as the 13th century. Woodwork and metalwork in brass, iron, and copper add to the province's cultural legacy.

Sind

The life and economy of Sind flows on the current of the river Sindhu, or Indus, for which the province is named. Yet despite its aqueous spine, this is among the hottest areas of Pakistan. Jaccobabad, in the north of the province, is one of the hottest places on earth, with daytime temperatures in the summer rising to over 120 degrees F (49°C). Comprising three divisions, the province covers 54,198 square miles (140,914 sq. km). Sindhi, an ancient language, is spoken by a great majority of the population.

The capital, Karachi, has been the nation's primary seaport since the 1700s and is the largest city in Sind. In addition to its position as a trading center, Sind is also an industrial powerhouse, producing up to half the nation's goods in some manufacturing sectors. Rice, cotton, and wheat give the province a strong agricultural base.

Important archaeological sites are scattered throughout Sind. Just east of Karachi, Bhambore marks the site of the seaport of Debal, where the first Arab armies came ashore in 711 C.E. and began their conquests in the region. Thatta, the former provincial capital, was once a center of learning and still contains notable historical architecture. About 60 miles (98 km) east of Karachi, it is also the site of the famed Makli Tombs, a sprawling necropolis built between the 15th and 17th centuries.

The town of Sehwan predates the Islamic era and includes the ruins of Kafir-Qila, a fort reputedly built by Alexander the Great during his invasion of the area in the fourth century B.C.E. It is also the site of pilgrimages by Shia who come to visit the tomb of the 12th-century mystic poet, scholar, and saint Shaikh Usman Marvandvi.

In the 18th and 19th centuries, Hyderabad was the capital of Sind, and today it is noted for colorful handicrafts including glass, lacquered furniture, and hand-loomed cloth, as well as several historic forts, buildings, and monuments. Crafts remain important throughout the province, which is noted for *ajrak*—local craftwork that includes pottery, carpets, leatherwork, and silk. Sind is also noted for its textiles in the form of blankets, gold and silver embroidery, and cotton cloth (*soosi*). As befitting the first outpost of Islam on the subcontinent, poetry has long been a part of Sind's cultural heritage.

North-West Frontier Province (NWFP)

The North-West Frontier Province (NWFP) boasts the largest concentration of high peaks in the world. Containing the restless tribal areas and situated astride key mountain passes, including the Khyber Pass, NWFP has long been an untamed and strategic corner of the region. Most of the invaders who swept into the area that is now Pakistan—including Alexander the Great, Timur, Emperor Babur, and Mahmud of Ghazni—passed this way on their journeys of conquest.

The province in its present configuration, covering 29,808 square miles (74,521 sq. km), was created in 1901 and divided into "tribal" and "settled" areas. The tribal areas are administered by the federal government, while the settled areas are ruled by the fairly autonomous provincial assembly, as are all the provinces. The province has five administrative divisions: Peshawar, Kohat, Hazura, Dera Ismail Khan, and Malakand. Each of these is divided into two or more districts. The provincial capital is Peshawar. This province was also the home of the Gandhara Civilization, noted for its art, which blended Greco-Roman and local traditions, often harnessed to glorify Buddha and the religion he brought to this region. The valley of Udiyana, in the Swat River valley, was important during the Buddhist era of this region.

Baluchistan

The largest of Pakistan's four provinces (131,051 sq. miles; 347,190 sq. km), Baluchistan is a generally inhospitable land, and its lack of resources left it relatively undisturbed by regional powers for most of its history. Its geography encompasses mountains, coastal plains, and rocky deserts on its high plateau. In the south, the Makran Range separates the coastal plain from the interior, a region of highland basins and deserts.

Southeast Baluchistan is cut by narrow river valleys. With little room for alluvial deposits to settle, there is little agriculture. Archaeological research in the areas of Mehrgarh, Nausharo, and Pirak in the Kachi Plain indicates that settlements existed from the Neolithic period through the Iron Age, beginning in the early seventh millennium B.C.E. Dams were common to many settlements. The final settlement phase of this culture lasted until about 2600 B.C.E., the period when the Indus Valley Civilization of the river plains to the east of Mehrgarh was beginning to develop. Evidence from this time period points to mass production of pottery and increasing trade and exchange. Near the middle of the third millennium B.C.E., traces of human habitation end.

In historic times the area was first claimed by the Persian Empire, when it was called Maka. Alexander the Great brought it under nominal Greek rule in the fourth century B.C.E. The province takes its name from the Baluchs, the last of the major ethnic groups to settle in what is now Pakistan. The Baluchis, who may have originated from the Caspian Sea area, arrived around 1000 C.E., displacing the Meds of Maran and other tribes. The great Persian poet Firdausi (Abdul Kasim Mansur; 932–1021) mentioned the Baluchs and their valor in his epic poem *Shah Namah* (*The Book of Kings*), along with the warlike Kuch.

Baluchistan became a full-fledged province only in 1969. It has six administrative divisions: Quetta, Sibi, Kalat, Makran, Loralai, and Nasirabad. Each of these is composed of two or more districts. The capital of Baluchistan is Quetta, located by the Bolan Pass.

Three main languages are spoken: Baluchi, Pashto, and Brauhvi. Urdu, Pakistan's national language, is understood as well. The Baluchi, the language of the Baluchs, has Indo-Iranian roots. The strong national identity of the Baluchis—their tribes extend into Iran and Afghanistan—along with the historic lack of government attention and services, has made them resistant to being incorporated into the fabric of Pakistan. The region has been marked by periodic insurrections that continued into the 21st century.

Though only about 1.2 million of its 85 million acres is under cultivation, the province's economy is based on agriculture. The production of fruit in Baluchistan gives the province the sobriquet Fruit Garden of Pakistan. With little rainfall in the region, irrigation depends mostly on wells, *karezes* (underground water conduits), and springs. Canals irrigate about 1,000 square miles (2,590 sq. km). Livestock, primarily sheep and goats, are also a mainstay of the agricultural sector. In the Arabian Sea to the south, a fishing industry flourishes.

Though rich in minerals including iron ore and copper, Baluchistan has lagged in development of these resources. Facilities for the textile, pharmaceutical, and gas industries have recently been constructed, and the government has established economic incentives to encourage investment in the province.

Languages

The language of the Indus Valley Civilization is unknown. The Dardic language came with the first wave of Aryans around 1800–1500 B.C.E. Once established, the upper classes spoke Sanskrit (an Indo-Aryan language), while the masses (composed of indigenous populations) spoke what is called North-Western Prakrit, or the language of Gandhara. This was possibly an amalgam of local pre-Indo-European, Indo-Aryan, Dardic, and East Iranian speech. Today, reflecting its polyglot past and the historic isolation of many of its peoples, Pakistanis speak a variety of languages. Urdu is the national language, and English is the official language, but other common tongues are Punjabi, Pashto, Sindhi, and Baluchi. Most of the myriad languages are thought to be offshoots of the Sanskrit spoken by the Aryans three millennia ago.

Prehistoric Pakistan

Among the earliest fossils found in Pakistan are those of several ape species, including *Ramapithecus* and *Sivapithecus,* and the larger *Gigantophithecus* dating to the Miocene period, some 9 million years ago, unearthed on the Potwar Plateau. The region was also habitat for species of pigs, giraffes, antelopes, and other grazing animals. Boars the size of contemporary hippopotamuses, sheep larger that horses, and mastadons also roamed the landscape. In wet areas, crocodiles, turtles, and anthrocheres, a hippolike creature, flourished. Many of these creatures became extinct between 5 million and 1.5 million years ago, though humanoid apes thrived. But among the apelike creatures that thrived here, only *Homo sapiens* would survive the ice ages. Finding shelter in caves, they would learn to control fire and make tools, and they left records of their passage and way of life in cave paintings found in the central subcontinent.

Early Humans

In the Rawalpindi district, southwest of Islamabad, and the city of Rawalpindi near the Soan River, evidence of habitation by pre–Stone Age humans who lived between 3 million and 500,000 years ago has been found. They were likely hunter-gatherers whose pebble tools are the only trace of their existence. Extensive evidence of Stone Age, or Paleolithic, cultures has also been found. The most primitive tools found, dating to the early Stone Age, are eoliths, large stone-flake tools labeled the "pre–Soan" type. Artifacts of the so-called Soan Culture have been found on the Potwar Plateau, in the Rawalpindi district, the Jhelum River, and tributaries of the Chenab River. Middle Stone Age sites, dating to 300,000 to 150,000 years ago, have been found near Nomad Lake. By this time, toolmaking had improved. Flat chips called flakes were used as spearheads and knives. During Late Soan Culture, the use of wooden traps to catch fish and small game may have been mastered. In the Sanghao Valley near Mardan, stone tools dating to 70,000 years ago have been found. The transition from Lower to Upper Paleolithic cultures makes one of the most vital evolutions of mankind, and the remnants of the Soan Culture show dramatic advances in the manufacture of bone and stone tools.

About 10,000 years ago the global climate turned more temperate, and the last ice age ended. Receding glaciers were replaced by herds of grazing animals and the humans who hunted them. Ultimately some of these grazing animals were domesticated. Agriculture, the Neolithic revolution, may have initially developed in order to feed these animals, freeing humans from the need to follow migrating herds and allowing the establishment of permanent settlements.

Roots of Civilization

The settlement and agricultural exploitation of the region took root about 6500–5000 B.C.E. Agriculture came from the west; the first farming villages in the subcontinent appeared in areas of Baluchistan closest to Iran and Afghanistan. Neolithic farming and pastoral communities dotted the plains and western highland regions of Baluchistan and Afghanistan. The oldest Neolithic site in the subcontinent, found in 1979, is at Mehrgarh in Dhadar District, six miles south of the Bolan Pass, a key route into the region of present-day Pakistan. It dates to about 6500 B.C.E. or earlier. The remains of houses of dried mud bricks and tools of stone and flint have been identified. Inhabitants cultivated barley, oats, and wheat, harvesting them with sickles with stone blades. They wove baskets and kept herds of cattle and flocks of sheep. Beads, shells, and stones were used to make ornamental items. Objects found include necklaces and bracelets made from beads of turquoise, marble, lapus lazuli, shell, and steatite, or soapstone. The use of stones and shells not native to the area evidence trade with peoples from the Arabian Sea to Afghanistan. A copper bead found in a grave dating to 5000 B.C.E. is one of the first metal objects found in the region.

Numerous Neolithic sites dating to 5000 B.C.E. and later have been found throughout Pakistan. Among the artifacts discovered are highly polished stone tools, and pottery with beautiful paintings of animals: deer, mountain goats, fox, and bison. This pottery, in its style and decoration, likewise shows influences from as far as Iraq. Boxes carved from soft stone and figurines believed to be deities, particularly the Mother Goddesses, have also been found. From here agriculture spread up the Indus Valley. Annual floods of the Indus made the ground rich and pliant enough to obviate the need for plows.

Sometime around 4000 B.C.E. a new ethnic group appeared in the Indus region, the Dravidians. Though thought to have come from the Middle East, their origins are unknown. Their appearance—not fair skinned, high nosed, or flat nosed—indicates they were not related to central Asians or Mongolians. Early urban centers began to appear in the area about this time. One such community, Rehman Dheri, a few miles north of Dera Ismail Khan in NWFP, had an estimated population of 10,000 to 15,000. Inscriptions found on pottery at the site indicate script was developing. Remnants of such settlements have been found from Sahiwal and Rupar in East Punjab to Karachi and Baluchistan to the west.

The Dravidians built planned towns with two-story buildings, underground drains, public water supplies and baths, and large grain storehouses. More than three dozen sites have been identified. After 4000 B.C.E. bronze, a combination of copper and tin, became common in present-day Pakistan, though stone tools remained the norm in Baluchistan.

By 3000 B.C.E. hundreds of farming communities were established along the Indus and its tributaries. Several towns were fortified. The wheel was in wide use, both for throwing clay on potter's wheels and on carts pulled by draught animals. Toy carts have been found in the ruins of Kot Diji and in surrounding areas of the Kot Diji culture. Examinations of the pottery found at various sites have led to speculation that much of the culture originated in farming settlements in Baluchistan and spread east.

The Indus Valley Civilization

Sometime around 2600 B.C.E. at least two cities were destroyed by fire. In both cases, a new city was built atop the ashes of the old. But these new metropolises were markedly different from what they replaced. Both were built according to a uniform plan. Two large sites, Mohenjo-Daro (Mound of the Dead), near Larkana in Sind, and Harappa, near Sahiwal in the Punjab, are the most notable.

Mohenjo-Daro's edifices were constructed of durable burned-mud brick. Built around a central citadel, wide thoroughfares divided the municipal district into large blocks. Large temple-like structures include a pillared public bath measuring more than 100 feet by 180 feet. In residential areas, blocks were smaller and bisected by narrower lanes. Houses ranged from small cottages to roomy two- and three-story dwellings, replete with indoor plumbing. A complex sewer system, unmatched until the Roman Empire, served the city's sanitation needs.

Since these two cities were discovered in the 1920s, the remnants of many more built the same way have been uncovered. All have straight north-south and east-west streets. An administrative area was built on a vast platform protected by thick-walled fortifications overseen by

Mohenjo-Daro, near Larkhana in Sind, is among the best examples of an Indus Valley Civilization city. (Courtesy Pakistan Tourism Development Corporation)

watchtowers. Public buildings, granaries, and auditoriums also appear to have been common to all.

The Harappans were prosperous agricultural traders known throughout the ancient world. They traded with Mesopotamia and with Arabian Gulf communities. Internal trade likely consisted of cotton, lumber, grain, livestock, and other comestibles. A highly standardized system of weights controlled trade. The economic growth accompanying urban expansion brought increasing social stratification and distinction. The appearance of elaborate ornaments of gold, silver, and ivory; terra-cotta figurines; and sculpture marked this evolution. They also produced finely painted pottery and carved seals similar to those found in Sumer. The seals were often engraved with animals, the most common being a unicorn inscribed with pictographic symbols. The symbology has yet to be deciphered.

Though peaceful, they also made weapons of bronze and stone. They worshipped many gods and goddesses, most prominently one similar to the later Hindu god Shiva. The dead were buried in wooden coffins with pottery vessels and simple ornaments. No elaborate or valuable items of gold, silver, or precious stones were interred with them.

The unity of style and symbology linked the region culturally, but individual areas developed distinct, identifiable styles. At the end of the era these regional differences hardened, signifying independence as well as isolation, limiting the opportunities for advancement that had accompanied the earlier interaction.

At its height, the Indus Valley Civilization incorporated an area larger than Mesopotamia or Upper Egypt, stretching almost 700 miles (684 miles; 1100 km) north to south, from the foothills of the Siwalik Mountains to the Tapti River, and the same distance east to west, from Quetta in Baluchistan to Bikaner in Rajasthan, India, and Alamgirpur in the Upper Ganga–Jamuna *doab*.

Seals engraved with animals and inscribed with pictographic symbols are common relics of the Indus Valley Civilization. (Courtesy Pakistan Tourism Development Corporation)

Decline

After 1900–1800 B.C.E. the Indus Valley Civilization began to decline. Changes in river patterns wrought by earthquakes are thought to have contributed to the downfall of Harappan culture. While the Indus River is regarded as the wellspring for the region's earliest true civilization, at the time the region's greatest river was the Sarasvati, often identified in later Aryan accounts as the Ghaggar-Hakra. The Sarasvati River dried up and disappeared about 1900 B.C.E., disrupting agriculture and the

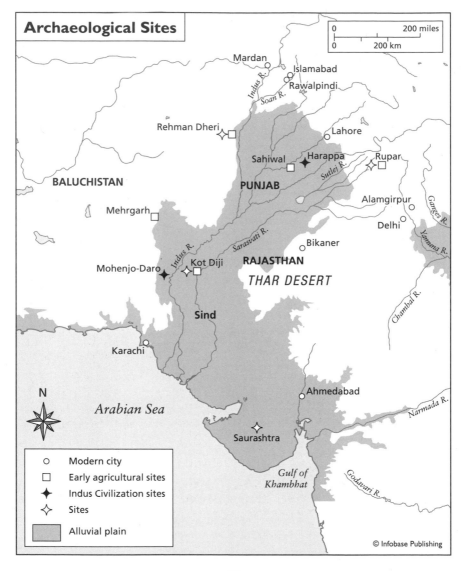

economy. The Indus changed course as well, causing destructive floods. The demise of the Indus Valley Civilization was mirrored in southeast Baluchistan, where settlements and irrigation systems were abandoned. Yet the area remained essentially habitable and hospitable, and the reasons for the depopulation are unknown. By about 1700 B.C.E. the Indus Valley Civilization had fragmented into smaller regional cultures called Late or Post-Harappan cultures.

The Aryans

A few hundred years after the urban centers of the Harappan culture had been abandoned, a people who called themselves the Aryans, or "noble ones" in Sanskrit, belonging to a large group of seminomadic tribes from Central Asia, migrated into the region. Before arriving on the subcontinent the larger group called Proto-Indo-Europeans had divided into three branches. One went west to Europe, the Iranian Aryans to Iran, and the third, the Indo-Aryans, to the subcontinent. Expert horsemen, aggressive fighters, and armed with iron weapons, the Aryans met little resistance. They arrived in the subcontinent in at least two major resettlements and ongoing, smaller migrations, the first in about 1,500 B.C.E. Their language, Dardic, or Old Indo-Aryan, composed of several dialects, was restricted to the Pamir mountain region at the time. The second wave came about six centuries later. In its aftermath their language, now evolved into Indic, became dominant in the Pakistan area. The Aryan language also became the root of Sanskrit, Pahlavi, Greek, Latin, and ancient forms of Teutonic and Slavic languages. By this time the Aryans had supplanted the Indus Valley Civilization. They may have driven the Dravidians south into what is now India.

The Aryans had chariots as well as weapons superior to those of indigenous forces. Aryans called those they conquered *dasyus*, meaning "inferior people born to serve." As Aryan society became more stratified, social laws evolved into a caste system of four classes. The highest were the Brahmans, priests who provided the link between men and god. Kshatriyas, the second caste, were warriors, commanders, leaders, and kings. The Vaishya caste consisted of artists, artisans, farmers, traders, and, later, minor officials. And the lowest caste, Shudras, were menial workers. Rule over Aryan tribes was primarily hereditary, though citizens had a voice through some elections. The king was crowned by Brahmans. The castes first developed as an open system, allowing Kshatriyas and Vaishyas to move up as their capabilities allowed. But over time the system became fixed.

The Epics

Knowledge of the Aryans primarily comes from their collection of sacred hymns, called the Vedas, meaning sacred knowledge. The Vedas include the Rig-Veda Samhita, Sama-Veda, Yajur-Veda, and Atharva-Veda. The Rig-Veda Samhita (Samhita means collection) is the source of all Vedic lore and religion. The Vedic pantheon contains 33 gods divided into groups of 11 in three categories: atmospheric (Indra), terrestrial (Agni), and celestial (Surya or Vishnu). Reference to astronomical phenomena leads scholars to believe the Vedas refer to incidents as early as 4500 B.C.E.

Two epic poems recount the heroic deeds of the early Aryans, and these traditions had a large influence on Hindu life and outlook. One, the *Ramayana,* was reputedly composed by Valmiki, a Hindu sage, although the date of its creation is unknown; the version that survives today is thought to date from between 500 and 100 B.C.E. The other epic, the *Mahabharata,* is a longer, episodic poem. The major portion of the *Mahabharata* is the Bhagavad Gita, a series of moral lectures from Lord Krishna to Arjuna, archer-prince, before going into battle.

Other sacred writings include the Brahmanas, commentaries on the Vedas that were written ca. 700–500 B.C.E.; and the Upanishads, considered among the greatest religious works in the world. These latter writings represent the height of Hindu culture.

The language of the religious texts, Sanskrit, was sacred and personified by a goddess. About 400 B.C.E. a grammarian, Panini, developed some 4,000 rules for the language. Later the scholars Ktayayana (ca. 250 B.C.E.) and Patanjali (ca. 150 B.C.E.) wrote commentaries on Panini's work, adding to the codification of the rules of Sanskrit.

The religion was polytheistic, with gods representing the sky, sun, moon, thunder, rain, earth, and rivers. Indra, god of war, sacker of cities, and bringer of rain, was the earliest of them and was originally the king of the deities. But over centuries a Hindu trinity emerged: Brahma, the creator; Vishnu, the preserver; and Shiva, the destroyer. Shiva ultimately evolved into both creator and destroyer. Vishnu was the savior of mankind.

Aryan Society

The basic Aryan political unit was the *grama,* or village, and its leader was the *gramani.* A *jana* was a larger area, and a *vis* was likely a subdivision of a *jana. Rashtra* was the state and was ruled by a *raja,* or king, who was also called *gopa,* or protector. *Samrat* was the supreme ruler.

Early Vedic society was nomadic and cattle herding the chief occupation. There were no coins or money at the time, and cows served as their currency. Families were patrilineal, with wealth passed from father to eldest son. The Aryan diet consisted primarily of grain and cakes, milk and milk products, and fruits and vegetables. Horse meat was consumed, but cows were seldom eaten due to their value, and their use as food declined over time.

Agriculture grew in importance and became the dominant economic activity as Aryan culture became more sedentary. Concurrently several small kingdoms emerged, often at war with one another. Some Vedic literature refers to 16 great kingdoms, or *mahajanapadas*. During this time two leadership groups emerged, the Brahmans and Kshatriyas. The former developed elaborate sacrifices and specialization, and proper enunciation of sacred verses became essential for divine intervention in granting wealth and victory in war. Over time the alliance between these two groups grew stronger.

From about 1500 to 1000 B.C.E. the area of present-day Pakistan where the Aryans ruled remained independent of the rest of what is now India. Once the Aryans migrated east to the Gangetic Plains, the area that is now Pakistan reverted to its insular existence. Little is known about the events that occurred in the region between 1000 and 500 B.C.E.

2

INROADS OF ARMIES AND IDEAS (500 B.C.E.–700 C.E.)

The migration of the Aryans from the Indus to the Ganges valley around 1000 B.C.E. left what is now Pakistan largely autonomous. But by the middle of the first millennium B.C.E. the region's isolation had given way to a series of invasions of ideas and armies. Jainism and Buddhism were the first of the former, which left indelible marks on the region's society and culture that still echo today. The armies came from Persia, Greece, and Central Asia, each earning a place in the region's history. Concurrently, the Hindu kingdoms that developed in India from Aryan roots periodically held sway over the Indus region from whence they originated.

The Path to Enlightenment

In the sixth century B.C.E., near the end of the Indus region's period of obscurity, spiritual and intellectual revolutions were reshaping the ancient world. New thinkers advanced ideas that profoundly changed views of life and religion. These guiding spirits included Zoroaster (ca. 628–551 B.C.E.) in Iran; Pythagoras (ca. 570–500 B.C.E.) in Greece; Confucius (551–479 B.C.E.) and Laozi (fl. sixth century) in China; and Siddhartha Gautama (ca. 623–543 B.C.E.), known as the Buddha, and Mahavira (ca. 599–527 B.C.E.), who spread Jainism, in India.

Jainism

Mahavira was born a prince at Vaisali, near Patna, India. The son of Siddhartha, chief of the Nat Clan of the Kshatriyas, his given name was Vardhamana. At age 30 he gave up his life of ease to embark on a spiritual quest and wandered as a monk for 13 years until attaining supreme knowledge. He spent the next 30 years preaching throughout the subcontinent, teaching the faithful how to achieve release (*moksha*) from earthly concerns by avoiding sinful thoughts and desires and by avoiding causing harm to others. As did Buddhists, he believed every living being was influenced by karma, the accumulated energy of all the individual's good and bad deeds. Followers called him Jina, the conqueror, and later Mahavira (taken from the Sanskrit word *mahavir,* meaning very brave and courageous).

Jainism and Buddhism are considered to have developed contemporaneously, as their founders lived at the same time. But Mahavira based his teachings on Jaina traditions that went back centuries in the Indus Valley. Within Jainism, he is regarded as the 24th, last, and most important of the *tirthankaras,* ford makers, or pathfinders. The previous *tirthankara,* Parshvanatha, or Parshva, and the first for whom historical evidence exists, probably lived in the ninth century B.C.E. Mahavira, over his years of preaching, brought many new adherents to the faith. His sermons were memorized by followers, and over hundreds of years they were collected in the Agam Sutras (canonical literature). Punjab eventually became a stronghold of Jainism, with a large community in Lahore. Most adherents moved to the Indian portion of Punjab following independence in 1947.

Buddhism

As Mahavira spread his message, another scion of nobility who would have even greater impact on the region was on a similar mission. Siddhartha Gautama was the son of the chief of Kapilavastu, a principality at the foot of the Himalayas. Gautama abandoned his life of ease and pleasure and set off on a search for truth, wandering first as a hermit and later attracting followers as he preached during his journey. His quest eventually brought him enlightenment and he was proclaimed as Buddha, a Sanskrit word meaning "enlightened one" or "awakened one." (The title applies to anyone who has received enlightenment, though is often used to refer to Gautama, who was also called by the religious name Shakyamuni.) Gautama believed in reincarnation and preached that karma, the accreted spirit of one's good and bad deeds, determines the quality of the next life. The key to enlightenment lay in connecting to dharma, the truth of the world's nature, which is only possible by elevating one's karma through thought and deed. This would allow the attainment of nirvana, an exalted state of bliss and understanding. Gautama also taught that there is no intermediary between humans and the divine spirit and that he himself was merely a guide.

The Buddha's message struck a responsive cord among those disenchanted with the rigid social stratification practiced by the Hindus. One of the Buddha's primary patrons was Bimbisara, the fifth Saisunaga ruler of the Hindu kingdom of Magadha, one of three larger kingdoms founded by the Aryan tribes who had migrated east from Pakistan. Magadha dominated the northeast region of the subcontinent. The king ruled from the capital at Rajgir. He married a Kosala princess and annexed the neighboring kingdom of Anga. According to legend, Bimbisara invited Gautama to visit his court at Rajgir before he had achieved enlightenment. When Gautama declined, Bimbisara invited him to return once his quest was completed. Having attained enlightenment, the Buddha and his monks visited Bimbisara's court, and the ruler awarded him property for use in his teachings. Bimbisara was later deposed by his son Ajatasattu, imprisoned, and starved to death. Ajatasattu (also spelled Ajatasatru and Ajatashtru) built a new capital at Pataliputra and made Magadha into the most powerful of the three Hindu kingdoms.

It was during this time of spiritual awakening that foreign incursions—Persian and Greek from the west, and later empires from the south—brought the Indus region under outside control.

Persian Conquest

The area that is now Pakistan may have come under Persian domination as early as the reign of that empire's founder, Cyrus the Great (ca. 585–529 B.C.E.). Under his grandson and second successor, Darius I (r. ca. 522–486 B.C.E.), the area of Sind and Punjab became the 20th *satrapy,* or province, of the Achaemenian Empire, as the Persian dominion was known. Darius called the new Persian province the Sind Satrapy, after Sindhu, the ancient name of the Indus River. References to Sindhu and Hindu figures are found on inscriptions in the ancient Persian cities of Kermanshah, Susa, and Persepolis and refer to Hapta Hindva (the Seven Rivers) as belonging to Darius's empire. Herodotus (ca. 484–420 B.C.E.), the Greek historian, wrote that Darius had dispatched Scylax to lead an exploratory mission to the Indus River valley in 517 B.C.E. Once under its suzerain, Sind was the richest of Persia's provinces and, according to Herodotus, "paid a tribute exceeding that of every other people" (Herodotus, *Persian Wars*, Book III, 204), due in part to the heavy rainfall and many rivers that nourished the land. Darius also conquered the *doab* between the Indus and Jhelum Rivers.

Commerce followed conquest. Trade increased, and several cities were established along caravan routes. With growing prosperity, the arts and philosophy took more prominent roles in society. Taxila, near Rawalpindi, which would later be renowned for its art and commerce, is thought to have first flourished as such a capital during this time. Charsadda, on Peshawar's trade route, is thought to have been another of the thriving metropolises of the era. An additional result of Persian influence was the introduction of the Kharoshthi script, read from right to left, to the subcontinent.

By the last half of the sixth century B.C.E. Gandhara (consisting of present-day Peshawar in NWFP and the Rawalpindi area of the Punjab) had been added to Persia's territory as a separate province. Portions of Sind west of the Thar Desert and the Punjab east of the Indus are also thought to have come under Persian rule, as did the entire length of the Indus River itself, from Upper Punjab to the Arabian Sea. However, the region remained administratively independent. The rajas who ruled the small kingdoms that comprised present-day Pakistan simply swore fealty to their Persian lords, paid their tribute, and provided military assistance when needed. This independence grew over time as the Persian Empire's power began to fade.

Darius used the region's military assistance to further expand his empire. He used Pakistani troops in his victorious first campaign against the Greeks, which expanded the Persian Empire as far west as the river Danube. And when Darius dispatched Xerxes (r. 485–465 B.C.E.) to lead a subsequent campaign against Greece, troops from Pakistan were again part of the invasion force. Herodotus wrote of the cavalry and chariots that came from the Indus satrapy, and of their bows and arrows of cane sheathed in iron. He also noted their garments of cotton.

Besides bringing the Indus region under foreign influence, its link with Persia also created a history and cultural identity for this area unique and independent from that of the rest of the subcontinent. It is among the divisions between what are now Pakistan and India that persist to the present. For almost two hundred years what is now Pakistan remained the collective vassal of Persia's rulers. But internal conflict still occurred as local kingdoms fought for greater regional dominance, and would-be rajas sought to usurp the power of established rulers.

Alexander the Great

In the fourth century the Persian Empire fell to another great invader from the west, Alexander the Great (356–323 B.C.E.). The son of Philip

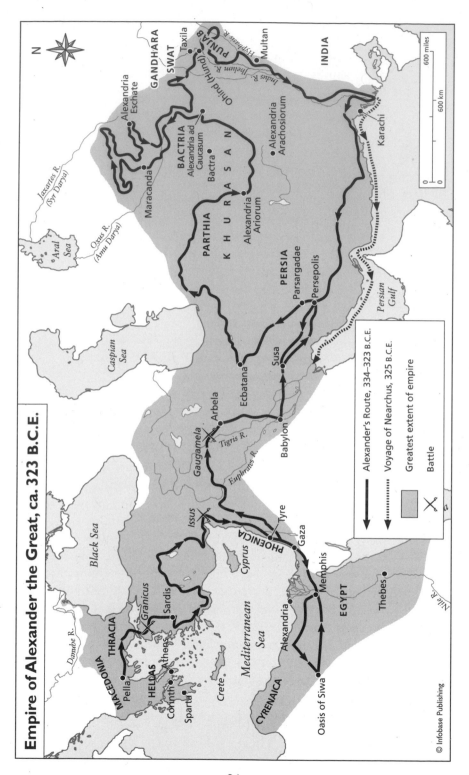

Empire of Alexander the Great, ca. 323 B.C.E.

Legend:
- Alexander's Route, 334–323 B.C.E.
- Voyage of Nearchus, 325 B.C.E.
- Greatest extent of empire
- Battle

© Infobase Publishing

Labels on map:

N

MACEDONIA · Pella · THRACIA · Granicus · Sardis · HELLAS · Athens · Corinth · Sparta · Crete · Black Sea · Mediterranean Sea · Cyprus · PHOENICIA · Tyre · Gaza · Issus · Danube R.

EGYPT · Alexandria · Memphis · Thebes · Nile R. · CYRENAICA · Oasis of Siwa

Babylon · Euphrates R. · Tigris R. · Gaugamela · Arbela · Ecbatana · Susa · Persian Gulf

PERSIA · Parsargadae · Persepolis · PARTHIA · KHURASAN · Alexandria Ariorum · BACTRIA · Alexandria ad Caucasum · Bactra · Maracanda · Alexandria Arachosiorum · Karachi

Caspian Sea · Aral Sea · Oxus R. (Amu Darya) · Iaxartes R. (Syr Darya) · Alexandria Eschate

GANDHARA · SWAT · Taxila · PUNJAB · Ohind (Hund) · Hydaspes R. · Hyphasis R. · Multan · Indus R. · Jhelum R. · INDIA

600 miles · 600 km

26

of Macedonia, Alexander took the throne upon his father's death in 336 B.C.E. As a prince he had harbored dreams of military conquest, and upon becoming king he put his plans into action. The Persian Achaemenian Empire, at the time the world's most powerful, was his first objective. After taking two years to organize his army, in 334 B.C.E. Alexander led his troops eastward. Darius III (ca. 380–330 B.C.E.), who ruled the Achaemenian Empire at the time, gathered forces from across the empire to battle the invaders. His forces included Bactrians and Sogdians from what is now Pakistan. Their assistance in this and previous campaigns pitting the Persians against the Greeks did not escape Alexander's attention.

Alexander defeated Darius at Issus in 333 B.C.E., though the Persians survived the defeat. Suspending his campaign long enough to conquer both the Phoenicians in present-day Lebanon, and Egypt in the years 332–331 B.C.E., Alexander returned to rout Darius at Gaugamela in 331 B.C.E. He looted and burned Persepolis and several other Persian cities.

The Indus Campaign

In 327 B.C.E., after adding Khurasan and Bactria to his conquests, Alexander marched his army toward Afghanistan and points east. Enlisting Pashtun tribesmen to join his forces, Alexander crossed into present-day Pakistan via the northern route through Bajaur and Swat. His campaign lasted from June through December. Consolidating his victories, Alexander married Kleophis, queen of the Assakenoi (Asvakas), the region's most powerful tribe. Continuing the advance, in February of 326 B.C.E. Alexander crossed the Indus River at Ohind, 12 miles north of Attock. He was welcomed by Taxila's ruler, Raja Ambhi. Alexander spent some time here enjoying the hospitality of this center of culture and learning. But the adjacent kingdom, middle Punjab, ruled by Porus (d. 317 B.C.E.), resisted the Greeks, gathering forces that included 200 war elephants, 300 chariots, 4,000 cavalry, and 30,000 infantry. Alexander met the Punjabi army at Jhelum ford that July and defeated Porus in what would become known as the Battle of Hydaspes. In recognition of Porus's valiance in battle, Alexander allowed him to keep his throne. (This also served to limit future insurrections among local populations.)

After defeating Punjab, Alexander advanced to the Hyphasis River (modern-day Beas River). He wanted to continue his conquests and defeat Magadha, the Hindu kingdom to the east, but his soldiers, weary

The invasion of Alexander the Great (326–324 B.C.E.) brought what is now Pakistan into direct contact with Western civilization. (Snark/Art Resource, NY)

from the long campaign, refused to go farther. Alexander spent three days cloistered in his tent before emerging to order his army's withdrawal, after having 12 pillars marking his conquests erected by the river. On his way back through Pakistan he marched south and fought the Malavas (Malloi in Greek), whose kingdom was in western and central India, before conquering Multan. His army suffered numerous casualties during the campaign. Along the route he established garrisons manned by troops he left in place and founded towns that would be populated by settlers who would come from Greece and other parts of the empire. Greek historian Diodorus Siculus (fl. first century B.C.E.) wrote that Alexander himself recruited 10,000 people to reside in a city he founded in the lower Indus region.

Continuing south in Multan, Alexander crossed the Hub River near Karachi. Upon arriving at the mouth of the Indus he divided his army in two. Half he sent back by sea, while the other half returned over land. He had spent 10 months in what is now Pakistan, traversing its length and breadth. History records that Alexander and his generals were much impressed with the culture they found in Pakistan and the prowess of its military, which was superior to the armies Alexander had faced in Asia Minor and Asia up to that point. On the way back to Macedonia, Alexander died. His generals fought over his empire. Seleucus I Nicator (358–281 B.C.E.) gained the largest part, extending from Asia Minor to Bactria, including present-day Pakistan. He continued Alexander's practice of building new towns in an effort to cement Greece's hold on the land.

Alexander's Legacy

Alexander's invasion brought Hellenistic culture to the area, notwithstanding the influences already absorbed by soldiers from the region who had battled on the Greek's home soil more than a century and a half before. Local soldiers who joined Alexander's armies or that of his successors quickly learned and adapted to Western customs and ways. But in the immediate aftermath of his invasion, Alexander's influence was negligible. With his limited resources, he left administrations as he found them for the most part and made no effort to recast the culture in the Macedonian mold. And unlike the barbarity that marked Alexander's assault on Persia, cities and civilians were spared the depredations of his army. He came, he conquered, he left. However, garrisons Alexander established to present a facade of Greek rule would play a role in the region's political and cultural future.

Chandragupta and the Mauryan Empire

Alexander had created a superb army. The lessons of his methods and strategies were adopted by local rulers, for whom warfare had been an art, science, and instrument of state for centuries. Chandragupta Maurya (r. 322–298 B.C.E.) was one such ruler. A Punjabi noted as remarkable, brave, and ruthless, he established a kingdom, the Mauryan empire, in the Ganges River valley. The first major Indian state, it ruled the upper half of the subcontinent until 185 B.C.E. His renowned court was at Pataliputra (near present-day Patna), the largest city in the east in its time, covering some 13 square miles (34 sq. km). Pataliputra was filled with palaces, temples, a university, gardens, parks, and other public buildings and spaces. The king, whose palace contained hundreds of rooms, was protected by a crack corps of formidable female soldiers. Chandragupta's minister Kautilya (Chanakya), author of a textbook on government administration and political strategy, was instrumental in the kingdom's expansion and administration.

Chandragupta had failed in an earlier effort to conquer Magadha, undertaken in an alliance with the Greeks when Alexander was in Punjab. After Alexander's death, Chandragupta again attacked Magadha, this time defeating the kingdom and claiming its throne.

In 305 B.C.E. Chandragupta battled Seleucus, Alexander's successor, near the Indus River, emerging victorious. In the subsequent peace treaty, Seleucus ceded all of present-day Pakistan and part of Ariana, present-day Afghanistan, to Chandragupta. To cement the treaty, Chandragupta married Seleucus's daughter and gave Seleucus 500 war elephants. This marked the end of Greek rule in Pakistan, though descendants of these Greek immigrants would one day rule the region. Cordial relations between the Greeks and Chandragupta were maintained. Megasthenes (350–290 B.C.E.), an ambassador sent to the court by Seleucus, wrote an account of Chandragupta's kingdom, reporting on the government, trade, the capital, and the army.

Greek influence had remained limited in the region, but under Chandragupta Hellenistic ideas and culture sparked an intellectual renaissance in the royal court, stimulating interest in the arts and sciences. A century later the descendants of Greek garrisons left in Bactria would invade Punjab and establish a line of Bactrian kings.

Ashoka

After Chandragupta's death his son Bindusara (r. ca. 298–273 B.C.E.) continued the empire's expansion, conquering the Deccan. But it was

Bindusara's son and successor, Ashoka (r. ca. 269–232 B.C.E.), who was regarded as the most able of the dynasty's kings, and, indeed, was one of history's great rulers. His first major conquest, in 261 B.C.E., was of the Kalinga kingdom in the present-day Orissa province of India. Though his kingdom was expanded with the sword, the blood shed in his war with the Kalingas so repulsed Ashoka that he became a Buddhist and, according to lore, a devout missionary. This turned all of Pakistan on a path toward Buddhism, on which it largely remained until Islam appeared about 1,000 years later. Thus Pakistan was under Hindu rule for only a relatively short time.

A paternal ruler, Ashoka regarded his subjects as his children and sponsored works of architecture and education. Greeks played a large role in these latter activities, and Ashoka also apparently relied on his Yavana, or Greek subjects, and Greek nobles to assist in his empire's administration. Ultimately Ashoka's kingdom stretched from Afghanistan to the Cavery River in south India. His death began the Mauryan empire's decline. Mauryan control over Pakistan had been limited, and the descendants of the Greeks who had come with Alexander and established themselves in northwest Pakistan gradually asserted their power.

The Bactrian Kingdom

Though Seleucus had ceded Greek territory to the Mauryans a century before, descendants of Greeks who had been garrisoned in the area gained control of Bactria (Balkh in northern Afghanistan) and areas west of the Hindu Kush under their ruler Demetrius I (fl. second century B.C.E.). Bactria's dominion expanded eastward, and by about 200 B.C.E. the Mauryans had been driven from the region. Local rulers asserted their autonomy and sought security, as they had each time an empire's retreat left them free and exposed. In about 185 B.C.E., under Appolodidus, the Greco-Bactrians began a series of campaigns of conquest in what is now Pakistan. In 175 B.C.E. Appolodidus's successor, Menander (r. ca. 155–130 B.C.E.), also known as Milinda or Menandros, invaded Punjab, establishing the Bactrian kingdom. At its height the kingdom extended from Kashmir in the north to the Arabian Sea. Indeed, Bactria's Greek rulers "had conquered more people than Alexander himself." (Gankovsky 1971, 72) Taxila became a renowned center of arts and sciences, drawing scholars from all the known world. The acclaimed sculpture subsequently produced throughout Gandhara (Peshawar Valley) and Taxila, called the Gandhara school of art, was a result of the mutual influence between Buddhist and Hellenistic artistic traditions.

Hellenistic influences are evident in the carvings and sculpture of the Gandhara school of art, which flourished in the Peshawar Valley. (Courtesy Pakistan Tourism Development Corporation)

Menander, Bactria's most powerful king, made his capital at Sakala (present-day Sialkot). His kingdom was noted for its seaports, mines, cities, and vibrant trade. Like Ashoka he eventually turned to Buddhism and was a great patron of Buddhist scholars and teachers. A theological discussion he held with the Buddhist philosopher Nagasena was the basis for a noted Pali text, *Milindapanha, Questions of Milinda.*

The Scythians (Sakas)

In the middle of the second century B.C.E. nomadic horsemen from Central Asia called Scythians—the first in a progression of these invaders—began to pour into what is now Pakistan. The nomadic tribe had invaded and conquered Persia and Khurasan in about 150 B.C.E. The Sakas were a branch of the Scythians.

Menander was on a military campaign to expand his kingdom eastward at the time, Mathura had already fallen, and Menander was preparing to advance on the grand city of Pataliputra when he learned of the Scythian incursion. He turned his army north to meet them. Menander was killed in the ensuing battle, and his death marked the end of the

Bactrian kingdom. Rent by internal rivalries and disputes and bereft of its greatest leader, it split into several minor kingdoms.

The Sakas quickly overran the patchwork of Greek-led kingdoms and set about building new settlements to accommodate their vast numbers. Such was the preponderance of these new arrivals that Greek geographers and cartographers began to refer to what is now Pakistan as Scythia, while Indians referred to it as Saka-dipa. The Sakas quickly assumed rule over the northwest subcontinent. Branches of the Sakas founded kingdoms in Taxila, Lower Punjab, Malwa, and Jujarat Kathiawar. Their rulers preferred to use the Persian title of *satrap*.

The first three of the Saka kings were Maues, Azes I, and Azilises. Gandhara was their principal stronghold and Taxila their capital. The scanty historical evidence indicates the Sakas initially showed deference toward the assimilated Greek rulers they conquered. The coins struck during their reigns, for example, closely resembled those of the Bactrian Greeks they supplanted. But after several decades the Saka rulers felt confident enough to assert their supreme authority and display their cultural roots. They followed the style of the Pahlavas, or Parthians of Iran, in time even turning the throne over to Pahlava princes. One of these princes, Gondophares (ca. 20–48 C.E.), announced his independence from Parthian control, establishing the Indo-Parthian Kingdom. Early ecclesiastical accounts suggest the Christian apostle St. Thomas was martyred here after coming to the region—and even Gondophares's court—to preach. Over some 100 years of the Indo-Parthian kingdom's existence, it grew at the expense of the Sakas to encompass present-day Afghanistan, Pakistan, and northern India. The capital, originally at Taxila, was relocated to Kabul shortly before the kingdom's demise.

Though Greek rule had ended, their language remained in use by the ruling and upper classes into the common era. In the second half of the first century C.E., the king of Taxila, for example, spoke fluent Greek.

The Kushans

While the Sakas were losing hegemony in what is now Pakistan in the middle of the first century C.E., another wave of Central Asian nomads appeared. The Yuezhi (Yueh-chih) had been pushed from China's border region by stronger tribes that seized their grazing lands. The branch of the tribe that overran Pakistan was the Kushans. After conquering Bactria they continued south across the Hindu Kush and seized the Kabul Valley. In 48 C.E., under the command of a Tokhari prince, Kujula Kadphises (30–80 C.E.), they invaded Punjab, Saka territory. Kujula's son,

33

Kadphises II, who succeeded him, completed the conquest of the Sakas. But the Saka princes were often allowed to retain their rule, and only had to swear their allegiance to their Kushan lords. Such was the retention of their power and status that this period of subjugation is called the Saka era, a name bestowed by the Kushans themselves. It began in 78 C.E., when Kanishka (d. ca. 126 C.E.), their most able ruler, took the throne and started a new calendar, dubbing it the Saka era. Kanishka established the Kushan capital in Purusapura, modern Peshawar, and continued the expansion of the empire. He extended its territory into Central Asia, all of Afghanistan, and much of northern India, in addition to all of Pakistan. The Kushans controlled the trade routes linking Rome and China from their capital. Their ambassadors were frequent visitors to Rome and China. The empire grew into one of the great civilizations of its time, noted for both its size and its power, and the advanced state of its social and cultural life. In addition to being a warrior-statesman, Kanishka was a great patron of the arts. And though the Kushan had traditionally been pagans, Kanishka, like Menander and Ashoka before him, became a Buddhist. The Gandhara school of art, which had first emerged under Bactrian rule a few centuries earlier, flourished during this time.

Thousands of petroglyphs are found in the Indus River valley, the majority created by Buddhists between the first and ninth centuries C.E. (Courtesy Pakistan Tourism Development Corporation)

Both Buddhism and Gandhara art achieved their greatest glories in Pakistan under the Kushans, and under Kanishka's patronage Buddhism spread to Central Asia and China.

Buddhism itself was undergoing a transformation. At first seen as a teacher, Buddha over time was elevated to the status of a god, worthy of worship. This led to a great deal of temple building. Hindus and Jains also made the ancestral heroes of their legends and lore into deities, human reincarnations of gods.

The figure of Buddha inspired generations of artists in the subcontinent, as his identity among adherents evolved from that of a teacher to a deity. (Courtesy Pakistan Tourism Development Corporation)

The Sassanians

Upon his death around 126 C.E. Kanishka was briefly succeeded by his son Huvishka, who was replaced that same year by Vasudeva I. By the end of the second century C.E. the Kushan empire was in decline. The power vacuum was filled by the rulers, or shahs, of Iran's Sassanid dynasty. The Sassanians conquered the Persians in 226 C.E. under Ardeshir (r. 226–241 C.E.). Soon after, his son, Shapur I (r. ca. 241–272 C.E.), laid claim to what is today Pakistan. Shapur's son, Narses, was made shah of Seistan, Baluchistan, Sind, and the coast of what is now Pakistan. However, the Kushans were able to retain their control of central Pakistan and the Kabul Valley (while the Saka rulers retained their kingdoms under them). The Kushans exercised this power until the fifth century, when their kingdom, along with all others around them, fell to new invaders from Central Asia.

The Guptas and the Great Age of the Hindus

After falling from importance and enduring three centuries of obscurity, Magadha, the once-powerful kingdom that had controlled the subcontinent's northeast, returned to the Indian stage. This occurred under a ruler who shared the name of the monarch who had established the

Mauryan kingdom: Chandragupta I (r. ca. 320–335 C.E.). The founder of the Gupta empire, Chandragupta I was the earliest king to have left a historical record of his rule.

His son Samudragupta (r. 330/335–380) was a poet and musician as well as a fearless and aggressive warrior. Under Samudragupta's rule, the Guptas, as the dynasty was later known, were accepted as the subcontinent's preeminent kings. Samudragupta conquered all of Upper India and counted the rulers of Punjab and Malwa among his vassals; these and other Hindu vassal states flourished under the Guptas' reign. Samudragupta expanded the Gupta empire southward to Kalinga (present-day Orissa Province).

Chandragupta II (r. 376/380–415), who took the title *vikramaditya* (son of valor), continued the empire's expansion. He conquered the holdout Saka kingdom of Ujjain (in present-day Madhya Pradesh Province, India) as well as the key seaports on the western coast of India—including Broach, Surat, Kalyan, and Sopara—that were crucial for the trade between the Mediterranean world and western Asia. The Gupta empire grew rich from its control of the sea trade, and Chandragupta II was highly regarded. The renown of his court and its splendors was such that, under the name Raja Bikram, he became the heroic subject of a cycle of popular folk tales.

Art of all kinds flourished under the Guptas, as did the sciences and religious writing. Hinduism itself underwent a revival during the Gupta years, a process that included the codification of the caste system. Leading literary works were reconfigured to reflect and bolster the revised tenets.

The empire retained its vigor and position under Kumaragupta (r. 415–455), who succeeded Chandragupta II. Kumaragupta's successor, Skandagupta (r. 455–467), was adjudged to be an even more skillful ruler. But, nonetheless, under his reign the empire would be lost as the region faced what would be its most ruinous invasion in history: the onslaught of the White Huns. When they first appeared in the mid-fifth century, sweeping down from the plains of Central Asia like so many before them, Skandagupta emerged victorious from several battles, killing tens of thousands of the invaders. But more came, and under repeated attacks the Guptas' empire declined. By the mid-sixth century their power had ended.

The Huns

Unlike previous invaders who added to established kingdoms, the Huns who swept into the subcontinent from Central Asia through the northwest mountain passes were nomads who are recorded as having enjoyed barbarity and bloodshed. These were Ephthalite, or White Huns, part of the same nomadic group that invaded Europe under the leadership of Attila (d. 453). With their ferocious assaults and terrifying reputations, the Huns quickly conquered Bactria, Kabul, and Gandhara. Their conquest of Kashmir, the Punjab, and Malwa soon followed.

The invasion of the Huns turned a new page in Pakistan's and the subcontinent's history. All the traditions of previous empires, of the Guptas, Kushans, Sakas, and Mauryas, would be forgotten, and from this time forward new traditions would evolve. As had happened with all previous invaders, the Huns changed as they became inevitably assimilated into the culture. The Huns and their brethren invaders eventually became Hindus. But first they wrought a complete reordering of the existing clan structures; some clans were stripped of all they had, while others that possessed nothing were elevated to positions of power under the new rulers. The remnants of the high caste assisted in the transformation. The Brahmans invested in the new ruling class the same qualities and spiritual purity they had previously applied to their traditional warrior-king caste, the Kshatriya of the Vedic scriptures. Mirroring this transference, the term Raja-putra, king's son, later shortened to Rajput, the designation for the members of the ruling clans and families, became the equivalent of the term Kshatriya. The Rajputs would found kingdoms of their own.

Malwa, taken by the Huns under the leadership of Toramana (ca. 448–510) in about 500, served as their headquarters. The rule of Toramana and his son Mihiragula (or Mihirakula; r. ca. 510–542) was so brutal and inept that it finally triggered a revolt. The prince of Malwa, Yasodharman (r. 520–530), and the Gupta king of Magadha, Baladitya, the son of Skandagupta, organized the Hindu rajas to rise up against Mihiragula. They met in battle around 532, and Mihiragula was defeated. Exiled from his former kingdom, Mihiragula settled in Kashmir, where he deposed the reigning king and ruled the area until his death a few years later.

The victory over Mihiragula thrust Yasodharman to the forefront of regional rulers. He conquered all the former Gupta lands and took the title *vishnuvardhan*. He also, like other Hindu kings before and after, took the title *vikramaditya*. A patron of the arts and literature, Yasodharman reigned over a court that, according to contemporary accounts, possessed "nine gems," the famed scholars and experts in his retinue, evoking the "nine gems" of Hindu mysticism; each of the latter was thought to possess astrological powers and could be worn individually or combined in a necklace or amulet for their powers at appropriate times.

Magadha, which had regularly served as a power center for regional rulers going back centuries, again became a dominant kingdom. Following Yasodharman's reign a dynasty of kings whose names were suffixed with *gupta* ruled from here for several decades, though their connection to the imperial Guptas is unclear.

The Maukharis of Kanauj

Since the time of the Maurya dynasty the Maukhari had been a prominent tribe. In the sixth century a new line of Maukhari kings arose. They had ruled as chieftains in the Gaya district as vassals of the imperial Guptas and had developed an independent kingdom that constantly fought with the second Gupta line. Toward the end of the sixth century the Maukhari succeeded in expelling the Guptas from Magadha and afterward dominated upper India.

Harshavardhana (ca. 590–648), raja of Thanesar (a holy Hindu town north of Delhi), was the younger son of Prabhakaravardhana, a ruler famed for victories against the Gujaras, Malavas, and other tribal invaders. Harsha followed in his father's footsteps and for several years fought to establish rule over the northern subcontinent. Prabhakara died in 604, and, after his elder son was assassinated in 606, nobles selected Harsha to be king.

About this time the heirless last ruler of the Maukhari dynasty, Grahavarman, was killed in battle and his army defeated by the Malwa king. Grahavarman was married to Harsha's sister, and after his death she and other Maukhari nobles invited Harsha to take the throne of their kingdom. Harsha agreed. He then raised an army said to number 100,000 cavalrymen and conquered Punjab, Bihar, Malwa, and Gujarat. He continued south to the Deccan, where he was defeated, and accepted Narmada River as the boundary of his empire. Making Kanauj his capital, he turned his efforts from expanding to administering the kingdom.

Though he reigned at a time when the region's fortunes were in decline, Harsha, a scholar, poet, and dramatist as well as a monarch, is regarded as the last of the great Hindu rulers. During an assembly Harsha convened in Kanauj in honor of a visiting Chinese chronicler, Xuanzang, an attempt was made on the king's life in a plot engineered by Brahmans. Nonetheless, Xuanzang wrote a vivid, complimentary account of the kingdom and Harsha's court.

Harsha died in 648 without an heir. A minister seized power. He attacked and robbed a Chinese envoy, who escaped to Nepal, which was Tibet's suzerain. Tibet's king was married to a Chinese princess and attacked Kanauj to avenge the ambassador's honor. After this incident the Maukhari empire disintegrated into small states that remained independent throughout the century.

The Rajput

Upper India remained in turmoil for a century after Harsha's death. The landscape was dotted with small kingdoms inhabited by descendants of the Huns, Gurjaras, and allied tribes that had invaded and since settled, and their rajas were in frequent conflict with one another. The Rajput, or sons of the king, inheritors of the Vedic Kshatriya tradition, came to power during this period. Their appellation was both literal and figurative. They were indeed the sons of the monarchs of assorted kingdoms when the title Rajput was adopted. But some began to claim divine descent, and the kings they cited as their fathers included the sun, the moon, and fire. Over time the name came to apply to all members of the ruling class and to all members of the tribes they led. The Rajput developed their own social order, founded on a strong code of conduct and honor. Boys were trained in the art of warfare and horsemanship from a young age. Much of their fighting was against other Rajputs.

The first major Rajput kingdom was founded in 816 by Nagabhata II (r. 805–833) on territory wrested from Kanauj. Kanauj had been under Kashmir and Bengal's control since Harsha's death, and its rulers served at the pleasure of these powerful neighbors. Pratihara, as the kingdom was known, grew to encompass much of northern India and retained its power until early in the 10th century. Raja Mahira Pratihara (r. ca. 836–890), also known more popularly as Bhoja, is considered the greatest ruler of the line. From his capital at Dhar he controlled territory stretching from the Himalayas in the north to the Nerbuda in the south, and from the now dried-up river Hakra in the west to Magadha, a vassal state in the east. A Hindu, Bhoja maintained a large army. His son, Mahendrapala (r. 890–910) took Magadha from the Pala kings of Bengal. Mahendrapala was in turn succeeded by his son, Mahipala (r. 910–940). But whereas Mahendrapala had been a worthy successor to Bhoja, Mahipala was a weak ruler who began to lose control over his kingdom. He suffered a grievous defeat in 916 when Indra III, the Rashtrakuta king of Deccan, raided the kingdom.

Mahipala's lack of power allowed other kingdoms along his borders to gain strength. One bordering kingdom helped the former ruler of Magadha regain his lost territory, continuing the decline of Mahipala's empire. The last of the line of this kingdom's rajas was overthrown by Mahmud of Ghazni in 1018–19.

3

THE COMING OF ISLAM
(700–1526)

Pakistan was founded as a haven for the subcontinent's Muslims, and today they comprise more than 95 percent of the population. But it took centuries before Islam gained more than a foothold here, and centuries more before native inhabitants took up the religion in great numbers. The roots of Islam in the subcontinent extend back to the campaigns of conquest waged by Arab armies in the first years after the birth of their religion in the seventh century. Its real impact began when Muslim rulers from Central Asia invaded the subcontinent through what is now Pakistan in the 11th century. For 500 years a succession of Islamic dynasties—the Ghaznavids, Ghurids, and Delhi Sultanate among them—ruled significant portions of the region, battling Hindu kingdoms and migrating nomads. These dynasties laid the foundation for one of the greatest kingdoms the world has seen: the Mughal Empire.

The subcontinent was accustomed to incursions from outsiders seeking land, treasures, and dominion. But unlike the nomads, Persians, or Greeks who preceded them, the Muslims introduced strong central government and many other social innovations. Their influence transformed the subcontinent and left a legacy of incomparable art and architecture, scientific knowledge, and other priceless contributions to world heritage. But in the process the Islamic tide created a schism with the subcontinent's Hindu majority that continues to define relations between Pakistan and India to this day.

Islam's First Wave

Islam, the religion brought forth by the prophet Muhammad (ca. 570–632) on the Arabian Peninsula, created a new social order and unified its formerly fractious adherents under a common faith and political community. Soon after Muhammad's death, Arab armies set off on campaigns of conquest, spreading his message in an effort to bring infidels—those who believed in neither Islam nor the religions Muhammad considered its forbears, Judaism and Christianity—into the flock. In little more than 100 years the Islamic Empire would be the largest the world had seen, stretching from the Atlantic Ocean to outposts on the Indus River. But the lands they conquered, particularly at the extremities of the empire, were often in revolt, as local rulers sought to preserve their authority. In the Pakistan region local populations frequently revolted following their subjugation. Periodic military campaigns were necessary to reassert control over restive territories.

The Islamic Empire was ruled by the caliph, the spiritual and political leader of the Islamic community, or *umma*. The caliphate, as his office and seat of power were known, was initially in Medina, in what is now Saudi Arabia. Over the history of the empire, control of the caliphate changed hands, and the caliphate moved from Medina to Damascus (in what is now Syria) under the Umayyads (660–750) and then to Baghdad (in present-day Iraq) under the Abbasids (750–1258); ultimately the caliphate resided in Constantinople under the Ottomans (1299–1922). Concurrently, rival claimants to leadership of the faith, based on lineage to the Prophet, created dynasties of their own, ruling smaller empires from Cairo (the Fatimids), Córdoba in Spain (the Umayyads as rivals to the Abbasids), and other capitals.

When Islam arrived on the doorstep of what is now Pakistan, Hun and Turkish nomads and warfare between the Persians and Byzantines had rendered the region unstable and travel unsafe. The trade between East and West along the Silk Route that previously enriched the area had dwindled.

The Arabs already knew the area from their knowledge of caravan routes and their extensive sea trade. Early in the period of Islamic conquests, between the years 637 and 643 during the reign of the Caliph Umar (r. 634–644), the Arabs mounted several campaigns in the region. Arab naval expeditions raided Debal in Sind and at Thana and Broach on the northwest coast of India. A small-scale raid against Makran in 643 paved the way for a larger invasion the following year, during which a Muslim army defeated the forces of the Hindu king of Sind near the Indus River. However, after receiving reports of the inhospitable land they had conquered, the caliph ordered the army to desist from further campaigns and make Makran the easternmost boundary of the empire.

Concurrently, the Arabs conquered Karman, an Iranian province that included southern Baluchistan, in 644, and the caliph appointed the commander of the force, Suhail ibn Adi, governor of the province. Ibn Adi mounted a campaign in Baluchistan that brought some of that region under loose Islamic control. Yet even Islamic rule in Karman was tenuous, and within a few years the inhabitants revolted. In 652 Majasha ibn Masood, who was sent by Caliph Uthman (ca. 580–656) to retake Karman, reconquered Baluchistan as well, extracting tribute payments from its subdued rulers.

In 654 an Arab army under Abdulrehman ibn Samrah was sent to pacify areas near Kabul and Ghazni, and by the end of the year all of what is now Baluchistan, with the exception of the heavily defended mountain redoubt of Kalat (then known as QaiQan), was under Islamic control. After 656 insurrections broke out in Baluchistan and Makran once more. But the *umma* was preoccupied with a civil war arising from disagreements over succession of the caliphate.

In 660, under the direction of Caliph Ali ibn Abu Talib (r. 656–661), Haris ibn Marah Abdi successfully led a large Arab force to reassert control over Makran, Baluchistan, and Sind. But in 663, while trying to suppress a revolt in Kalat, ibn Marah and most of his army were killed, and Islamic control over the Baluchistan region was lost. By then the caliphate had been relocated to Damascus under the dynastic control of the Umayyads, descendants of one of Muhammad's early followers. Caliph Muawiya ibn Abi Sufyan (r. 661–680), founder of the Umayyad dynasty, dispatched an overland expedition to recapture the region.

Kabul and the Buddhist holy land of Gandhara, which encompassed Kashmir and what is now northern Pakistan, including the Peshawar plain, Taxila, and Swat, had been under the rule of the Shahi dynasty since the decline of the Kushan empire in the late second century. Between the dynasty's founding—likely by descendants of the Kushans—and its decline in the ninth century, some 60 Shahis, as the kings were known (a title believed to be derived from the Persian *shah* or *shao* of Kushan's rulers, and meant to denote kinship with the Persians, either actual or aspirational), ruled the territory, though not without interruption. The first of the Shahis were Buddhists. An Arab army arrived at Kabul in 663 demanding its king accept Islam. For two years the Islamic warriors fought throughout the kingdom and laid siege to Kabul, bombarding it with catapults until, in 665, the city fell. The king converted, and the Arabs withdrew. The Turkish king of Gandhara, who had been Kabul's vassal, sensed an opening for himself and killed the ruler of Kabul, proclaiming himself the kingdom's lord, or Kabul Shahi. He ceded Ghazni-Kandahar in southeastern Afghanistan to his brother, and for the next two centuries this Turk Shahi dynasty controlled the

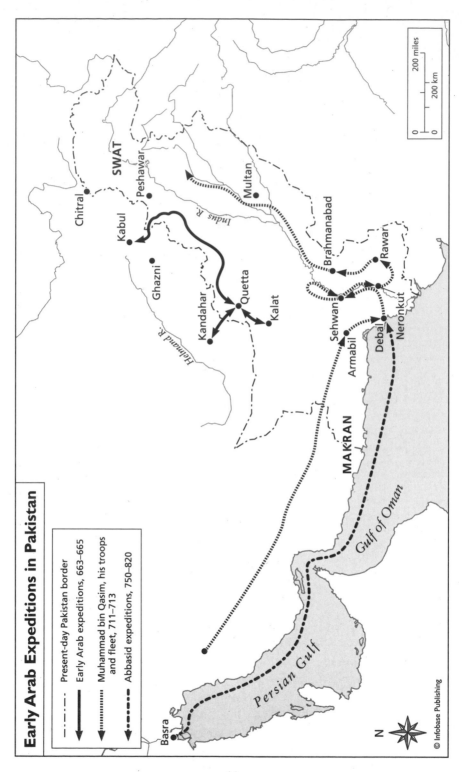

Early Arab Expeditions in Pakistan

- — · — · — Present-day Pakistan border
- ⟶ Early Arab expeditions, 663–665
- ·······▶ Muhammad bin Qasim, his troops and fleet, 711–713
- – · – · – Abbasid expeditions, 750–820

200 miles

200 km

SWAT

Chitral

Peshawar

Kabul

Ghazni

Indus R.

Multan

Brahmanabad

Rawar

Kandahar

Quetta

Kalat

Helmand R.

Sehwan

Armabil

Debal

Neronkut

MAKRAN

Gulf of Oman

Persian Gulf

Basra

N

© Infobase Publishing

44

area, serving as a buffer between the Arabs and contemporary northern Pakistan. The Arabs made efforts to collect tribute from the two Shahi kingdoms, which could only be extracted by waging war, and victory in their collection campaigns was often elusive. Indeed, Muawiya ordered several campaigns against the region, and only the last, which gained a foothold in Makran in 680, achieved any lasting success.

That same year a major schism erupted in Islam, again diverting attention and resources from the expansion and consolidation of the empire. A battle over the succession of the caliphate resulted in the killing of Husayn, grandson of the Prophet, and one of the contenders for the caliphate. This led to the establishment of the Shi'i branch of Islam and its estrangement from the Sunni branch that continues to this day. In the aftermath of this upheaval, rulers who had been subjugated by Arab conquerors reasserted their independence. To reclaim these territories Umayyad caliph Abd al-Malik ibn Marwan (r. 685–705) sent Hajjaj bin Yousuf (661–714), governor of Iraq, to restore the caliphate's rule over the northeast corner of the empire. General Qutaibah bin Muslim (d. 715) led the campaign in 699/700. He reconquered a large area of Transoxiana (located between the Oxus and Syr Darya Rivers in modern Uzbekistan) but was unable to defeat the Kabul Shahi. They reached a truce, exempting the kingdom from any tribute payments for seven years. Again, the Pakistan region escaped Arab domination and ongoing attention.

For the next three centuries (ca. 700–1000) Kabul, Peshawar, and Swat were settled by Afghan tribes who migrated from their ancestral lands west of the Sulaiman Range. At first the Kabul Shahi tried to drive the immigrants back. When that failed, the Shahi enlisted them in their battles with the Arabs and awarded the tribes villages between Kabul and Peshawar, in a region known as Lamghan, in return. The Afghanis constructed a fort in the Khyber Pass to block the advance of Arabs.

Arabs in Sind

As noted, the Arabs were familiar with the coast of the subcontinent, having sailed along its western shores plying a bustling trade with Ceylon (today's Sri Lanka) for centuries. In addition to the challenge of the elements, pirates and hostile coastal kingdoms made the voyage perilous. At the mouth of the Indus River (called the Mehran by the Arabs), the port city of Debal served as the stronghold of the Meds, one such kingdom. Noted seafarers, they engaged in trade, fishing, and piracy and extorted seafarers for protection payments.

The Meds seized the ships of any who attempted to navigate the waters they claimed without paying for safe passage. In 710 news reached Arabia that Debal pirates had seized an Arab ship, stolen its cargo, and imprisoned its crew and passengers, Arab families returning home from a visit to Ceylon. Exacerbating the outrage, the ship had been carrying gifts from the king of Ceylon to Caliph Walid I (r. 705–715).

Hajjaj bin Yousuf, then governor of the Islamic empire's eastern end, demanded the kingdom's ruler, Raja Dahir (d. 712), pay for the ship and its cargo and free its passengers. Dahir claimed he held no sway with the pirates, and negotiations broke down. Two limited campaigns against Dahir subsequently failed. Finally Yousuf received permission for a major campaign against all of Sind. His young nephew, Muhammad bin Qasim (695–715), was given command.

The Campaigns of Muhammad bin Qasim

By age 15 Muhammad bin Qasim was one of his uncle's most trusted assistants, from whom he received his education in warfare. At age 16 he served under General Qutaibah bin Muslim, where he distinguished himself with his military planning. Six months of preparation preceded Qasim's Sind campaign. Before commencing the assault, Qasim married his uncle's daughter. His attack force included 6,000 Syrian horsemen, 6,000 troops on camels, and 3,000 Bactrian camels to carry supplies. Ships carried five large catapults. The largest, called Uroos, Arabic for bride, required a force of 500 men to operate. A network of couriers was organized for battlefield communications.

The coastal strip of Makran was the first region of Sind attacked and the first to fall. Armabil (contemporary Bela in Baluchistan) was next. Joined by the troops from the previous two unsuccessful Arab attacks on the Hindu kingdom, Qasim set out for Debal on the Indus River delta, where a naval expedition from Basra (in present-day Iraq) was also directed. The sea and land forces arrived at Debal on the same day, the former having been about a month in transit. They dug trenches and awaited orders to attack.

Residents of Debal believed their gods would protect them as long as the flag waved from their central temple. Qasim, learning this, made the flag his primary target and had the catapult arm of Uroos shortened to hit the target. Debal's flag was soon knocked down, the fortifications breached, and the town conquered, though its leader fled. Qasim issued a decree:

All human beings are created by Allah and are equal in His eyes. He is one and without a peer. In my religion only those who are kind to fellow human beings are worthy of respect. Cruelty and oppression are prohibited in our law. We fight only those who are unjust and are enemies of the truth. (Hussain 1997, 103)

A treaty was promulgated by one of the officers: On behalf of the Commander of the Faithful, I, Habib bin Muslim, grant amnesty to all the people of Daibul [Debal] and hereby ensure their personal safety, security of their temples, women and children and their property. So long as you will pay jizya [a tax of protection levied on non-Muslims] we shall abide by this agreement. (Ibid.)

Hindu rule in the region had been marked by oppression and cruelty toward both the large Buddhist population and lower-caste Hindus. By their tolerance the Muslims, as they had in other conquered regions, soon won over the populace, who had little regard for their previous rulers.

Continuing the campaign, Qasim next attacked Neronkut, a predominantly Buddhist city farther upriver on the Indus, near present-day Hyderabad, which was under the rule of Raja Dahir's son, Prince Jay Singh. Siege equipment was loaded back on the ships and floated up the Indus. After a six-day march the troops arrived at the city. Dahir ordered his son to vacate the city and join him at Brahmanabad, leaving Neronkut in the command of a Buddhist priest who turned the city over to Qasim and provided fodder for the Arab's camels and horses.

Qasim now marched on Sehwan, under the rule of Dahir's cousin, Bhoj Rai. The city's Buddhist community asked Bhoj to capitulate, but he attempted an attack on the rear of Qasim's forces. While the Arabs planned their counterattack, the Buddhists secretly sent Qasim word that the commoners did not support Bhoj Rai and advised the Arab commander their army was largely ineffective and unready to fight. After another week of battle, Bhoj Rai fled. Qasim organized an Islamic administration of the conquered city. The fortress was later retaken by its former ruler, but was won back by Muhammad Khan, one of Qasim's generals. Sehwan became a center of Islamic power in Sind.

With losses mounting, local rulers and governors began offering submission to Qasim and providing supplies for his army. Leaders who submitted were treated generously. All were allowed to continue practicing their religion.

Final Victories

Meanwhile, the Arab's advance bogged down at the Indus. Blocked by Dahir's son from crossing the river at Brahmanabad, the army encamped on its banks. After several weeks their supplies began to run out. Horses were slaughtered for food, and soldiers weakened from hunger. Qasim sent Yousuf a request for supplies and received 2,000 horses along with vinegar-soaked cotton, intended perhaps as a palliative for the rampant vitamin deficiency. The Arabs finally built a bridge of boats and after 50 days crossed the Indus, making for Rawar, joined by more local rulers who switched sides against Dahir. In June of 713, following several days of skirmishes, Dahir, leading his forces from atop an elephant, came out to face Qasim in a battle that would decide the fate of Sind. Early in the battle a blazing arrow struck the trunk of Dahir's elephant, setting its ornamental silk covering on fire. The panicked elephant ran, leaving Dahir's abandoned forces frightened and confused. Returning to the battle on horseback, Dahir tried to lead his troops but was decapitated by an Arab swordsman. His army was routed by the Islamic army and their newfound local allies. After the battle the city of Rawar surrendered, as did Brahmanabad. But strongholds remained. The Multan fort resisted the Arabs' months-long effort to conquer it. Finally the channel that supplied the fort with its water was discovered and cut off, and the fort surrendered. To secure the protection of their temple, the Multanis gave a fortune in treasure to Qasim, a sum large enough to help pay for the entire expedition. From here Qasim sent forces to Kashmiri strongholds on the Jhelum River and to the borders of the Kanauj kingdom in northern India.

During the campaign Yousuf died, as did Caliph Walid I soon after Multan had fallen. The new caliph, Sulaiman (r. 715–717), ceded power in the empire's east to a rival Arab faction. Yousuf's family members were now regarded as enemies by the new ruler. Qasim was recalled and executed before further advances were made. Nonetheless, Sind became Islam's path (*bab-al Islam*, or door of Islam) to the subcontinent.

Sind after Muhammad bin Qasim

Despite the halt in the advance of the Arab forces, for the next 200 years Sind remained part of the Islamic Empire, under the direction of at least 37 Arab governors who oversaw the administrations of local rulers. Islam spread while Buddhists and Hindus continued to practice their faith. Local revenue officials collected *jizya* and *zakat* (a tax on Muslims). Mosques sprouted in every city, joining the Hindu and

Buddhist temples and shrines. Disputes between Muslims were settled by *qadis,* Islamic judges, according to Islamic law. Disputes between Buddhists and Hindus were settled by Brahman priests of the local *panchayat,* or council. Over time the Islamic and Sindi customs intertwined to create a new culture. Underscoring the deep bond that grew, Sindi became the first language into which the Qur'an was translated.

Some 10 years after Qasim's conquests, Junaid, an Arab governor, tried to expand Sind's empire to the east by annexing Kutch, the coastal area between the mouth of the Indus and the Gulf of Kutch, and Malwa. But in 738 the Arabs were defeated at the Battle of Rajasthan by the Pratihara Rajputs of the Thar Desert. A northward expansion into Punjab from Multan was halted with Kashmiri help under the leadership of Laladitya (724–760), one of Kashmir's greatest rulers. Laladitya maintained an alliance with the Tang dynasty in China, as did Turkish Shahi rulers in Kabul who sought allies against the Arabs.

The Arabs were not the only force seeking to gain territory in the region. Tibet ruled much of Nepal, northern India, and what is now Bangladesh. In about 726 Tibet conquered Skardu, which lay to Gilgit's east. Seeking to counter their growing power, in 747 the Chinese sent troops to southern Chitral, an area in modern northwest Pakistan, where they replaced the pro-Tibet ruler, putting his brother, who was closer to the Chinese, on the throne. But Tibet's westward expansion continued, finally winning dominance over the Gilgit Valley and upper Chitral.

Such was the importance of maintaining strong ties with China that before the leader of Kabul and Swat passed rule to his son, he sought approval from China. Underscoring China's interest in defending its flank, China also granted the son the title "Brave General Guarding the Left" in approving the succession.

Meanwhile the resurgent Arabs resumed efforts to expand their empire in Central Asia. The conflict between the Arabs and Chinese for control of this area ended at the Battle of Talas in 751, with the Arabs emerging victorious. In the aftermath most of the Turkish nomads who had settled in the region converted to Islam. Yet despite the Arab victory, the area encompassing Gandhara, Swat, and Kabul remained largely independent.

The Abbasids

By this time the caliphate, the office of the political and spiritual ruler of the Islamic Empire, had moved to Baghdad, and the Abbasid dynasty of caliphs was in power. It was under the Abbasids that the intellectual flowering called the Golden Age of Islam took place. The Golden Age reached its height during the reign of the Abbasid Caliph Harun al-Rashid (r. 786–809). His death created unrest throughout the empire, as local rulers sought to assert independence while his sons Muhammad al-Amin (r. 809–813) and Abdullah al-Mamun (r. 813–833) fought for control of the empire. While the two were thus occupied, the governor of Transoxiana proclaimed his independence, backed by allies including Qarluq Turks, the Shahi of Kabul, and the Tibetan empire. Al-Mamun finally prevailed in the struggle for succession and quickly dispatched forces to subdue Transoxiana's rebellious ruler and his allies.

In 817 the Arab forces captured Kabul's ruler, Ispabadh Shah, at Merv, in present-day Turkmenistan. Taken to Baghdad and brought before the caliph, the shah converted to Islam. His successor as *lagaturman,* another title by which Kabul's rulers were known, was allowed to rule the Kabul region, but was assessed twice the normal tribute, which he paid to the governor of Khorasan, the Islamic Empire's northeastern frontier state.

A second campaign sent Muslim troops to upper Chitral as far as the Indus River to forestall future attacks from Tibet. Here they planted the black flags of the Abbasid caliphate.

In suppressing local rebellions throughout the empire, al-Mamun came to rely on several generals. In Khorasan the general who directed al-Mamun's victory over his brother, Tahir ibn Husain (d. 822), a Persian by birth, was so effective he became the de facto ruler of the region, though he continued to swear fealty to the caliph. Like Tahir himself, his troops were primarily Persian Muslims. This marked the first time the Islamic Empire came to depend on non-Arabs for its security. The increasing reliance on non-Arab Muslims would have a dramatic impact on the empire, as eventually these military leaders took over the empire while retaining the Abbasid caliphs as figureheads. The Turks in particular, as a result of the Abbasid practice of capturing Turkish boys and educating and training them in the military arts, would come to occupy premier positions in the Abbasid power structure.

However, in the late ninth century Tahir's successors lost control of the territory to a Muslim coppersmith from Sistan (now eastern Iran), Yaqub bin Laith (r. ca. 867–879). Unable to defeat Yaqub, the Tahirid governor gave him authority over eastern Persia and Afghanistan, creating the Saffarid (from *saffar,* coppersmith) Emirate.

In 870/1 Yaqub attacked and defeated the Hindu Shahi ruler of Kabul, even though Kabul was nominally a suzerain of the Islamic

THE REGION'S PART IN ISLAM'S GOLDEN AGE

The region that is now Pakistan played a prominent role in the era of inquiry and discovery known as the Golden Age of Islam. Numerous works that had been created in what is now Pakistan when it was part of the Sassanian Persian Empire (224–651) were now translated from Pahlawi into Arabic. This includes the tale of Sinbad the Sailor, later collected in *A Thousand and One Nights*. Chess, which became popular throughout the Arab world, also originated in the Indian subcontinent and came to Persia under the Sassanians. A family from Punjab, the Barmakids, played a key role in the transfer of knowledge from the region to the Islamic Empire. Originally Buddhist priests, the Barmakids were masters of the medical arts. They settled in Balkh, along the current Afghan-Uzbekistan border, and converted to Islam. Later they became secretaries and advisers to the Abbasid caliphs until they lost power in 803.

A raid against Kashmir by the governor of Sind during this time brought the famous Sanskrit scholar Mankha to Baghdad. After studying its tenets, Mankha converted to Islam and thereafter spent his life translating works from Sanskrit into Arabic. Mathematics also benefited from Islam's exposure to India. What are commonly called Arabic numerals in the West originated in a numbering system from the subcontinent. The numeral zero was part of this system and was probably invented centuries earlier in the Taxila region. Some 700 years later this knowledge passed to the Western world during the Renaissance.

Empire. To win favor, Yaqub sent treasures back to the Abbasid caliph in Baghdad. In return the caliph extended Yaqub's authority over all of Persia and Sind. For the next decade Yaqub appointed the governor of the Hindu Shahi kingdom. By 876 Yaqub was threatening the Abbasid caliphate itself. He marched his army to Baghdad but was defeated near the city. Though not routed, Saffarid power began to decline. By 903 his descendants' rule was again confined to Sistan.

Another Persian group, the Samanids, composed of nobles and landowners, played a large role in pushing the Saffarids back to Sistan. For their service the caliph ceded them rule of eastern Muslim territories including Persia and Afghanistan. Samanid rule lasted from 903 to 999 and marked a rare period of tranquility and prosperity in Central Asia.

With the Saffarids gone, by 900 the Kabul Valley was free of Muslim governance, and the Hindu Shahis' rule was restored. The Hindu Shahi dynasty had been founded by the Brahman minister Kallar in 843. The Turk Shahis who preceded him had been mostly Buddhists. Kallar had moved the capital east from Kabul to Ohind, seat of one of the Hindu kingdoms that dominated the region, on the west bank of the Indus River, near present-day Attock. Ohind had historically been a major crossing point of the river. With Central Asian trade routes now under Arab control, overland trade again flourished, and the city became an important trade city. Here precious gems, textiles, perfumes, and other goods made their way west from the northern subcontinent. Illustrating the importance the region played in international trade of the era, coins minted by the Shahis have been found throughout the subcontinent, Central Asia, and even eastern Europe. The city also became a center of education and culture. But education at this time was confined to preservation rather than expansion of knowledge. Great Hindu temples were built by the Shahis and filled with idols, many of them later taken by Arab raiders. Some of their temples can still be seen in the Salt Range at Nandana, Malot, Siv Ganga, and Ketas. Ruins of these shrines are also on the west bank of the Indus, while the remains of old fortresses dot the hills of Swat.

While the Hindu Shahi kingdom flourished in the northwest of present-day Pakistan in Sind and Makran, small Muslim kingdoms developed. Mansurah and Multan were the two main principalities. The ruins of Mansurah attest to its former grandeur, while the Hebadi dynasty of Multan was well known for its devotion to learning and the welcome it gave scholars.

Kashmir's power continued to grow during this period, and it came to control parts of Punjab. The Hindu Shahi kingdoms formed an alliance to block any further Kashmiri expansion. Under Jayapala Shahi (r. 964–1001), the most celebrated Hindu Shahi ruler, the Hindu Shahi kingdom extended from west of Kabul to east of the present Pakistan-India border, and in the north from the valleys of Bajaur, Buner, and southern Kashmir to Multan in the south.

Islam's Second Wave

For some 350 years Islamic rule in what is now Pakistan and India was confined to small areas or exercised through local vassals. But beginning in the 11th century, after campaigns of conquest waged by Muslim rulers from Central Asia, direct Islamic rule would extend over large swaths of the subcontinent.

The Ghaznavids

The Hindu Shahi kingdom's western border abutted Ghazni, ruled by Turkish Muslims and their king, Sebüktigin (r. 977–997). Seeking to expand his kingdom, Jayapala, the Hindu shahi, raised an army and marched on Ghazni. After days of battle the Turkish Muslims had gained the upper hand. Sebüktigin accepted Jayapala's promise of money, territory, and elephants in exchange for peace. But Jayapala reneged on the agreement, incarcerating the Turkish officers sent along to assure his compliance. Sebüktigin marched his army in pursuit, burning temples and destroying property along the way. Though outnumbered by Jayapala's massive force, skillful deployment of the Turkish cavalry earned victory for the Muslims The defeated Jayapala ultimately committed suicide.

Mahmud of Ghazni

Sebüktigin was succeeded by his son, Mahmud of Ghazni (r. 998–1030). Under Mahmud the Ghaznis extended their rule into non-Islamic northern India, adding great wealth to their kingdom. Concurrently Islam spread throughout the region and became the dominant social and political force in what is now Pakistan.

By this time the Islamic Empire had split into rival caliphates: the Abbasids, who ruled from Baghdad, and the Fatimids in Cairo, whose hereditary rulers claimed legitimacy to the caliphate through their descent from Fatima, daughter of the prophet Muhammad. Multan had been under the control of Fatimid loyalists. Mahmud, who supported the Abbasids, attacked and defeated Multan and its Hindu allies. He also continued his battles against the Hindu Shahi dynasty, which gradually lost ground, from 1000 to 1026. In 1001 he conquered Peshawar, and it became an important center of the empire. As he conducted his military campaigns, Mahmud also built his capital of Ghazni into the greatest city east of Baghdad. The Persian scholar al-Beruni (973–1048) accompanied Mahmud back to Ghazni after his conquest and annexation of Khorasan and also on campaigns in the subcontinent, becoming the first Muslim scholar to study Indian society and languages.

For nearly 200 years Mahmud and his successors ruled what is now Pakistan. During the Ghaznavid period Muslim missionaries

The mausoleum at Ghazni is a relic of the Ghaznavids, the first major Islamic kingdom in Central Asia. (Borromeo/Art Resource, NY)

and scholars traveled throughout the kingdom spreading the prophet Muhammad's message. One of the first, Shaikh Ismail Bohkari, began preaching in Lahore in 1005. Islam was embraced by more Afghan tribesmen as well as the Janjuas rajputs of the Salt Range and others in the Punjab. Gradually it was accepted throughout the population.

Today Mahmud is considered a hero in Pakistan but reviled in India for forcing Hindus and Buddhists to convert to Islam and for the sacking and plundering of Hindu temples.

In 1018 Mahmud conquered Kanauj, marking the end of the Gurjara-Pratihara dynasty. The Pratiharas were superseded by another Rajput clan, the Rathors, who ruled under Mahmud and his successors.

With the stability wrought by the Ghaznavids, trade along the silk routes in Punjab that had been disrupted by warfare among local kingdoms revived. Ghazni became an important trade center, and Mahmud minted coins to facilitate commerce. Among Hindus trade had always been an occupation of the lower castes. But with the growing profits, by 1030 Brahmans were also involved in mercantile activities.

Masud I

Mahmud was succeeded by his eldest son, Masud (r. 1031–41), who reorganized the administration in Lahore, a Ghaznavid vassal state, to assure control over the new territories. Masud sought to keep Muslim leaders separate from their Hindu subjects without alienating the masses. He instructed Turkish officers not to drink, play polo, or socialize with Hindu officers, nor display religious intolerance toward them. When the governor of Lahore raided Banares (modern Varanasi) and failed to give Masud any of the spoils, Masud showed his own tolerance by selecting a Hindu general, Tilak, to lead a retaliatory attack on Lahore.

However, the empire began to crumble. Multan regained its independence after Mahmud's death and again allied itself with the Fatimids. The western part of the empire began to fall to the Seljuks, the Turkish mercenaries who had taken the reins of the Abbasid caliphate. Masud's father, Mahmud, had always kept a Seljuk prince as a hostage to gain leverage over the Turks. But a hostage was insufficient to deter them now. The Seljuks continued their onslaught, and at the Battle of Merv (1040) they drove the Ghaznavids from Khorasan. Masud was prepared to accept defeat, but his own Turkish troops rejected his submissive attitude and, during their retreat, rebelled at the Indus River crossing at Ohind. Masud was arrested along with his wife and some followers, and a month later he was beheaded.

After Masud

The Ghaznavid dynasty survived Masud's execution. While the Seljuks assimilated their gains in Khorasan, Masud's son Maudud (r. 1042–49) defeated Masud's younger brother to take control of the empire. During Maudud's reign three Hindu rajas made repeated attempts to drive the Ghaznavids from the Punjab. The Hindus succeeded in regaining Kangra and Thanesar but were thwarted at Lahore during their siege. A Turkish marksman killed the Hindus' leader, and his troops withdrew in disarray. Maudud later sent one of his sons to oversee Peshawar, and another to run Lahore.

During this period southeastern Sind was ruled by the Sumras, one of the first clans to accept Islam following Qasim's campaigns. They assisted the Arabs in their governance of Sind, though they later developed an allegiance to the Fatimids. By the mid-11th century they had assumed independent rule of southeastern Sind, making their capital at Kutch. More than a score of Sumra rulers presided over the Sumra kingdom over the next two centuries.

Ghaznavid rule in what is today northern Pakistan continued under Ibrahim (r. 1059–99) and his son Masud III (r. 1099–1115). Though the Seljuks had increased their power in the Islamic Empire, treaties with them kept the western flank of the Ghaznavid kingdom secure. Lahore became a major cultural center in the Muslim world during this time. Among its important figures was Syed Ali Ibn Usman of Havver, also known as Data Ganj Bakhsh (d. 1077). A noted Muslim theologian, he wrote poetry and scholarly works, helping spread Islam in the region. His treatise on Sufism was the standard text on the subject for centuries. His former home in Lahore is still visited by thousands annually. Lahore's prominence as a center of learning and the arts continued into the reign of Ibrahim's grandson, Shirzad (r. 1115).

The Ghurids

In a region called Ghur, the desolate hill country south of Herat, Afghanistan, a blood feud precipitated by Bahram Shah (1118–52), the ruler of Ghazni, gave birth to a new kingdom that would supplant Ghaznavid rule. Bahram executed a prince of Ghur, provoking one of the prince's brothers to attack Ghazni and force Bahram into a temporary retreat. When Bahram again set upon the Ghurid forces, he captured the Ghur prince who had led the assault and barbarously put him to death. The remaining Ghurid princes, determined to avenge the deaths of their brothers, mounted an overwhelming attack on Bahram's kingdom in 1150/1, completely destroying Ghazni and earning their leader the honorific Jahan-Soz, or Earth Burner. The Ghaznis moved their capital to Lahore.

The Ghurids, now independent of Ghazni rule, attacked Herat but were defeated by the Seljuk governor. But in 1153 the Seljuks fell to another Turkish tribe, the Ghuzz, who went on to conquer most of Afghanistan, including Ghazni. After 1160 the Ghuzz kept the Ghaznavids confined to what is today northern Pakistan.

In 1173 the Ghurid ruler, Sultan Ghiyas-ud-din Muhammad, assisted by his younger brother, drove the Ghuzz from the Ghazni region. The younger brother, Muhammad of Ghur (1162–1206), began raiding the subcontinent, using the Gomal Pass as his transit point. In 1175 Muhammad of Ghur occupied Multan and Uch (near present-day Bahawalpur). Following in the footsteps of Mahmud of Ghazni, he set out across the Thar Desert in Rajputana to raid Gujarat. He was defeated by Chalukya Raja of Kathiawar (today's northwest India) in 1178. Bloodied but unbowed, Muhammad of Ghur attacked Ghaznavid lands, taking Peshawar in 1179. He defeated both the Gakkars, powerful tribes that lived in the hill country between the upper Indus and Jhelum Rivers, and the Ghaznavid ruler Khusrau Malik (r. 1160–87), taking Sialkot in 1185 and occupying Lahore in 1186/7. Muhammad's conquest of Lahore marked the end of the Ghaznavid dynasty.

In 1190/1 Muhammad conquered Bhatinda, India, in the territory of the Chauhan. But once Muhammad set off to return to Ghazni, the Chauhan ruler, Raja Prithviraj (1165–92), sent forces to retake the fortress at Bhatinda. Muhammad reversed his course and met Raja Prithviraj's army at Tarain (also Taraori, near the present-day city of Thanesar, India). Muhammad's forces lost the battle, though Muhammad survived. Seeking revenge, he returned in 1192. At the Second Battle of Tarain, Muhammad captured Prithviraj and completely routed his numerically superior forces. The victory opened northern India to Muslim conquest. The raja's queen and attendants immolated themselves in the style of defeated Rajput women. Delhi was now under Muslim rule, as it would remain for more than 650 years, the capital of a series of powerful Muslim dynasties, until the last Mughal was deposed by the British.

By 1203 Muhammad had established Ghurid rule of the Ganges River basin. From his capital in Firoz Koh in Ghur, Afghanistan, he ruled over much of the subcontinent, sharing power with his older brother. To the west lay Khwarezm, extending from Persia into Central Asia, ruled by a Turkish Muslim dynasty. Shortly before his death in 1206, Muhammad failed to defeat the shah of Khwarezm, Ala-ud-Din Muhammad II (r. 1200–20, d. 1231) in battle. He was assassinated in his sleep, bringing the Ghurid empire to its end. The shah of Khwarezm gained control of all of Transoxiana (Turkestan), then conquered the Ghurid territories west of the Indus. Muhammad of Ghur's governors established independent fiefdoms east of the river. A top Ghurid general, Qutb-ud-Din Aibak (r. 1206–10), or Aybak, who had conquered and been appointed governor of Delhi, made that city his capital. He founded the first of a series of Muslim dynasties that would be known as the Delhi Sultanate.

The Delhi Sultanate

The Delhi Sultanate (1206–1526) established Islamic rule throughout much of the subcontinent, and it maintained its predominance in the region for more than three centuries. The sultanate's formative period, 1206–90, is often called the Slave dynasty because the rulers of this era were Turkish generals who began their lives as slaves. They took the title *sultan*.

The Slave Dynasty

Qutb-ud-Din Aibak, the first sultan of Delhi and the first Muslim ruler to make his capital in India, was born in Transoxiana. Captured and sold into slavery as a child, he received a good education and was schooled in archery and horsemanship. Upon the death of his owner, the chief *qadi* of Nishapur, in Khorasan, Aibak was sold to Muhammad Ghuri, eventually becoming his most trusted general. Aibak conquered much of northern India during the Ghurid campaigns of conquest. A builder as well as battler, he constructed mosques in Delhi and Ajmer, Rajasthan. Aibak was in Lahore subduing a Gakkar uprising when Muhammad died, and he established his capital in that city before moving it to Delhi. He died in an accident while playing polo in 1210.

SUFISM

Sufism developed in the 10th century as a reaction to the increased worldliness of Islam in the aftermath of the empire's expansion and growing secularism. It was enthusiastically adopted in the Sind and Punjab. Sufis practiced asceticism and eschewed the trappings of materialism. The populations in these regions were familiar with these practices, as they had a history of asceticism under Buddhists. By the 13th century Multan and Uch were flourishing centers of both trade and Sufism, drawing many merchants, Sufis, and scholars. Here Sufi saints and Muslim trade and craft guilds were closely linked. Indeed, during Iltutmish's reign, Multan became the site of the first Sufi center, or *khanqah,* established by Shaikh Bahand-din Zakariyya, or Baha-ud-din Zakariyya (ca. 1170–1267). He introduced the Suhrawardi order of Sufism to the subcontinent. The Suhrawardis were fervent proselytizers, responsible for converting many Hindus to Islam.

The Chistiyya order of Sufis was the second to establish a *khanqah.* The order was founded in Chist, a village near Herat, Afghanistan, by Khwaja Muin-ud-din Chisti (b. ca. 1141–1236). By the time of his death Chistiyya *khanqahs* had been founded throughout the Delhi Sultanate. Baba Farid Shakar Gunj, or Farid-ud-din Ganjshakar (ca. 1180–1266), his successor, is considered the first great poet of the Punjabi language.

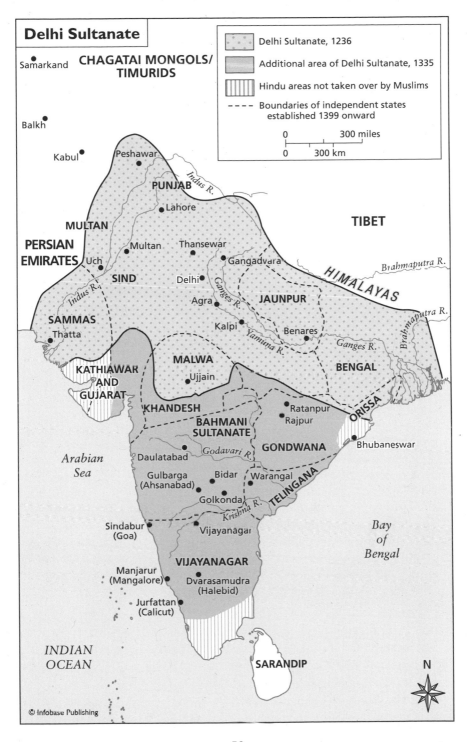

Delhi Sultanate

- CHAGATAI MONGOLS/TIMURIDS
- Samarkand
- Balkh
- Kabul
- Peshawar
- PUNJAB
- Indus R.
- Lahore
- MULTAN
- PERSIAN EMIRATES
- Multan
- Uch
- Thansewar
- SIND
- Indus R.
- Delhi
- Gangadvara
- TIBET
- Brahmaputra R.
- HIMALAYAS
- Agra
- Ganges R.
- JAUNPUR
- SAMMAS
- Thatta
- Kalpi
- Yamuna R.
- Benares
- Ganges R.
- Brahmaputra R.
- KATHIAWAR AND GUJARAT
- MALWA
- Ujjain
- BENGAL
- KHANDESH
- BAHMANI SULTANATE
- Ratanpur
- Rajpur
- GONDWANA
- ORISSA
- Bhubaneswar
- Arabian Sea
- Daulatabad
- Godavari R.
- Gulbarga (Ahsanabad)
- Bidar
- Warangal
- Golkonda
- TELINGANA
- Krishna R.
- Bay of Bengal
- Sindabur (Goa)
- Vijayanagar
- VIJAYANAGAR
- Manjarur (Mangalore)
- Dvarasamudra (Halebid)
- Jurfattan (Calicut)
- INDIAN OCEAN
- SARANDIP
- N

Legend:
- Delhi Sultanate, 1236
- Additional area of Delhi Sultanate, 1335
- Hindu areas not taken over by Muslims
- Boundaries of independent states established 1399 onward
- 0 — 300 miles
- 0 — 300 km

© Infobase Publishing

59

Aibak was briefly succeeded by his son, Aram Shah (r. 1210–11), but owing to his reputed laziness and incompetence, Turkish officers deposed him in favor of Aibak's son-in-law, Shams-ud-Din, who ruled under the name Iltutmish (r. 1211–36). Iltutmish was faced with insurrections throughout the empire, but methodically took on the young sultanate's former vassals and then began expanding the empire's territory. He defeated Taj-ud-Din Yalduz, or Yulduz, in Lahore in 1215 and Nasir-ud-Din Qubacha (r. 1206–28), who ruled Multan, upper Sind, and portions of Punjab, in 1215 and again in 1228. Both these foes were former slave generals who served under Muhammad of Ghazni, as had Iltutmish's father-in-law, Aibak, founder of the Delhi Sultanate. The Khalji in Bengal, a kingdom also founded by slave generals formerly allied with Aibak, were defeated after Iltutmish mounted three campaigns against them. The Abbasid caliphate recognized Iltutmish's rule and sent envoys to Delhi from Baghdad in 1229. By the time of his death in 1236, the Delhi Sultanate's territory was consolidated.

Mongols on the Doorstep

Under the reign of Iltutmish the sultanate—and the region that is now Pakistan—contended with the depredations of armies of Mongol nomads that swept into the region led by Chinggis, or Genghis Khan, (ca. 1162–1227). Chinggis Khan and the Mongols first came to the area in 1221 in pursuit of Jalal–ud-Din Mengüberdi, son of the shah of Khwarezm, Ala-ud-Din Muhammad II. The Mongols had overrun Khwarezm in 1220. Ala-ud-Din Muhammad had escaped but died soon after, and Mengüberdi (r. 1220–31) fled east with a small army. The Mongols caught and defeated them at the Battle of the Indus. Mengüberdi and some of his followers escaped into India. Chinggis Khan continued into the subcontinent as well, plundering and sacking his way through Punjab and Multan. Iltutmish is said to have declined Mengüberdi's request for sanctuary in Delhi.

By the end of Iltutmish's reign the Mongols controlled much of what is now Pakistan as well as most of Central Asia and parts of Europe. Now that the silk routes were under their jurisdiction, the Mongols switched from raiding caravans to taxing them. In the Pakistan region, towns west of the Indus submitted to Mongol rule while the Delhi Sultanate claimed all lands east of the river. Local rulers in the Indus region tried to remain neutral.

After the death of Chinggis Khan the Mongol empire split into four parts. Present-day Pakistan came to be known as Chaghatai, named after the descendants of Chaghatai, Chinggis Khan's second son. Mongol raids continued to ravage the region, ultimately depopulating the provinces of today's Baluchistan and NWFP. Marco Polo (1254–1324) was held prisoner here, and after his escape wrote of the Chaghatai: "They know well the localities . . . they come here by the dozen thousands, sometimes more, sometimes less. Once they seize a plain, no one escapes, neither men nor cattle. If they make their mind to plunder, there is nothing that they cannot take hold of. When they take a folk in captivity they slay the old and take away the young whom they sell as slaves" (Hussain 1997, 145). The raids also drew Baluchi and Afghan tribes into the western Pakistan area, as the land was now emptied, introducing two important ethnic groups into the population of Pakistan.

On the east side of the Indus Iltutmish was succeeded by his daughter Razia Sultana (r. 1236–40). But military leaders were unwilling to recognize her rule. Turkish nobles rebelled against her and seized power, but were unable to agree on a leader. Iltutmish's youngest son, Nasir-ud-Din Mahmud (r. 1246–66), was his last descendant to rule the sultanate. He spent most of his time in prayer, turning the affairs of the state over to a Turkish slave, Ghiyas ud Din Balban, who gradually gained control of the empire. Balban (r. 1266–87) took the throne upon Nasir-ud-Din's death.

The sultanate had grown in part due to the ambitious corps of Turkish officers that led its military victories. Their contributions were reflected in the rule by consensus previous sultans had observed. Balban dispensed with this practice and shifted composition of the military garrisons from Turkish to Afghan forces, lessening the chances of an attempted coup by these officers. Concurrently he introduced pomp and ceremony into the state's affairs. From his subjects' point of view, his major contribution was the construction of forts from the Indus to Delhi, built to protect the region from the Mongols. He also rebuilt towns and villages throughout Punjab the marauders had destroyed, including the reconstruction of Lahore. Balban's eldest and most capable son, Muhammad, governor of Multan and Sind, engaged the Mongols successfully in several skirmishes, but died in battle.

Balban was succeeded by his inexperienced and undisciplined 18-year-old grandson, Muiz ud din Qaiqabad (r. 1286–90). Four years later, after suffering a debilitating stroke, Qaiqabad named his three-year-old son Kayumars (r. 1290) as ruler in his stead. A group of Turkish nobles asked Jalal-ud-din Firuz Khalji (r. 1290–96) to step in, and the elderly general accepted. But the sultanate was in decline, as it had been since the reign of Iltutmish. The corps of ambitious Turkish officers who helped create the kingdom now gave in to avarice over the spoils of the dynasty's demise, further fragmenting the empire. Some resented the increasing power of the Khalji clan, considered to be of Afghan rather than Turkish origin.

The Khalji Dynasty

The Delhi Sultanate continued battling the Mongols after the fall of the Slave Dynasty. By the time Jalal-ud-Din Khalji took the throne, he had spent years battling the Mongols. Now old and nonthreatening, he was unable to keep either his officers or the Mongols in check. He appointed his battle-hardened and ruthless nephew Ala-ud-Din Khalji as governor. Later Ala-ud-Din Khalji (r. 1296–1316) succeeded him to the throne. Battles with and victories against the Mongols marked his rule.

Soon after Ala-ud-Din assumed rule, Punjab was invaded by an army of 100,000 Mongols. Ala-ud-Din drove off this first wave. A year later the Mongols returned and captured Sehwan, but Ala-ud-Din reclaimed the city, capturing thousands of Mongols and their leader. In 1299 the Mongols laid siege to Delhi. Advisors urged Ala-ud-Din to make peace with the Mongols, but he refused: "If I were to follow your advice, how could I show my face, how could I go into my harem, what store would the people set by me?" (Hussain 1997, 151). Instead he attacked and defeated the Mongol army.

An able administrator as well as warrior, Ala-ud-Din reorganized the state, ending local insurrections by reorganizing local rule and creating a centrally paid army that could stave off Mongol attacks anywhere in the kingdom. Ultimately he drove the Mongols from all of Pakistan and carried the war to their strongholds, pillaging Kabul, Ghazni, and Kandahar. Ala-ud-Din also conquered the Sumra kingdom and expanded Muslim rule deep into the subcontinent. Expeditions in 1307, 1309, and 1313 brought victories as far as the tip of the Deccan peninsula. Local rulers held their positions but paid tribute to Delhi.

Ala-ud-Din's conquest of southern India brought an infusion of new cultural elements into the Delhi Sultanate. Artisans and craftsmen from the conquered areas flocked to the prosperous cities of the kingdom. This infusion resulted in cultural advances that included the sitar, purportedly invented by Amir Khusro, or Khusrau, Dehlawi (1253–1325), a Muslim intent on creating a separate Islamic art tradition based on the subcontinent's own cultural roots. The stringed instrument was derived from the Persian *tanpura* and the South Indian vina. Amir Khusro is also credited with inventing the tabla ("drum" in Arabic), a percussion instrument based on the South Indian drum. (Amir Khusro makes no mention of creating these instruments in his own writings.)

A long illness compromised Ala-ud-Din's administrative and leadership capabilities, and he ceded control of the empire to his general, Malik Kafur, a former Hindu slave. Confusion reigned after Ala-ud-Din's death until 1320, when Punjab's governor, Ghias-ud-Din Tughluq, accepted the request of Muslim nobles to take the throne.

The Tughluq Dynasty

A former governor of Punjab, Ghias-ud-Din Tughluq (r. 1320–25) reasserted the power of the sultanate in Delhi, the Deccan, and Bengal, which had ebbed while Al-ud-Din focused on his southern conquests. A bold general and able administrator, he reversed some of Ala-ud-Din's unpopular policies, granting *iqtadars*—local administrators who raised land revenues and maintained troops for the sultanate—greater control over their lands and lower tribute payments. His short reign ended when he died in the collapse of a poorly built pavilion.

Muhammad ibn Tughluq (r. 1325–51), Ghias-ud-Din's son, was similar to Ala-ud-Din in his ruthlessness and ambition, but unthinking in his application of those traits. He reimposed the unpopular local governance policies of Ala-ud-Din that his father had reversed. To exercise greater control over the Deccan, he moved the capital from Delhi to Deogir, renaming it Daulatabad, and ordered all inhabitants to move from Delhi to the new capital. Many died during the trip south. Ibn Tughluq also planned to have all the inhabitants of Multan move south. When the governor refused, Ibn Tughluq came to the city and demanded that all its citizens be put to death. The inhabitants were later pardoned after the intercession of Shah Rukn-e-Alam (1251–1335), an influential cleric whose mausoleum is today one of Multan's most famed edifices. In 1347 Ibn Tughluq restored Delhi as the sultanate's capital and allowed people to return to the city.

Ibn Tughluq's attempt to introduce a new copper and brass currency was a failure. He raised a large army, intending to mount a campaign against Khorasan, under the rule of Persian-allied Muslim rulers, and Tibet in the north, possibly to gain gold and horses, as rebellions were reducing the kingdom's income. However, he was unable to follow through on his plans. Natural disaster added to his people's misery. A drought during the years 1335–42, one of the worst in the subcontinent's history, caused widespread famine and led to a revolt, despite Ibn Tughluq's efforts to provide relief.

Where his father and grandfather had been content to leave local rulers in place and collect tribute, Ibn Tughluq tried to institute direct governance, a policy that provoked rebellions. Hindu rajas created an alliance to resist Delhi rule. By 1344 tribute payments in the Deccan were off 90 percent. An independent sultanate in the south, the Bahmani Sultanate, was formed in 1347 by Muslims who remained in the Deccan after Ibn Tughluq restored Delhi as the empire's capital. That same year Gujarat and Kathiawar revolted, uprisings that Ibn Tughluq successfully suppressed.

In 1349 the Sammas, a group of Muslim chiefs, seized power from the Sumras. Both the Sumras and Sammas are thought to have originally been Hindu Rajputs. Though they were now Muslims, they kept pre-Islamic names. Sammas territory encompassed Sind and parts of Baluchistan and Punjab, and its capital was Thatta. Ibn Tughluq set

Daulatabad Fort guarded Daulatabad, the city that Muhammad ibn Tughluq tried to make the capital of the Tughluq dynasty. (SEF/Art Resource, NY)

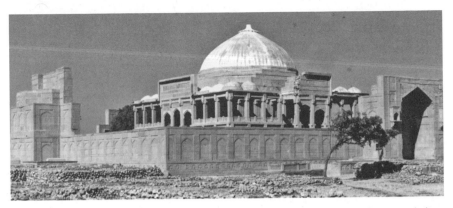

Thatta, near Karachi, is noted for its abundance of monuments and historical sites, including this nearby necropolis at Makli. (Courtesy Pakistan Tourism Development Corporation)

off for the capital where the Sammas had given a rebel chief sanctuary. But during the expedition Ibn Tughluq took ill near Thatta and died in 1351.

With Ibn Tughluq's death no suitable descendant of Ala-ud-Din existed to take the throne. A group of nobles and religious leaders invited Firuz Tughluq (r. 1351–88), a cousin of Ibn Tughluq, to take the throne. He accepted the appointment, and one of his first acts was to withdraw the army from Sind. Firuz became known for his concern for his subjects and their welfare. Taxes were lowered and the empire's infrastructure repaired and expanded. Sind was now basically independent, though in a display of fealty rulers sent a prince to the Delhi court as a resident. In the decade after Firuz's death at age 80 in 1388, eight different Tughluq kings ruled the sultanate, which had seen its hold over the territories loosen during the Firuz reign. Mahmud Nasir-ud-Din Tughluq (r. 1395–98) was the last of the Tughluq sultans. During his reign the Gakkar chief Shaikha created an independent state in Punjab and for a time extended his territory to include Lahore. Nasir-ud-Din's rule ended when he was temporarily driven from Delhi by a new invader from Central Asia: Timur Lenk.

Timur and the Sayyid and Lodi Dynasties

During this time the power of the Mongols, like that of the sultanate, was weakening. By 1320 almost all the Mongols had been driven from their former stronghold in Transoxiana. In 1369 a Turkish chief, Timur (1336–1405), took power as the grand emir of Transoxiana. Son of a minor chief, as a young man he had received a leg wound that gave him a permanent limp, and he was called Timur Lenk (the lame), anglicized into Tamerlane. A devout Muslim, he sought to conquer all Mongol lands for Islam. But his ambitions were not limited to retaking Mongol holdings. After conquering lands in Persia and Russia, in 1397 he invaded the subcontinent. He took Delhi from Mahmud Tughluq in 1398 and sacked the city, then withdrew to his capital at Samarkand, modern Uzbekistan, from where he administered the territory.

Mahmud Tughluq returned to the throne of Delhi after Timur's departure and occupied it until his death in 1413. However, the Tughluq dynasty is considered to have ended with Timur's conquest of Delhi. During Mahmud's final years the sultanate continued to disintegrate, and governors declared their independence.

By the end of the short-lived Sayyid dynasty (1414–51), which succeeded the Tughluq dynasty, the sultanate's dominion was basically confined to Delhi and its immediate surroundings. During the rule of its last ruler, Alam Shah (r. 1444–51), Multan claimed independence, but the attempt by Multan's populace to name their own ruler was thwarted when a local Afghan chief, Rai Siphera, or Sarha Langa, staged a coup, founding the Langa dynasty of Multan, which survived for 80 years.

The last dynasty to rule the Delhi Sultanate was the Lodi dynasty (1451–1526). Bahlul Lodi (r. 1451–89) restored the sultanate's authority in much of the northern subcontinent. But Multan remained independent, despite Lodi's efforts to conquer it. He finally recognized its ruler, Hussain Langha (1456–1502), the son of Sarha Langa, under whom Multan expanded its territory.

Once again the Delhi Sultanate declined. But this time it would not recover. By about 1500 independent Muslim kingdoms had arisen in Multan, Gujarat, Malwa, Sind, and Khandesh, in central India. With the death of Ibrahiml Lodi (r. 1517–26) the Delhi Sultanate came to an end. It gave way to a kingdom that would be among the grandest the world had seen: the Mughal Empire.

4

THE MUGHAL PERIOD
(1526–1748)

The Mughal Empire marked a high point in the history of the subcontinent. While its hold over present-day Pakistan wavered, the empire's military campaigns, governance, trade policies, and cultural achievements had a large impact on the region. Mughal rule rose from the decay of the Delhi Sultanate, a power that never fully recovered from its destruction by Timur in the late 14th century. Yet, paradoxically, it was one of Timur's great-grandsons, Babur (1483–1530), who led the Mughals' ascension. Today he is celebrated as the first of the Six Great Mughals: Babur, Humayun, Akbar, Jahangir, Shah Jahan, and Aurangzeb. The empire grew under an enlightened administrative system, *mansabdari*, that included policies of advancement based on ability rather than birth, and religious tolerance for expressions of Hindu devotion and Shi'i ritual. It became one of the largest centralized states in premodern history. The empire's golden age lasted into the 18th century. But poor governance, military setbacks, religious intolerance, and European incursions ultimately brought down the empire by the middle of that century. Mughals would occupy the kingdom's throne for another century, but by then it had neither the size, the power, nor the glory of its former years.

Rise of the Mughals

By the early 16th century what remained of the declining Delhi Sultanate faced threats from traditional enemies—tribal kingdoms, regional dynasties, and Central Asian invaders—and a new foe: the Europeans. These last outsiders came by sea, seeking a direct trade route to Southeast Asia bypassing the hazardous overland Silk Route. Portuguese explorer Vasco da Gama, who pioneered the route around Africa's Cape of Good Hope, was the first; he landed near Calicut (present-day Kozhikode), on the southwest coast of the subcontinent, in 1498. In 1503 he established the first Portuguese "factory," as the trading posts were called, at Cochin, on the southwestern tip of India. In 1510 the Portuguese took possession of Goa, farther up the coast, and soon established a factory at Diu, in Sind.

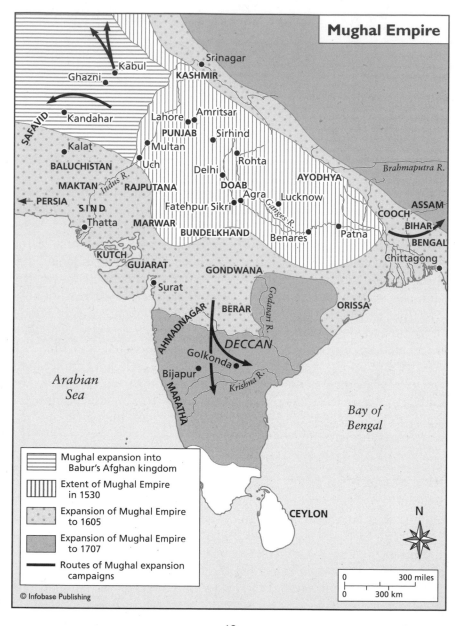

Mughal Empire

Legend:
- Mughal expansion into Babur's Afghan kingdom
- Extent of Mughal Empire in 1530
- Expansion of Mughal Empire to 1605
- Expansion of Mughal Empire to 1707
- Routes of Mughal expansion campaigns

© Infobase Publishing

0 — 300 miles
0 — 300 km

At the time, what is today's Pakistan was a patchwork of independent Muslim and Hindu fiefdoms. Many leaders of these small states aspired to regional dominance. Babur of Ferghana was among them. Babur founded the Mughal Empire, and his son, Humayun, spent years reestablishing its rule after rebellions splintered the kingdom in the wake of Babur's death. These two monarchs set the foundation upon which the crowning achievements of the Mughal Empire were later built.

Babur

Zahir-ud-Din Muhammad—Babur of Ferghana—was a great-grandson of Timur, the Mongol conqueror. Babur's father was the Timurid king of Ferghana, a Turk-dominated region in present-day eastern Uzbekistan. Though raised in a Turkic culture, Babur was a Mongol. It was this once nomadic group that would give name to a state renowned for its wealth, military prowess, artistic achievement, and enlightened government: the Mughal Empire. Babur inherited the throne of Ferghana at age 12 upon his father's death. He also inherited his father's dream of reconquering Timur's empire and ruling from Samarkand, the capital of Ferghana. But enemies, including his own relatives and the Uzbek Turks, deposed and exiled 14-year-old Babur from Samarkand in 1497.

Over the next few years Babur retook and lost Samarkand twice while building an army, and in 1504 he captured Kabul and Ghazni. After he realized how little income the poor area could generate, in 1505 he proceeded through the Khyber Pass to attack what is now Pakistan, returning with nothing more than some livestock.

In 1507 Babur set out from Kabul to battle the Khalji tribesmen of southeast Afghanistan, going as far south as Kalat in central Baluchistan. Now in control of the trade routes, like his forebears he switched from plundering caravans to taxing them.

The Timurid's greatest adversaries were the Uzbek khans, and the khan in Babur's time was Muhammad Shaybani (r. 1500–10). Shaybani had driven the Timurids from several of their strongholds, including Babur from Samarkand. Babur enlisted as an ally the ruler of Persia, Shah Ismael (ca. 1485–1524), founder of the Shi'i Safavid dynasty, and their forces defeated Shaybani's at the Battle of Merv in 1510, killing the Uzbek khan as he tried to escape. Babur led the allied forces to take Samarkand once more the following year. But Babur, a Shia, did not enjoy the support of the Sunni populace, and, after renewed attacks by the Uzbeks, he abandoned Samarkand again in 1514. For the next five years Babur confined his campaigns to Afghanistan and

Babur, founder of the Mughal dynasty, conquered and lost Samarkand twice in his bid to gain his father's throne. In this leaf from Baburnama, produced in the late 16th century, he is depicted fleeing the city in 1501–02 with two companions. (The Pierpont Morgan Library/ Art Resource, NY)

Baluchistan, but these forays had repercussions in other parts of what is now Pakistan, as well.

Reoccupying Kandahar and Kalat, Babur drove the Mongol ruler of the area, Shah Beg Arghun (r. 1507–22), into Sind, where Jam Firoz, son of the great Samma ruler Jam Nizamuddin (d. 1509), held the throne. Shah Beg defeated the Samma forces, and Jam Firoz retreated to Thatta. Shah Beg built an island fortress at Bhakkar in the Indus River, between present-day Sukkur and Rohri. From here he continued his conquests in Sind. In 1520–21 Shah Beg conquered the Samma capital of Thatta, and Jam Firoz fled to Gujarat, a city in northwestern Punjab and capital of the Gujarat Sultanate, centered in what is today the Indian state of Gujarat. The Arghuns' control of Sind lasted until 1555 and restored the region's cultural ties to Persia.

Conquest of the Punjab and Delhi

In 1519 Babur acquired muskets and artillery and set off for the subcontinent. He first captured the Yusufzai Fort at Bajaur, in what is today the North-West Frontier Province, but failed to conquer the Yusufzai, one of the most powerful Pashtun tribes. Most of northwest Pakistan was under the control of the Gakkars at the time, and Babur next staged a surprise attack on their bastion, Pharwala Fort, near Rawalpindi in Punjab. The Gakkar chief surrendered, and in return Babur recognized their rule of the Potwar Plateau. Thereafter the Mughals could count on Gakkar support for their rule. Returning to his goal to pacify the frontier tribes, Babur married the daughter of the Yusufzaisi's chief, but the tribemen remained rebellious. Changing tactics, Babur mounted a military campaign in the Hashtnagar region of NWFP. Campaigns against tribes along the tributaries of the Indus in Punjab followed, including an effort to eradicate Afghan nobles, many of whom had settled in Punjab during Lodi rule. Punjabis, whom the Afghans had taxed, welcomed their elimination.

Babur's leadership and military prowess drew the attention of nobles seeking a regime change in Delhi. Lodi family members requested Babur's aid in overthrowing Ibrahim I Lodi (r. 1517–26), the sultan of Delhi, in part due to his policy of replacing respected military commanders with young loyalists. Timur's lands had included Delhi, and as his direct descendant Babur considered the sultanate his birthright. Allying himself with various Lodi leaders, Babur assembled an army and in 1525 marched toward Delhi. Ibrahim Lodi advanced with an army of 100,000 soldiers and 100 elephants to intercept him. The forces met in 1526 at the First Battle of Panipat, about 30 miles north

POLO

Along with many other traditions, the Mughals introduced polo to the subcontinent. The game originated in Central Asia sometime between the sixth century B.C.E. and the first century C.E. Its name is believed to be derived from the word *pulu* or *phulo,* meaning "ball" or "ballgame," respectively, in the Balti language of Baltistan, in what is today Pakistan-administered Kashmir. In polo two teams mounted on horseback try to drive a small ball through the opponent's goal using long-handled mallets. It is often compared to the traditional Afghani sport *buzkashi* (goat grabbing), in which two teams of equestrians attempt to grab the carcass of a headless goat and throw it into a scoring circle.

Now often called the sport of kings, polo became the sport of Persian nobility, and teams might have as many as 100 horsemen. It was also used as a training game for cavalry, as the expert horsemanship required was highly adaptable to the battlefield. Babur is credited with establishing the game in the subcontinent. But by the 19th century polo had largely been forgotten, relegated to a few mountainous pockets in the northern subcontinent. English tea planters and military personnel in Manipur, Bengal, rediscovered it in the 1850s. The British developed today's rules (which include having four players per team and dividing the contest into

of Delhi. Lodi had superior numbers, but Babur's forces were better equipped and more disciplined. On the first day of battle Ibrahim Lodi and 15,000 men were killed. Babur was proclaimed emperor of Delhi the next day.

Babar's great-grandfather Timur had conquered Delhi and returned to Samarkand. Babur planned to rule from the subcontinent. He recognized that it had resources that made it an advantageous seat of power: an abundance of cultivatable lands, plentiful gold and silver, and large numbers of skilled workers in every profession and craft.

Babur's plan to rule from Delhi provoked Rana Sanga of Mewar (r. 1509–27), northern India's strongest ruler and head of the Rajput Confederacy, to raise an army of some 210,000 soldiers to oppose Babur. In 1527, at the Battle at Khanua, near Agra, Babur defeated the numerically superior Rajputs, becoming the master of the northern subcontinent. He granted rule of Rajput territories to his followers,

periods called *chuckers*) and organized polo clubs throughout the subcontinent. From there it spread to England, South America, and beyond.

Surrounded by spectators, Mughals play polo, attended by grooms with spare polo sticks. (HIP/Art Resource, NY)

who included Rajput and Afgan nobles and Gakkar chiefs. Among his first acts was to construct a road from Kabul to Agra, passing through Lahore to ease travel in the territory.

Throughout this time Multan had retained its independence. But in 1526, following a 15-month siege, the Arghun rulers of Sind conquered the city, sacked it, and massacred the survivors. The remaining inhabitants united behind the former commander of the Multan army and expelled the Arghun governor, then pledged their loyalty to the governor of Punjab, a suzerain of Babur's.

Meanwhile, allies of the former Delhi sultan, Ibrahim Lodi, tried to regain their kingdom. Under the leadership of his brother, Mahmud, during his brief reign as king of Bihar (r. 1528–29), Afghan chiefs of Bihar and Bengal, raised an army to fight Babur. The opposing forces met at the river Ghaghara in 1529 in Babur's last major battle. He emerged victorious, ending the last regional threat to his power.

Humayun

Babur died in 1530 at age 47. He left his Indian territories to Humayun (1508–56), his eldest son, and the Kabul kingdom to his youngest son, Kamran (1509–57). But Babur's hold over the northern regions was weak, and with him gone, restive rulers asserted their independence, among them Bahadur Shah (r. 1526–35, 1536–37), the Afghan ruler of Gujarat; Rajput chiefs; and Sher Khan (1486–1545). The son of a minor Afghan ruler, Sher Khan, who had briefly served in Babur's forces, assumed control of Bihar by the early 1530s.

Determined to regain control of his inherited kingdom, Humayun (r. 1530–40, 1555–56) fought Bahadur Shah and the rebellious Rajputs in a series of skirmishes. He defeated Bahadur Shah in 1535. But Sher Khan led a campaign into Bengal and defeated Humayun's forces at Chausa on the banks of the Ganges in 1539. Taking control of Delhi, he proclaimed himself Sher Shah Sur. At a subsequent encounter at Kanauj in 1540, Humayun's troops fled before the battle even began. Humayun escaped to Lahore and sought protection from his brother, Kamran. With Sher Shah Sur in pursuit, both brothers left Lahore but split up after a dispute at the Jhelum River at Khushab. Kamran went to Kabul, and Humayun went south and joined his mother and brother Hindal in Sind. Here he met his future wife, Hamida Bano. Seeking either an alliance with the Rajput chiefs or their conquest, he and his new wife and followers set out across the Thar Desert to Rajasthan, where they received protection from the rajas of Umarkot (today's Tharparker District in Sind), whose territory included parts of what is today Rajasthan state in India. His son Jalal-ud-Din Akbar was born at Umarkot Fort in 1542.

Seeking more secure refuge in his brother Kamran's domain in Afghanistan, Humayun led his group to Kandahar but came under attack there as well and once again fled, finally finding sanctuary in Persia. Akbar, his son, was left with an aunt in the Kabul kingdom territories.

Sher Shah Sur

Having chased Humayun to Punjab, Sher Shah Sur (r. 1540–45) demanded obeisance from the Gakkar rulers, and when they refused he awarded their land to thousands of Afghan tribesmen who had recently settled in the area and to three Baluchi chiefs: Ismael Khan, Fateh Khan, and Ghazi Khan. The Gakkars gathered an army to fight Sher Shah, but were defeated at the Fort of Rewat in Rawalpindi.

Sher Shah built the fort at Rohtas, with a three-mile circumference, to protect his kingdom from Mughal and Gakkar invaders. (Courtesy Pakistan Tourism Development Corporation)

During his brief, five-year reign Sher Shah's empire stretched from the Indus Valley through Bengal, and from Kashmir in the north to Chanderi and Benares in central India. He was more concerned about outside invaders than regional rebellions and considered the Mughals a greater threat than Chinggis Khan or Timur had been in their time. Balban and Ala-ud-Din Khalji had established the Delhi Sultanate as a bulwark against Mongol invaders. Sher Shah in turn developed his kingdom to defend the region against the Mughals. He built a massive fort at Rohtas (current-day Rohtak, in the Indian state of Haryana), some three miles around, to defend his kingdom's western borders from the Mughals and Gakkars.

However, his successes as a ruler outshined his military victories. He introduced many reforms embraced by the Mughal rulers and the British colonial overseers who succeeded them. He effectively reorganized the state's administrative system, built a network of roads (one of the them, the Grand Trunk Road, extending from the Indus to eastern Bengal, is still in use today), stimulated commerce by overhauling the customs system, and promoted religious tolerance. He also established a professional, salaried army and introduced a system of coins, the *rupayya,* whose name is still used for coinage in Pakistan, India, and neighboring countries to this day.

Sher Shah was killed in 1545 in an explosion while storming the Rajput hill fortress at Kalinjar in present-day Uttar Pradesh state in central India. On his deathbed he declared his sorrow that he had not destroyed Lahore, eliminating this tempting target of conquerors who used its spoils to continue to fuel their invasions. Some consider Sher Shah the last of the Delhi sultans, and perhaps the greatest.

After Sher Shah's death, his younger son, Jalal Khan, took control as Islam Shah (r. 1545–53) and ruled until his death in 1553. Four more descendants of Sher Shah ruled the dynasty until the last among them, Sikander Shah Sur (r. 1555), was defeated in battle by Humayun.

It was during the final years of the Sur dynasty that Europeans first took military action in the area that is now Pakistan. In 1554 the last of the Arghun, the family that ruled Sind, died. Two Turkish chiefs divided Sind between them, making Thatta and Bhakkar (near present-day Rohri on the Indus) their capitals. Thatta, a port strategically located at the apex of the Indus delta, had served as the capital of lower Sind since the 14th century. By this time the Portuguese had established trading posts along the west coast of the subcontinent. One of the new Turkish chiefs sought an alliance with the Portuguese against the other, and the Portuguese agreed to come to his assistance. But by the time the Portuguese sailed into the Indus and anchored, the two chiefs had made peace. Angered that the alliance had been called off, the Portuguese sacked and burned Thatta and the surrounding countryside, slaughtering many.

Humayun's Return

Humayun, now in Persia, persuaded the shah of Persia to back him, as Humayun's father Babur had done with the shah's predecessor. With the shah's support, Humayun attacked and took Kandahar and Kabul from his brother, Kamran. Akbar, Humayun's son, was in his uncle's custody at the time of the attack, and Kamran exposed Akbar at the walls of Kabul Fort during the assault, trying to induce his father to stop the bombardment. Nonetheless Humayun took Kabul and appointed nine-year-old Akbar governor of Kabul. With the city secured, Humayun set off for the subcontinent with Akbar, still eager to reclaim his inherited empire from the ashes of Sher Sur's kingdom. They arrived in 1554.

Kamran had tried to ally himself with Sher Sur's successors but was arrested by the Gakkars and held for Humayun's disposal. On Humayun's orders he was blinded and sent on a pilgrimage to Mecca to contemplate his sins. Humayun conquered Rohtas Fort without a fight, as the Afghan governor and garrison had fled. Humayun captured Lahore, then Sirhind, where he defeated Sikander Sur before claiming Delhi and Agra in 1555.

Inspired by the Safavid art he had encountered while in exile in Persia, Humayun recruited court artists who developed the celebrated Mughal school of painting. He also oversaw the construction of grand edifices that helped define the Mughal style of architecture. But his enjoyment of the regained throne was brief. Humayun died in 1556 after falling down stairs in his library. His tomb in Delhi is one of the finest examples of Mughal architecture in the subcontinent. Some of the details of his life come from memoirs of his sister, daughter of Babur, Gulbadan Begum.

With the Mughal Empire's borders secure, its army powerful, and the framework for its administration in place, the next three emperors—Akbar, Jahangir, and Shah Jahan—would engineer and preside over the empire's greatest achievements. But during the reign of the last of the Great Mughals, Aurangzeb, the empire's power would begin to decline, never to recover.

Akbar

Akbar the Great (r. 1556–1605) was 13 at the time of his father's death in 1556. His guardian, Bairam Khan, proclaimed him emperor of Hindustan, a term used historically to refer to the Indian subcontinent.

Sher Shah Sur's two nephews, Sikander and Adil, could not overcome their mutual animosity to join forces against Akbar. Adil's army was led by Hemu, a Hindu minister and general. Hemu conquered Agra in October of 1556 and conquered Delhi immediately after when the Mughal general Tardi Beg fled. Hemu took the title of Raja Vikramaditya, literally "sun of valor," borrowing the name of a legendary Hindu king. The day after Akbar learned Delhi had fallen, news came that Kabul was in revolt. Against the counsel of all his advisers except his guardian, rather than returning to Kabul to put down the uprising, Akbar marched on Delhi and decisively defeated Hemu's army at the Second Battle of Panipat in 1556.

Akbar's Early Years

In 1560 Akbar took full control of the kingdom from his guardian, whom he sent on a pilgrimage to Mecca to eliminate any possibility of meddling. During the years 1561–76, Akbar reconquered Malwa and

Gondwana (in the present-day Indian state of Maharashtra), the Rajput kingdoms, Gujarat, Bihar, and Bengal. This marked the end of the first phase of his campaigns of conquest.

Akbar instituted reforms and treated with respect Rajput rulers who submitted to him, allowing them to retain their power. He used intermarriage between members of the ruling family and Rajput princesses to cement relationships. He gathered detailed records on agricultural production and prices in an effort to regulate the economy. For assessing taxes and collecting revenue he adopted the system developed for Sher Shah Sur by Todar Mal, a Rajput king (r. 1560–86). Revenue went mostly to pay military officers, who were responsible for providing for their soldiers and members of the court. Officers, or *mansabdars*, as these overseers were known, were rotated every three years from territories to keep them from becoming feudal lords. Previously the Arabic term *iqta* was used for these territorial assignments. By Akbar's reign it had been replaced by the Persian term *jagir*, as the system would henceforth be known.

The assignment of lands to administer was prone to corruption, as those who made the assignments expected bribes to grant a *jagir* where productivity was high and the population was not restive. The demand for kickbacks created discontent among military officers. In 1574 Akbar ended the assignment system in the provinces with the oldest links to the empire, including Lahore, Multan, Delhi, and Agra. These areas were managed as *khalsa* (state-controlled land) for the next five years. Officers in charge got cash salaries rather than a percentage of revenues. But the plan failed, as officers had no incentive to stimulate productivity, and land fell out of cultivation in these areas. Meanwhile, local rulers oppressed and taxed the peasants, leading to depopulation. In response Akbar changed the tax system. Through detailed studies of soil quality, water availability, and other factors for individual parcels, along with local market conditions, assessments were based on what the land was capable of producing. This spurred investment in the land and renewed efforts to improve its productivity.

State and Religion

Tolerant of other religions, in 1563 Akbar removed the tax imposed on those who visited Hindu shrines and in 1564 eliminated the *jizya*, the tax on non-Muslims. He attempted to have local rulers emulate his

(opposite page) Bullocks drag siege guns uphill during Akbar's attack on Rathanbhor Fort in 1568. Illustration from the Akbarnama, produced ca. 1590. (Victoria & Albert Museum, London/Art Resource, NY)

THE MANSABDARI AND JAGIRDARI SYSTEMS

Akbar instituted the civil service system upon which the Mughal Empire's administration was based. The system had its roots in the Delhi Sultanate, when rulers such as Ala-ud-Din Khalji and Muhammad ibn Tughluq created a prototypical revenue and payroll plan. Sher Shah Sur reorganized it, and Akbar refined it.

Government officers were organized in 33 levels or grades. Each government officer held the honorific *mansabdar* (because he had rank) or *mansab,* if he had sufficient rank. Royal family members typically had exclusive rights to the very top ranks. Those with the rank of Commander of the Five Hundred and above held the title of emir, or "noble." Most officers initially received cash allowances generated from the *khalsa,* or state-controlled lands, dispensed by the royal treasury. Akbar believed cash payments encouraged loyalty, but the government found it increasingly difficult to manage enough *khalsa* lands to raise the revenue.

Over time a growing number of officers received *jagirs,* assigned lands they administered and from which was generated income to pay their salaries and that of their troops as well as to meet other expenses. Akbar and later rulers were eager to prevent officers from creating fiefdoms. Thus the positions were not hereditary, and *jagirdaris* (those who administered the *jagirs*) were rotated to new assignments every few years. The system helped stabilize the empire by maintaining government control of property. But it also led to exploitation of the lands since the *jagirdaris* cared only to maximize income during their tenure. Their oppression led farmers, and later merchants and artisans, to flee *jagirs* for lands controlled by rajas and *zamindars* (lords of the land). These local rulers retained their hereditary positions from pre-Mughal times and were allowed to keep their power as long as they remained loyal and provided troops and tribute to the empire. Over time these independent tribal chiefs and kingdoms came to present a major threat to the Mughals as their power declined.

nondiscriminatory practices. Though a Muslim himself, after listening to ongoing disagreements of the ulama, or Muslim religious leaders, Akbar became disenchanted with Islamic orthodoxy, and created the Hall of Worship, where religious thinkers could come to discuss their religions. He invited Zoroastrians, Christians, Jews, Hindus, and Jains to explain the tenets of their faith. In 1579 he promulgated his Infallibility Decree, which mandated that any conflict among the ulama would be decided by the emperor.

In 1580 nobles and religious leaders in Bihar and Bengal revolted, upset at Akbar's religious unorthodoxy and reduction of their allowances. Akbar's half-brother, Mirza Hakim (d. 1585), ruler of Kabul, seized the opportunity and marched on Punjab, but was unsuccessful in his effort to capture the Rohtas fort or Lahore. He retreated to avoid Akbar's advancing army, which had arrived at the Sutlej River. Akbar dispatched the great Hindu general Man Singh (1540–1614) to chase Mirza Hakim, while Akbar headed for Kabul, which he occupied, installing his sister, Bakhtunissa Begum, as governor.

By 1582 Akbar had proclaimed himself God's representative on earth and the leader of a new religion, Din-i-Ilahi, the Divine Faith, which combined elements of Islam and Hinduism. He created new rites and ceremonies, some of which offended Muslims. His flirtation with unorthodox theosophies ended by 1590, when he was again practicing Islam. But his tolerance created a long-standing backlash in the Muslim community, which demanded that future emperors be unwavering in their Islamic faith. Leaders would find the most convincing way to demonstrate their orthodoxy was by practicing intolerance toward other religions as well as any unorthodox form of Islam. Thus Akbar's efforts to encourage tolerance and diversity drove the sociopolitical climate in the opposite direction.

Akbar's Middle Years

It was in this period that Akbar built Attock Fort at the point he crossed the Indus, usurping the town of Ohind's position as a major crossing point of the river as well as the Rohtas fort's importance as a frontier bastion.

Punjab and Upper Sind, whose fortunes had declined during the years the *jagir* system was modified, were now rebounding. Multan retained its importance as a religious center and trade capital, while Sehwan held its position as a commercial hub bustling with trade and industry.

During the years 1584–98, Akbar ruled from Lahore, which remained a center of commerce as well as government. Abdul Fazal (d. 1602), Akbar's friend and court historian, claimed the city had a thousand shops that made sheets and shawls alone. Akbar built a new mint to produce coinage for the realm and constructed a red brick wall around the old city. Some of its original 12 gates still stand.

Akbar's campaigns to subjugate the frontier in Kashmir, Lower Sind, Baluchistan, and parts of the Deccan continued during these years. Much of the agricultural land in Punjab at this time was under direct state control. *Jagirdars,* as those who oversaw the *jagirs* were known, were more closely monitored here than those at the fringes of empire.

Akbar was eager to secure the Kabul area for the Mughal Empire. Mirza Hakim had been ruling Kabul under his sister's nominal governorship. When he died in 1585, Akbar set out to conquer it, in part to keep it from falling to the Uzbek Turks, who likewise coveted the territory. Akbar, encamped at Attock, sent Man Singh to take over Kabul. Boatmen were brought from the east to ferry forces across the Indus. But Akbar was unable to subdue the border area, primarily due to resistance of the Afridi tribe. The Afridi and others in the area were adherents of the Roshanaya movement, a Sufi offshoot, so called for the adopted name of its founder Bayazid Ansari (ca. 1525–82/85), who called himself Pir-i-Roshan (the enlightened one or pir of [Mount] Roshan). Ansari's son Jalala refused to recognize Mughal rule and to permit Akbar's passage through the area. Akbar finally forced Jalala to flee to Chitral, a town in today's NWFP, where he died in 1601. But his absence and death did not dampen restiveness in the frontier area.

Akbar also attempted to expand the empire northward, but his campaigns in 1585 to conquer the Yusufzais and Kashmir, mounted to take advantage of internecine fighting among Muslim sects there, were unsuccessful. Though the attack failed, a resulting treaty gave the Mughals the right to buy Kashmir's saffron crop. In 1586 Akbar finally conquered Kashmir, making the Mughals the sole purveyor in the saffron market. Profits were vast. But high tax rates imposed on the peasant farmers caused a rebellion in Kashmir, and the tax rates were rolled back.

Akbar's Later Years

Following the Portuguese destruction of Thatta, the city was rebuilt. But renewed civil war among Turkish chiefs of Sind broke out. Sensing an opening, Akbar, back in Lahore from Attock, ordered the governor of Multan to attack lower Sind, and by 1592 the region had been annexed by the Mughal Empire. Baluchistan and Makran were annexed in 1594. The following year the shah of Persia, who had seized Kandahar after helping Humayun regain his empire, gave it to Akbar. All of the northern subcontinent was now under his rule, and thus in 1595 Akbar commenced the third and final phase of his campaigns of conquest: marching his forces southward to the Deccan. By 1601 almost all of the subcontinent was Mughal territory.

Under Akbar security was enhanced throughout the empire, leading to increased trade. Commerce was also stimulated by the currency system and mints he founded. A private banking system with letters of credit evolved. Goods from Kashmir and Kabul were shipped through Multan to Thatta's principal port of Larri Bunder. European appetite for dye brought Portuguese and Dutch traders to the region, and the manufacture of indigo dye became a major industry, enriching the kingdom.

Akbar's contributions to the arts are likewise remembered. Though he could neither read nor write, he collected literature and art from around the world and commissioned buildings and monuments. These edifices range from the tomb of his father, Humayun, in Delhi, considered the first great Mughal monument, to the entire city of Fatehpur Sikri (City of Victory), which served as his capital from 1569 to 1584. For his legacy of accomplishments in war and peace, Akbar is considered the greatest Mughal ruler.

Jahangir

Akbar's sole surviving son, Salim, had rebelled against him and tried to set up a kingdom of his own in the Deccan. Akbar nonetheless anointed him as his successor, and Salim ascended to the throne upon Akbar's death in October 1605. He took the title Jahangir (r. 1605–27). Jahangir had spent his formative years around Lahore, his father's capital for much of his reign. His companion as a youngster at home in nearby Sheikhupura was Abdullah Bhatti, the son of a tribal chief whom Akbar had executed. Akbar also killed, in a fit of rage, a woman in his harem, Anarkali, whom Jahangir had fallen in love with. Her tomb is in her eponymous bazaar in Lahore.

Soon after Jahangir's ascension his eldest son, Prince Khusrow, tried wresting control of the empire by laying siege to Lahore. Somewhat paradoxically, Khusrow's attempted coup was supported by nobles angered by the disloyalty Jahangir had shown to his father in trying to establish an independent state in the Deccan. Jahangir came from Agra to battle his son, and their armies met at the Chenab River, with Jahangir's forces prevailing. Prince Khusrow was captured trying to flee the area. As punishment he was blinded and incarcerated, and 700 of his followers were impaled in Lahore.

The leader of the Sikhs, Guru Arjan Dev (1563–1606), was suspected of aiding the prince, and his lands were confiscated; he and his sons were imprisoned. Up to that point the Sikhs had been apolitical. Jahangir had Arjan executed in prison, but, after his release, his son Guru Hargobind (1595–1644) formed a Sikh self-defense force, which became a longstanding opponent of the Mughal dynasty.

Meanwhile Abdullah Bhatti, Jahangir's childhood friend, led a force against him to avenge his father's death. Jahangir tried negotiating a settlement, but when that failed, he reluctantly suppressed the uprising. Meanwhile, resistance by the Roshanaya movement, which had begun under his father's reign, continued, and Jalala's successors attacked Peshawar in 1613. The town of Shikarpur in upper Sind became a center of resistance to the Mughals.

Jahangir's reign was a time of peace and prosperity within his kingdom. The Mughal style of painting reached its zenith under him. But agricultural production began to decline during his reign because of the growing corruption within the *jagir* system. Jahangir's rule was assisted by his ambitious and beautiful wife, a Persian princess he dubbed Nur Jehan (Light of the World). She had a large hand in administering and ruling the kingdom, as did her family members, including her father, a Persian, and her brother Asaf Khan. Jahangir's third son, Prince Khurram, also part of Nur Jehan's inner circle, married Asaf Khan's daughter, Mumtaz Mahal. In 1615 Prince Khurram conquered the last Rajput fortresses in Mewar. However, the state of Ahmadnagar resisted conquest, and during the campaign Ahmadnagar Fort, which had been captured during Akbar's rule, was retaken from the Mughals. Prince Khurram succeeded in regaining the fort and was given the title Shah Jahan, Lord of the World.

Jahangir's fondness for alcohol was now affecting his health. Nur Jehan wanted her youngest son, Prince Shahriyar, to succeed Jahangir, as he would be the easiest for her to control. Signaling her intent, she gave the hand of her daughter, conceived in an earlier marriage, to Shahriyar. Shah Jahan, who was the popular choice to take over Jahangir's throne, revolted in 1622. But his army was defeated in 1625 by Mahabat Khan, Nur Jehan's general. Nur Jehan, now worried about Mahabat's growing power, accused him of corruption. In response, Mahabat staged an insurrection and captured Jahangir in 1626 while he was en route to Kashmir. Nur rescued Jahangir, but the ruler died in 1627. Asaf Khan, Nur's brother, arrested her, and Shah Jahan was named emperor. Shahriyar was blinded and imprisoned, and Nur gave up statecraft, spending her time overseeing construction of her tomb.

European Trade

During the Mughal era European powers established footholds in the subcontinent. A century after the Portuguese had successfully established trading posts along the west coast of India and Pakistan, the English, French, and Dutch, hearing of vast profits, followed suit. In 1600, a group of London merchants formed the East India Company (EIC) to trade with India under a charter from Queen Elizabeth I (1533–1603).

In 1615 an ambassador from England, Sir Thomas Roe (1581–1644), arrived at Jahangir's court. He was the second such emissary. Seven years earlier England's king James I (1566–1625) had sent Turki-speaking Captain William Hawkins with a request to Jahangir for a trade concession at Surat on the Gujarat coast. Though Hawkins was received graciously and remained for two years, the Portuguese held sway, and permission was denied. Roe had better luck. After three years in residence he won concessions for the EIC as well as permission to build a factory in Surat. Jahangir's largesse to the English angered the Portuguese, who attacked Mughal shipping in retaliation. Jahangir in turn arrested all Portuguese in the empire, closed their churches, and declared war. The Portuguese sued for peace. The English built Surat into a thriving trade center and sought additional outposts in other parts of India.

The Dutch and French formed East India companies of their own, in 1602 and 1664, respectively. Most of the outposts were on the east coast of the subcontinent, putting them closer to the East Indies (present-day Indonesia) spice trade. Bengal and Bihar became economic centers. The Portuguese and the Dutch went on to fight for control of the East Indies, a war the Dutch would win. The British and French battled over the subcontinent, with the British finally prevailing in the mid-18th century.

Shah Jahan

Shah Jahan (r. 1627–57) pursued a westward expansionist policy, relocating his court to Kabul for two years in pursuit of this goal. During the height of Shah Jahan's reign, the Mughal Empire was the most advanced in the world, the leading light in commerce, culture, and architecture, wealthy beyond the ability to catalog its riches. Among the architectural works created during his reign was the Taj Mahal, the tomb of Jahan's beloved wife, Mumtaz Mahal. But Shah Jahan's reign also marked the beginning of the empire's decline, signaled by rebellions in lower Sind, the collapse of Mughal rule in the Deccan, and a stagnating economy. After crippling the agricultural sector by overtaxing farmers, the Mughals began raising taxes on urban enterprises, traders, and artisans. The government entered into trading agreements with European companies to raise revenue. With wealth becoming concentrated and revenues falling, the nobility sought wars as a way of expanding Mughal territory and gaining more revenue, but wars proved increasingly expensive and unsuccessful. Still, the royal court continued in its lavish ways.

One region in which warfare did prove successful was the Deccan, which had slipped from the empire's grasp since Akbar's conquests of 1595–1601. Three of the five Deccan Sultanates—Ahmadnagar, Berar, and Bidar—were reabsorbed into the Mughal Empire. The other two, Golkonda and Bijapur, became tribute-paying states.

Aurangzeb

In 1657, with Shah Jahan suffering a serious illness, a battle for succession erupted among his four sons—Aurangzeb, Shah Shuja, Murad Bakhsh, and Dara Shukoh—from which Aurangzeb emerged victorious. He took over Agra and imprisoned his father in Agra Fort until his death in 1666 at age 74. He then pursued his three brothers. Murad was arrested and in 1661 executed. Shah Shuja fled into the jungles of Burma. Dara Shukoh, the eldest, raised an army to fight Aurangzeb but was deserted by erstwhile allies, and in 1569 was captured and executed for heresy by Aurangzeb's forces.

Aurangzeb (1618–1707) was the last of the great Mughals. Under his rule (r. 1658–1707) the Mughal armies led almost constant wars of conquest, and the empire expanded to its largest size. In 1661 the eastern kingdom of Cooch was annexed by the Mughals. Portuguese pirates were driven from the area after the Mughals conquered the Bengal port of Chittagong in 1666. But the warfare almost bankrupted the empire, and the empire's hold on the new territories was weak. An unpopular ruler, Aurangzeb faced rebellions by the Yusufzais near Peshawar (1667, 1672–76); the Sikhs in Anandpur, in what is today the Indian state of Punjab (beginning in 1668 and lasting for several years); and the Marathas, beginning in 1670. Shivaji Bhonsle (1630–80), the leader of the Maratha Hindu kingdom, had risen to take over Deccan territory. By 1663 Shivaji controlled Bijapur territory in the Deccan and Mughal territory in Ahmadnagar. The Mughals' inability to deal effectively with Shivaji was emblematic of their declining fortunes. Aurangzeb

Aurangzeb, who ruled for almost half a century, is depicted on his throne as an old man in this early 18th-century Mughal miniature. (Erich Lessing/Art Resource, NY)

dispatched his uncle, Shaista Khan, to attack Shivaji. The Mughals won the initial engagement, but Shivaji counterattacked and expelled the Mughal forces from the region. Aurangzeb then ordered one of his most powerful generals, the Rajput Jai Singh, to carry on the fight against the Marathas, and the campaign was a success. Shivaji accepted the terms of surrender and was placed under house arrest at the royal court in Agra. But Shivaji escaped and regained power in his old territory. He recaptured forts and expanded his dominion to the south, forming a strong independent state.

Meanwhile, Aurangzeb adopted religious policies that created schisms within the empire, further weakening it. A devout Sunni Muslim, he ended the practice of religious tolerance and tried to force the conversion of Hindus to Islam. He changed the legal system, making sharia, Islamic law, the law of the land. With the exception of construction of the Badshahi Mosque he also turned his back on the promotion of great works of art and architecture that had characterized Mughal rule up to this time. He banned singers, musicians, and dancers from his court and built few grand monuments or buildings.

The English also gained stronger footholds in the subcontinent during this period. They received Bombay, which the Portuguese had held, as the wedding dowry of Catherine Henrietta of Braganza (1638–1705),

The Badshahi Mosque in Lahore is one of the few grand public buildings built during Aurangzeb's rule. (Courtesy Pakistan Tourism Development Corporation)

a Portuguese princess who married King Charles II (1630–85). By then Surat had proved vulnerable, having been sacked twice by Shivaji (in 1664 and 1670). The English relocated their headquarters to Bombay. They cleared its swamps and by 1677 created a more substantial factory.

Sir Joshua Child, the chairman of the EIC at the time, wanted to strengthen Britain's position in the subcontinent. In 1685 12 English warships were sent to take establish and control fortifications at Chittagong. Mughal forces met and defeated them. In retaliation England blockaded several ports on the Indian west coast. They seized Mughal ships and kept pilgrims from making the hajj to Mecca. Aurangzeb ordered his forces to attack English trading posts. Several including Surat were taken by the Mughals. EIC representatives were killed. The company appealed to Aurangzeb for an end to the attacks and agreed to pay for the seized ships and compensate the Mughal ruler for other damages. In return Aurangzeb pardoned the English and granted them a new trading license in 1690.

At the time, English pirates were active in the region, but the EIC did little to stem their activity. In 1695 English pirates seized a Mughal ship carrying pilgrims and trade profits. In response the Mughal governor of Surat arrested the local head of the EIC and put the city's English citizens under custody—in chains—to protect them from angry Muslim residents. On India's east coast, the English were allowed to create a trading post on the Hooghly River in Bengal in 1697. This became the city of Calcutta (present-day Kolkata), the capital of British India from 1858 until 1912. Another major British trade center on the east coast was Madras (present-day Chennai). The British hired local soldiers they called sepoys and formed armed forces for their own protection. Over time local rulers asked the British to lend them the sepoy forces to help with security. In return for concessions and land, the British often agreed; they increasingly became more involved in local affairs and took control of more land.

The frontier area in what is now northwest Pakistan was another region that tested Mughal domination. The Yusufzai had been in rebellion since the beginning of Aurangzeb's reign. In 1667 a force of 5,000 Yusufzai mounted a series of invasions into Pakhli (present-day Hazara district). Mughal forces responding to the uprising soundly defeated the rebels. A 1672 revolt by the Satnamis of East Punjab, a fanatical Hindu sect, was also brutally put down. Meanwhile the Jats (not to be confused with the Jats of Afghanistan), an ethnic group in the northern subcontinent whose kingdom centered around Agra, continued causing havoc as they had since Akbar's reign.

Affairs of State

Corruption of the administration system became endemic under Aurangzeb, driving more peasants from the land, lowering state income, and further weakening the empire. Aurangzeb tried to improve the lot of peasants, but his orders were often ignored by landowners and administrators. At the same time his anti-Hindu policies, which included restrictions on religious practices and the desecration and destruction of temples, further alienated his subjects. This encouraged more anti-Mughal activity and helped fuel the Marathas' rebellion. Aurangzeb also alienated the Rajputs by trying to put them under greater state control, which led to a Rajput uprising. Unhappy with the way his son, Prince Akbar, handled the rebellions, Aurangzeb replaced him, and Prince Akbar was subsequently recruited by the Rajputs to lead their forces in revolt against Aurangzeb. But Aurangzeb tricked the Rajput forces into deserting Akbar. However, the war with the Rajputs continued, and Aurangzeb had to cede them some degree of autonomy.

Aurangzeb tracked his rebellious son into the Deccan. Prince Akbar escaped pursuit, but the empire's forces remained in the Deccan for 26 years (1681–1707), and during this time finally captured the Marathas' leader, Shivaji. The Mughal army boasted 170,000 men, but the force was unwieldy, and its officers were more interested in pursuing leisure at home than engaging in foreign campaigns. Thus the army's power was blunted. Losses mounted in the Deccan. The conflict sapped the empire's strength and will, and it began to suffer setbacks in the north as well. The upper classes were dissatisfied because of deteriorating economic conditions. In 1690, Aurangzeb tried to placate the nobility by promising them ownership of lands under their control. But the flight of the peasants was making land less productive, and, by 1700 the nobles were demanding cash rather than land, and all the local chiefs were in revolt.

The Sikhs coexisted with the Mughals at the beginning of Aurangzeb's reign, mostly due to their own internal dissension. But after Aurangzeb ordered the execution of the ninth Sikh guru, Tegh Bahadur (1621–75), the 10th and last guru, Guru Gobind Singh Gurdwara (1666–1708), formed the Khalsa, the movement's military arm, in 1699. The Khalsa were baptized with water stirred with a dagger. Wearing "the five K's" was mandated: *kesha*, uncut hair, symbolizing spirituality; *kaccha*, short pants, signifying self-control and chastity; *kangha*, comb, symbolizing hygiene and discipline; *kara*, iron bangle, signifying restraint of action and remembrance of God; and *kirpan*, dagger, a symbol of dignity and struggles against injustice. Aurangzeb mounted a campaign of suppression against them near the end of his reign, and Mughal forces laid siege to the Sikhs at Amandpur in 1704. The siege was unsuccessful, and the Sikhs were promised safe passage, but the Mughals and their allies slaughtered them once they left their fortifications.

Decline of the Mughals

As Mughal power declined, small independent principalities emerged in the frontier area, Baluchistan, and Sind. Indeed, the Kabul-Ghazni-Peshawar area had never been totally under Mughal control. Aurangzeb had futilely spent more than a year at Hasan Abdal in the frontier area trying to suppress the Yusufzai and other Pashtun tribes.

In 1695 the Ahmedzai clan established a dynasty in Kalat in central Baluchistan that ruled the region's nomads, primarily Baluchis and Brahuis. The ruler was known as the khan of Kalat, and the state as the Khanate. (The British later called this the Brahui Confederacy.) Kalat was strong enough to assert independence from the Persians and the sultans of Delhi who had alternately claimed control of the area in preceding years. Mughal efforts to conquer the area failed. Ahmedzais would remain khans of Kalat until Kalat agreed to join the newly independent Pakistan in 1948.

Maritime commerce, which had been an important part of the empire's economy, was also in decline during this period. The harbor at Thatta and other Sind ports were filling with silt despite Mughal efforts under Aurangzeb and his successor to clear them. And ports in nearby Gujarat faced attacks by Marathas, who gained control over western coastal waters.

Aurangzeb died in 1707 at the age of 80. After brief infighting 63-year-old Shah Alam (r. 1707–12), Aurangzeb's most capable son and the former governor of Kabul and Peshawar, took the throne. He assumed the title Bahadur Shah but ruled only five years before he died in Lahore. Bahadur Shah's death marked the end of the Mughal Empire's glory. Looting broke out in Lahore as armies of those vying for succession converged on the city to gain control of the empire.

Of Bahadur's four sons, Prince Azam was most admired. His three brothers were encouraged by a nobleman to challenge him for rule. Azam drowned with his elephant, and the nobleman arranged for the least capable of the siblings, Jahandur Shah, to take the throne so his backers could control the empire. Azam's son, Farukkhsiyar (1683–1719) defeated Jahandur with the help of two officers, the Sayyid brothers. When Farukkhsiyar took the throne in 1713, it was under the control of the Sayyid brothers. During his reign the Europeans, especially the British, were able to get favorable treatment for their trading ventures by bribing officials. In 1715–16 the Mughals achieved a final victory in eastern Punjab over the Sikhs, who were led by Banda Singh Bahadur (1670–1716). Banda and thousands of Sikhs were tortured and killed. But Sikh unrest continued, destabilizing the kingdom and compromising trade, with bands of Sikh robbers raiding the caravans.

In 1719 the Sayyids had Farukkhsiyar incarcerated and killed. The Sayyids installed two subsequent puppet regents in the same year before Muhammad Shah (r. 1719–48), a 20-year-old grandson of Bahadur Shah, was named ruler. The Sayyid brothers' ruthless machinations caused their own deaths, which came within a year of Muhammad's ascension. Muhammad's rule lasted almost 30 years, marked by continued loss of territory and power as those around him grabbed what they could from the disintegrating empire.

The mid-18th century marked the nadir of Muslim fortunes in the subcontinent. One of the leading reformers who attempted to halt the decline of Muslim rule and revive its intellectual traditions was Shah Waliullah (1703–62). After completing Islamic studies in Mecca in 1734, he returned to the subcontinent and began preaching, calling on Muslims to return to the pure life as exemplified by the words and deeds of the prophet Muhammad. His most important accomplishment was the translation of the Qur'an into Persian. After Shah Waliullah's death, his son, Shah Abdul Aziz (1746–1823), continued his work with the help of dedicated assistants.

As the Mughal Empire dissolved, it was kept from chaos by the able administration of the now-autonomous states that were taken over by local governors. But the weakened territory was again vulnerable to invasion. In 1735 the Persian king, Nadir Shah (r. 1736–47), took advantage of the power vacuum. He acquired European arms, which he used in a campaign of conquest of his neighbors to the east and former Mughal strongholds. He defeated Kabul and then advanced on Punjab. The territory submitted without resistance, but Nadir Shah plundered and looted Punjab nonetheless. Lahore was spared carnage after the rich inhabitants paid for their city's safety. Nadir Shah next conquered Delhi. He kept Muhammad Shah on the throne as a puppet, receiving in return a very rich tribute that included the famed Koh-i-noor diamond and the Peacock Throne of Shah Jahan. But Delhi was not spared as Lahore had been, and the city was depopulated between 1738 and 1739. Karachi, today Pakistan's major port, was first mentioned in an account of Nadir Shah's officers who made use of the harbor.

A decade after Nadir Shah's incursion, Ahmed Shah Abdali (ca. 1723–73), an officer under Nadir, followed a similar invasion path, but was defeated at Sirhind, in southeast Punjab, by Muhammad Shah's son. The Persians retreated across the Indus. This was the last victory the Mughals achieved over foreign invaders. The death of Muhammad Shah in 1748 marked the end of Mughal power.

Half a dozen more Mughals took the throne after Muhammad Shah, but they presided over an empire in name alone, continuously shrinking and losing power, under siege by regional rulers and the European powers that were increasingly gaining power over the subcontinent.

5

TRADING COMPANY WARS
(1748–1858)

European powers had been competing with one another since the 16th century to gain control of the Asian trade routes that bypassed the Arabs, who had long dominated the commerce. In the mid-18th century one power achieved hegemony: Britain. Over the next century the English East India Company (EIC), under the patronage of the Crown, would establish control over the subcontinent, its objectives often achieved by military force. The British saw domination of the subcontinent as a national destiny, a God-given mandate similar to the conviction that fueled Islamic warriors in spreading their religion. But the British goals were political and mercantile. They sought to establish the subcontinent as a larder for their resource-starved homeland and to block competing European powers from establishing footholds in the region.

Having bested Portugal, Holland, and France in claiming dominance on the subcontinent, the British established supremacy over native powers with the defeat of the Mughal forces at the Battle of Plassey in Bengal in 1757. Though the Mughal Empire would survive for another century, it was increasingly subservient to Britain's agenda, which included reforms in government and society that remain a part of Pakistan today. Yet British influence and rule incited deep animosity, culminating in the Indian, or Sepoy, Rebellion, also called the Indian Mutiny, an uprising that spread across northern India and what is now Pakistan. It would lead to direct British control over the subcontinent.

The Battle of Plassey
In the mid-1700s, the chartered European trading companies in Asia and the Pacific transformed their trading posts into fortresses. With their parent nations engaged in political and military skirmishing in

Europe, this was done as much to defend against each other as to fend off Maratha attacks. In 1756 Siraj-ud-Daula (r. 1733–57), the young nawab of Bengal, as the region's Muslim rulers were known, ordered the Europeans to dismantle their fortifications. All but the British complied. In response, Siraj seized the English trading post at Kassim Bazaar and laid siege to the British post at Calcutta (Kolkata). After four days, the English commander there fled with some of his men, abandoning the rest of the garrison. Those left behind were captured and put in the post's stockade. According to a survivor, by the next day 123 of 146 prisoners had suffocated. (Some historians have questioned the reliability of his account.) The stockade became known as the Black Hole of Calcutta. The few British who escaped Calcutta spent six months waiting for rescue at Diamond Harbor, where many succumbed to disease.

During this time the British were actively engaged in countering French power throughout the world. On the subcontinent French holdings included settlements on the southeast and southwest coasts and in Ceylon (today's Sri Lanka) as well as in Bengal. Their headquarters were at Pondicherry, on the southeast coast. As part of the British Crown's initiative against the French in Pondicherry, a British fleet and army happened to be in the harbor at Madras, 100 miles (160 km) north, when word of Siraj's attack was received. The fleet was sent to avenge the disaster under the command of Robert Clive (1725–74), a former civil servant who had become a military leader in the subcontinent, and the troops successfully reconquered British Calcutta in January 1757. That same year Clive negotiated a treaty with Siraj-ud-Daula with more favorable terms for the British and also took the opportunity to destroy the French trading post at Chandernagore (present-day Chandannagar).

Despite the new trade agreement with Siraj, Clive desired a more pliant ruler on the throne. Many of the merchants and bankers of Bengal also wanted a more business-friendly leader. Clive conspired with Siraj-ud-Daula's opponents, including Mir Jafar, Siraj's commander in chief and father-in-law. Clive organized a small British force to attack Siraj-ud-Daula's army. Fought in a mangrove swamp in Bengal in 1757, the Battle of Plassey marked the true beginning of British control of the subcontinent. Though far outnumbered, the British possessed superior cannons, and with deceit wracking Siraj-ud-Daula's forces, Clive's forces won an easy victory. Siraj-ud-Daula was tracked down and killed, and Clive made Mir Jafar the new nawab of Bengal (r. 1757–60). In the aftermath of the victory, the British would reap untold riches, while the area, at the time among the most fertile in the world, began to experience an economic decline from which it has still not recovered. Henceforth the British appointed and discharged the nawabs of Bengal at their discretion.

The Carnatic Wars

The victory at Plassey opened the door for more British military conquests on the subcontinent. Rather than administer these territories, Clive formed alliances with corrupt and malleable local rulers, squeezing them for ever greater profits made on the backs of their increasingly downtrodden subjects.

From 1744 to 1763 the British, French, and Marathas engaged in a series of military engagements for dominance of the Carnatic, a coastal strip in southeast India stretching from just north of Madras to the southernmost tip. These were known as the Carnatic Wars. By the end of the Second Carnatic War (1748–55), French power in the subcontinent had dimmed.

The third and final Carnatic war (1756–63) was a direct outgrowth of the Seven Years' War waged across Europe during those same years. A French fleet commanded by Thomas-Arthur, comte de Lally (1702–66) arrived at the subcontinent in April 1758 to regain control of the region. Lally first captured the British headquarters for southern India, Fort St. David in Cuddalore, a few miles south of Pondicherry. His next goal was Madras. But the French fleet that was to assist him had been bloodied in a recent encounter with the British, and the commander of the fleet refused to take part in an attack. Meanwhile, lack of provisions and money to pay the troops greatly demoralized the French forces, and Lally's quarrelsome, overbearing manner alienated civil authorities. Furthermore his lack of respect for local religious traditions antagonized the Indians. By the time he was able to mount his assault in 1759, his depleted forces were unable to take the city. Lally sent for the marquis de Bussy-Castelnau (ca. 1718–85), who led a French force in Hyderabad, to come to his aid. But even with de Bussy's help Madras eluded capture.

Lally and his forces returned to Pondicherry. In 1760 they tried to retake their nearby fort at Vandavesi and were defeated by British Lt. General Sir Eyre Coote (1726–83) in the Battle of Wandiwash (the anglicized version of *Vandavesi*). It was a defining battle of the war. In its aftermath the French were restricted to Pondicherry, where in 1761 Lally and de Bussy surrendered after a long siege.

Consolidating British Control

In Bengal the British also defeated a Dutch expeditionary force sent to challenge them and conquered Dutch troops at Bedara in 1759. The British consolidated their control in the region by replacing Mir Jafar,

India, 1805

Kabul
DURRANI EMPIRE
Peshawar
Rawalpindi
Kandahar
Lahore
Indus R.
SIKH KINGDOM
Brahmaputra R.
Multan
Kalat
BALUCHISTAN
Delhi
NEPAL
Kathmandu
OUDH
RAJPUT STATES
Ganges R.
SIND
Karachi
BENGAL
Calcutta
Chandernagore
MARATHA CONFEDERACY
MARATHA CONFEDERACY
Daman
Diu
Godavari R.
Bombay
NIZAM OF HYDERABAD'S DOMINIONS
Arabian Sea
Krishna R.
Yanaon
Goa
Bay of Bengal
Madras
MYSORE
Pondicherry
Mahe
Karikal
Cochin
TRAVANCORE
KANDY
Kandy
N

British territory
British protected/ dependent states
Portuguese territory
Independent kingdoms
European settlements
▲ British   ■ French
□ Portuguese   O Dutch
Note: Contemporary boundaries are provided for reference.

INDIAN OCEAN

0   250 miles
0   250 km

© Infobase Publishing

the nawab they had installed, with the seemingly more pliant Mir Qasim (r. 1760–63). With Bengal secure, in 1760 Robert Clive retired to England to enjoy the vast fortune he had acquired in the subcontinent. As great a profiteer as he had been, the British who took charge of the subcontinent for the EIC after Clive were even more rapacious.

By the conclusion of the Seven Years' War in 1763, the British had all but eliminated the French from the subcontinent. Lack of unity among local rulers now gave the British an almost free hand in dominating the region. Up to this time Europeans had played a relatively small role in the economy of the subcontinent. But the demands of the British would overwhelm the economy, particularly in Bengal, leading to the famine of 1770, one of a series of food shortages that occurred under British control that claimed the lives of millions.

The Durrani Empire

While the British were gaining control in Bengal and along the subcontinent's coasts, their actions caused little stir in the region that is now Pakistan. Here local rulers engaged in power struggles in the wake of the collapse of the Mughal Empire. In the power vacuum left by the demise of Mughal authority the Marathas, Sikhs, and Afghans all sought hegemony in the area that is now Pakistan.

Afghanistan had been under the rule of the shah of Iran, Nadir Shah. Following his assassination in 1747, Ahmad Shah Durrani (ca. 1722–92) became the first ruler of Afghanistan's Durrani Empire. Ahmad Shah led eight major military campaigns in the Pakistan area between 1748 and 1768. In 1757 he seized lands east of the Indus, including Lahore and Multan in the Punjab. His son, Prince Timur Shah (r. 1772–93), whom he placed in charge of the newly conquered territories, then attacked the Sikh's sacred city of Amritsar. Provoked by the sacrilege, the Sikhs seized the region around Lahore and allied themselves with the Mughal governor of the Punjab, Adina Beg Khan (d. 1758), who was eager to preserve his own power. Adina Beg in turn asked the Marathas to help drive off Timur Shah. In 1758 the Marathas and the troops of Adina Beg arrived in Lahore, and the Afghan prince retreated westward.

Ahmad Shah Durrani was dealing with a tribal rebellion in Baluchistan at the time, but broke off that campaign to counterattack Punjab. Though Adina Beg Khan eluded capture by seeking refuge in the nearby hill country, awaiting the Afghan emperor's withdrawal, he died soon thereafter. The Marathas returned to Lahore in 1759 to secure the rudderless city. But rather than supporting the Mughals, the Marathas supplanted them. They reached the height of their power at this time, their empire embracing almost all of the subcontinent but for the lands west of the Indus; eastern Bengal, which was under British control; and the southern tip of the subcontinent, the Mysore kingdom. What is now Pakistan was increasingly dominated by the Marathas in the southeast and the Afghans in the north and west.

Some in the area preferred the Islamic rule of the Afghan Muslims to that of Hindu Marathas from the Deccan. Those who favored the Afghans included the influential figures Shah Waliullah, the Islamic reformer, and Malika-i-Zamani, the widow of the late Mughal ruler Muhammad Shah. Their pledges of support convinced Najib-ud-Daula (d. 1770), of the Rohilla (literally "mountaineer") Afghans—the Pashtun inhabiting the highlands from Swat west to Kabul and Kandahar—to form a Muslim Confederacy to cooperate with Ahmad Shah Durrani. In 1759 Ahmad Shah Durrani, his army fortified with Rohilla Afghan fighters, advanced on Lahore, vanquishing the Marathas and expelling them from the Punjab. The armies met two years later at Paniput, about 80 miles (130 km) north of Delhi, and again the Afghans prevailed, ending Maratha hopes of inheriting the mantle of the Mughal Empire. Ahmad Shah Durrani returned to Kabul with his army. To secure his conquest of Delhi, he installed Shah Zada, the son of the previous Mughal head, Alamgir II (r. 1754–59), as the ruler of the ailing Mughal Empire and Oudh, a region of north central India to the east of Delhi, giving him the title Shah Alam II (r. 1759–1806). By this time the empire had dwindled to Delhi and the surrounding areas. Najib-ud-Daula was appointed regent of Delhi. In the ensuing decade the area enjoyed some respite from the invasions and battles that had characterized its past.

Conflicts in Punjab

Northern Punjab and the Peshawar region were important parts of the Durrani empire. However, Ahmad Shah's rule in Punjab faced ongoing opposition and restiveness from the Sikhs, culminating in a Sikh uprising in 1760 and 1761. After suppressing the rebellion, Ahmad Shah allowed the Sikh chief Ala Singh (1691–1765) to rule in east Punjab.

In 1762 Ahmad Shah annexed Kashmir, bringing the Durrani empire to the height of its power and size. He used existing tribal structure to administer his domain, while major decisions were made by a council of *sardars*, a Punjabi term for "chiefs" or "leaders." But Sikh opposition in the Punjab continued. That same year Ahmad Shah, fearful of losing his Indian territory to the restive Sikhs, launched a campaign to not merely defeat but to exterminate the Sikhs. This only united the Sikh community and strengthened their resolve to resist Afghan rule. In 1764 the Sikhs attacked Lahore, dividing it among their three conquering chiefs. Lahore would remain under Sikh rule until the arrival of the British in 1849.

In 1773 Ahmad Shah Durrani died, succumbing to the cancer that had already forced him to relinquish most of his administrative duties. His death ended Afghan dreams of an empire in the mold of the Mughals or Persians. His son Timur Shah had taken on the responsibilities of the state. He allowed the Sikhs to continue their control of Punjab, recognizing the difficulty of maintaining Afghan rule of the region by military means. The empire's reach simply was not great enough. But the lands of the northwestern subcontinent from which the Afghans retreated did not automatically fall to the westward expansion of the Sikhs' dominion. The Sikhs had to defeat the Gakkars, who took Rawalpindi, as well as gain the upper head over other local tribes and chiefs—often strongly Muslim and staunchly anti-Sikh—who sought to establish their own kingdoms.

Rule in Sind and Baluchistan

Sind had long been part of the Mughal Empire, but by the latter half of the 17th century local tribes rather than a central authority controlled the region. The weak Mughal hold invited periodic raids and efforts to exercise dominion by Afghan and Maratha forces. By the beginning of the 18th century the leaders of one Sind tribe, the Kalhora, were recognized as rulers of Sind, suzerains of whatever larger power claimed the realm. The Kalhora dynasty (r. 1701–83) achieved its zenith during the reign of Ghulam Shah Kalhora (r. ca. 1757–72). This coincided with the period of Afghanistan's weakest grip on the region. Ghulam's rule expanded southward to the Arabian Sea. Karachi was taken peacefully after he negotiated a land exchange with the khan of Kalat in Baluchistan. During this time the Indus River changed course, possibly as a result of earthquakes. The shift made much of the Indus delta unnavigable, effectively shutting Sind's port at Shah Bunder. As a result the nearby city of Thatta, the capital city, lost its position as a major trade center. In about 1768 Ghulam founded a new capital city, Hyderabad, located farther north along the new route of the Indus. Instability and a bitter civil war between the Kalhoras and the Talpurs, a powerful Baluchi tribe, followed Ghulam's death in 1772.

In 1773 Timur Shah relocated the capital of the Durrani empire from Kandahar to Kabul. This put the empire's center even further from Sind and Baluchistan. Chiefs of Baluchistan, formerly under tight Afghan rule, became semi-independent. Indeed, most of what is now Pakistan was briefly free of both invasions and the requirement to pay tribute to the Afghans, activities that had become the norm over the preceding quarter century. But in the chaos following Ghulam's death, Sind again became the target of Afghan invasions, and tribute payments were reinstituted. By 1775 continual warfare made the economic situation in Sind so bleak that the British withdrew their merchants from the region. The Sindis revolted against Afghan rule in 1779, provoking yet another invasion by Afghan forces determined to collect tribute.

Meanwhile local rivals continued battling for rule of Sind as Afghan proxies. After a decade of bloodshed, the Talpurs finally defeated the Kalhoras at the Battle of Halani in 1782. The Afghan emperor gave them a *firman,* or royal mandate, in 1783 to rule most of Sind, which they continued to do until 1843. Five years later, with the Afghan empire in further decline, the Talpurs stopped paying tribute. The Afghans continued trying to collect revenue by force for another 20 years.

Changing British Policies

The region that would become East Pakistan before gaining independence as Bangladesh was a center of the British presence on the subcontinent. In 1763 a violent dispute erupted in Bengal between EIC traders and their Bengali hosts. Some of the British claimed they were not being accorded the trading privileges the Mughal emperor Farukhsiyar had extended to them during his rule 50 years earlier; they believed these privileges applied to their personal business dealings as well as to those conducted on behalf of the EIC. With Clive back in England, his replacement as commander in chief of India, John Caillaud (r. 1760/61), negotiated a compromise with Mir Qasim, the British-installed nawab of Bengal. The English traders, however, refused to accept the compromise. The same year the sepoys the British used as troops mutinied for the first time. The British harshly put down the insurrection. Their actions provoked Mir Qasim to seek support against the British from the Mughal ruler Shah Alam II and the nawab of Oudh, Shuja-ud-Daula (r. 1753–75). The forces met at the Battle of Buxar in 1764, where the British defeated the Mughal army.

By this time the EIC was facing serious economic problems. Individual traders in the company's employ were becoming wealthy from their private dealings, while the company itself was losing money, spent on military campaigns against native rulers and competing European powers rather than on trade activities. With turmoil wracking the EIC, Robert Clive returned to India in 1765. He negotiated a peace agreement that granted the British the right of revenue collection in Bengal, Bihar, and Orissa and brought Oudh into their sphere of influence. But Clive's efforts to rein in the employees' private dealings were deemed insufficient to reverse the company's fortunes. In an effort to trim expenses the company cut the salaries of its European military officers, provoking a mutiny. Clive sent some of the rebellious officers back to England as prisoners, where he himself returned in 1767.

As EIC agents, eager to amass personal fortunes, plundered the subjugated populations of the subcontinent, they showed less dedication to the EIC's business, and the company's profits turned to losses. In 1771 the EIC asked the British government for a loan to pay its taxes. In 1773 Parliament granted a £1.5 million loan to the EIC and passed the Regulating Act of 1773 to gain greater control over the EIC. The act placed oversight of the EIC's operations in the subcontinent under a governor-general. Warren Hastings, governor of Bengal, was chosen by company directors as the first governor-general of India (r. 1773–85), charged with reforming the company and restoring profitability. Hastings, who had joined the company as a young clerk, was a more enlightened administrator then most of the British of the time, knowledgeable and respectful of both Hindu and Muslim cultures. But

THE BENGAL FAMINE

Whatever reversal of fortune the EIC experienced was minor compared to what its policies wrought in Bengal. "Dual Rule," one of Britain's bedrock policies, put the peasant class under two rapacious regimes. Not only were they taxed by the British, who received most of the income from all taxes collected, the corrupt and servile proxy rulers the British installed taxed the peasants again to pay for the running of their own administrations. Between 1756 and 1770 these policies turned Bengal, a formerly rich and fertile region with a sound economy, into an impoverished land where one-third of the population died of starvation or accompanying disease. Though drought was the immediate cause of the Bengal famine of 1770, British policies had left no reserves to alleviate the starvation.

the Dual Rule policy, whereby peasants in Bengal had to pay taxes both to EIC authorities and to local rulers, continued during his tenure, as did the periodic famines and dislocation of local economies caused by British policies.

The EIC had built its administration on the framework developed by the Mughals. Revenues were collected by representatives of the regional rulers the EIC supported or installed. The British had also adopted the Mughals' legal system to apply to their subjects. Under Mughal tradition Muslims and Hindus were subject to the laws prescribed by their respective religions. As part of his administrative reform efforts Hastings tried to incorporate these indigenous legal codes into British laws for the subcontinent. But Mughal jurisprudence was based on the ability of judges to know and interpret the law on a case-by-case basis. As adapted by the British, the new law was incapable of capturing such nuance, and it institutionalized differences between Muslims and Hindus that had previously been more malleable.

Efforts to overhaul jurisprudence would take their largest step with the British parliament's Charter Act of 1833, considered the beginning of legal reform in the subcontinent. Though its primary purpose was to recertify the administrative authority of the East India Company, the act also created the framework for codification of laws, based on the British model of justice, throughout India. It also guaranteed rights of the indigenous population, stipulating, for example, that no Indian in the employ of the EIC could be barred from any office in the company due to religion, place of birth, descent, or color.

The Government of Charles Cornwallis

British general Charles Cornwallis, whose defeat at Yorktown in the American Revolution had effectively given the American colonies their freedom, replaced Hastings as the EIC's governor-general (r. 1786–93, 1805). He brought order to British affairs and won salary increases for EIC officers to compensate for the rules barring them from engaging in extortion and illegal trading. The gulf separating the British and the locals grew. The British and the Mughal aristocracy shared mutual interests in trade, sports, and ceremonial ritual, but the EIC's upper ranks were closed to locals of any status, further isolating the British from both the masses and the upper-class Indians.

Cornwallis ignored diplomacy in favor of political maneuvering. Hyderabad, the capital of the kingdom of Golconda, in southeastern India (not to be confused with the city in Sind of the same name), was ruled by a dynasty whose monarchs took the title *nizam*, or *nizam-ul-mulk,* administrator of the realm. The nizam of Hyderabad, Asaf Jah II (r. 1762–1803), gave territory to Cornwallis in return for the use of local Deccan troops in British employ for his war (r. 1782–99) with Tipu Sultan, the ruler of Mysore, a Hindu kingdom that dominated southern India. In retaliation for their support Tipu Sultan (r. 1782–99) attacked the British, and Cornwallis ultimately took command of the British forces. The British allied themselves with the Marathas as well, turning the tide of the conflict. In March 1792 Tipu Sultan capitulated, agreeing to give up half his territories, return prisoners of war, pay war reparations, and surrender two of his sons as hostages. His lands were distributed to the EIC and its allies.

In an attempt to stimulate agricultural production and create a landowning class, Cornwallis introduced the Permanent Settlement of land taxes. The Permanent Settlement fixed tax rates for agricultural land, freeing landowners from concerns that increased production would result in higher taxes. However, droughts occurring soon after the new tax law was adopted made it impossible for them to pay what they owed. They were forced to sell their land to absentee landlords who were more interested in making quick profits than in long-term increases in productivity.

British Interests in the Pakistan Region

The EIC had trading posts on the west coast of the subcontinent as well as on the east. The west coast settlements were primarily commercial enterprises, largely uninvolved in political matters, unlike those in Bengal and Madras. It was not until the late 1700s that the British gained a political interest in what is today Pakistan, aroused by Afghanistan and its hold on the region.

With the relocation of the Afghan capital from Kandahar to Kabul, the frontier, and the Peshawar region in particular, took on critical importance to the Durrani empire. Timur Shah escaped an attempt on his life in Peshawar in 1791 and executed the chief of the Mohmands, a Pashtun tribe living in southeastern Afghanistan (now the NWFP), for his role in the plot. However, the Sikh rulers of Lahore and Rawalpindi were firmly in the Afghans' orbit. The kahn of Kalat recognized Afghan suzerainty as well, as did other local rulers in Baluchistan and Persian Khorasan. Timur Shah died of natural causes in 1793, leaving no designated successor despite having several sons. Another period of instability ensued. Zaman Shah (r. 1793–1800), Timur's fifth son, succeeded his father and soon launched a campaign against the Talpur chief of Sind, Mir Fath Khan (r. 1783–1802), to collect overdue tribute. But trouble stirred by an elder brother, Mahmud, required Zaman to negotiate a hasty agreement with the Talpurs and quickly return home.

Lord Mornington, the marquis of Wellesley, the new British governor-general (r. 1797–1805), reestablished the British trading presence in Sind in order to monitor the area. Karachi had by now overtaken Thatta's position as the area's premier port. Once the Indus changed course, and the delta began to silt up, Thatta could no longer provide a gateway to and from the region's interior. Additionally Karachi was less rigidly controlled than Thatta, where Sindi officials were rigorous in their enforcement of trade rules, collecting tariffs and duties on all goods coming or going through the city and anywhere in the territory. Karachi had been alternately ruled by the Kalat, Kalhoras, and Talpurs, and the trade routes to Afghanistan from here passed through Baluchistan rather than Sind, making it preferable to the British. The agents engaged in the political mission in Sind discovered rich economic opportunities, and their report extolled the bustling activity of Karachi's port. But unlike the welcome originally accorded the British in Bengal on the east coast, local merchants had resisted foreign presence going back to the time

The Derawar Fort in Cholistan, Punjab, changed hands repeatedly during the 18th century. (Courtesy Pakistan Tourism Development Corporation)

of the Portuguese 250 years before. The locals refused to do business or associate socially with the Europeans. The British representatives sought a meeting with Sind's ruler, Mir Fath Khan, to gain his support, and they were granted permission to open a factory. However, within a year of establishing their factory in 1799, Mir Fath Khan ordered it closed, concerned about the British reputation for seizing power and working against local merchants.

By this time the glory days of the khan of Kalat were over. Its most heralded ruler, Naseer Khan Baluch (r. 1749–94), had died in 1794. Local principalities such as Karachi, Las Bela, Kharan, Jhalawan, and others mounted periodic insurrections against Kalat. Thus British interest in Pakistan's economic and political potential was growing at a time when Pakistan was without a dominant power.

The Sikhs in Punjab

Any hopes the Sikhs harbored of being done with the Afghans ended with an invasion marshaled by Zaman Shah in 1795, followed by similar incursions in 1797 and 1798. In 1799 Zaman Shah survived an assassination attempt in Peshawar, and like his father, had the plotters, in this case Barakzai tribal chiefs, executed. In Punjab the absence of outside authority ignited a power struggle among local chiefs. By 1800 most of the 12 Sikh *misls,* or divisions of the Dal Khalsa, the Sikh army, had staked out land for fiefdoms. (The word *khalsa,* from the Arabic for "pure," was used by Muslim rulers to signify state lands; later, Sikhs used the term to mean practicing members of the faith, after which it was applied to their military force and soldiers.) Half of these fiefdoms were in what is now Pakistan. Most of Pakistan's Punjabi territory was ruled by local Muslim aristocracies. Some of these ruling families, of Pashtun descent, had roots in the area that dated back centuries, while others came during more recent invasions.

One of the most powerful Punjabi rulers, Ranjit Singh (r. 1801–39), was also one of the most unlikely. A small man—illiterate, blind in one eye, his face scarred by small pox—Ranjit Singh inherited lands in the Gujranwala area, north of Lahore, initially acquired by his grandfather, a Sikh chief allied with Ahmad Shah Durrani at Amritsar. Ranjit's father had led the border chiefs who extended Sikh rule to the Margalla Pass (between Islamabad and Taxila) and Hasan Abdal in northern Punjab during Zaman Shah's reign.

Ranjit was 12 years old in 1791 when his father died. He took part in raids the following year, and his stature among the Sikhs grew.

Ranjit fought Zaman Shah's first invasion of the Punjab, but as much a diplomat as a warrior, he helped negotiate the latter's retreat from Punjab. When cannons were lost in a river during Zaman's withdrawal, Ranjit retrieved and returned some of them to Afghanistan. In gratitude Zaman awarded him Lahore, though the Afghan ruler's hold on the city was weak. The chiefs who ruled Lahore, and their sons, refused to give up the city, but the local elite opened Lahore's gates and welcomed Ranjit, and he took over the city in 1799. Meanwhile, the power of the Sikh armies was increasingly impinging on the sovereignty of Punjab's Muslim chieftains.

At the beginning of the 19th century a nascent power struggle in the Punjab pitted Ranjit Singh against four allied Sikh chiefs from Amritsar, Gujarat, Wazirabad, and Ramgaon, along with the Muslim leader of Kasur. The alliance foundered with the death of Amritsar's ruler, and his army disbanded. But his widow, who inherited his position, assembled an army. Ranjit sought sovereignty over all Sikhs, and control of Amritsar, their holiest city, was essential for his quest. In 1802 the three other Sikh chiefs allied themselves with Ranjit in defeating the widow's

In this 1820 painting, officers of the British East India Company are entertained by musicians and dancers, as one of their number smokes a hookah. (Werner Forman/Art Resource, NY)

forces. Over the next two decades Amritsar's fortunes improved as Ranjit rebuilt its temple and improved its fortifications.

During the first years of the century the Marathas were engaged in battles with the British across the subcontinent. The Holkar, a powerful central Indian state and member of the Maratha confederation, sought an alliance with Ranjit against the British. Determined not to be on the wrong side in the war, in 1806 Ranjit instead signed a treaty with the British pledging not to aid the Holkar. In return the British promised not to interfere with the internal affairs of Ranjit's territory, leaving him free to expand his empire. Among his first subsequent conquests was Kasur, in 1807, a city about 55 miles (80 km) southeast of Lahore. Not only was it of cultural importance to Muslims, the city had long resisted the Sikhs. Such was Ranjit's growing power that in 1808 rival Sikh chiefs asked the British Resident—the EIC representative—in Delhi to prohibit Ranjit from attacking them. The British would soon have their own reasons for checking Ranjit's expansion.

International Affairs

In July 1798 French general Napoleon Bonaparte invaded Egypt with the goal of cutting off England from India. A year later, in May 1799, the British fought their last battle against Tipu Sultan, defeating him at his fortress at Seringapatam, on an island of the same name in the Cauvery River. The British were now the major power in much of India, a position cemented by Napoleon's defeat in Syria that same month, ending the French threat to the British position in the subcontinent.

However, in 1807 Russia and a resurgent France signed a treaty to cooperate against the EIC's possessions. By 1808 the French army was advancing on Persia; Sindi rulers had granted the French access to their ports. The British mounted a diplomatic counterattack, dispatching envoys throughout the region, including Sind, Baluchistan, the Punjab, and Afghanistan. Ranjit Singh was, of course, on the list for visits. He welcomed the approaching envoys by mounting a display of force, attacking Amritsar, Ambala, and Patiala in Punjab. Ranjit hoped his campaign would pressure the British into recognizing him as the leader of the Sikhs as well pledging nonintervention in actions he undertook in Afghanistan, in return for supporting the British against the French. But by the time the envoys reached Ranjit, the British felt less threatened by the French and were more interested in suppressing the growth of regional powers such as Ranjit represented. Siding with the other Sikh rulers, they forbade Ranjit from expanding his empire by force anywhere but northwest of the Sutlej River. Ranjit prepared to resist the ultimatum, gathering his forces at Ludhiana (in today's Indian state of Punjab) for a showdown with the British, but then agreed to a treaty rather than fight. The 1809 Treaty of Amritsar that Ranjit signed left the Sikh community permanently divided. Some were vehemently opposed to capitulation to British demands and preferred a military response. Others felt Ranjit had taken a prudent course that preserved the kingdom. That same year statesman and historian Mountstuart Elphinstone (1779–1859), the first Englishman to visit Peshawar, went to the court of Shuja Shah Durrani, the Afghan ruler (r. 1803–09, 1839–42). Elphinstone was impressed with the reception and the tribal *jirga,* or council system of village government. (The clan *jirga* was called *khel,* and the *loya jirga* advised the emir of Kabul.) A few weeks after Elphinstone's visit, Shuja Shah was deposed by his brother Mahmud, who had previously ruled the kingdom. For the next 42 years Shuja Shah tried to regain the throne. His claims to the kingdom were used by Ranjit Singh and later the British to justify their own actions against the Durrani empire, which they claimed were undertaken on Shuja's behalf.

From 1809 to 1819 Ranjit Singh annexed all the territories allowed by his treaty with the British. Ever the opportunist, he conquered independent Muslim areas, claiming to be acting on behalf of the Durrani empire, though he kept most of the spoils of his conquests for himself. He did, however, mount a cooperative mission with Mahmud's Afghan forces to punish Kashmir for supporting one of Shuja Shah's attempts to regain his throne. The Afghans were the first to conclude a peace agreement with Kashmir and collect tribute, which they later refused to share with Ranjit's Sikh forces. But the Sikhs defeated the Afghans in the Battle of Haidaru in 1813, and in 1814 Rawalpindi came under Ranjit's rule.

The Jihad

Muslim reform efforts continued after the death of Islamic scholar and activist Shah Waliullah, carried on by his son and spiritual heir, Shah Abdul Aziz Muhaddith Dehlavi (1746–1823), and others. The downturn of the fortunes of the subcontinent's Muslims mirrored the decline of the Mughal Empire. In the early 19th century efforts by Christian missionaries to convert Muslims, and the loss of lands they had controlled for centuries to the Sikhs, roiled the Islamic community. Shah Waliullah's call for spiritual jihad, or holy struggle to live more piously, was now being supplanted by the military jihad urged by his descendants. Although Waliullah too had endorsed holy wars, he had directed Muslim rulers of his era to wage battle against the Hindu kingdoms; now Sikhs were the target of Muslim militancy. After Ranjit's conquest of Rawalpindi in 1810, rumors spread that the Sikhs were persecuting and attacking Muslims in Punjab. In response Shah Abdul Aziz launched a jihad. Sayyid Ahmad Barelwi (1786–1831), a military and religious leader noted for his organizational skills, was appointed to run the movement. Muslim mujahideens, or holy warriors, gathered throughout the region of today's Pakistan. Bands of volunteers made their way through Bahwalpur, Sind, and Baluchistan. In Peshawar, they overran and captured the town.

Ranjit Singh sent an army under the command of Jean-Baptiste Ventura (ca. 1792–?), a French mercenary of indeterminate background whom Ranjit had made a general, against the mujahideens. Meanwhile, his agents spread rumors claiming that Ahmad Barelwi's reforms were un-Islamic and that he was a Wahhabi, a practitioner of a rigid form of Islam. (Wahhabism is followed in contemporary Saudi Arabia.) Other potential supporters were bought off with bribes and presents. The jihad began to lose support. Many Afghans deserted, and local Pathan chiefs killed many of the mujahideens, seeking either economic or spiritual gain. Ahmad Barelwi was driven to the foothills of Kashmir, and on May 6, 1831, at a battle at Balakat, Ahmad Barelwi and many of the movement's leaders were killed and his army vanquished. The movement went underground and continued to foment anti-Hindu and, increasingly, anti-British sentiment.

British Wars in Afghanistan

With the Russians continuing to make overtures to Afghanistan, George Eden, first earl of Auckland (1784–1849), arrived from England with orders to install a pro-British regime to keep the Russians at bay. He dispatched an army that marched through Sind on the way to Afghanistan, ignoring a treaty with the Mirs, as the Talpur chieftains of Sind were known. The 1832 treaty forbade passage of British forces or military stores along the Indus River or across Sind. Lord Auckland's army joined another British force in Baluchistan. Once in Kabul the British installed their puppet, Shuja Shah, on the throne, but in 1841, while the British were on their way back to Jalalabad, near the Khyber Pass, a rebellion broke out. The retreating British forces were attacked, and most were slaughtered. Lord Auckland was recalled to England, though not much changed under his replacement, Edward Law, earl of Ellenborough (r. 1842–44). The British returned to Afghanistan to take Ghazni and Kabul, then withdrew. This marked the conclusion of the First Afghan War, which lasted from 1839 to 1842.

The Mirs of Sind allowed the British to penetrate their territory unimpeded. Perhaps emboldened by the lack of protest, the British forced a new, more onerous treaty on the Mirs, reducing their property and income. Sir James Outram (1803–63) was sent from England to enforce the treaty. The Mirs protested strongly, but their objections were met with a brutal British response from an army dispatched by Lord Ellenborough under the command of Sir Charles Napier (1782–1853). The British assault sparked an uprising in Baluchistan that culminated in an attack on the British residency in Hyderabad, Sind. Napier used the attack as a pretense to attack the rebel forces nearby at Miani and Dabo (1842–43), thereby conquering Sind. The Mirs were exiled, and Napier became Sind's first British governor, provoking the anger of Muslims and Hindus alike.

The Sikh Wars

Ranjit Singh died in 1839. After his death Punjab fell into chaos under the brief reigns of a succession of rulers. In response to the anarchy of the post-Ranjit years, the army played a growing role in political affairs. The degree to which the EIC was seeking an excuse to gain more control in the region has been debated, as has the notion that it was only concerned about the effects of instability on its nearby settlements. But whatever the EIC's motives, the Sikh army's growing assertiveness provided a spark that ignited armed conflict between the British and the Sikhs known as the Anglo Sikh, or, simply, Sikh Wars.

Ranjit Singh had signed a treaty with the EIC pledging to keep Sikh forces northwest of the Sutlef River. As the Sikh kingdom began to crumble, the EIC had built up its military forces along the river, to which the Sikhs objected. After negotiations broke down, and the EIC sent a large force to reinforce the area, in late 1845 the Sikh army crossed the Sutlef, igniting the First Anglo-Sikh War (1845–46).

The Sikh army was well equipped and had been trained by European mercenaries. Still, ultimately the British resoundly defeated the Sikh army, and the war officially ended with the Treaty of Lahore, signed in March 1846. Under the terms of the treaty the Sikhs paid the British an indemnity and ceded them Kashmir, and the British kept the current ruler, Ranjit's son, the young Dalip Singh (r. 1843–49) on the throne.

But the British Resident controlled policy. The Sikh's army was reduced to 20,000 infantry and 12,000 cavalry, retained primarily to keep the region from falling to Afghanistan. The British sold Kashmir to Raja Gulab Singh for 8 million rupees, the equivalent of about US$2,640,000 at the time.

The defeat, terms of the treaty, and British presence bred anger and resentment among many Sikhs. In August 1848 Sikh forces stationed in Hazara, in what is now Pakistan's NWFP, rebelled, as did those in Multan the next month when the British tried to choose the successor to the ruler of the Sikh territory. Two British officers sent to Multan to install the EIC-backed governor were killed, precipitating the Second Sikh War (1848–49). The Sikhs initially won several battles, but the British rebounded to win a decisive victory under the command of Lord Hugh Gough (1779–1869), formerly Sir Hugh. The uprising ended with a second Treaty of Lahore, signed March 9, 1849, under which the Sikhs ceded Punjab to the British, and the Sikh army was disbanded. Raja Dalip Singh moved to England in 1854. Sir John Lawrence (1811–79), later Lord Lawrence, was named chief commissioner of the Jullundur district, in today's Indian state of Punjab.

The British were led at the time by James Broun Ramsay, first marquis of Dalhousie (r. 1848–56). Young, short-tempered, and arrogant, Lord Dalhousie had boundless energy and willpower despite his frail constitution. Convinced of the superiority of Western ways and the need for British rule on the subcontinent, he pursued a policy of bringing princely states under British rule through the doctrine of lapse. According to this policy rulers without sons and under the direct control, or paramountcy, of Great Britain surrendered their right to appoint a successor to the British. This alienated the feudal aristocracy and sparked a revolt by deposed princes. British support for missionaries, who were seen by some as corrupting Hindu religious and cultural traditions, exacerbated popular opposition to the British. Hindus also objected to the mixing of religions and castes in prison, which was contrary to their faith, as well as to laws prohibiting sati, the practice of burning widows alive on their husbands' funeral pyres. Muslims were angered by the exclusion of Arabic and Persian from schools.

However, under the modernization efforts spearheaded by Dalhousie, roads, schools, and canals were built. British administrators John Lawrence in Punjab and the frontier, and Henry Bartle Frere (1815–84) in Sind and Baluchistan, played a large role in these projects. Sikh leaders were given *jagirs,* and relations with them gradually normalized.

Only the Muslim state of Oudh, now part of Utter Pradesh in north India, was still intact, the last vestige of the Mughal Empire. This too would be annexed by the British. First, though, the growing antipathy toward the British and their policies would erupt in an uprising. The short-lived Indian Revolution would profoundly change British governance in the subcontinent and further set back the fortunes of its Muslim population.

6

THE RAJ ERA (1858–1909)

The Sepoy Rebellion, or Indian Mutiny—the culmination of growing resentment and anger toward the British and their policies—marked a turning point in the subcontinent's history. In its aftermath the British Crown dissolved the EIC and assumed direct control over Indian territories. This ushered in the era referred to as the Raj. Under colonial rule the British attempted to introduce some forms of democratic institutions while simultaneously denying the people of the subcontinent any meaningful representation in the government. The Raj was also the period when seeds of an independent Pakistan were sown. Upper-class Muslims were living in economic and political isolation due to British perception of their support for the Sepoy Rebellion. Concurrently nationalist sentiment grew throughout the region and coalesced in 1885 in the foundation of a united independence movement led by the Indian National Congress. As the independence movement grew, so did divisions between Hindus and Muslims. A call for a separate Muslim state was heard, along with the rising demand for the subcontinent's independence from Britain, exemplified by the formation of the Muslim League. In 1909 Muslims gained a greater voice with the Government of India Act, also known as the Morley-Minto Reforms, marking a crucial juncture in Pakistan's history.

The Sepoy Rebellion

British control over the subcontinent had grown incrementally. The patchwork of states and fiefdoms that comprised the subcontinent's political landscape enabled the British to pursue a divide-and-conquer strategy, pitting ruler against ruler and lord against his subjects. It also allowed the British to rely on Indian troops for the great majority of its military force in the region, a weapon that played an important role in establishing Britain's rule. The ethnic and cultural diversity of the subcontinent and its history of internal warfare minimized the potential for the indigenous population to unite against the British. But a confluence of events finally ignited anti-British sentiment across the subcontinent, leading to sufficient unity against the British and thus the outbreak of the Sepoy Rebellion in 1858.

Roots of Rebellion

Britain's Indian troops, called sepoys, were divided into three main armies, headquartered in Bengal, Madras, and Bombay. The soldiers had been periodically restive since the beginning of the century. The Madras army had revolted in 1806 in Vellore, in what is now southern India, after changes in dress code that offended native religious sensibilities were instituted. Hats made of leather, a material forbidden to Hindus, who venerate cattle, were issued to the troops for headgear, while Muslims were required to shave their beards and trim their mustaches. The Bengal army, which had many high-caste Hindu troops, mutinied four times between 1843 and 1856 over a variety of grievances. During the 1840s, the British led troops from Bengal into newly annexed Sind and Punjab. But high-caste Hindu troops objected to crossing the Indus River, since this crossing traditionally resulted in a loss of caste. The sepoys also chaffed at the gradual loss of their overseas allowances, paid for serving across borders; the extra pay provided important financial support for their families while soldiers were away on duty. As more previously foreign territories were annexed, the sepoys increasingly served within their own borders, no matter how far from home their mission. And there were some theaters of operation—for example Burma, with its unpleasant jungles—where sepoys simply did not want to serve.

Numerous other causes for complaint existed. British officers often made a conscious effort to evince their own superiority, while humiliating local soldiers. And the Crimean War (1853–56), which pitted France, Britain, and the Ottoman Empire against Russia, had decimated the ranks of seasoned British officers, leaving less experienced and capable commanders in their place. At the same time, the British army's requirement that new officers study the native languages were dropped, further distancing British officers from Indian troops.

In February 1856 Charles Canning, first earl Canning (r. 1856–62), replaced Lord Dalhousie as governor-general of India. The hard-line policies Lord Dalhousie had championed—"lapse" and "paramountcy," annexation, and economic exploitation—had helped sow the seeds of anger and discontent that drove the Sepoy Rebellion. That same year the British instituted a mandatory deployment policy that required troops to serve wherever ordered in the empire; it was aimed at troops refusing to serve in Burma. Other military policies perceived by sepoys as anti-Hindu were also announced.

"Biting the Bullet"

In January 1857 the British gave Indian troops cartridges for their newly issued Enfield rifles. Sepoys had been taught to bite the tips of the cartridges before loading to prepare them for firing. Muslims thought the grease on the cartridges tasted of forbidden pork fat, while, to the Hindus, the grease smelled of cattle, which were sacred to them. Soldiers at Dum Dum, near Calcutta, refused to use the cartridges. Soon the resistance spread. Though animal fat was indeed used as lubrication, the British denied the fact and attempted to force use of the bullets. The British command surrounded groups of sepoys with British artillery and ordered them to "bite the bullet." Soldiers who refused—and most did—were immediately separated, stripped of their insignia, and dismissed without pay. They had to walk home to their villages, in some cases hundreds of miles away.

The British finally allowed soldiers to supply their own grease and rescinded the order that cartridges had to be bitten. But unrest among troops across northern India simmered. Fires of mysterious origin broke out on army bases. Some units mutinied, others were disbanded by the British to preclude uprisings. Oudh was a scene of particular restiveness, the result of a British-mandated inspection of landholdings, viewed by the indigenous population as a veiled effort to expropriate native property. EIC Resident Sir Henry Montgomery Lawrence (1806–57) was dispatched to Oudh as part of the inspection and established a residency at its capital, Lucknow, in March.

Rebellion Begins

At Meerut, in north central India, 85 soldiers had been incarcerated earlier for refusing to bite the bullet. On May 10, 1857, while the British officers were in church, the sepoys revolted, freeing their imprisoned comrades. After killing several officers they marched to Delhi, 30 miles (48 km) south, where they were met by other Indian troops who joined the insurrection. The last Mughal emperor, Bahadur Shah II (r. 1838–58), was then 82 years old, and his authority was limited by the British and largely confined to Delhi, but he was the one figure behind whom both Muslim and Hindu could unite. The rebellious troops asked Bahadur Shah II to lead a campaign for restoration of Mughal rule, and he agreed. With most of the European forces off fighting the Crimean and Persian wars (the latter fought with Persia over Afghanistan in 1856–57), their ranks between Bengal and Meerut were thinned, and the British began disarming native troops. Lucknow, Agra (in north central India), Lahore, Peshawar, and Mardan (in what is now the NWFP) were among the places were the sepoys were relieved of their weapons.

On May 13, 3,600 Indian troops were disarmed in Lahore and put under the guard of 400 Europeans, augmented by Sikh troops. The Sikhs had suffered defeats in the two Sikh wars at the hands of British-led Indian troops, so they had little sympathy or fondness for either the Indian troops or the Mughal emperor the troops supported. Meanwhile, British interception of sepoy mail revealed that troops were communicating with followers of Sayyid Ahmad Barelwi, the late revolutionary Islamist, in Swat and Sithana (in north central India), and that the Sithana revolutionaries in turn were in communication with mutineers in Bengal. In response the British sent the Bengal Native Infantry across the subcontinent to the edge of the tribal area, where they would have more difficulty inciting or drawing support from locals. Still, the revolt expanded and by late May had spread as far as Bombay. The Corps of Guides, made up of Indian troops loyal to the British, was dispatched to meet and reinforce the British forces in the Delhi area. A few weeks later some Indian soldiers at Mardan and Nowshera (in today's NWFP) refused orders. Both forces were disarmed, an action some British officers strongly opposed, feeling the loyalty of all the troops had been unfairly maligned by the actions of a few. Some of these British officers gave up their own swords and spurs in protest. Two of the deserting Mardan sepoys were captured in the Hazara District in the frontier region a few weeks later. On June 13, they were blown from the mouths of cannons as an example before a large assembly.

Most of the Mardan troops were eventually executed. The north area now seemed secure. Sir John Lawrence (1811–79), chief commissioner of Punjab and brother of Sir Henry Lawrence, considered asking Dost Mohammed Khan, ruler of Afghanistan (r. 1818–39, 1843–63), to take control of Peshawar, which would have freed the Europeans to go to Delhi. But the senior officers felt the British would lose face by requesting such help. Lord Canning agreed, sending an urgent message on the new telegraph line that instructed the British commander to hold Peshawar at all costs. The British, meanwhile, had taken to keeping pistols by their sides at mealtime and in church.

Rebellion Spreads

In Lucknow, which was the center of the rebellion, the Europeans had been besieged since early June, as they were in Kanpur, on the Ganges in north central India. On July 16 some 400 European residents of Kanpur, promised safe passage downriver, were instead shot and hacked to death in a spasm of violence. British troops recaptured the city the following day.

In July 1857 mutinies broke out in Sialkot and Jhelum in Punjab and in other cities. On July 30, a violent dust storm swept Lahore, where the 26th Native Infantry had been under detention for three months. During the storm the British commander was killed, and the incarcerated troops were liberated. Most fled, and the few who remained were killed by the British, as were those who surrendered the following day. Some 500 sepoys were executed within two days. Others were sent to Lahore and executed by cannon fire. Sir John Lawrence and Robert Montgomery (1809–87), lieutenant-governor of Punjab, commended the executions. Still the revolt spread. A British attempt to retake Lucknow was unsuccessful, and the revolt continued through the fall.

The rebels' most able military leader was Lakshmibai (ca. 1828–58), the queen, or rani, of Jhansi, a Maratha state in North India. Sir Hugh Rose (1801–85), British army field marshal, considered her the most dangerous of all rebel leaders due to her bravery, cleverness, and perseverance. She died in battle against Sir Hugh's forces at Gwalior in north central India, ending her threat.

The decisive battle of the insurrection was waged at Kanpur, scene of the massacre of British citizens the previous December. The British, led by Commander-in-Chief Colin Campbell (1792–1863), defeated Tantia Topi (1814–59), commander of the rebel forces. Following the victory, the British razed villages in retribution for the slaughter.

The End of the Revolt

Fighting continued into 1858, but the rebellion failed, and with it the last hope to drive out the foreign interlopers from the subcontinent. On July 8, 1858, Lord Canning proclaimed peace. The subcontinent was left in chaos. Several factors contributed to the revolt's failure. There was no central command. The spontaneous eruption of hatred and anger, powerful though it was, had no organization or coordinated way to channel its energy. The insurrectionists failed to mount any form of guerrilla warfare. What leaders they had were dethroned princes eager for return to old feudal ways, rather than enlightened figures with a progressive vision. Moreover, the Westernized, educated classes supported the British. And unity was elusive, with some rebels seeking restoration of Mughal power, while others wanted a return of the Marathas' authority.

The British took swift steps to punish those they held responsible and to reassert the rule of law. Tantia Topi was captured and hanged in April 1859. Emperor Bahadur Shah II was tried and exiled to Burma. His sons had already been killed by the British.

The Sepoy Mutiny was especially disastrous for British India's Muslim community. The British assigned them the brunt of the blame for the uprising, and subsequently limited opportunities for advancement to Muslims that Hindus of the subcontinent enjoyed, widening the chasm between the two societies. A decade after the rebellion, British Orientalist William Wilson Hunter (1840–1900) stated:

> There is no use shutting our ears to the fact that the Indian Muhammedans arraign us on a list of charges as serious as have ever been brought against a government . . . They accuse us of having closed every honourable walk of life to the professors of their creed. They accuse us of having introduced a system of education which leaves their whole community unprovided for, and which landed it in contempt and beggary. They accuse us of having brought misery into thousands of families by abolishing their law officers, who gave the sanction of religion to marriage, and who from time immemorial have been the depositories and administrators of the Domestic Law of Islam. They accuse us of imperiling their soul by denying them the means of performing the duties of their faith. Above all, they charge us with deliberate malversation of their religious foundations, and with misappropriation on the largest scale of their education funds (Hunter 969, 145).

Government of India Act of 1858

In the aftermath of the uprising the British reexamined their policies toward their colonies. The insurrection was blamed on misrule by the EIC, and the British government was now determined to take charge of the EIC's management and operations. The British parliament passed the Government of India Act of 1858, creating the position of secretary of state for India to whom the governor-general of India would report. Previously, the governor-general was under indirect British government control, which made it easier for EIC directors and agents to ignore the government's wishes. Henceforth, the governor general, while retaining this title, was also now known as viceroy, and considered a representative of the British monarch. The act also created councils to draft and pass laws with the viceroy's approval. The governor-general's council was composed of an executive council, which proposed laws for British-held areas, and a legislative council, which enacted them. These councils were mirrored at the provincial level and were to include Indians appointed by the viceroy's office.

The act vested the British monarch with ultimate authority over the subcontinent's states and Parliament with responsibility for dictating their policies. But the viceroys exercised a high degree of independence in establishing the tone of their administrations. They would retain their role as the titular heads of the subcontinent until its independence in 1947.

Lord Canning

Charles John Canning, first earl Canning, who had become governor-general in 1856, retained his post and became the first viceroy (r. 1858–62). The military was among the first institutions he reformed in the wake of the strife. Lord Canning disbanded the Bengal Army, numbering more than 100,000 soldiers (a *lakh* in the traditional Indian numbering system), most from what is now Uttar Pradesh in north central India, and many of them Muslim. Loyal Sikhs, Rajputs, and Gurkhas (an ethnic group from Nepal and North India) were enlisted in their place. The percentage of British personnel in the army was increased, and the proportion of high-caste Hindus decreased. Only British troops manned artillery. Though all officers were British, a viceroy's commission for native recruits introduced three ranks: jemadar, subedar, and subedar major. These junior officer ranks gave prestige to locals and enabled a better chain of command from officers to troops.

Lord Canning promoted a policy labeled conciliation, aimed at fostering good relations with leading princes and feudal aristocrats. By restoring their feudal authority he hoped these proxy powers, by their local connection and history, would keep their subjects in check. Even rulers of tribes participating in the revolt were restored to power. Lord Canning also reversed Dalhousie's efforts to appropriate feudal principalities. The Right of Adoption was restored, allowing feudal rulers without natural heirs to adopt one in order to preserve their kingdoms after death.

The conciliatory policy of feudal appeasement the British pursued in the aftermath of the revolt did not extend to Punjab. The British viewed

Lord Canning arrives in Lahore in February of 1860, as depicted in this painting by William Simpson (1823–99) (HIP/Art Resource, NY)

Punjab's feudal rulers, most of them Hindu, as obstacles to social progress, contributing little, taking more than their share in taxes, and short-changing the British on their due. The British wanted to levy taxes directly on peasants and eliminate the feudal landlords altogether. As a result, they gave preference to small landlords in determining the outcome of land ownership disputes, and rather than improving relations with the land barons in Punjab, the British curtailed their power. Peasants working the land, primarily Muslims, sold their crops to merchants, who, like the feudal lords, were mostly Hindu. Freed of the rulers' heavy hand, the economy expanded. By the 1870s Hindu merchants and other businessmen were developing into a middle class in Punjab. Mostly composed of members of lower castes, this emerging class sought Western education as a way to better themselves, a path eschewed by Muslims. Muslims, already blamed for the revolt, found themselves even further estranged from the mainstream of the subcontinent by a growing education gap.

Large numbers of insurrectionists were under detainment at the conclusion of the revolt. In 1858 the British reopened the penal colony at

Port Blair, in the Andaman Islands in the Bay of Bengal, to house some of them. To appease the upper classes, the Indian Councils Act, passed in 1861, added more members to legislative councils in the provinces. Indians nominated for membership by the British were from the upper classes, chosen for their loyalty to the Crown. In reality the legislative councils had no authority over the executive council, which determined policy. But it furthered the cause of reconciliation, demonstrating Britain's desire to make at least cosmetic changes to its rule of the subcontinent. Also in 1861 the Indian Penal Code proposed by Thomas Babbington Macaulay (1800–59), based on the laws of England, was enacted, establishing high courts in major towns.

Lord Canning convened two durbars, or ceremonial gatherings, where loyal princes' rank and titles were affirmed, as was Britain's pledge not to annex their territories. At his second durbar Lord Canning read out Queen Victoria's Proclamation of 1858. Considered the first constitutional reform of the British government's control of India, the proclamation expressed a desire to better the lives of all on the subcontinent. It promised that the civil service would be open to all. However, in practice, high-level administrators selected in England served to exclude well-educated Indians from senior positions.

Lord Elgin

In 1862 James Bruce, eighth earl of Elgin, became the second viceroy (r. 1862–63). The British policy of alliances with the aristocracy had not completely pacified the population. Muslims chaffing at their treatment in the wake of the Sepoy Rebellion revolted in Punjab and in the frontier areas. The insurrection was an offshoot of the movement founded by followers of Islamic reformer Shah Waliullah, primarily his son and spiritual heir Shah Abdul Aziz Muhaddith Dehlavi, and Sayyid Ahmad Barelwi. Though Sayyid Barelwi and many of the leaders had been killed at the Battle of Balakat in 1831, the movement lived on, inspiring a new generation of Islamic holy warriors willing to battle the British. The unrest in the frontier lasted from 1858 to 1863, requiring four British expeditions—a total of 27,000 troops—to finally suppress the uprising.

Sir John Lawrence

After the reign of Lord Elgin, a pair of provisional viceroys were appointed in succession before Sir John Laird Mair Lawrence (r. 1864–69) was named viceroy. He had been the chief commissioner in Punjab following the 1857 revolt. Lawrence continued to improve the infrastructure system initiated by Lord Dalhousie in the 1850s, including large construction projects to expand the railway and irrigation systems. Concern for public health led him to upgrade sanitation systems and water supplies. The Punjab and Oudh Tenancy Act was passed in 1868, which gave tenants ownership of lands they had lived on and cultivated for a requisite period of time. Yet with the many changes the British had wrought in the agricultural system, the subcontinent had still not recovered its ability to feed all its people. In 1866–67 a famine occurred in Orissa, the first in a series of famines over the next few decades. Sir Lawrence proposed supplying grain to those affected, but his council rejected the proposal on the grounds it would interfere with the laws of supply and demand. Moreover, council members felt it would be demeaning to offer charity to the population. Thus nothing was done, and almost one-quarter of Orissa's population starved. When a famine later occurred in Rajputana, Lawrence ignored his council's opinion and mounted a relief effort, which was credited with saving many lives.

Afghanistan still cast a large shadow over the area that is now Pakistan, even as British interest in this area grew. In 1863 Dost Mohammad Khan (b. 1793) had died, and Sher Ali Khan (1825–79), one of his sons, emerged as the ruler after defeating his brother; however, his brothers continued trying to wrest leadership from him. Sher Ali asked Lawrence for help in securing the throne, but as the British had a policy of noninterference in the succession battle, he declined. Sher Ali was ousted in 1866, but regained control of Afghanistan in 1868, which he held to his death in 1879. Throughout the reign his hold on the throne was tenuous, and the memory of Britain's lack of support remained with him.

Lord Mayo

Sir John Lawrence was succeeded by Richard Southwell Bourke, sixth earl of Mayo (r. 1869–72). A major policy change he initiated transferred more control over finances to regional authorities, shifting decisionmaking to the provinces. At the regional level, budgetary needs could be more accurately gauged and spending more carefully monitored. Lord Mayo also initiated large public work programs for the construction of roads, railways, canals, and sanitation projects. The rails were becoming a key part of the subcontinent's landscape, drawing together the disparate regions. By 1870 rails connected Multan with Calcutta and Bombay. Railways played a key part in territorial dominance as well, allowing for the quick movement of military assets over large distances. When Russia, which was conquering territories to the north, built a rail link to the Oxus River, on Afghanistan's border, Britain responded by building a rail link to its frontier on the border

SIR SAYYID AHMAD KHAN

Regarded as one of the fathers of Pakistan, Sir Sayyid Ahmad Khan (1817–98) was one of the first to push for Muslim education and representation. After the Sepoy Rebellion he wrote forcefully on its causes, blaming British inability to understand Indian thinking for the violence. A visit to England convinced him the only path toward progress for Muslims in India lay in Western education. He believed accommodation with the British was in Muslims' best interests. Many Muslims

were reluctant to have their sons educated at schools without Islamic teaching, and the subsequent lack of education kept many from pursuing career paths that provided opportunity for advancement. Ahmad Khan believed Western education was compatible with Islamic teachings. He was the driving force behind the creation of the Muhammadan Anglo-Oriental (M.A.O.) College (later renamed Aligarh Muslim University), founded in 1875 in Aligarh in northern India. Khan made Arabic language and Islamic studies compulsory courses at M.A.O. The university fomented the thinking and shaped the minds of future leaders who would father an independent Pakistan.

Sir Sayyid Ahmad Khan was one of the first to call for separate representation for the subcontinent's Muslims and Hindus in institutions of self-governance. (Courtesy Pakistan Tourism Development Corporation) with Afghanistan. This further opened what is now Pakistan to British incursion and domination. After the opening of the Suez Canal in 1869, Karachi became Europe's closest Asian port, and sea trade increased in volume and importance.

In 1869, his first year in office, Lord Mayo traveled to Ambala in North India to meet with Sher Ali Khan, with whom relations had been strained since Britain's failure to help Sher secure the throne in Afghanistan. The earl also improved relations between Indian princes and the government. However, his efforts to impose an income tax, instituted in 1869, drew widespread opposition, and the tax was ultimately unsuccessful in generating projected revenues. He established the Department of Agriculture to boost agricultural production. And during his tenure Chiefs' Colleges, created to offer Western education to the sons of princes and chiefs, were founded in Lahore, Rajkot (in the present-day state of Gujarat in western India), and Ajmer (in modern-day Rajasthan state in northwest India). Lord Mayo also helped lay the groundwork for the Muhammadan Anglo-Oriental (M.A.O.) College, founded in Aligarh in 1875, shortly after his time as viceroy came to a premature end. The college, later renamed Aligarh Muslim University, was founded by Sir Sayyid Ahmad Khan (1817–98), a leading Muslim reformer who believed that access to Western education was essential for Muslim progress in British India.

Lord Mayo also initiated prison administration reforms during his tenure. Paradoxically, he was stabbed and killed by a Pashtun prisoner—a Muslim—at the prison colony in the Andaman Islands in 1872. The British incorrectly believed Muslims were bound by religion to resist British rule, and incidents such as this assassination reinforced this view.

Lord Northbrook

Two provisional viceroys succeeded Lord Mayo before Thomas George Baring, second baron Northbrook (r. 1872–76) was appointed viceroy. In the 1870s Baluchistan remained restive, with tribes throughout the area staging border raids on Punjab and Sind. During the previous decade, as part of their efforts to work with local rulers in the wake of the revolt of 1857, the British had encouraged the new khan of Kalat, Khodada Khan (r. 1857–63, 1864–93), then a teenager, to consider himself an absolute monarch. The British created a standing army for the young khan and with their blessing he had spent the intervening years in a failed attempt to establish his dominance over the tribes of

Baluchistan. With Khodada Khan unable to control them, the British had then dispatched their agent Sir Robert Groves Sandeman (1835–92) to negotiate with tribal leaders, paying the tribes to act as border guards. These payoffs reduced, but did not eliminate, raids, which continued to vex border villages. The British had finally ceded the responsibility, again, to Khodada Khan, treating him as the ruler of the tribal lands and providing money to pay tribal leaders to cease their attacks. In a further effort to promote law and order, the frontier and other tribal areas in the region had been brought under jurisdiction of the Frontier Crimes Regulations in 1871. The laws it codified were different from those in force in the rest of the subcontinent; they included the stipulation that internal disputes would be settled by *jirgas,* or tribal councils of elders, while ceding British administrators ultimate authority over all matters. In 1876 Sandeman received a concession from Khodada Kahn to establish a frontier trading post at Quetta, a location that would give the British another access point to Afghanistan and control of the Bolan Pass. The khan also gave the British permission to post a resident in Kabul. Lord Northbrook unsuccessfully objected to the posting, asserting it would subject England to the risk of another war in Afghanistan, a conflict he believed would be both costly and unnecessary.

Lord Northbrook staunchly supported the development of business and commerce in the subcontinent. He abolished the unpopular income tax imposed under Lord Mayo and also sought to protect India's nascent textile industry. The British were intent on wringing as much revenue as possible from India. Under the banner of free trade, British manufacturers, who had the benefit of industrial production, flooded India with cheap imports. Lord Northbrook felt British goods brought into the colony should have a higher import duty to protect Indian manufacturers and in 1875 made his views known to Parliament. However, a conservative government had been elected in England during his tenure, and instead of raising Indian import duties on British textiles, Parliament reduced the duties to make them more competitive with locally produced goods. His policy differences with the government too profound to bridge, Lord Northbrook resigned in protest in 1876.

Lord Lytton

Lord Northbrook was replaced by Robert Bulwer-Lytton, second baron Lytton (r. 1876–80), who set about undoing the reforms Northbrook instituted. Lord Lytton tried to restore the authority of the feudal princes who had been most disaffected by the previous viceroy's reforms. His primary goal, however, was to regain British control over India and avoid the possibility of losing the colony entirely. In 1877 Lord Lytton convened a great durbar at Delhi to impress local aristocrats. The guests were required to pledge an oath of loyalty in return for the award of honors and multigun salutes. During the gathering Queen Victoria was proclaimed empress of India.

In response to a famine that began in 1876 and that had by 1877 claimed the lives of tens of thousands, Lord Lytton established the Famine Commission, which recommended building roads and railways for shipment of grain to famine-plagued areas and instituting updated irrigation methods. Though the subcontinent would experience subsequent famines in 1896 and 1899, the adoption of the commission's recommendations was credited with minimizing the severity of these later crises.

Meanwhile, discontent was growing in British-ruled areas. More opportunities in the civil service and other reforms had been promised to Indians in the Charter of 1833, the Queen's Proclamation of 1858, and other laws. But Lytton sought to renege on these pledges in an effort to maintain Britain's hold on power. The British made a cosmetic attempt to placate locals by creating a separate statutory civil service, as opposed to the covenanted civil service, in 1879. It included one-sixth of the minor posts from the covenanted civil service. Appointments were made based on education and social position. This essentially closed the ranks to all but loyal members of the aristocracy. So rather than quell protests, the new civil service further inflamed educated Indians.

Discriminatory taxes and import and export duties angered the business class, and the British felt they needed to take steps to forestall unrest. The Vernacular Press Act of 1878 reduced freedom of expression in newspapers printed in non-English languages, effectively stifling reporting of news that put British actions in a negative light. The same year the Arms Act forbade Indians from carrying arms without a license. Both laws aroused further resentment and anger throughout the subcontinent.

Throughout the viceroyships of Lawrence, Mayo, and Northbrook, the area of present-day Pakistan had received less attention than other regions of the subcontinent. That changed under Lord Lytton, who supported the "forward policy," a strategy of containing Russia's expansion toward Afghanistan; the policy's most notable proponent was British prime minister Benjamin Disraeli (r. 1868, 1874–80). The treaties struck by Sir Sandeman in 1876 with Khodadad Khan gave the British a foothold for their military by permitting their annexation of Quetta and its surrounding territory. By this time the khan viewed the British as the ultimate arbiters of his disputes, as stipulated by treaty.

The Second Anglo-Afghan War (1878–1880)

The ruler of Afghanistan, Sher Ali Kahn, continued his weak hold on power. Despite Lord Mayo's visit in 1869, the British still refused to support him militarily or financially, and Sher Ali resisted British efforts to post an envoy in Kabul. Russia, meanwhile, made overtures of assistance to Sher Ali, although he had also refused Russia's request to post an envoy. Concerned about his developing relationship with Russia, Lytton dispatched a British officer to meet with the Afghan ruler, but Sher Ali refused to grant the emissary an audience and threatened to turn back any British diplomatic mission. In response, Lytton declared war on Afghanistan. Three forces consisting of 35,000 troops and camp followers under the command of Major General Frederick Roberts (1832–1914), General Samuel Browne (1824–1901), and General Donald Martin Stewart (1824–1900) advanced on Afghanistan. Traversing what is now Pakistan, the British army made a show of force that implicitly demonstrated their control over the area. Sher Ali fled to Turkestan, from where he dispatched a letter agreeing to allow a British envoy in Kabul. Despite his acquiescence, the British occupied Kandahar and Jalalabad. On his way back to Afghanistan, Sher Ali died. The British struck a treaty with his son, Yaqub Khan (r. 1879), at Gandamak, a village in southeast Afghanistan, in 1879.

Under the terms of the Treaty of Gandamak, the British were allowed to place a British resident in Kabul and British agents in Herat and Kandahar. In return, Yaqub Khan received a subsidy of six *lakhs* (600,000) of rupees a year. Parts of Afghanistan and the whole of the Khyber Pass were ceded to Britain. Yaqub Khan also agreed to accept British counsel in conducting his foreign policy. But many Afghans wanted no British presence in their capital, and in 1879 mutinous troops stormed the house of the British Resident, Sir Pierre Louis Cavagnari (1841–79), and killed him and his staff. Lord Lytton dispatched an army under the command of generals Roberts and Stewart. Another of Sher Ali's sons, Ayub Khan (1857–1914), engaged the British army at the Battle of Maiwand in southern Afghanistan in July 1880. The largest battle of the Second Anglo-Afghan War, it ended in a British defeat, though the Afghan forces also lost many soldiers. Ayub Khan's remaining forces next laid siege to Kandahar, where a British resident was stationed. General Roberts hurried to relieve Kandahar, marching his forces more than 300 miles from Kabul. The British defeated the Afghans at the Battle of Kandahar in September 1880, the last major conflict of the Second Anglo-Afghan War. During the conflict, without the draft animals the British appropriated for the campaign, agriculture in the Punjab region suffered, costing the government a fortune in lost revenue. Lord Lytton resigned.

Lord Ripon

Following the Second Anglo-Afghan War, Lord Lytton was succeeded by George Frederick Samuel Robinson, first marquis of Ripon (r. 1880–84), a more enlightened viceroy. In the same year British Liberal Party leader William Gladstone (r. 1868–74, 1880–85, 1886, 1892–94) was beginning the second of his four terms as prime minister of Britain. He moderated the "forward policy," pursuing a less confrontational strategy toward Afghanistan. Instead of large settlements and forces, the British sought to counter Russian influence by the posting of small forces and extensions of existing fortifications. They agreed to recognize as emir of Afghanistan Abdur Rahman Khan (r. 1880–1901), a grandson of Dost Mohammad, who had long battled Sher Ali, Abdur Rahman's uncle, for the throne. The new emir brought stability to the region and retained good relations with the British throughout his reign, which lasted until 1901. He was succeeded by his son, Habibullah Khan (r. 1901–19).

The Second Anglo-Afghan War brought large areas of Baluchistan and the frontier into the British Empire. Yet British objectives in Baluchistan were fundamentally different from those in Sind and Punjab. In Baluchistan, the British were interested in the military and geopolitical value of the land; in the rest of the subcontinent, they sought primarily to extract income. But the local populations still bore significant costs from the British incursions. British development of cantonments, or military quarters, at Quetta and other areas required evicting many locals from their lands, creating an army of landless peasants. This action led to the suppression of local tribes and increased resentment of the British throughout the subcontinent, particularly among Muslims. Indians also had to endure tax increases, levied in order to pay for the war.

During his tenure as viceroy, Lord Ripon abolished the Vernacular Press Act established by his predecessor, posted Indians in high government posts, broadened the powers of local governments, and made municipal offices elective positions, giving locals experience in democracy. Laws were passed to safeguard working conditions in factories. He encouraged education of the subcontinent's people, appointing the Hunter Education Commission, whose report of 1884, among other accomplishments, helped focus attention on the plight of Muslims in the subcontinent. The viceroy also attempted the radical step of allowing Indian judges to try Europeans under the Ilbert Bill, enacted by the Indian Legislative Council in 1884, but loud European opposition forced him to back down.

However, economic exploitation continued throughout Lord Ripon's tenure. In the years following the reduction of import duties on British textiles in 1876, economic manipulation of tariffs and trade became common. In 1879 all tariff duties for English goods were abolished, primarily to help the British fabric industry. In 1895, after the British placed an excise duty of 5 percent to raise revenue, Parliament imposed a similar excise duty on Indian cotton goods. Foreign exchange between the Indian rupee and the British pound was fixed in such a way as to stimulate imports of British goods into India and curtail exports from the subcontinent.

As Indian demands for autonomy and freedom began to grow, Muslims continued their political awakening. Sir Sayyid Ahmad Khan spoke out forcefully for separate representation for Muslims in self-governance institutions. He won recognition in 1882 for the principle of separate electorates for Muslims on Lord Ripon's municipal councils. In a speech before the Governor-General's Council in January of 1883, Ahmad Khan explained the need for separate representation: "So long as differences of race and creed, and the distinctions of caste form an important element in the socio-political life in India, and influence her inhabitants in matters connected to the administration and welfare of the country at large, the system of election, pure and simple, cannot be safely adopted. The larger community would totally override the interests of the smaller community, and the ignorant public would hold Government responsible for introducing measures which might make the differences of race and creed more violent than ever" (Symonds 1950, 30–31).

Lord Dufferin

Liberalization of policies that began under Lord Ripon continued under Frederick Hamilton-Temple-Blackwood, the earl of Dufferin (r. 1884–88, later first marquis of Dufferin and Ava), his successor. The

Bengal Tenancy Bill, proposed during Lord Ripon's viceroyalty, passed in Bengal in 1885 under Lord Dufferin's stewardship. The law defined and improved the rights of farmers under their landlords. Working conditions and exploitation of the subcontinent's labor force had come to the attention of the British public, which had already grappled with similar homegrown abuses springing from its industrial revolution. In response, Parliament passed the Factor Act, which limited the number of hours employees could be required to work, and forbade children under age nine from employment in factories.

In 1886 Lord Dufferin appointed a commission to explore ways to expand public services. The viceroy also wrote *A Report on the Condition of the Lower Classes Population in Bengal,* called the Dufferin Report, published in 1888, which countered claims that the poor had benefited from British rule in the subcontinent. His wife founded a charity fund that built Lady Dufferin hospitals for women, staffed by female doctors, which took all patients regardless of ability to pay. Today, Lady Dufferin Hospital in Karachi is the largest women's hospital in Pakistan. However, as viceroy Lord Dufferin also sought to ease concerns of the British population of India, which viewed the reforms introduced by Lord Ripon with unease.

For most Indians, British reforms came too late and did not go far enough. In 1885 the Indian National Congress (INC) was founded, established by a new generation of Indians educated in Western-style educational institutions. Consumed by nationalist zeal, INC members met regularly and, though they had no legal authority, passed resolutions recommending actions and policies for the British-run government to follow. Several British helped in founding the Congress Party (as the INC is otherwise known), viewing the organization as a way to monitor the opposition, and as a relief valve for political discontent.

The INC began as a moderate political party, supported by the educated middle classes—lawyers, teachers, and journalists—as well as by some members of the business community and landed gentry. They sought increased British assistance in training and education, not independence. But as moderate voices within the INC were ignored by the British, more radical leaders gained power. Some Hindu extremists played on anti-Muslim prejudices, and their incendiary rhetoric went largely unchallenged. Muslims watched mute while shrill INC members who denounced British rule were received with cordial respect by the viceroy. Leaders of the Muslim community were reluctant to strike a militant stance, since the financial well-being of educated professionals and landlords was in the hands of the British. But with the establishment of educational institutions such as the M.A.O., a new generation of educated Muslims was coming of age, eager to pursue its own path. After 1884 Ahmad Khan began to support Muslim separatism, advising Muslims to boycott the Indian National Congress, and in 1886 he formed a rival institution to the INC, the Mohammedan Education Conference, a predecessor of the All India Muslim League that would form 20 years later. In 1887 a Muslim was named president of the INC; Ahmad Khan denounced the appointment. He felt the appointment would lead Muslims into what he saw as a false belief that they and the Hindu majority could work together and peacefully coexist in one nation independent of the British. His opposition to the INC coincided with that of the British: As the INC as a whole adopted a more independent stance, British support evaporated. However, many Muslims continued to support the stance of the INC's less militant members and favored a nonconfrontational approach to their differences with the British. Following the fourth annual session of Congress, government officials were banned from joining the organization.

Lord Landsdowne and Lord Curzon

Henry Charles Keith Petty-Fitzmaurice, fifth marquis of Lansdowne, succeeded Lord Dufferin as viceroy (r. 1888–94). His tenure and that of his later successor George Nathaniel Curzon, first marquis Curzon of Kedleston (r. 1899–1905), underscored the fact that liberalization accorded to the majority of the subcontinent was withheld in the frontier areas of what is today Pakistan. The Indian Councils Act, passed by Parliament in 1892, increased membership in the central and provincial legislative councils in the Punjab and Sind, but not in Baluchistan or the frontier area. These western provinces were deemed too untamed to permit such reforms.

Defining the Border

As kingdoms in the region grew and declined, their territories were often in flux. The border between Afghanistan and British India had never been fixed. That boundary was delineated by the Durand Line, created during Lord Lansdowne's time as viceroy. Sir Henry Mortimer Durand (1850–1924) was an officer in the corps when he requested permission from Abdur Rahman, the emir of Afghanistan, to determine a line of demarcation between Afghanistan and the British Empire. Abdur Rahman could not well refuse, as the British controlled trade routes in and out of Afghanistan and paid the emir subsidies. When completed in 1893, the Durand Line moved the border of the British territory from the foothills west to the crests of the highest peaks and ridges in the mountains dividing the territories. This brought several tribes, including the Afridis, the Mahsuds, the Wazirs, and the Swat, under nominal British rule if not control. The British launched several military campaigns to subdue the tribes and demonstrate their regional dominance. In 1895 an uprising broke out in Chitral and soon spread to the rest of the tribal area. During the campaign a force of allied tribesmen besieged 400 British troops in the Chitral Fort; they also succeeded in closing the Khyber Pass. It took British forces 48 days to come to their countrymen's rescue and relieve the siege.

In the early 1890s the chesslike maneuvering the British and Russians engaged in as each attempted to gain power and influence in the area became known as the Great Game. The Pamir Mountains, which extend from the Hindu Kush into Afghanistan, took center stage in their contest. The Great Game came to an end with the Pamir Boundary Agreement of March 1895, signed by Russia and Great Britain. It established the Wakhan Corridor, a narrow sliver of Afghanistan in the Pamir Mountains, as a buffer between Russia (now Tajikistan) and British-held India in what is today Pakistan. The corridor, about 300 miles (480 km) long and less than 10 (16 km) miles wide in some places, borders China on the east. In 1896 the border between the British and Persian territory of Baluchistan was established.

Lord Curzon, who became viceroy in 1899, took a different tack in dealing with the rebellious tribes. He saw the frontier Pashtun as a unique population, independent and strong willed, whose heritage fell far outside of social norms not only in Britain but even in this corner of the subcontinent. He recognized that raiding and plundering, the basis of their livelihood, had long been the only means of survival in the frontier. In 1900 Curzon established the area as the North-West Frontier Province, placing it under the direction of a seasoned chief commissioner.

Cultured and well traveled, Curzon instituted numerous reforms. He emphasized improvements in university education, overhauled the police department, bolstered farmers' rights, and pushed credit societies and agricultural banks to give financial assistance to the poor. Under his direction thousands of miles of railway were built.

An Agrarian Revolution

In the last quarter of the 19th century agrarian reforms and improvements to the infrastructure introduced by the British showed some results. Before this time, much of the Indus Valley was dry and sparsely inhabited. A canal system the Mughals built to irrigate the area had fallen into disrepair. Changes in the course and flow of the Indus had added to depopulation. The British undertook large-scale projects to repair and expand the ancient canal system and engineered massive additional irrigation systems that made vast areas of formerly uninhabited lands in Punjab arable. An expanding railway system transported grain from Punjab for shipment to England. After 1879 Lahore and Karachi were linked by rail. By 1883 it was possible to travel from Karachi to the Khyber Pass by rail. During construction of the Lahore-Multan track, engineers discovered the lost city of Harappa. They used the ancient brick they found to build 100 miles (160 km) of the railway's embankment. Curzon recognized the region's archaeological importance. The Ancient Monuments Preservation Act, passed during his tenure, made the government responsible for maintaining historic buildings and investigating archaeological sites. Taxila and cities of the long-lost Indus Valley Civilization were first excavated as a result of this act.

From the 1880s onward peasants settled on these newly fertile lands. This set in motion a new political dynamic in the region as agrarian landlords came to accumulate land and power. Peasants were limited to plots of 100 to 150 acres, with landlords receiving a percentage of crops in rent. Sometimes the rents were usurious, and tenant farmers often fell into debt, their plots seized by the landlords. Other peasants lost their lands to moneylenders. By the late 19th century some of these holdings became mini–feudal states and their owners strong supporters of the British, whose policies served their interests. The situation was antagonizing many Muslims, who comprised a majority of sepoys in Punjab. To help address the problem of small farmers having their lands repossessed and stem the unrest it was stirring, Parliament passed the Punjab Land Alienation Act in 1900. The act defined tribes as either agricultural or nonagricultural and forbade nonagricultural tribes from acquiring the land of agricultural debtors.

Partition of Bengal

Despite the fact that it was the region first exposed to the British presence—or because of it—Bengal, the northeast corner of the subcontinent, lying east of the Ganges, remained backward and undeveloped. The eastern portion of Bengal was predominantly Muslim, the western portion Hindu. The religious dichotomy had complicated administration of Bengal, as did the large population. To break the administrative bottleneck, in 1905 Lord Curzon partitioned Bengal into two parts:

A European is engaged in a tiger hunt, a pursuit of nobles and the upper class, in this 1892 painting from Punjab. (Victoria & Albert Museum, London/Art Resource, NY)

West Bengal encompassed Bihar and Orissa, with Calcutta as its capital, and East Bengal incorporated the province of Assam, with Dacca (modern-day Dhaka) as its capital. From the start, Hindus objected to the partition, feeling their land was being taken away. The protest was more widespread and sustained than anticipated by the British and increasingly included Hindu nationalist overtones as well as violence. The opposition to the partition also spawned the *swadeshi* movement, which advocated boycotting British goods, a form of protest that turned out to be surprisingly effective.

Toward Muslim Independence

As viceroy Lord Curzon enjoyed the customary control over the Indian Army's commander in chief (CIC). But in 1905 the secretary of state for India in England changed the policy, taking direct oversight of the CIC for himself. Lord Curzon resigned in protest. Gilbert John Elliot-Murray-Kynynmound, fourth earl of Minto, succeeded Lord Curzon as viceroy (r. 1905–10).

Political change, both peaceful and violent, was in the air. Muslim aspirations were being expressed in Muslim-majority areas, and the concept of self-government for Muslims began to take root. In 1906 the All India Muslim League was founded, a political party that would play a major role in the future of the subcontinent's Muslims. Formed in Dacca (now Dhaka) at the annual meeting of the Muhammadan Educational Conference, attended by 3,000 delegates, it was created in answer to concerns that Muslims would be oppressed by the Hindu majority if the British ever vacated the subcontinent. Sultan Muhammad Shah, Aga Khan III (1877–1957), hereditary leader of a large Shia sect, was appointed first honorary president. The league's principles were spelled out in its *Green Book*, though its goals did not initially include a separate state for the subcontinent's Muslims. Instead of independence, the group's principles stressed the protection of Muslim liberties and rights, and encouragement of understanding between Muslims and other Indians. Indeed, its initial platform included the goal of promoting feelings of loyalty to the British government among Muslims, which caused some of the more militant voices in the community to shun membership.

Despite the appearance of liberalization, heavy-handed British policies had fed rising tension and opposition throughout the subcontinent. Attempts to placate the population by providing the appearance of increased local political power were failing. The British hoped to mollify the upper classes sufficiently to win their tacit support for continued British rule. Viceroy Minto worked with the British secretary of state for Indian affairs, John Morley, First Viscount Morley (1838–

1923), to develop a framework that would give Indians more direct control over their government while keeping the ultimate authority in the hands of the British. In 1906 Lord Morley announced the government's intent to cede greater legislative power to local rule. Parliament approved the changes as the Government of India Act of 1909, more commonly called the Minto-Morley Reforms. The reforms would be a landmark in the subcontinent's constitutional history and begin a new chapter in its march to independence.

7

THE ROAD TO INDEPENDENCE
(1909–1947)

During the last half of the Raj, nationalist sentiment and violence weakened Britain's grip on the subcontinent, the crown jewel of its global empire. Calls for a separate nation for Muslims on the predominantly Hindu subcontinent began to be heard alongside growing demands for an independent India.

As British power ebbed, more control was ceded to local populations. The Hindu majority's voice was amplified by Muslim reticence to engage in the political process. The British supported the concept of legal assurances for the recognition of Muslim rights in the overwhelmingly Hindu subcontinent. Through the All India Muslim League and the Indian National Congress, or Congress Party, efforts to reconcile Muslim and Hindu political aspirations were repeatedly made, but all ended in failure. With the inability of Indian and British institutions to protect the rights of the Muslim minority, many politically active Muslims saw a divided subcontinent with a separate nation for Muslims as the only way for them to achieve equality. As Britain prepared to cede independence to the subcontinent, the political battle between Muslim and Hindu led to growing sectarian strife. The monumental struggle for Muslim rights saw its conclusion in the creation of the Republic of Pakistan in 1947.

The Government of India Act of 1909 (Minto-Morley Reforms)

The Government of India Act of 1909—also called the Minto-Morley Reforms for its sponsors, Gilbert Elliot-Murray-Kynynmound (1845–1914), fourth earl of Minto, viceroy of India, and John Morley (1838–1923), Viscount Morley, secretary of state for Indian affairs—was aimed at answering growing Indian demands for self-government. Its sponsors intended it to provide cosmetic changes to British rule rather than any real power sharing. Yet it was noteworthy in that the British had previously ignored popular aspiration in formulating governmental policy. The reforms mandated that legislative councils be established in all provinces and that their members be elected by the population each represented. However, the councils had only advisory power. Membership in the Viceroy's Legislative Council was increased from 25 to 60. Additionally, Indians were to be appointed to the Viceroy's Executive Councils and the Secretary of State's Council and were to take over the governorships of Bombay and Madras. Minority groups, including Muslims, Sikhs, landowners, and the tea and jute industry, would have their own representation in provincial legislative councils. This encouraged more Muslim participation in politics. Many Hindus viewed the changes as proof the British had become pro-Muslim.

Partition of Bengal Annulled

At the beginning of the 20th century Muslims were considered politically pro-British, as British support for Muslims' basic rights countered the Hindu nationalist stance of many Hindu politicians. Since its formation in 1906, the All India Muslim League reflected that pro-British bias in its moderate voice. However, British policies after the first decade of the century led to a gradual hardening of the Muslim position. The 1905 partition of Bengal had led to sustained political protests by Hindus, which increasingly included violence and acts of terrorism against the British. In December 1911 Britain's king George V (r. 1910–36) unexpectedly annulled the partition, caving in, as Muslims saw it, to "bombs and bullets" (Stephens 1967, 72). Muslims were shocked and angry. Besides being a betrayal of the Muslims, the reversal cast doubt on all the British stood for. From the day of partition, the decision was portrayed as irreversible, as permanent as the empire itself.

"We told the Mussalmans that the partition was a settled fact, over and over again; there could have been scarcely a civil servant who had not declared that it would be impossible for the British Government to reverse the decision," Lord Minto remarked in the House of Lords in 1912 after his return (Stephens 1967, 72). If British steadfastness over so important an issue could be suddenly reversed, what of its insistence on the limits of independence?

In addition to the annulment of Bengali partition, other British actions contributed to the increasing resistance among Muslims. A turning point came in 1913 when the British destroyed part of a mosque in Kanpur, in north central India, to facilitate road construction. Muslims gathered to protest, and security forces opened fire.

Many of the young Muslims educated at the Muhammadan Anglo-Oriental (M.A.O.) College (now Aligarh Muslim University) and similar institutions had previously avoided joining the Muslim League, preferring to identify themselves with political aspirations for the subcontinent as a whole, rather than for Muslims as a separate group. However, this now began to change. Among the new members who joined in 1913 were Muhammad Ali Jinnah (1876–1948), an English-trained lawyer and member of the Indian National Congress, and Maulana Abul Kalam Azad (1888–1958), also a member of Congress noted for his revolutionary zeal. These new leaders not only hardened the league's stance against the British but advocated greater cooperation with Hindus through the Congress Party as well. In 1913 the league changed its platform from support for British rule to the goal of self-government for the subcontinent. The growing militancy alienated some moderate members of the league. Aga Khan III, Sultan Muhammad Shah (1877–1957), the first president of the league, resigned in 1914 because of his discomfort with its growing anti-British attitude. Jinnah was elected the league's president in 1916 and would go on to play the principal role in the creation of an independent Pakistan. He is popularly known in Pakistan as Quaid-e-Azam, or Great Leader, and is considered to be the father of the nation.

Muhammad Ali Jinnah, the Quaid-e-Azam, or great leader, is regarded as the father of Pakistan. (Courtesy Pakistan Tourism Development Corporation)

Lucknow Pact

Hindus were also chaffing under British rule, and the mutual opposition drove the two religious groups together. Reflecting the growing solidarity between the Muslim League and Congress Party, in December 1915 both organizations held their annual sessions in Bombay, and their leaders met for the first time in history, linked by their desire to end British rule of the subcontinent. In October 1916, a group of 19 Muslim and Hindu elected members of the Imperial Legislative Council sent the viceroy a reform memorandum. The British ignored the memorandum, but it became the basis for an agreement on electorates and representation reached by Congress and Muslim League leaders at Calcutta in November 1916 and ratified at Lucknow in December. Called the Lucknow Pact, the agreement established an alliance between the Muslim League and the Indian National Congress. It mandated self-government in India with separate electorates for Hindus and Muslims, and it guaranteed a minimum number of representatives to adherents in areas where they were a minority. Muslims were to have one-third representation in the central government. The Muslim League dropped its claim to majority status in Punjab and Bengal in exchange for the promise of extra seats in the Muslim minority areas. The spirit of cooperation was relatively short-lived, but it marked the first time Congress recognized the Muslim League as a legitimate representation of the Muslim community.

Montagu-Chelmsford Reforms

During World War I (1914–18), which pitted the Allied forces (Great Britain, the United States, Russia, and France, among others) against the Central Powers (Germany and Austria-Hungary, joined by others, including the Ottoman Empire), Indians of all backgrounds supported Great Britain. In August 1917 Britain had promised the subcontinent a transition to self-governance in recognition of its people's contribution to the war effort. Keeping that pledge seemed a necessity: At the war's end the Defense of India Act would expire, and conscripts from the subcontinent, combat tested and out of work, would return home. Retaining control of the subcontinent might not be possible.

In 1918, following six months in India, Edwin Samuel Montagu (1879–1924), secretary of state for Indian affairs (1917–22), unveiled his constitutional reform plans, drafted with the viceroy, Frederic John Napier Thesiger, third baron Chelmsford (r. 1916–21). Parliament approved them as part of the Government of India Act of 1919, commonly known as the Montagu-Chelmsford Reforms. They introduced diarchy, a system of double government for the provinces of British India. This marked the first appearance of democratic principles in the executive branch. In coming years the democratic principles would be expanded until the subcontinent ultimately achieved independence. But these first reforms were limited. Both the Muslim League and Congress initially favored the constitutional reforms the British promised.

However, at the same time, efforts at repression continued. In February 1919 the British passed the Rowlatt Acts, named for Sydney Rowlatt, an English judge who chaired the investigative commission on seditious activities, which allowed preventive detention without charges or trial.

The Khilafat Movement

Although many leading Muslims supported Great Britain during the war, some backed the Ottoman Empire, the last vestige of the Islamic Empire that had begun with the conquests of the prophet Muhammed (ca. 570–632) in Arabia some 1,300 years before. The Islamic Empire once reached from Spain and North Africa to China. During the Muslim Mughal Empire, Muslims of India ignored the Ottoman Empire's claim to leadership of the Islamic community. (Tipu Sultan was the first Indian Muslim ruler who, having been frustrated in his attempts to gain recognition from the Mughals, had turned to the sultan of Turkey to establish a legal right to his throne.) But the Muslims of India now had no political power. The Ottoman sultan, Mehmed VI (r. 1918–22), whose office had long laid claim to leadership of the world's Muslims, now appeared to them as a suitable caliph. Though the caliphate bore little connection with its historical antecedents—particularly since the Young Turks, a political movement that eschewed Islamic ties, had moved the Ottoman Empire in a more Western, secular direction—the office nonetheless represented the only Muslim political power in the world. Some among India's Muslims supported Germany as well, because Germany was allied with the Ottoman Empire. Paradoxically, many of the troops from the subcontinent who joined the war effort on behalf of Britain were Muslims from the present-day Pakistan area.

As the end of World War I approached, the dissolution of the Ottoman Empire became imminent. Muslims of South Asia mounted an effort to save the empire, joining in the Khilafat movement. They sought preservation of the caliphate and protested the Allied treatment of the Ottoman Empire. In December 1918 the Muslim League passed a resolution to work for the preservation of the caliphate. Support was not unanimous. Jinnah and the raja of Mahmudabad (r. 1914–73), another influential leader, opposed involvement in international affairs, as Sir Sayyid Ahmad Khan had done earlier. Nonetheless, the emotional appeal was unstoppable. The anti-British sentiments of the Khilafat movement overlapped with the interests of the wider Indian nationalist movement, and, when the Rowlatt Acts were passed in February 1919, they sparked widespread protest throughout India. On April 10, 1919, riots erupted in Amritsar in Punjab. In response, a ban was imposed on public meetings. Unaware of the new edict, demonstrators gathered at the Jallianwala Bagh gardens in Amritsar on April 13, 1919. The British opened fire on the crowd, resulting in 379 dead and 1,200 wounded, according to official tallies, though other accounts put the number of casualties considerably higher. The incident became known as the Jallianwala Bagh Massacre, or Tragedy. Unrest spread to other cities in Punjab, where martial law was declared from mid-April to early June. The law was enforced with public beatings and humiliations.

Leaders of the Khilafat movement and the Congress Party issued a joint statement in 1920 calling for a boycott of British goods, schools, and institutions. This noncooperation movement was led by Mohandas K. Gandhi (1869–1947), who emerged as the leader of the Indian nationalist movement around this time. Gandhi supported the Khilafat movement as a way to bring Muslims and Hindus together in the movement for independence. Jinnah and other Western-educated Muslims, on the other hand, feared that a religious focus would ultimately divide Muslims and Hindus. He favored a secular political leadership, called the movement unconstitutional, and resigned from the Congress Party in protest.

Despite the movement and threats of noncooperation against the British, the Ottoman Empire disappeared with the signing of the Treaty of Sèvres in 1920. Yet the Khilafat movement remained alive for more than a decade, finding resonance in Punjab, Baluchistan, and Sind. It ended when the sultan, the figurehead of a much-reduced Turkey, was removed in 1922, and the Turkish government itself abolished the caliphate the same year.

The collapse of efforts to save the Ottoman Empire spawned the ill-fated Hijrat, or emigration, movement. Since the British failed to support the caliphate, Islamic scholars concluded that it was sinful to live in British-ruled territory. Hundreds of ulama, or religious leaders, signed a fatwa urging Muslims to immigrate to Islamic lands. In August 1922 thousands of Muslims abandoned their homes and possessions and began trekking to Afghanistan. Most were Pashtuns from the frontier area, Baluchis, and Sindis. Afghanistan, bowing to British pressure, closed its border, leaving the would-be émigrés homeless and destitute.

Third Afghan War

Reverberations from Russia's Bolshevik revolution added to the chaos of the post–World War I years in the subcontinent. The revolution's message of power to the downtrodden gave tribal elements in the frontier areas an ideological basis for resisting colonialism and expelling the British. Habibullah Khan, the emir of Afghanistan (r. 1901–19), was assassinated in 1919, and rule passed to his son, Amanullah Khan (r. 1919–29). While Punjab was under martial law, Amanullah declared war on Britain, which he believed was responsible for his father's death. The Afghan army began marching toward its border with India. Frontier tribes rose against the British, and Indian troops mutinied, deserted, and looted. The Afghan army reached Punjab before being driven back by stiff British resistance. However, the light British forces were not a great offensive threat, incapable of carrying a war to Afghanistan, despite their threats to the contrary. The Third Afghan War ended with an armistice treaty, the Rawalpindi Agreement, signed in August 1919. The agreement reconfirmed the Durand Line as the border between Afghanistan and British India and recognized Afghanistan's right to noninterference within its borders.

The entire NWFP area had been left out of the reforms of 1892 and 1909, as had Baluchistan. With disorder spreading through the tribal areas, the British continued denying self-rule to the border region, despite a commission finding in 1922 that self-rule might help quell the unrest. The British found other ways to consolidate control over the tribal areas: More roads were built; a railroad now ran through the Khyber Pass; and the routes were increasingly traveled by military convoys, as local militias charged with protecting British interests were replaced by professional soldiers under direct British command.

In March 1927 Jinnah convened a meeting in Delhi with some 30 of the subcontinent's Muslim leaders in an effort to close the gap between Hindu and Muslim aspirations. At the meeting's conclusion the leaders unanimously agreed to relinquish the demand for a separate electorate for India's Muslims if the Hindu leadership accepted what became known as the Delhi Proposals. These four proposals were that Muslims in Punjab and Bengal have representation in the legislative council in proportion to their population; that one-third of the seats in the Central Legislature be reserved for Muslims; that Sind be made a separate province; and that government reforms adopted in the subcontinent be extended to NWFP and Baluchistan. It was the first and only time the leadership of the Muslim League agreed to joint electorates.

Simon Commission and the Nehru Report

The Montagu-Chelmsford Reforms had stipulated the formation of a commission to study the results of the reforms at the end of 10 years. The commission would then recommend the next steps toward the subcontinent's self-rule. An all-British delegation, the Simon Commission (named for its director, British statesman John Allesbrook Simon; 1873–1954) was appointed in 1927. It was widely seen as a self-serving effort by the British to avoid meaningful change. No Indians were appointed to the commission. As a result many political parties refused to participate in the commission's work. In 1927 the Muslim League split into two factions, the Jinnah League and the Shafi League, over the issue. The organization's president, Mian Muhammad Shafi (1869–1932) favored cooperation with the British, while Jinnah and his allies and other Muslim organizations supported a boycott. The arriving British delegation was met with protests. Almost all major political parties boycotted the commission's hearings, and its mission ended in failure. At the end of 1927 Congress Party adopted complete independence from Britain as its objective.

With the Simon Commission failing to come up with a workable political reform plan, the British turned the problem over to local political leaders. In February 1928 some 100 representatives of Muslim political organizations and Congress met at the All Parties Conference to draft a constitution. As usual a resolution of the differences between Muslim and Hindu leaders was beyond reach. Minority rights—separate political representation for minority communities—was the primary issue of contention, with Muslims in support and Hindus, who controlled Congress, opposed. In March the second meeting of the All Parties Conference was held, with the same lack of progress. At the third All Parties Conference, in Bombay in May 1928, delegates appointed a small committee headed by Motilal Nehru (1861–1931) to draft a constitution. Two Muslims were on the nine-person committee.

After three months, the committee issued the Nehru Report. It recommended abolishing separate electorates, eliminating any weightage given to minority communities and populations and making Hindi the national language. It further called for reducing Muslim representation in the Central Assembly (from one-third to one-quarter) and rejected the recent acceptance by Congress of the Delhi Proposals. Muslims refused to accept the report, and an attempt to find a compromise solution failed. Despite pleas from Jinnah, Congress ultimately adopted the report and threatened the British government with a disobedience movement if the terms were not implemented into law by December 31, 1929.

The Nehru Report reunited the Jinnah and Shafi wings of the Muslim League, divided since 1924, as they took a common stand against the proposals. In early 1929, the All Parties Muslim Conference convened in Delhi under Aga Khan to counter the report with Muslim demands. The conference was a turning point in Muslim political attitudes and expression. Jinnah, who had championed cooperation with the Hindus, announced his split with Hindus and Congress.

In March 1929 Jinnah articulated an alternative course in a set of tenets that became known as the Fourteen Points. Most of the principles had already been advanced. The points stated that the government should be federal, with provinces exercising residuary powers. They called for all legislatures in the country and other elected bodies to be constituted on the principle of adequate minority representation without reducing the majority in any province to a minority or even equality. These precepts became a blueprint for Muslim political aspirations for most of the next decade. The Muslim League made inclusion of the demands expressed in the Fourteen Points a prerequisite for their agreement to any constitution.

A final effort by Jinnah to end the deadlock with the Hindus over the Nehru Report, made at the All Parties Convention at Calcutta in 1929, failed. As the new decade dawned, the divide among Muslims, Hindus, and the British was sharp and deep. At its annual meeting in 1930 in Lahore, Congress demanded Britain make a pledge that the subcontinent would receive dominion status (a self-governing nation with the British Commonwealth), like Canada and Australia, as a prerequisite for participating in discussions with the Simon Commission. Britain's rejection sparked a second noncooperation movement in 1930. The Simon Commission released its report early in 1930.

Despite the framework of the Fourteen Points Muslims now clung to, some began to doubt any accommodation could ever be reached, given Hindu intransigence and British indifference to Muslim demands. At a meeting of the All India Muslim League at Allahabad in 1930, its president, Allama Muhammad Iqbal (1877–1938), a noted poet and philosopher, raised the possibility that peace would be impossible between Muslims and Hindus unless Muslims were given the status of a separate nation. He stated that the predominantly Muslim northwest region of the subcontinent was destined to form a self-governing unit. This was the first public call for statehood for the subcontinent's Muslims.

Badshah Khan and the Khudai Khidmatgar

In the frontier areas the noncooperation movement was led by a charismatic Pashtun pacifist, Khan Abdul Ghaffar Khan (1890–1988),

FOURTEEN POINTS OF
M. A. JINNAH (1929)

Muslim opposition to the Nehru Report had a galvanizing effect on Muslim unity. At a meeting of the All India Muslim League on March 28, 1929, Jinnah proposed an alternative to the Nehru Report contained in a series of positions on issues of government and minority rights. These became known as his Fourteen Points. They were:

1. A federal, rather than a unitary, form of government
2. Electoral safeguards for minorities in all provinces
3. Equality for each province
4. Separate electorates for religious and other groups
5. In the Central Legislature, Muslims would have at least one-third of the seats.
6. No resolution or bill shall be passed in any elected body if three-quarters of the members of any community in that particular body opposes it.
7. Muslim majorities in Punjab, Bengal, and NWFP should not be altered by territorial changes or redistributions.
8. Sind should be separated from Bombay and be made a separate province.
9. NWFP and Baluchistan should enjoy the same reforms as all other provinces.
10. All religions should have full liberty of belief, worship, observance, association, and education.
11. Muslims should have an adequate share of employment in all the services of the state and in local self-governing bodies.
12. The constitution should guarantee the protection of Muslim culture and the protection and promotion of Muslim education, language, religion, education, and charitable institutions.
13. Cabinets at both the central and the provincial level should have a proportion of at least one-third Muslim ministers.
14. Any changes to the constitution by the Central Legislature require the consent of all the federating states.

The All India Muslim League made inclusion of the principles contained in these 14 points a requirement for Muslim acceptance of any constitution.

called Badshah Khan "king of chiefs," who founded the Khudai Khidmatgar ("servants of God") organization in the 1920s. A close ally of Gandhi, Badshah Khan joined the Congress Party, rather than the Muslim League, which he saw as pro-British. Badshah Khan managed to unite the various Pashtun tribes behind his movement—at its peak the organization had 100,000 members—and the Khudai Khidmatgar became famous for its pacifist opposition to the British. However, the movement provoked violent British efforts at suppression that affected the entire NWFP. Seeking political partners with the power to pressure the British to rein in their aggressive tactics, the Khudai Khidmatgar formed an alliance with the Congress Party. To counter the Khidmatgars' influence in the area the Muslim League sought supporters from among the wealthy landlords, who opposed the Khidmatgars.

Round Table Conferences

The British central-left Labour Party, had traditionally given more support to the concept of independence for the subcontinent than the Conservatives. With the Labour Party's return to power in Britain in 1929, prospects for a headway to the independence impasse improved. In November 1930 the British convened a Round Table Conference in London involving Hindus, Muslims, Sikhs, and Christians to discuss new constitutional reforms. But all Congress Party leaders were in jail on charges related to the civil disobedience movement. They passed the word that they would boycott any future constitutional discussion unless the Nehru Report was enforced in its entirety as the constitution of India. Still, 73 delegates attended the conference, including Jinnah. The Muslims insisted on keeping weightage and separate electorates, while the Hindus wanted to end these electoral processes. The Hindus sought a powerful central government, with the Muslims preferring a loose federation of autonomous provinces. The Muslim majority status in Punjab and Bengal was also a point of contention, with Hindus opposing their imposition. The conference ended in January 1931 with an agreement to provide safeguards for minorities in the constitution under a federal system of rule.

The British government saw the Indian National Congress as the key to developing a constitution that would pave the way for independence. Muslim-Hindu conflict was not as important to the British as Hindu-British cooperation. Nonetheless, the British employed a "divide and rule" strategy in the subcontinent as they (and other powers throughout history) had in other lands under their control, stoking regional rivalries and undermining efforts of indigenous solidarity to prevent the formation of a powerful, unified opposition. The historic animosity between Muslim and Hindu made this approach particularly potent and useful in the subcontinent. Under Sir George Cunningham, governor of NWFP (r. 1937–46; 1947–48), British government agents continuously exhorted the Pashtun to avoid conspiring with Hindu revolutionaries. Yet it is noteworthy that the population to whom they preached had indeed allied themselves with Hindus through the Khudai Khidmatgar's alliance with the Congress Party, rather than forging ties with the Muslim League. Edward Frederick Lindley Wood, Lord Irwin, the viceroy at the time (r. 1926–31), invited Gandhi to discuss the subcontinent's political future, and Gandhi agreed. After subsequent talks, in March 1931, the two signed the Gandhi-Irwin Pact, which restarted the stalled constitution-drafting process. Under its terms Congress would discontinue the civil disobedience movement and participate in a second Round Table Conference. The British government, for its part, would withdraw all ordinances issued to curb Congress, cease prosecution of all offenses relating to nonviolent civil disobedience, and release all persons serving sentences for their activities in the civil disobedience movement.

The second session of the Round Table Conference, convened in London in September 1931, was intended to address the composition of the central government and, more vexingly, minority rights, or the communal issue, as it was known. Jinnah, Iqbal, the Aga Kahn, and Gandhi attended. However, the conference ended without results. On his return to India, Gandhi resumed the civil disobedience movement.

British prime minister Ramsay MacDonald (r. 1924, 1929–35), proclaiming himself a friend of the Indian people, proposed his

PAKISTAN

The idea of a separate homeland for the subcontinent's Muslims had been advanced, but the name of the nation-to-be was coined by a student at England's Cambridge University. Chaudhuri Rahmat Ali wrote a pamphlet, *Now or Never,* calling for a federal state encompassing the Punjab (P), Afghania (A), the NWFP; Kashmir (K); Sindh (S); and Baluchistan (Stan). His tract found its way to delegates at the Third Round Table Conference, but it was belittled as a schoolboy's fantasy by delegates. Nonetheless, Pakistan soon became the term applied to the subcontinent's Muslim majority area in the northwest.

own solution to the minority rights problem in August 1932. The Communal Award, as he called it, guaranteed all minority communities, not just Muslims, the right of a separate electorate. The sudden recognition of the political rights of the Untouchables and lower castes was even more alarming to Hindus than the rights the communal awards bestowed on Muslims. Meanwhile, the weightage principle was misapplied in Punjab and Bengal, giving the majority Muslims minority representation in the provinces' assemblies. In short, the Communal Award was unpopular among all Indian political organizations. Nonetheless, the Muslim League agreed to accept it, while reserving the right to demand future changes. For Hindu political groups, the rights it would grant lower castes made the Award completely unacceptable.

The final session, the Third Round Table Conference, in November 1932, was limited to discussing committee reports and accomplished little. Jinnah was not invited to the conference, because Conservatives, restored to power in England, considered him anti-British for his insistence on equality and self-rule in the subcontinent. The ongoing antipathy between the Muslims and Congress overcame him. Discouraged, he moved to England and practiced law. But his retirement from politics and the independence movement was relatively brief. In 1934 Jinnah was reelected president of the Muslim League and that same year was elected to the Legislative Assembly. In October 1935 he sold his house in London and returned to the subcontinent.

What came out of the Third Round Table Conference was a white paper, published in March 1933, that became the basis for a reform constitution. Parliament voted it into law two years later as the Government of India Act of 1935.

The reformed constitution granted almost complete autonomy to the 11 provinces while preserving British control over the central government. Muslims were given one-third of the seats in the central legislature, and another third would go to nominees of Indian princes. The right to vote was expanded to include about one-sixth of India's adult population. This led to a transformation of subcontinental politics. Political parties now had to appeal to commoners. They began retooling their messages as they sought viable candidates for the upcoming provincial elections. However, Muslim populations and leadership in Punjab, the frontier area, Bengal, and the new province of Sind were disunited. Some factions and power groups opposed the Muslim League. Baluchistan, under the rule of the latest of the khans of Kalat, Ahmad Yar Khan (r. 1933–55, 1958), even refused to participate in the provincial elections.

Elections of 1936–37

Elections were held in the winter of 1936–37. The Congress Party won about 70 percent of the popular vote and 40 percent of the provincial government seats, but through coalitions gained an upper hand in the rule of most provinces. The Muslim League won only 5 percent of the total Muslim vote and not a single province, including the Muslim-majority provinces, in which regional parties (in Bengal, Punjab, and Sind) and Congress (in NWFP) gained control. The Congress Party soon proved unwilling to include Muslims in their administrations. At the national level, Congress refused to work with Muslims unless they resigned from the Muslim League. Paradoxically, the reversal of Muslim fortunes revitalized the Muslim League. From a few thousand adherents in 1937 membership grew to a few hundred thousand by 1938, and a reported 3 million by the end of 1939.

At a meeting in Karachi in Sind, a province in which Muslims were still divided, 20,000 delegates gathered and heard the first official pronouncement of the two-nation theory. Attendees resolved that it was essential to the interests of peace, cultural development, and the economic, social, and political self-determination of Hindus and Muslims to revise the entire concept of the constitution.

As the decade ended, World War II began in Europe. Without consulting Indian government officials, the viceroy, Victor Alexander John Hope (r. 1936–43) announced that India would join the Allied cause. Congress answered by demanding immediate independence in return for its approval of the alliance. Britain refused, and in response Congress resigned on December 22, 1939. Jinnah declared it a day of deliverance and celebration marking the end of Congress's rule.

The Lahore Resolution

In March 1940 in Lahore, Jinnah told 100,000 at a public meeting, "Muslims are not a minority as it is commonly known and understood . . . Muslims are a nation according to any definition of a nation, and they must have their homelands, their territory, and their state." The position became Muslim League policy on March 24, 1940, as the Lahore Resolution. The resolution declared:

> *No constitutional plan would be workable or acceptable to the Muslims unless geographical contiguous units are demarcated into regions which should be so constituted with such territorial readjustments as may be necessary. That the areas in which the Muslims are numerically in majority as in the North-Western*

and Eastern zones of India should be grouped to constitute independent states in which the constituent units shall be autonomous and sovereign.

Though the name Pakistan was never mentioned in the speech, the Indian press called the speech the Pakistan Resolution. The stakes and parameters of the political discussion of the subcontinent's future had been irrevocably changed.

The Muslim League negotiated with British representatives over the terms of a future constitution and Muslim representation in return for their support of the British war effort. The viceroy proffered what became known as the August Offer of 1940, promising that no constitution would be adopted without the consent of Muslim India, while denying the Muslim League the representation they sought on the Defense Council, an advisory war council under development. The Muslim League declined the offer.

Unrest spread in 1940 and into 1941. In Sind Muslim extremists waged jihad against the British. The British declared martial law and established

Muslims rally during a 1940 meeting of the All India Muslim League, in Lahore, where a resolution demanding a separate homeland for the subcontinent's Muslims was passed. (Courtesy Pakistan Tourism Development Corporation)

internment camps, confining people without food or water, and razing villages and farms. By mid-1941, some 20,000 people had been arrested.

As the conflict in the Pacific theater intensified, the British worried that Japan would invade India and realized local support needed to be shored up. In March 1942 Richard Stafford Cripps (1889–1952) arrived in India on a high-level mission to appease Muslim concerns. More than 1 million men from the subcontinent were now in the British Indian Army, and most were Muslims. Cripps offered independence for the subcontinent at war's end, an assembly to draft a constitution, protection for minorities, and choice for the provinces as to whether to join the new Indian state. But without a guarantee for an independent Muslim state, the Muslim League rejected Cripps's offer. Congress rejected the plan as well. Meanwhile the disruption wrought by war impacted the subcontinent in other ways: In 1943 famine swept Bengal, and some 3 million died of starvation.

Jinnah and Gandhi

Against this backdrop of war and famine, the Muslim League, with its staunch demand for independence, gained more support in Muslim-

Muhammad Ali Jinnah and the architect of Indian independence, Mohandas K. Gandhi, who was opposed to a separate homeland for Muslims in the subcontinent, meet over this issue in September 1944. (Courtesy Pakistan Tourism Development Corporation)

majority areas. It was now the dominant power in Punjab, Sind, and Assam and by spring 1943 had taken power in Bengal. The majority of those on the subcontinent were eager for an end to the clash between Muslims and Hindus. Gandhi was adamantly opposed to a two-nation solution. In July 1944, Gandhi, just released from prison, proposed he and Jinnah meet. That September the two conferred in Bombay for six days. Gandhi had come, he said, on a personal mission, and not as a representative of either Congress or the Hindus. Gandhi tried to convince Jinnah that Muslim demands for a separate state were folly. Gandhi argued that the subcontinent's Muslims were descendants of Hindus, proving the subcontinent's historic unity. Gandhi was also worried that if Muslims pressed their demands, other minority groups would seek independence as well.

Simla Conference

In May 1945, with the end of the war in Europe in sight, Archibald Wavell, first viscount Wavell, the viceroy of India (r. 1943–47), returned to London to discuss the subcontinent's future. After the conflict in Europe ended, in June, the Viceroy's Council demanded immediate dominion status. Instead, Wavell, back from England, unveiled the so-called Wavell Plan at a conference in Simla in northern India at the end of June 1945. With the war all but over, the British no longer felt the need to appease the Muslims, who had comprised a major portion of the troops from the subcontinent. The British preferred to revert to positioning the Congress Party as the sole political representative of Indians. This preference was bolstered by close ties between Britain's Labour government and the leadership of the Congress Party. At the Simla Conference, as it became known, all parties agreed that general elections would be held for central and provisional assemblies. But the Congress Party refused to recognize the Muslim League's claim to be the sole representative of Muslim political aspirations; Congress wanted to be able to nominate Muslim candidates of their own in the upcoming elections. Meanwhile, the Sikh party Akali Dal and the Panthic Party opposed elections, which they saw as a step toward an independent Pakistan. These groups feared that a subcontinent divided along religious lines between Muslim and Hindu would have less tolerance for the aspirations of the subcontinent's other religious and ethnic constituencies than would one unified nation. Additionally, many Pashtun political elements had stronger ties to the Congress Party, with whom the Khudai Khidmatgar had been allied, rather than the pro-partition Muslim League. These and other disagreements and concerns scuttled the conference, and at its end, in mid-July, Wavell pronounced it a failure.

Despite the lack of agreement on the subcontinent's political future, central and provincial legislature elections were scheduled for the winter of 1945. Wavell's plans also called for the formation of an executive council and a body charged with drafting a constitution after the election. Jinnah rejected the plan, as it failed to provide for a Muslim state. Congress opposed it as well. Yet both parties recognized the results of the upcoming election would be critical in establishing their legitimacy and position in the subcontinent's future. The Muslim League's primary campaign platform was independent Muslim statehood. The Congress Party campaigned on the platform of a united India. Muslim League candidates won all 30 seats reserved for Muslims in the central assembly. Congress also did well, winning 80 percent of the general seats.

Cabinet Mission Plan

In 1946 the British dispatched three cabinet ministers to settle the dispute between the Muslim League and the Congress Party. The envoys first stipulated that the creation of two separate states was not a negotiable option. The Cabinet Mission Plan, as it was called, proposed a single nation with a national government that would leave provinces virtually autonomous and free to write their own constitutions. The Muslim League accepted the proposal in principle, but when Congress refused to give the league what it felt was an adequate role in the proposed interim government, the Muslim League refused to endorse the plan. The British authorized Congress to form an interim government without the Muslim League's participation, though it was agreed some league members would be part of its final constitution. Muslim representatives protested bitterly.

The Muslim League proclaimed a Direct Action Day on August 16, 1946, calling for *hartals*—massive displays of noncooperation that would bring business and commerce to a standstill—demonstrations, strikes, rallies, and meetings. The display of Muslim unity brought a Hindu backlash. In Calcutta, where Muslims were a minority, sectarian violence that became known as the Great Calcutta Killing erupted. As many as 4,000 people of both faiths died. Some 15,000 were injured, and 100,000 left homeless. The violence spread and continued into the fall.

Intransigence of Congress

In late August Wavell met with Gandhi and Jawaharlal Nehru (1889–1964), son of Motilal Nehru and president of the Congress Party, and accused the Congress Party of reneging on its commitment to include the Muslim League in a national coalition government. He asked for their pledge in writing. Gandhi and Nehru rejected the request and sought to have Wavell recalled. Instead, the British instructed Wavell to form an interim government. In early September he announced the posts, naming Nehru as vice president and giving one of three key cabinet posts, that of the finance portfolio, to a member of the Muslim League, Liaquat Ali Khan (1896–1951).

A close ally of Jinnah, after graduating from Aligarh Muslim University Liaquat Ali Khan attended Oxford University and two years later returned to India with a law degree. His birthplace in eastern Punjab was among the first areas to agitate for a restoration of Muslim rights. The minority status of Muslims in this region made them acutely aware of the inequality they faced. But most of Punjab was a Muslim-majority area, and here Muslims felt little need for political activism. The Unionist Party, dominated by landowners, had established what most saw as an equitable power-sharing arrangement. Khan joined the All India Muslim League and quickly rose in the ranks. He was also a member of the urban United Provinces Legislative Council, elected in 1926, in which he served until 1940.

The Constituent Assembly was scheduled to go into session on December 9, 1946. Still, Congress remained opposed to a power-sharing arrangement, leading the Muslim League, the Princely States, and the Sikhs to refuse to take part in the Constituent Assembly. Before the assembly began, the British prime minister summoned the viceroy, Jinnah, Liaquat Ali Khan, Nehru, and Sikh political leader Baldeve Singh (1902–61) to London to forge a power-sharing arrangement. Congress gave its approval to a plan the leadership agreed to, but again failed to implement the agreement. More minority groups boycotted the assembly.

The British were committed to handing over power no later than June 1948, but who would get the power and whether it would be one government or more was unknown. The British began a campaign to suppress Muslim protests and groups. The Muslim National Guards, the volunteer corps of the Muslim League, was banned, and league leaders in Lahore were arrested. Muslim League offices in Punjab were raided. In response, the league called for a civil disobedience campaign. The British banned assemblies, and tear gas met those that occurred.

But a Pakistan movement had built into an unstoppable force, spreading across all facets of Muslim society.

Sectarian Violence Spreads

Across the subcontinent tens of thousands of Muslims, Hindus, and Sikhs lost their lives in sectarian riots and violence. Amidst this background of chaos and religious schism, the newly elected government took office. Predictably, progress on legislative matters was virtually impossible in this atmosphere. The finance ministry was now led by the Muslim League's Liaquat Ali Khan, giving the league effective control of the government. The league was determined to leverage this power to fight for its objectives. Liaquat introduced what was called a "poor man's budget," calculated to hamstring the Hindu business class.

In March 1947 Louis Mountbatten (1900–79), first earl Mountbatten of Burma, was named the new and last viceroy (r. 1947). He toured the subcontinent upon his arrival, meeting its leaders. Some of what he saw, such as massive demonstrations in the frontier, convinced him of the depth of Muslim nationalism. Moreover, Jinnah told Lord Mountbatten that an independent Pakistan now had the support of Muslims across India and that Jinnah could not abandon the goal. The Hindu political community also recognized the depth of Muslim determination. On March 8 the All India National Congress called for the division of Punjab. This was equivalent to sanctioning the partitioning of the subcontinent. Congress was unwilling to work with the Muslim League, but realized the league was powerful enough to thwart any of its aims. The lesser of two evils was to jettison the Muslims, while doing everything possible to block the development and success of their state.

Lord Mountbatten's Plan

Lord Mountbatten developed an alternative plan to partitioning India. The details were completed at the Governor's Conference in April 1947 and approved in Britain in May; the plan called for the right of the Indian provinces to choose independence. The details of what became known as the June 3 Plan were to be kept secret until announced publicly, but Nehru was able to see the document before its release. Fearing the plan would lead to a balkanization of the subcontinent, Nehru rejected it. The plan was hastily revised by Lord Mountbatten and a Hindu assistant on his staff and refined by Nehru; it now proposed a transfer of authority to the independent dominions of India and Pakistan. Lord Mountbatten himself took it to London, where Prime Minister Clement Attlee (r. 1945–51) and his cabinet quickly approved the partition plan. Both Congress and Britain wanted to limit Pakistan's size, and the Pakistan envisioned was smaller than the five provinces the Muslim League sought to include in the new nation.

On June 4, 1947, Jinnah, Nehru, Baldeve Singh, and Lord Mountbatten addressed the public in a radio broadcast and announced a plan to draw borders for the two new nations. Elected representatives in Sind, West Punjab, and East Bengal would determine territorial borders for their provinces. In the NWFP and parts of Assam, a plebiscite would be held. Baluchistan's borders would be determined through a consultative arrangement. And in Bengal and Punjab, a commission would be appointed to delineate the boundaries between Muslim and non-Muslim areas. The decisions on borders would remain secret until after independence. Mountbatten also made a surprise announcement about accelerating the transfer of power. Instead of June 1948, as previously planned, the transfer would take place on August 15, 1947—little more than a month from the date of the broadcast.

In late June 1947 Baluchistan decided to join Pakistan, as did the NWFP in a vote in early July. After Bengal chose to become part of Pakistan, a referendum in Sylhet, Assam, determined the parts of Assam that would join with Bengal.

Muhammad Ali Jinnah (third from right), Liaquat Ali Khan (second from right), and leaders of Congress met with Lord Mountbatten (fourth from right) in June of 1947 during the final phase of planning for the partition of India. (Courtesy Pakistan Tourism Development Corporation)

Muhammad Ali Jinnah announces the impending independence of Pakistan in a radio address on All India Radio in June 1947. (Courtesy Pakistan Tourism Development Corporation)

The Indian Independence Act

On July 10 Parliament passed the Indian Independence Act, providing the foundation for establishing Pakistan and India as dominions of the British Commonwealth. The act also established the office of a governor-general for each of the two new dominions.

With partition imminent and sectarian passions further aroused, violence flared. But the road to independence now moved in only one direction. On August 11 the Pakistan Constituent Assembly, which served as both the federal legislature and the creator of the constitution, held its first session. On August 13 Lord Mountbatten arrived in Karachi bearing a message from King George he read to the assembly. On August 15 both Pakistan and India became independent. The dream of independence had been achieved. But the new nation of Pakistan would find its real challenges lay ahead.

8

THE CHALLENGES OF
INDEPENDENCE
(1947–1958)

Pakistan had won its independence, but the chaotic, violent state of the new federation created little cause for celebration. Born in spasms of massacre and flight, Pakistan was a nation physically divided, its East Wing (present-day Bangladesh) and West Wing separated by some 1,000 miles (1,600 km). Among the issues the new nation confronted: Could it exist as two separate areas linked by little but religion? Was Pakistan to be secular or an Islamic state? How could it deal with the refugee crisis of Muslims spilling into its territory from India, and how to cope with the brain drain as Hindus and Sikhs fled Pakistan for India?

The India Independence Act, which granted statehood to both Pakistan and India in 1947, left it to principalities along border areas to decide which of the two new nations to join. Some that had been designated as part of Pakistan tried to assert their own independence, requiring military action from Pakistan to bring them forcibly into the union. The battle over the future of one, Kashmir, would provoke a war with India within two months of Pakistan's statehood and remain unsettled into the following century. Pakistan would also fight a trade war with India, forcing it to find new sources for basic supplies that previously had come from its neighbor.

In yet another blow Muhammad Ali Jinnah, Pakistan's founder and leader, died little more than a year after independence, creating battles over succession that also roiled the country. As the fractious divisions grew more visible and seemingly intractable, a senior military officer, General Mohammed Ayub Khan, seized power in a coup a decade after independence. These tumultuous events served as the milestones of the first years of the independent nation of Pakistan.

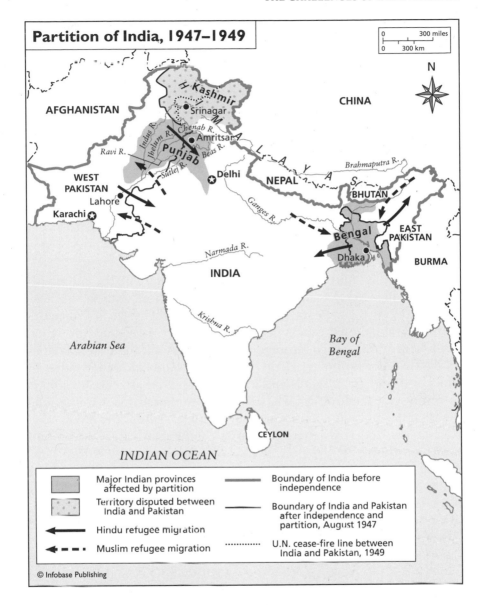

Partition of India, 1947–1949

0   300 miles
0   300 km

N

CHINA

AFGHANISTAN

Kashmir

Srinagar

Indus R.

Jhelum R.

Chenab R.

Amritsar

Ravi R.

Punjab

Beas R.

Sutlej R.

Delhi

NEPAL

Brahmaputra R.

BHUTAN

WEST
PAKISTAN

Lahore

Karachi

Ganges R.

Bengal

EAST
PAKISTAN

Dhaka

BURMA

Narmada R.

INDIA

Krishna R.

Arabian Sea

Bay of
Bengal

CEYLON

INDIAN OCEAN

	Major Indian provinces affected by partition		Boundary of India before independence
	Territory disputed between India and Pakistan		Boundary of India and Pakistan after independence and partition, August 1947
	Hindu refugee migration		
	Muslim refugee migration		U.N. cease-fire line between India and Pakistan, 1949

© Infobase Publishing

Pakistan's Difficult Birth

With the passage of the Indian Independence Act by the British parliament on July 18, 1947, Pakistan and India became sovereign states. The transfer took place on August 14, 1947, which is today celebrated as Pakistan's Independence Day. (India chose August 15 as its independence day, so it would not celebrate on the same day as its Muslim neighbors.) The Muslim dream of a homeland had been achieved.

Pakistan was a dominion within the British Commonwealth of Nations. Muhammad Ali Jinnah was named its first governor-general. Jinnah selected the port of Karachi as the nation's capital. Liaquat Ali Khan, Jinnah's primary aide and political ally, was appointed the first prime minister.

The birth of Pakistan spelled the death of several political parties that had maintained power in the area by allying themselves with the Congress Party. These included the Unionists in Punjab and the Khudai Khidmatgars in the NWFP. Meanwhile, some formerly marginal groups gained power, such as the *muhajirs,* the refugees who had fled India at partition, in Karachi and lower Sind, and the middle classes of urban Punjab.

Communal Riots

The wrenching split from India defined Pakistan in the aftermath of independence. The antipathy toward its new neighbor, the hostility between the two states, was an inseparable part of Pakistan's identity and national psyche. Sectarian violence continued to wrack both new states, as communal riots erupted throughout Pakistan and India. Newly independent Muslims in Pakistan and Hindus in India, inflamed by religious and nationalist fervor, attacked members of minority communities. The violence prompted mass migrations of Muslims from India to Pakistan, while Hindus and Sikhs fled Pakistan for India. Massacres in Punjab alone resulted in almost half a million deaths in a matter of months. By the time Pakistan conducted its first census in 1951, it determined some 14 million people had moved across the frontier: 8 million Muslims coming to Pakistan from India, and 6 million Hindus leaving Pakistan for India. Most of these people had to abandon all their possessions in their flight. No reliable survey of the number of people who lost their lives in the violence has ever been attempted, but it has been estimated that about 1 million people were killed. Additionally, as many as 50,000 Muslim and 33,000 non-Muslim women were abducted by some estimates (Menu and Bhasin 1998, 70).

The riots and sectarian strife destroyed property and infrastructure and created a vast sea of refugees who had to be clothed, housed, and fed by the poor nation. Pakistan had no real administration, as the civil service had been predominantly Hindu, and anyone of rank who had lived in what became Pakistan resettled in India. Moreover, the British had turned over most of their assets to India.

The partition of India caused great dislocation. Muslims fleeing India swarmed aboard trains bound for Pakistan, which became targets for marauding bands of Hindus. (Courtesy Pakistan Tourism Development Corporation)

Regional Challenges

Even the pieces of the nation remained to be assembled in the aftermath of independence. The day after partition, the khan of Kalat, Ahmad Yar Khan, declared Baluchistan an independent state. In October the khan traveled to Karachi to discuss Baluchistan's future and the transferability of its treaties with the British should the Baluchis choose to align themselves with Pakistan. The two houses of the Baluchistan Assembly vetoed a merger with Pakistan. Jinnah traveled to Baluchistan in an attempt to convince legislators to approve unification. But after hearing demands regarding recognition of Baluchi customs and privileges, Jinnah turned the matter over to his cabinet to resolve.

An autonomous government continued to enjoy support in the North-West Frontier Province (NWFP), whose leadership encouraged followers to ignore the edicts of Pakistan's new rulers. Afghanistan's government also claimed rights within Pakistan, leading to a rupture of diplomatic and commercial relations between the two countries.

State Language Movement

The issue of the state language created a schism between East and West Pakistan during these first years of nationhood. Many in Bengal had hoped the area would gain independence as a separate state when the British withdrew from the subcontinent. When Lord Mountbatten announced the post-British division of the subcontinent on June 3, 1947, he made Bengal a province of Pakistan, forestalling if not shattering those dreams. Eager to ensure their voices would be heard in the new nation, many in East Pakistan wanted Bengali, the language of Bengal, to be the state language of East Pakistan and to share the distinction of the state language with Urdu, the language that dominated West Pakistan. West Pakistanis, who controlled the political power, planned to make Urdu alone the state language. In the months after independence the issue grew more acute. In November 1947 university students in Dhaka, the capital of the province of East Pakistan, staged a protest, demanding Bengali be made the state language. When the new nation's coins and stamps were issued, they were in Urdu and English alone. Government officials explained it was an oversight, but in February 1948 the Constituent Assembly, formed the previous August to draft a constitution, refused to approve the resolution to make Bengali the state language of East Pakistan. Demonstrations continued, and a general strike was called.

Muhammad Ali Jinnah arrived in March of that year for a visit to East Pakistan. In a speech on March 21 he declared that Urdu alone would be the national language of Pakistan, further inflaming the public.

Indus Water Crisis

In another major challenge Pakistan's water supply was disrupted by East Punjab in India. Pakistan was largely an agrarian society, and about 80 percent of its agricultural production was in the Indus River basin. The plains of Punjab were the world's largest irrigated agricultural area, comprising more than 28 million acres, and the partition line cut across this unique irrigation network, just as it split Punjab. The extensive canal system in West Pakistan dating to the British era in the late 19th and early 20th centuries was dependent on the waters of the Indus. At the time of partition the British awarded the area in Kashmir that contained the upper basin of the Indus River, which had traditionally been in Muslim control, to India. The source rivers of the Indus—the Ravi, Beas, Sutlej, Jhelum, and Chenab—also remained on the Indian side of Punjab. In the aftermath of partition, negotiators representing the two nations were unable to agree on how the water from the Indus would be shared, and in a unilateral action, on April 1, 1948, the East Punjab government cut off the flow of water to every canal whose source it controlled.

Prime Minister Liaquat Ali Khan called for an immediate restoration of the water supply and proposed an interdominion conference to resolve the dispute. Indian prime minister Jawaharlal Nehru (r. 1947–64) prevailed upon the provincial government of East Punjab to restore the flow of water, the lifeblood of Pakistan's canals and irrigation system. An arbitration panel was appointed, but no agreement was reached by the time the panel's mandate ended in March 1948. In May representatives of the two nations met in New Delhi to take up the issue and at the conclusion of the talks signed the Inter-Dominion (Delhi) Agreement, which did little more than affirm that each country claimed rights to the waters of the rivers in East Punjab.

Progress on the water dispute came to a standstill as tensions over Kashmir, and the two states' general animosity, overtook negotiations. Pakistan proposed submitting the water dispute to the International Court of Justice, but India refused. Even the Delhi Agreement yielded conflicting interpretations from each party. As positions hardened, the possibility of the dispute escalating into a major confrontation grew. India continued to block access to the water until Pakistan signed, under duress, an agreement on the division of the water. The issue would again be taken up in 1952, when India agreed to allow the World Bank to negotiate a new treaty. The final agreement, the Indus Waters Treaty—a landmark treaty in water-dispute resolution—would not be signed until 1960. In subsequent years Pakistan frequently cited the Indus water dispute as evidence of the necessity of third-party involvement in resolving differences between the two nations.

The Princely States

The future of the Princely States, historically independent kingdoms, had yet to be determined. Some 560 of these semiautonomous principalities existed at the time of independence, some in Pakistan and some in India. Lord Mountbatten, the last viceroy, had stipulated that the states would decide for themselves which nation they would join. But at the time of independence, four had yet to make their choice: Junagadh and Jodhpur in northwest India, Hyderabad in the southeast, and Kashmir in the north. The first three had Hindu majorities and Muslim rulers; Kashmir's population and rule were the opposite.

Junagadh was 80 percent Hindu, but in September 1947 its Muslim ruler, Muhammad Mahabat Khanji III (r. 1911–48) chose to join Pakistan. Neighboring Indian states reacted violently, and India sent troops to force him to reverse his decision. Khanji fled to Pakistan, and Junagadh joined India. In Jodhpur, the Muslim maharaja, Hanwant Singh (r. 1947–52), new to the throne, bent to Mountbatten's pressure to join India.

Hyderabad, the largest and richest state in India, had a similar demographic profile, some 85 percent Hindu, led by the Muslim nizam Osman Ali Khan Bahadur Fateh Jung (r. 1911–48), who was reluctant to choose one nation over the other. Mountbatten again interceded, forcing the nizam's approval of accession to India. However, remnants of Hyderabad's independence were to be observed under a standstill agreement between the two states. Hindus who favored total absorption by India rioted against the agreement. India deployed troops to the region in Operation Polo, citing the need to restore order. Again, the display of military power forced capitulation, and Hyderabad completed its union with India.

The Kashmir Crisis

Kashmir was the last and most contested of the holdout Princely States. Here a Hindu, Maharaja Hari Singh (r. 1925–51), ruled over a Muslim majority of some 78 percent. The maharaja favored maintaining independence, but Mountbatten urged him to join one of the new states by mid-August of 1947. Two Muslim parties, the Muslim Conference and the National Conference, dominated the debate. The Muslim Conference favored union with Pakistan, while the National Conference took a more secular approach to statehood, willing to accede to India in exchange for de facto autonomy.

In the interim the maharaja sought standstill agreements with both Pakistan and India, seeking pledges of nonintervention. Pakistan agreed, but India refused. Local Muslims began agitating for accession to Pakistan. They staged a large demonstration in August. Hindu troops opened fire on the crowd, killing several hundred. The action caused a revolt in the region of Poonch, which declared itself Azad Kashmir, or Free Kashmir. The revolt sparked a Muslim guerrilla war against the maharaja, and Pakistan suspended supply shipments to the principality. On October 23, 1947, some 5,000 Pashtun tribesmen—Afridi, Waziri, and Mahsud from the NWFP—crossed the border into Kashmir, carried by Pakistan army vehicles. The irregulars reached as far as the outskirts of the Srinagar Valley. This area was the heartland of Kashmiriyat, the meaning and values of Kashmiri Muslim identity founded on traditions of Sufism and characterized by tolerance for their high-caste Hindu neighbors. The maharaja fled to his winter palace in Jammu, and the Kashmiri prime minister asked India to send troops to stop the attack. Nehru agreed under the condition that the maharaja accede to having Kashmir join India. By some accounts Mountbatten had an understanding with Nehru that a referendum on the region's future would be held later. On October 26 the maharaja chose to join India, and the following day India began airlifting troops to Srinagar, where they engaged the Pashtun tribesmen in battle.

The attack and occupation by Indian troops outraged Pakistan, which termed the accession coerced. Pakistan asked the United Nations (UN) Security Council to broker a cease-fire, so that a referendum or plebiscite could be held among Kashmiris, the results of which would determine which state they would join. With a large Muslim majority, a decision in favor of joining Pakistan was widely expected in any such referendum. Meanwhile, a large assault by Indian troops drove the Pashtun fighters back to the Pakistani border. In response Pakistan sent its own troops into Kashmir in May 1948, commencing a war with India.

UN Action

In August 1948 the UN Security Council called for an immediate cease-fire under four guiding principles: withdrawal of Pakistani troops, withdrawal of armed tribal groups, installation of an interim civilian government under UN control, and withdrawal of most Indian forces after the departure of Pakistani and tribal forces. Additionally, after the terms of the agreement had been met, a referendum would be conducted under UN supervision. Pakistan and India agreed to the terms. However, the resolution was not implemented until January 1, 1949. In March U.S. admiral Chester Nimitz (1885–1966) was appointed to oversee the referendum.

The cease-fire line was established in July 1949. The line is basically oriented east-west and then south. Jammu and Kashmir, which encompasses the Srinagar Valley, lies south of the border and is a member state of the Indian Union. Pakistan calls this Kashmiri Muslim heartland India-Occupied Kashmir. Hindus also cherish this region, for it is said to have been the scene of the development of important Hindu traditions. North of the cease-fire line lie the former tribal lands of Gilgit and Baltistan, now the Northern Areas, which are directly governed by the Pakistan government. West of the line, Azad Kashmir, the former Poonch, is a semiautonomous state under Pakistani control. India refers to these areas as Pakistan-Occupied Kashmir.

The referendum on Kashmir's future was never held. The UN administrator who tried to engineer the vote concluded that the sole option to settle the dispute was to split Kashmir, while putting off decisions on the future of the hotly contested Srinagar Valley area. Thus began a volatile stalemate that would last into the 21st century and become the most contentious issue and flashpoint between the two nations.

A Change of Leadership

Jinnah had seen himself as uniquely capable of achieving independence for Pakistan. He also believed he was the only individual capable of overcoming Pakistan's fractious political landscape and surmounting the problems plaguing the new nation. Many political observers at the time and since then have agreed. As Pakistan's governor-general, Jinnah wielded much more power than authorized under the Government of India Act of 1935 or the India Independence Act of 1947. After

Prime Minister Nawabzada Liaquat Ali Khan assumed leadership of Pakistan after the death of Muhammad Ali Jinnah. (Courtesy Pakistan Tourism Development Corporation)

Prime Minister Liaquat Ali Khan chaired the first cabinet meeting, the cabinet asked the Quaid, or leader, as Jinnah was commonly called, to take charge of the gatherings. Jinnah's role was so central that on December 30, 1947, the cabinet accepted the Adoption of Convention, which decreed that no policy or major decision should be made unless Jinnah chaired the meeting. But Jinnah's health had been deteriorating for several years, beset by tuberculosis and cancer. He tried to conceal his condition, fearing that any perceived weakness would encourage potential opponents to block his efforts. Despite the warnings of doctors, he maintained a rigorous schedule, and the appearance of vitality. When he died on September 11, 1948, Pakistan plunged into shock and grief.

Liaquat Ali Khan, Jinnah's prime minister, emerged as the nation's leader. Yet he could not replace Jinnah's power and stature. Liaquat Ali Khan had to forge coalitions and win the support of various factions. Three of the most important were his base supporters in the community of Karachi, the Muslim League constituency in Punjab, and the Muslim League constituency in East Pakistan. To win the support of the Punjabis and Bengalis, he delegated leadership roles to Muslim League figures such as Malik Ghulam Mohammad (1895–1956), from Bengal, who became finance minister; and Chaudhri Mohammad Ali (1905–80), from Punjab, who became the highest-ranking member of the Civil Service of Pakistan. He also offered the position of governor-general to Khawaja Nazimuddin (1894–1964), a powerful Muslim League leader and chief minister of the province of East Bengal.

The Civil Service of Pakistan

Though the government seemed paralyzed, the business of state carried on through the Civil Service of Pakistan (CSP). The institution had its genesis in the prepartition Indian Civil Service (ICS). This had been the primary institution through which locals could attain advancement and position in the British-controlled society of the Raj; it attracted some of India's best and brightest sons. At the time of partition, of the 1,157 senior members of the ICS and the police service, only 101 were Muslims. Of the latter, 83 opted to relocate to Pakistan, as did some 7,000 lower-level civil servants. But getting to Pakistan was difficult and dangerous, as the trains were unsafe, with marauding bands of Hindus hunting for Muslims. In a mission called "Operation Pakistan," Pakistan chartered 26 British airliners to fly the civil servants from Delhi to Karachi.

The civil servants arrived in a nation that had no administration to speak of. Managers who could staff senior posts were desperately needed, but none of the refugees held a senior rank equivalent to secretary. The CSP, struggling to meet the need for technocrats, gave rapid promotions and paid some British administrators to remain on payroll. The CSP was sometimes called the "steel frame," as it acted as the backbone of the nation. But early on its potential to achieve political power was also recognized. Jinnah instructed CSP members to stay out of politics. But after Jinnah's death, no one had sufficient clout to keep the CSP on the political sidelines, and the institution came to have a large part in forging the nation's policies.

In 1973 various services were combined into one administrative system, and the CSP was disbanded. Former CSP members, however, retained critical positions in the country's administrative apparatus even as subsequent governments came and went.

Economic Challenges

The new nation had little industry or industrial development plans. A total of 14,677 factories were registered in the subcontinent at the time of partition, but only 1,414 were in Pakistan. Of 394 textile mills, 14 were in Pakistan. There were 106 mills to process jute, a major crop; none of the mills were in Pakistan. And what little economic power existed—banks and insurance companies—were mostly Hindu owned. Pakistan also had little cash on hand. Cash assets belonging to the subcontinent were to be divided, but the division of assets favored India. Moreover, India had control over the disbursements and delayed remitting Pakistan's share, concerned that the money would be used to finance the conflict in Kashmir. For the same reason India also held up transferring military equipment that was due Pakistan. British general Claude Auchinleck (1884–1981), in charge of the transition to partition, was supposed to apportion military equipment between the two states, but, accused of being partial to Pakistan, he was recalled to England before Pakistan received its share of the hardware.

Liaquat-Nehru Pact

The ongoing violence between Muslims and Hindus continued to strain relations between Pakistan and India. In April 1950 Liaquat Ali Kahn and Indian prime minister Jawaharlal Nehru met in Delhi to seek a solution to the sectarian strife. Both agreed their respective countries would protect the rights of their minority citizens and guarantee their equality, including the freedom of speech and worship. They also agreed that both nations would establish minority commissions to enforce these rights and punish those who tried to abrogate them. The agreement became known as the Liaquat-Nehru Pact. It was one of the first high-level demonstrations of the leaders' awareness that the ongoing animosity between the two states and their citizens had to be reined in for the benefit of both nations.

Foreign Affairs

Since independence Pakistan's foreign policy has been based on a perceived need to defend itself against its larger, richer, and better militarily equipped neighbor and rival, India. This has required large budgetary expenditures for defense, impinging on the nation's ability to make progress in other key domestic areas, such as health and education.

During his brief tenure Jinnah had no real opportunity to put his stamp on foreign affairs. As prime minister, Liaquat Ali Khan pursued a policy of nonalignment. He tried to keep the nation neutral in the cold war between the Soviet Union and the United States. Soviet leader Joseph Stalin (r. 1922–53) invited Liaquat Ali Khan to Moscow in 1949, but he declined. In 1950, however, Liaquat Ali Khan called on U.S. president Harry S. Truman (r. 1945–53) in Washington, D.C., where he portrayed Pakistan as a democracy pursuing an independent foreign policy. Rather than recognize the nation as such, both the Soviet Union and the United States ignored Pakistan. Its neutral status proved costly at a time when Pakistan was desperate for assistance and allies. During his visit to the United States, Liaquat also sought Truman's assistance in resolving the Kashmir dispute, without success.

Objectives Resolution

Another important task facing the new state was the creation of a legal framework for its governance. The new nation had no constitution of its own. Under the terms of Britain's Indian Independence Act, the Government of India Act of 1935 became the working constitution of both new nations. However, Pakistan's leaders were anxious to draft their own constitution.

Liaquat Ali Khan drafted the Objectives Resolution, which laid the groundwork for adopting a constitution. Also known as the Magna Carta of Pakistan's constitutional history, the resolution was adopted by the legislative assembly on March 12, 1949. It asserted that Pakistan's constitution would be based on democratic representation and Islamic ideals:

> Wherein the State shall exercise its powers and authority through the chosen representatives of the people; wherein the principles of democracy, freedom, equality, tolerance and social justice, as enunciated by Islam, shall be fully observed; wherein the Muslims shall be enabled to order their lives in the individual and collective spheres in accordance with the teachings and requirements of Islam as set out in the Holy Qur'an and Sunna; wherein adequate provision shall be made for the minorities freely to progress and practice their religions and develop their cultures.

The Constituent Assembly, established to create and ratify a constitution and pass legislation until a constitution's adoption, formed committees to draft the document, led by the Basic Principles Committee. But Liaquat was unable to create a sufficient base of support to achieve a consensus on a plan for the constitution, and discussions and negotiations progressed slowly.

The Basic Principles Committee laid out the preliminary plan in 1950. It included provisions for equal representation in the upper house of the Central Legislature for East and West Pakistan, and that declared Urdu the national language. The plan met immediate opposition from representatives of East Pakistan, who objected to the equal division of power. East Pakistan contained the majority of the nation's population but was given only half of the seats in the upper house of the Central Legislature. Disagreements over the Islamic nature of the republic created more dissension. Public comment was invited to assist in reformulating the plan for the constitution.

The Military

Monitoring the civil discontent, high-ranking members of the military were also growing restive. Major General Akbar Khan (b. 1912), a veteran of the war in Kashmir, was among them. He was angered by Liaquat's failed efforts to resolve the conflict over Kashmir and believed Pakistan could remove Indian troops from disputed territory by military means. On February 23, 1951, he met with several other senior Pakistani army officers at his home in Rawalpindi. Many senior officers had experienced rapid advances in the wake of Pakistan's independence as the army expanded and top ranks were filled. Now that the military had been established and staffed, the lack of further advancement made some officers dissatisfied with civilian rule. The inability of the government to create a constitution and stable government institutions—which India had already accomplished—was another source of military discontent. At the meeting at his home Akbar Khan and his guests planned a takeover of the government with subsequent rule by a military council of senior generals. The meeting and its aims, which became known as the Rawalpindi Conspiracy, were discovered by the government later that year. Several prominent civilians with ties to leftist causes were also involved, including poet Faiz Ahmad Faiz (1911–84) and Sajjad Zaheer (1904–73), a Communist Party member. The conspirators were tried by a special military tribunal, convicted, and jailed. Most of them were released in 1955.

Growing Unrest

The domestic political situation, never very stable or marked by integrity, was deteriorating rapidly. Punjab and Bengal were both beginning to chafe under Muslim League rule. And the Muslim League itself was rent by dissent. The political leaders Liaquat had relied on to forge stability were becoming primary destabilizing elements. The military was no longer trustworthy. Liaquat decided he would try to bypass the political bosses and seek support directly from the public. He set off on a series of public rallies around the nation. At a large public meeting in Rawalpindi on October 16, 1951, he was shot at close range by an unemployed youth from the NWFP and died instantly. Liaquat's assassination did not plunge the nation into turmoil. It had already descended into chaos and political instability bordering on anarchy.

After Liaquat's assassination, Governor-General Khawaja Nazimuddin was named prime minister (r. 1951–53), as no other person was deemed suitable for the post. Finance Minister Malik Ghulam Muhammad was elevated to the post of governor-general (r. 1951–55). Born in Dhaka, in Bengal, in 1894, Malik Ghulam Muhammad attended Aligarh Muslim and Cambridge Universities. In 1929 he became provincial education minister in Bengal, where he championed educational reforms for rural people. In 1937 he was appointed as the home minister, and he became chief minister of Bengal in 1943. In 1947 he was elected leader of the Muslim League Party of East Bengal.

Work on the constitution continued. Nazimuddin was not a strong leader and was unable to gain control as political power struggles among subordinates increased. At the time of independence the economic and social disparity between the East Wing and West Wing of Pakistan was immense. The unity Islam brought to the two wings barely overcame the physical and economic distance between them. The majority—55 percent—of the new nation's population lived in East Pakistan. So its citizens believed the nation's capital should be in the east. Additionally, the sale of jute, grown in East Pakistan, was a major source of foreign earnings, yet the profits were spent on projects that did little to benefit the east. Bengali nationalism began to rise. The Awami League, formed in 1949, answered nationalist political yearnings in Bengal. One of its founders and later its leader, Sheikh Mujibur Rahman (1920–75), championed more autonomy for the provinces, especially for East Pakistan.

The issue of the state language burst forth again in 1952, when thousands of low-echelon government employees in East Pakistan staged a demonstration demanding Bengali be named their official language. In January Nazimuddin came to Dhaka and, despite his ties to Bengal, reiterated that the national language of Pakistan would be Urdu. He argued that Urdu was the only language that could facilitate communication among the provinces, as most people in both West and East Pakistan had some knowledge of Urdu, while Bengali was spoken primarily in East Pakistan. He emphasized that Bengali should be used in the administrative and educational systems of East Pakistan. His statement further inflamed the public. On February 21 students staged an illegal protest that was broken up by police, who used tear gas and fired into the crowds. Some students were killed. As a result of these events public support for the Bengali independence movement increased dramatically.

The report finally prepared for and endorsed by the Basic Principles Committee called for a bicameral legislature. It proposed the nation be led by a Muslim serving a five-year term and chosen by a joint session of the Central Legislature. The leader would select the prime minister. A board of ulama, religious leaders, would vet all proposed laws to ensure they were compatible with the tenets of Islam. However, this revised report, presented to the national assembly in December 1952, and its adoption as the Objectives Resolution did not close the growing rift between East and West Pakistan that the first report provoked. A stalemate ensued as politicians representing each wing held up progress on writing and adopting a constitution.

The Government Is Dissolved

Ghulam Muhammad, who had made adoption of a constitution a priority, was frustrated by the lack of progress. The national assembly, showing its own pique, passed a bill reining in the governor-general's powers. Meanwhile, religious turmoil was spreading, stoked by Islamic theologians opposed to a sect they believed to be heretical, the Ahmadiyya. The Ahmadiyya sect was founded in 1889 by Mirza Ghulam Ahmad (1835–1908), who claimed to have received revelations from God and proclaimed himself a prophet. This ran counter to Islam, which held that Muhammad, who brought forth the Qur'an, was the last of God's prophets. Nonetheless, the sect had survived, and its adherents generally supported independence for Pakistan; many became *muhajirs* after partition, moving their headquarters from the Indian province of Punjab to a small town southwest of Lahore the Ahmadiyya founded, Rabwa. The Ahmadiyya believed that jihad was not a struggle against infidels but a battle to spread the word of God, a belief that made them fervent proselytizers. Many thousands in Pakistan, as well as in Africa, East Asia, and North America, joined the sect. Mainstream Muslim leaders felt threatened by the Ahmadiyya's growing power and organization. In 1953 a group of ulama founded the Khatam-e-Nabuwat (Seal of the Prophets) movement in opposition. The group organized public demonstrations demanding that the government declare the Ahmadiyya to be non-Islamic. The riots spread, and the violence is believed to have claimed some 2,000 lives.

Responding to the violence and the assembly's efforts to curb his power, Ghulam Muhammad declared a state of emergency and dissolved the Constituent Assembly in October 1953. He thus became the first of several presidents who would remove democratically elected governments over the next half century. The Supreme Court upheld his action, determining the governor-general had the authority to dismiss the assembly and veto any legislation it passed. Ghulam Muhammad invited Muhammad Ali Bogra to resume the office of prime minister and to form a new cabinet dubbed "Ministry of Talents."

The Bogra Administration

Muhammad Ali Bogra (r. 1953–55) was Pakistan's ambassador to the United States at the time he was installed as prime minister. An aristocrat from East Bengal, he had been Nazimuddin's parliamentary secretary, and finance and health minister prior to independence. Muhammad Ali Bogra pronounced formal adoption of the now-written constitution a priority but promulgated an alternate plan called the Bogra Formula. It attempted to redress the imbalance of power between East and West Pakistan by setting aside an equal number of seats in the two houses of Parliament for each wing and stipulating that either the head of state or the head of government had to be from East Pakistan. It also provisioned that the Supreme Court, rather than the ulama, had the authority to decide if proposed laws were compatible with the tenets of Islam. The report was presented to the Constituent Assembly in October 1953, and a committee was appointed to draft the constitution under the Constituent Assembly's auspices.

In 1954 Muhammad Ali Bogra named the commander in chief of the army, General Muhammad Ayub Khan (1907–74), minister of defense, marking the first time the military was directly involved in the country's political process. Muhammad Ali Bogra also tried to settle the Kashmir dispute with India and met Jawaharlal Nehru in London in June 1953 in an attempt to reach a settlement. Although the two established cordial relations, Nehru refused to discuss the Kashmir dispute. That same year India forcefully suppressed a Muslim uprising in Kashmir, heightening tensions between the two countries. In August Muhammad Ali Bogra went to New Delhi to meet again with Nehru, this time wresting an agreement from him to hold a plebiscite in Kashmir. A series of communiqués between the two sides over the next several months further refined plans for the vote.

Alliances with the West

Three days after Muhammad Ali Bogra's nomination as prime minister, U.S. president Dwight Eisenhower (r. 1953–61) ordered thousands of tons of wheat shipped to Pakistan. That same year Ghulam Muhammad visited Eisenhower and came away from the meeting with a commitment from the United States to consider providing military assistance to Pakistan.

At the time Eisenhower was seeking cold war allies along what was called Asia's Northern Tier, which included Turkey, Iran, and Pakistan. In 1953 the United States offered economic and military assistance in return for Pakistan's agreement to join an alliance designed to check the spread of communism. In 1954 Pakistan signed the Mutual Defense Assistance Agreement and became a member of the Southeast Asia Treaty Organization (SEATO). Pakistan saw an alliance as a form of protection against India, though the agreement provided no guarantee that the United States would assist Pakistan in the event of aggression from India. But it obligated Pakistan to join in mutual defense against communist aggression. This was the price for the military and economic assistance from the United States, which Pakistan saw as vital to whatever military force Pakistan could muster to counter India's might. From 1954 to 1965 Pakistan received more than $1.3 billion in U.S. military assistance (Noor, n.p.). Defense minister Ayub Khan played a key role in negotiating Pakistan's entry into its military alliances.

India reacted strongly and negatively to the pact. Nehru reneged on his promise to support a plebiscite in Kashmir. The Soviet Union threw its support behind India's renouncement of a referendum.

Continuing its quest for international allies, in 1955 Pakistan joined Iraq, Turkey, and Iran in the Baghdad Pact. The administration saw the alliance as a way to strengthen relationships with other Muslim countries to foster more stability in the region. But the pact was bitterly opposed by Egyptian president Gamal Abdel Nasser (r. 1956–70), the leading political figure in the Arab world and a vocal pan-Arabist. Nasser's condemnation of Pakistan's participation in the Baghdad Pact earned it the rebuke of the Arab world. The Baghdad Pact was renamed the Central Treaty Organization (CENTO) after Iraq withdrew in 1959. Pakistan leased military installations to the United States as well, posts used for gathering intelligence and communications. The United States's U-2 reconnaissance aircraft that was shot down over the Soviet Union in 1960, creating a cold war crisis, took off from a base near Peshawar in Pakistan.

Stabilizing the Economy

Fitful steps were taken to stabilize and expand the economy during Pakistan's first decade. In July 1953 an economic planning board was given responsibility for identifying the human and material resources available to the country for a five-year period starting on April 1, 1954. But the repeated shake-ups of the government—five administrations between 1953 to 1958—left the government without ongoing economic expertise or stewardship. The board was unable to complete a draft of its five-year development plan until May 1956. It called for a 15 percent increase in national income over the period 1955–60, which, after allowing for population growth, amounted to a slim 7 percent increase in per capita income. The plan advocated a more equitable distribution of land in agricultural areas and called for opening more administrative jobs currently available only to Civil Service of Pakistan personnel to other technical-service professionals. At the time, however, political power was shifting to an alliance of landowners and the CSP, dooming chances for such reforms. Recommendations were debated for another two years. Finally, in May 1958 the plan was approved.

In August 1955 Ghulam Muhammad, beset by deteriorating health, resigned as governor-general. Major General Syed Iskander Ali Mirza, minister of the interior, succeeded him as governor-general (r. 1955–56). A civil servant, Iskander Mirza felt Pakistanis were not ready for true democracy because of lack of education and democratic traditions. He favored a partial democracy, with the majority of power vested in civil servants. That same month Iskander Mirza dissolved the national assembly and dismissed Muhammad Ali Bogra and his government. Called on to rule on the legality of the removal, the supreme court showed the compliance to those in power it would repeatedly display in acquiescence to military takeovers. "That which is otherwise unlawful, necessity makes lawful," the justices proclaimed (Raza, 1997, 8).

Muhammad Ali Bogra returned to his position as the nation's ambassador to the United States, replaced as prime minister by Chaudhry Muhammad Ali (r. 1955–56).

Chaudhry Muhammad Ali and the First Constitution

Like prime ministers before him, Chaudhry Muhammad Ali placed a priority on creating a constitution. To resolve the imbalance of power between the West and East Wings of Pakistan, the four provinces of West Pakistan—Baluchistan, Punjab, Sind, and the NWFP—were merged into one province called West Pakistan, with Lahore as the new provincial capital. At the same time East Bengal became the province of East Pakistan, with Dhaka as its provincial capital.

A constitution was approved by the Constituent Assembly on March 23, 1956. The constitution of 1956, as it became known, established Pakistan as an Islamic republic, ending its status as a British dominion. It had a parliamentary form of government with a unicameral legislature. The Constituent Assembly became the Legislative Assembly, and Iskander Mirza was made the nation's first president (r. 1956–58), the

ONE UNIT SOLUTION

The problem of how to balance resources and political power between the East and West Wings was never far from center stage. A school of thought advocated a "One Unit" approach to West Pakistan's organization, uniting the four provinces of West Pakistan. It was thought this would help minimize the problems between East and West Pakistan by dealing with two wings instead of four provinces in the west and one in the east. Prime Minister Chaudhry Muhammad Ali announced this merger concept and plan in October 1955. Iskander Mirza was an advocate of this approach. But regional rivalries within the West Wing complicated consensus. The populations of Baluchistan, Sind, and the NWFP were mostly opposed to the One Unit solution, fearing it would dilute what little voice their respective provinces had. Sind and the NWFP in particular chaffed at Punjab's political and economic dominance. Nonetheless, the four provinces of West Pakistan—Baluchistan, Punjab, Sindh, and the NWFP—were merged in October 1955. Lahore was made the new provincial capital.

office that replaced that of the governor-general. Seats in the national assembly were evenly divided between East and West Pakistan representatives. All citizens 21 years of age and older were given the right to vote. Urdu and Bengali were both recognized as state languages, while English was designated as Pakistan's official language for its first 25 years. The president was given the power to suspend provisions of the constitution in times of emergency.

Adoption of the constitution failed to stifle the dissension that made its creation so difficult. The parliamentary system created by the constitution needed disciplined political parties, and the nascent democracy of Pakistan had no such institutions. The sole political party that could serve as a model, the Muslim League, was losing its focus and power, and its decline fragmented the political landscape.

The Muslim League, the only major political party in Pakistan at the time of independence, had been largely identified with its goal of an independent homeland for Muslims on the subcontinent, as well as by its two major figures, Jinnah and Liaquat Ali Khan. With independence achieved, the two leaders dead, and its surviving leaders split by regional rivalries, the party lost its broad-based support. It slowly came to be dominated by Punjabi landowners and bureaucrats. The party had been further split by the impasse over the constitutional debate. Regional disagreements over representation and the Islamic values the country would adopt as its spiritual foundation were stronger than party loyalties. Muslim League politicians in East Pakistan, with a larger Hindu population, sought to establish a more secular state, which they saw as key to retaining broad support and power. But the Muslim League was adamant in making Pakistan's Islamic identity a core issue.

Political Repercussions

Chaudhry Muhammad Ali was unable to unite the spectrum of leadership to support the new constitution. Furthermore, he appointed a former Congress Party member who had opposed the creation of Pakistan, Khan Abdul Jabbar Khan (1882–1958), known by the honorific Dr. Khan Sahib, as chief minister of the newly unified province of West Pakistan. Jabbar Khan purged Muslim League politicians from his cabinet and formed a new party, the Republican Party. Muslim League members in the national assembly urged Chaudhry Muhammad Ali to rein in Jabbar Khan's actions in West Pakistan, but he refused, believing Jabbar Khan was acting in the best interests of the country rather than of an individual party.

In 1954 two former members of the Muslim League from East Pakistan, Husain Shaheed Suhrawardy (1892–1963) and A. K. Fazlul Haq (1873–1962), joined a coalition of opposition parties called the United Front with the aim of defeating the Muslim League in upcoming elections. Suhrawardy was the leader of the Awami League, which he had cofounded in 1949, and Fazlul Haq had established the Krishak Sramik (Workers and Peasants) Party.

Both men had held important positions in their abandoned party. Fazlul Haq had made the motion to adopt the historic Pakistan Resolution in 1940, and Suhrawardy had seconded it. But the West Wing's control over the Muslim League drove both away from the party. Suhrawardy was chosen as the leader of the opposition in the second Constituent Assembly.

Bereft of support, Chaudhry Muhammad Ali resigned as prime minister and as a member of the Muslim League. He was replaced by Suhrawardy (r. 1956–57), who became the first non–Muslim League politician to hold the office. By now the Muslim League had even lost its majority in the West Pakistan Legislative Assembly to the Punjab-centered Republican Party. Suhrawardy formed a coalition cabinet at the center that included the Awami League and the Republican Party. Though Suhrawardy enjoyed wide popularity in East Pakistan, he had no political base in the west, and his strong endorsement of the One Unit Plan cost him the support of all its provinces save Punjab.

Among his first challenges was the growing antipathy among the Muslim League and religious parties in West Pakistan to the joint electorate provisions he championed and the national assembly passed in October 1956. These provisions accorded greater voting power and rights to the nation's minorities. Opposition to the One Unit Plan was becoming better organized. And the ongoing economic inequality between East and West Pakistan was another source of friction. Suhrawardy tried to balance the fortunes of the two wings, but was met by opposition from business interests in West Pakistan, who saw their power being diluted. President Iskander Mirza asked for Suhrawardy's resignation; Suhrawardy agreed to give up his role in October 1957. Iskander Mirza selected Ibrahim Ismail Chundrigar to serve as interim prime minister (r. Oct.–Dec. 1957). Chundrigar presided over a coalition government that included the Muslim League, the Republican Party, the Nizam-i-Islam Party, and the Krishak Sramik Party. Though the Muslim League and the Republican Party typically worked in opposition, the Muslim League consented to taking part in the coalition under the condition that the Republican Party support its efforts to have separate electorates. But after Chundrigar formed his cabinet, in the fall of 1957, the Republican Party began opposing the legislative amendments required to overturn the joint electorate provisions. Unable to make headway from atop this crumbling coalition, Chundrigar left the prime minister post. In December 1957 he was replaced by Malik Feroz Khan Noon (r. 1957–58), a leader of the Republican Party in the national assembly. His ruling coalition included the Awami League, the National Awami Party, the National Congress, the Scheduled Caste Confederation, and the Krishak Sramik Party. Despite the large number of parties in his coalition government, Feroz Khan Noon was able to form a stable government and political chaos began to subside.

Military Rule

Iskander Mirza, who had exploited the divisions in Chundrigar's coalition to retain the upper hand in leadership, felt threatened by Khan Noon's stronger and more stable ruling alliance. Religious and ethnic tensions also persisted. In West Pakistan chief minister Khan Abdul Jabbar Khan was assassinated. In the NWFP his brother, Khan Abdul Ghaffar Khan (1890–1988), declared his intent to work for independence for the Pashtuns. And in Baluchistan, the khan of Kalat again declared his independence, requiring the intercession of the Pakistani army. Iskander Mirza, who already had the support of civil servants due to their distrust of politicians, tried to strengthen his position by forging alliances with politicians from other parties, including Khan Abdul Ghaffar Khan. But he was unable to undermine the coalition created by Feroz Khan Noon. With his attempts to assert control through political means failing, Iskander Mirza turned to extralegal means. On October 7, 1958, with the cooperation of the commander in chief of the armed forces, General (Field Marshal) Muhammad Ayub Khan, Iskander Mirza declared martial law. Ayub Khan assumed the position of chief martial law administrator. The Constitution of 1956 was abrogated, the central and provincial assemblies dissolved. Elections scheduled for January 1959 were cancelled. The Muslim League was dissolved, never to be revived again.

Iskander Mirza and Ayub Khan presented themselves as dual leaders, but the real power rested with Ayub Khan due to his control over the armed forces. Within days Iskander Mirza realized he had little control over Ayub Khan or the government. Iskander Mirza sought, unsuccessfully, to cultivate Ayub Khan's rivals in the armed forces as a balance against the general's power. Attempting blunter measures, on

October 24 Iskander Mirza removed Ayub Khan as head of martial law, appointing him as prime minister. On October 27, 1958, Ayub Khan had Iskander Mirza arrested and declared himself president. Ayub Khan was now the undisputed ruler of Pakistan and its military-run government.

9

MILITARY RULE
(1958–1971)

Pakistan's first efforts at civilian rule ended with the imposition of martial law under President Iskander Mirza, enforced by General Muhammad Ayub Khan. The public, tired of political gridlock and economic stagnation, was ready to welcome change that promised stability and forward movement. Ayub Khan, who soon replaced Iskander Mirza in a coup d'état, promised to restore democracy but instead took greater authority for himself and failed to deliver democracy or progress. This set the pattern for all later military rulers who seized power from elected leaders, as Pakistan lurched between democracy and dictatorship for the next half century.

Pakistan's problems would have been a challenge to any administration, with its poor, uneducated population; lack of public services and economic development; disparate ethnic and religious groups and sects that resisted assimilation; and intensifying estrangement between East and West Pakistan. All led to growing disenchantment with Ayub Khan. Within a decade of his coup, demands for freedom brought a temporary restoration of civilian rule. Yet Pakistan remained unsettled, the violent search for its identity and destiny leading to the 1971 secession of the nation's East Wing, which proclaimed its independence as Bangladesh. The West Wing's use of military force to end the rebellion led to a war with India, which came to the aid of the erstwhile East Wing, soundly defeating Pakistan's army. The loss of both territory and the war with India shook the soul of Pakistanis. Political upheaval would wrack what remained of the nation in the wake of these events.

Ayub Khan Seizes Power
Within three weeks after President Iskander Mirza, attempting to retain power against a restive legislature, declared martial law on October 7,

1958, Commander in Chief Muhammad Ayub Khan seized power in a military coup. Ayub Khan was a Pashtun from a region of the NWFP close to Punjab and its more urban cultural influences. He had joined the British Indian Army, as had his father, and, by the time of British withdrawal in 1947, Ayub Khan was a brigadier general, one of the most senior Muslims in the corps. During partition he was appointed a member of the boundary commission, responsible for maintaining order in disputed territories whose borders had yet to be determined. He was later accused of being lax in preventing violence that swept these areas during partition.

After partition Ayub Khan was placed in charge of the army in East Pakistan, where he developed a contempt for politics and politicians, as he later related in his autobiography, *Friends Not Masters*. He believed politicians were corrupt and undisciplined and political institutions inherently inefficient. A professional military man, he favored a structure in which commands were obeyed without question, a far cry from the fractious world of Pakistan's politics. He became convinced that democracy had to be limited in order to avoid being counterproductive in a struggling, fledgling nation. This view would become a cornerstone of his "Basic Democracies" governing policy after 1959.

In 1950 Liaquat Ali Khan asked Ayub Khan to be the nation's first commander in chief, and in 1954 he became minister of defense. Unhappy with the civilian government, many Pakistanis supported his coup d'état against Irkander Mirza, and Ayub Khan used this goodwill to institute major reforms in the political, social, and economic fabric. Corrupt administrators were put on trial as part of his first demonstration of government reform. In all, some 3,000 public officials were dismissed, and many more were demoted. The military government also promulgated the Elective Bodies Disqualification Order, or E.B.D.O, which allowed the government to bar select politicians from serving in elective bodies until 1967, some nine years hence. Many politicians who enjoyed widespread popularity, such as Hussain Shaheed Suhrawardy and Abdul Qayyum Khan, former chief minister of the NWFP (r. 1947–53), were "E.B.D.O.-ed" from office.

On October 27, 1959, Ayub Khan introduced the Basic Democracies Order, a plan that replaced the parliamentary system of democracy of the now-suspended 1956 constitution with an indirect elective government system. The doctrine was based on Ayub Khan's belief that Pakistan's largely illiterate population required a more limited form of democracy, one with reduced political and social freedoms. The system was intended to slowly introduce the population to the workings of the government by limiting its decision-making powers to local government and rural development. Ayub Khan called the form of governance "Basic Democracies," while others called it representational dictatorship. The order created some 80,000 elective council seats, whose holders were charged with electing senior government officials. The public voted for the 80,000 representatives, members of village and town councils, who then elected members of the national assembly. Eighty thousand representatives may seem like a large number, but being officials, they were prone to pressure from Ayub Khan and his proxies more than anonymous citizens, and they represented less than one-thousandth of the population.

In an effort to curb the influence of landlords, whose concentration of wealth and power was deemed a threat to the government and an impediment to economic progress, Ayub Khan also undertook major land reforms in West Pakistan. The reforms limited the size of land holdings to 1,000 acres for nonirrigated lands and 500 acres for irrigated lands; for properties exceeding these limits, the excess land would be distributed to people chosen by the government.

The port of Karachi, Pakistan's commercial center, was initially also the nation's capital. During General Ayub Khan's rule, the decision to relocate the capital to Islamabad was made. (Courtesy Pakistan Tourism Development Corporation)

Islamabad

After his coup d'état in 1959, General Ayub Khan was determined to relocate the capital from Karachi to an inland location. For Ayub Khan, a military leader, Karachi had several drawbacks as a capital. It was 1,000 miles (1,600 km) from Rawalpindi, the site of the military's general headquarters. Karachi was a cosmopolitan city, whose luminaries were business and industrial leaders; it was home to many *muhajirs* (refugees from India), who were often better educated and more literate than the people of Pakistan's interior, and held more worldly views of events and news. Ayub Khan had little in common and no desire to associate with such people. And Karachi had little connection to the heartland of Punjab, where Ayub Khan had grown up. Ayub Khan appointed a commission under Agha Muhammad Yahya Khan, chief of the army staff (1917–80), to recommend a site for a new capital. The commission suggested a location just north of Rawalpindi. A Greek urban planning firm, Doxiadis, designed the city, laying it out in a triangular grid pointing toward the Margaila Hills. The name Islamabad, or "city of Islam," was chosen in an effort to placate conservative religious figures concerned about the secular tilt of the Ayub Khan regime. Work on the new city began in 1961, and the first residents arrived in 1963.

Islamabad, or "the city of Islam," was created to serve as Pakistan's capital. Residents began arriving in 1963. (Courtesy Pakistan Tourism Development Corporation)

The Constitution of 1962 officially made Islamabad the federal capital. But only the executive branch was based here. The legislative branch would inhabit a new city near Dhaka, in East Pakistan, in order to demonstrate to the East Wing its importance to Pakistan as a whole.

Resolving the Indus Water Dispute

Finally resolving the long-standing dispute between Pakistan and India over the Indus River's water, in December 1958 Pakistan unconditionally accepted the World Bank's plan on the division of the waters. India had already accepted these terms. With Pakistan's approval, the Indus Waters Treaty was drafted and, on September 19, 1960, signed. It gave Pakistan exclusive rights to the Indus, Jhelum, and Chenab Rivers, which flow through West Punjab; India was granted exclusive rights to the Ravi, Beas, and Sutlej Rivers up to the point they enter East Punjab. Additionally, during a 10-year transition period India was to supply Pakistan with waters from the eastern rivers. Pakistan used the transitional period to build and renovate massive water projects. These included dams at Warsak in the Federally Administered Tribal Areas; Mangla in Azad Kashmir; and Tarbela, some 30 miles (50 km) northwest of Islamabad. The projects, which also linked canals, barrages, and other water works, were funded with $900 million in World Bank loans, monetary compensation from India, and contributions from Australia, Canada, West Germany, New Zealand, the United Kingdom, and the United States.

The Constitution of 1962

The Basic Democracies system, with its relatively limited local representation, left council seat holders vulnerable to Ayub Khan's interference and manipulation. Using these council members as electors, Ayub Khan held a referendum in February 1960, winning their approval to remain as president for five years and draft a new constitution. With his victory in hand, Ayub Khan established a commission to draft a new constitution and examine the reasons for the failure of the parliamentary form of government he had terminated.

Since Pakistan had been founded in the name of the Muslims of India, appealing to religion was akin to appeals to Pakistani nationalism itself, and politicians often aligned themselves with Islam as a way to win over voters. The ulama, meanwhile, tried to wield influence over the political process, using their sway over the masses and the politicians' need of their support to maintain power. General Ayub Khan was the first ruler to attempt to counter the power of the religious establishment, setting the government on a secular course. In his book *Friends Not Masters* Ayub Khan accused the ulama of fomenting discontent and anger at the government: "They succeeded in converting an optimistic and enthusiastic people into a cynical and frustrated community," he wrote (Ayub Khan 1967, 209).

The Muslim Family Laws Ordinance, passed in 1961, made religious law subservient to secular rules. For example, the ordinance made it more difficult for men to take more than one wife, requiring the consent of the first wife for such a union. Ayub Khan discouraged the wearing of the burqa, the body-covering garment associated with religious conservatism, and he sought to reduce the birth rate through family planning.

The commission's recommendations for the constitution, delivered in May 1961, did not match Ayub Khan's views. He consigned the recommendations to a series of committees, and, by the time the document emerged for approval by the legislature, the constitution conformed to Ayub Khan's blueprint.

The constitution of 1962, adopted in March of that year, consolidated authority in the hands of the nation's president. The president was to be a Muslim, his term would last five years, and he could serve a maximum of two consecutive terms. As head of state, head of the government, and commander of the armed forces, the president enjoyed absolute power. He had the power to appoint federal ministers and department heads, members of administrative commissions, and provincial governors. He anointed chief justices and judges of the supreme and high courts.

The constitution also mandated that Pakistan be renamed the *Republic of Pakistan* and the word *Islamic* be dropped from the nation's name, hewing to Ayub Khan's preference for a secular government. However, the majority of the National Assembly favored restoring *Islamic* to the republic's name, and the first amendment to the 1962 constitution, passed in December of that year, made the nation the Islamic Republic of Pakistan once again. The constitution mandated the establishment of the Advisory Council of Islamic Ideology to generate ideas for ways Muslim citizens could hew more closely to Islamic principles. The constitution also incorporated Ayub Khan's Basic Democracies plan and its system of indirect representational government.

The unicameral legislature consisted of a National Assembly of 156 members. The president had veto power over any legislation approved by the assembly and had the power to dismiss its members. He could also make law when the legislature was not in session. And though these laws needed the eventual approval of the assembly, the president also had absolute power to declare a state of emergency, which abrogated the need for legislative approval.

Any future constitutional amendment would require a two-thirds majority of the National Assembly and presidential approval. The Constitution of 1962 retained the principle of parity from the 1956 constitution, providing for equal representation for each of the two wings of the nation. It retained the One Unit concept for West Pakistan. Urdu and Bengali remained national languages, and English the official language for 10 years.

With the new constitution in place in March 1962, martial law was ended. A civilian government took the place of the military leaders who had ruled since Ayub Khan had gained power.

The Economy

The new decade marked the conclusion of the country's first five-year plan, which had been belatedly implemented more than halfway into its intended time span. Economic growth had fallen short of its goals during the 1955–60 period. Per capita income had increased by less than 1 percent. The growth in the industrial, agricultural, housing and settlement, transport, and communications sectors was below the very modest targets.

Ayub Khan had promised Pakistan an improved economy, but failed to deliver results. Having not achieved his initial objective, he appointed himself chairman of the planning commission overseeing the second five-year economic plan. The staff was strengthened, and more foreign advisers were added to the roster of those already providing planning assistance. Approved in June 1960, a few days prior to the start of the 1961 fiscal year, the new plan was focused on accelerated economic growth. It contained no provisions for increasing social services or alleviating poverty. The plan's budget of 29 billion rupees ($6.1 billion), allotted just under half (48 percent) of expenditures to public services such as water and power, agriculture, transport, and communication. Only 8 percent was earmarked for health, education, and social welfare, though Ayub Khan stressed the need for educational reform. "There exists a fundamental justification for inequality of income if it raises production for all and not consumption for a few," the commission's chief economist, Mahbubul Haq, wrote in the plan "The road to eventual equalities may inevitably be through initial inequalities" (Burki 1980, 73).

Of the rest of the development budget, the private sector would receive 39 percent of available funds, and 10 percent would be spent on Indus waterworks. Local councils established under the Basic Democracies would get 3 percent to spend on rural works programs of their choosing.

The plan achieved its goal of accelerating economic growth. Between 1960 and 1965 the nation's gross national product (GNP) grew at an annual rate of 5.2 percent. However, population growth was greater than anticipated, resulting in a small growth in income—barely a 2.7 percent per capita annual increase. Notably, East Pakistan's economy grew slightly faster than the more industrialized and prosperous West Wing. (West Pakistan's increase in per capita income for this period was a slight 2.4 percent.) The economic expansion and superficial political tranquility made the Ayub Khan regime a model for third world developmental success, cited by many international experts and chroniclers of the era.

1965 Presidential Elections

The 1965 elections were not only a presidential contest but a referendum on the autocratic government Ayub Khan instituted and embodied. The Convention Muslim League, of which Ayub Khan was president, and the Combined Opposition Parties were the two political parties in the election. The Combined Opposition Parties consisted of five different opposition groups. Its platform included a return to direct democracy and restoration of constitutional democratic principles. But the parties were combined in name alone. Unable to select a candidate from the party leaders among them, they turned to Fatima Jinnah, sister of Pakistan's first president and father of the nation, Muhammad Ali Jinnah, the Quaid. Fatima Jinnah, herself a veteran of the Freedom Movement, was known as the Madar-i-Millat, or Mother of the Nation. She had been absent from the political landscape since independence and largely quiescent to Ayub Khan's rule, despite her support of democratic ideals. The only other presidential contestants were two largely unknown candidates unidentified with any political party.

The names of the presidential candidates were made public before the Basic Democracies elections took place. The 80,000 electors (a number that would grow to 120,000 under the eighth amendment to the constitution) chosen in that contest would vote for the president and legislators. One month was allotted for the campaign, which was restricted to nine meetings open only to electors and the press. The campaign process hobbled the candidates. Nonetheless, Fatima Jinnah's campaign generated great public enthusiasm. Large crowds greeted her as she traveled through the East and West Wings of the nation. She declared Ayub Khan a dictator and claimed he had signed over Pakistan's water to India in the Indus Waters Treaty. Some major orthodox religious parties, which had previously maintained a woman could not lead an Islamic republic, supported Jinnah's candidacy. But despite her popular appeal, the Basic Democracy system of electors almost guaranteed Jinnah's defeat, due to the president's ability to influence and manipulate the votes of the 80,000 Basic Democrats who elected National Assembly members. This assured Khan's backers gained the majority of seats in the assembly, whose members in turn elected the president. Ayub Khan was reelected president on January 2, 1965.

A New Foreign Policy and the 1965 Indo-Pakistan War

At the beginning of the 1960s Pakistan and the United States maintained their military alliance. The United States had leased three air bases from Pakistan that played a key part in the cold war. However, Pakistan's interest in the alliance was not so much to counter communism but to offset India's might. Relations deteriorated when leaders in Islamabad began to feel a U.S. tilt toward India; to address the military disparity Pakistan began to explore relations with China and the Soviet Union.

Zulfikar Ali Bhutto (1928–79), then Ayub Khan's minister of fuel, power, and natural resources, was the first government official to turn Pakistan toward the Soviet axis. Bhutto believed Pakistan had large reserves of oil and gas and was frustrated that the Western oil companies with concessions in Pakistan were not exploring and finding these resources. In 1961 Bhutto negotiated an exploration agreement with the Soviet Union. The Soviets also agreed to provide technical and financial assistance to Pakistan's Oil and Gas Development Corporation. The agreement had little lasting impact on Pakistan or its energy industry.

Closer ties to China were also forged in the early 1960s. China and Pakistan shared a common border, and China was eager to foster improved relations, neutralizing whatever threat SEATO (Southeast Asia Treaty Organization) member Pakistan, at its back door, represented. Throughout these years Pakistan had continued efforts to resolve the Kashmir crisis, primarily by seeking the long-promised plebiscite, which had been approved by the United Nations and agreed to by Pakistan and India. But India refused to schedule a plebiscite, finding reason upon reason for its intransigence. A former Indian defense minister, Krishna Menon, once candidly explained why: "Kashmir would vote to join Pakistan and no Indian government responsible for agreeing to plebiscite would survive" (Mahmood 2000, 191). In fall 1962 a long-standing border dispute between India and China turned into open warfare. Western nations pressured Pakistan to assure India it would not use the distraction of the conflict with China to engage in any military adventures in Kashmir. At the same time India used the border war with China, an archenemy of the United States, to leverage more military assistance from the United States. Pakistan feared the purpose of the massive buildup in the Indian military was to create an army capable of conquering Pakistan. Seeking to counter India's suspected intentions, Pakistan began efforts to normalize relations with China. Angered at what it saw as Pakistan's new communist partiality, the United States suspended economic aid to Pakistan, though not all military assistance. During its war with China, India invited Ayub Khan to discuss a resolution to the Kashmir situation. The two sides met in November 1962, but soon after China announced a unilateral cease-fire following a quick defeat of the Indian army. With an end to the Sino-Indian border dispute, the talks over Kashmir stalled, ending in May 1963.

Upon the death of Foreign Minister Muhammad Ali Bogra in 1963, Zulfikar Bhutto convinced Ayub Khan to appoint him foreign minister. Under Bhutto's foreign-policy leadership, a border agreement with China was reached, and closer commercial links were established. Scheduled airline service between the two countries was instituted, and China pledged to build a major military-industrial complex near Wah, in Punjab. In February 1964 Ayub Khan made a state visit to China and won its support for a plebiscite in Kashmir.

In March 1965 Kashmir's legislative assembly adopted constitutional amendments that ceded the power to select the region's ruler to India. Kashmir's Muslim majority strenuously objected and set up a government of their own, a national government of the people of Jammu and Kashmir. In April confrontations between India and Pakistan erupted at the Rann of Kutch. Occupying some 3,500 square miles (9,100 sq. km) between Sind and the princely state of Kutch, the Rann (Hindi for "salt marsh") had been disputed territory before joining India at the time of partition. Pakistan easily defeated India and a United Nations–brokered cease-fire ended the conflict.

Encouraged by its military success in southern Pakistan and believing that the population of Kashmir could be incited to rise up against Indian occupiers, the Pakistani government decided to seek a military solution to Kashmir. Starting on August 5, 1965, under a plan code named "Operation Gibraltar," thousands of mujahideen were infiltrated into Kashmir. The mujahideen were to provide weapons and leadership once the revolt began. But the operation failed to incite an insurrection and only escalated tensions in the region. Indian prime minister Lal Bahadur Shastri (r. 1964–66) tried to control contested Kashmir by imposing presidential rule and asserting the right to enforce legislation. Kashmir's Muslim ruler, Sheikh Muhammad Abdullah (1905–82), was arrested for trying to block India's efforts. Protests against India's attempt to impose rule erupted in Azad Kashmir. In response, the Indian army crossed the cease-fire line to battle Muslim forces.

Kashmiri Muslim women practice marksmanship in 1965 to provide civil defense against the Indian army. (AP/Wide World Photos)

Full-scale war began on September 6, when India launched a massive air, armor, and infantry attack on Lahore, Sialkot, and Rajasthan. Pakistani troops invaded India at several points along the border. Seeking to contain the conflict, both the United States and the Soviet Union sought UN intervention. In Pakistan much of the public was in favor of going to war with India over Kashmir, particularly since Pakistanis thought they had the upper hand in the conflict and would defeat the Indian forces. The United Nations arranged a cease-fire, which took effect on September 23, 1965. Afterward, the Soviet Union sponsored a peace conference at Tashkent, in what is today Uzbekistan. Attended by Ayub Khan and Indian prime minister Shastri as well as Soviet premier Aleksey Kosygin (r. 1964–80), the Tashkent Conference commenced on January 4, 1966. Under the Tashkent Declaration, issued at its conclusion, Pakistan and India agreed to withdraw their

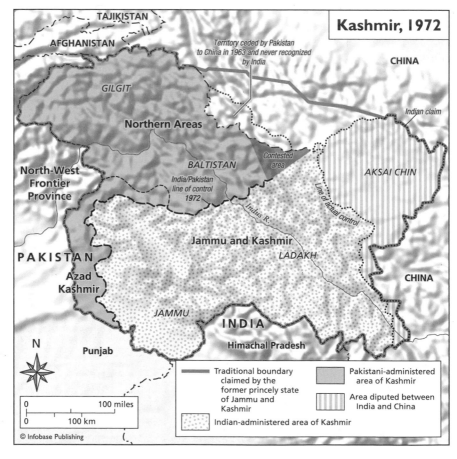

forces by February 25 to positions held prior to August 5, 1964, and agreed to attempt to normalize relations and renounce the use of force to settle disagreements. The agreement, which favored neither nation, stunned many Pakistanis, who felt they were winning the war. For them the declaration represented a humiliation. Public protest and riots broke out across Pakistan. On January 14 Ayub Khan addressed the nation on the reasons for signing the declaration. Though he was able to make his case to the majority of Pakistanis, his position was greatly weakened in the wake of the peace negotiations.

Economic Fallout

The Indo-Pakistan War was disastrous for Pakistan. It strained Pakistan's economy and drained the treasury at a time when the country was preparing to implement the Third Five-Year Plan. Eager to improve upon Pakistan's economic record, the Second Five-Year Plan became the model for the third, covering the years 1965–70. In addition to accelerating economic growth, the plan sought to reduce the economic disparity between the East and West Wings. By the end of the Second Five-Year Plan, East Pakistan was getting half of all Pakistan's investment in public-sector development. But when the war with India over Kashmir broke out in the first year of the third plan, developmental resources were diverted to the military. The drain slowed even the development of the new capital, Islamabad. The presidency and several departments took temporary offices in Rawalpindi. Ultimately the plan's basic economic goals were realized. By the last year of the plan the GNP increased at the rate of 5.5 percent annually, and per capita income rose 2.7 percent. But the rising income was not shared equally, and many Pakistanis were experiencing economic stagnation.

Meanwhile, the failure to unite the two wings successfully and widespread corruption plaguing Pakistan's institutions left the public disillusioned with the government. The war also convinced many in the East Wing that their country was incapable of providing adequate military protection, bolstering supporters of greater rights and even independence for Bengal.

Growing Unrest

People were looking for new leadership, and it came from a charismatic, energetic populist, Zulfikar Ali Bhutto. One of Ayub Khan's key aides, at age 30 Bhutto became the youngest cabinet minister in the nation's history, holding several posts. Born in Sind in 1928 on the banks of the Indus, Zulfikar Bhutto was the only son of a wealthy landowner and noted politician, Sir Shah Nawaz Bhutto (d. 1949), a supporter of Pakistani independence. His mother was a Hindu of lower social standing who converted to Islam before her marriage. Zulfikar Bhutto inherited most of the landholdings upon his father's death. He attended the University of California at Berkeley and Oxford University, earning a law degree. Returning to Karachi in 1953, he began to practice at the bar. Two of his four children, daughter Benazir (1953–2007) and son Shahnawaz (1958–85), named for his grandfather, would themselves play large roles in Pakistan's politics.

Zulfikar Bhutto became the first politician to turn Pakistan toward the Soviet Union. In 1961 he engineered an oil and mineral exploration agreement with the Soviet Union. Bhutto's ability to get Ayub Khan to agree to his plan was a sign of Bhutto's growing influence. The project itself had little lasting impact on Pakistan or its energy industry. In 1963, he was appointed foreign minister. In a book he published after resigning from Ayub Khan's government, *The Myth of Independence,* Bhutto made a case for his foreign policy, asserting any relationship between unequal powers such as Pakistan and the United States was destined to produce autocratic, subservient leaders in the weaker country. It was Bhutto who championed Operation Gibraltar, the failed effort to stir an uprising in Kashmir that preceded the war with India over the disputed territory. He adamantly opposed the Tashkent Declaration, and left Ayub Khan's government and party in 1966 over its acceptance. After weighing offers from several opposition groups, in 1967 Bhutto founded his own party the Pakistan People's Party (PPP). It was already a tradition in the short history of Pakistani politics for noted opposition figures to found their own parties rather than play a secondary role in someone else's organization. The cult of personality and lack of party strength and durability contributed to the fractious history of Pakistani politics then as it does now.

Despite public anger over the war's aftermath, Ayub Khan felt secure enough in office to schedule elections. He also arranged a celebration in 1968 to mark a decade of his rule. But he failed to grasp the depth of opposition to his government. Zulfikar Bhutto's populist platform of nationalism, socialism, and Islamic revivalism generated vigorous support. Making the defeat of Ayub Khan his priority, Bhutto embarked on a nationwide tour, denouncing Ayub Khan along the way. In November 1968, Bhutto and several supporters were arrested for their campaign activities and incarcerated for three months. The detentions further inflamed the opposition. The Awami League in East Pakistan also stood against Ayub Khan, accusing him of being unconcerned with East Pakistan's problems. The nation's other political parties banded together in an alliance, the Democratic Action Committee, to bring down Ayub Khan's regime. By the end of 1968, dissatisfaction with Ayub Khan's regime had spread across the middle class. The Joint Labor Council called for a labor strike to protest Ayub Khan's rule.

Ayub Khan tried to diffuse the growing opposition by releasing several jailed political figures in 1969, including East Pakistan's most popular politician, Sheikh Mujibur Rahman (1920–75). In 1966 Mujibur Rahman had proposed a six-point program for provincial autonomy and had been imprisoned since being implicated in a 1968 conspiracy to gain independence for the East Wing.

Attempting to rein in the growing political unrest, Ayub Khan scheduled a Round Table Conference in Rawalpindi in March 1969, bringing together all the major Pakistani political figures. But opposition remained steadfast. With protests and demonstrations convulsing the country, he resigned on March 25, 1969, turning power over to the army's commander in chief, General Agha Muhammad Yahya Khan (r. 1969–71). Yahya Khan proclaimed martial law, but soon announced

"22 FAMILIES"

In a speech in April 1968, noted economist and member of the planning board Mahbub ul Haq (1934–98) spoke out about the concentration of wealth that had occurred during Ayub Khan's regime. He presented data regarding ownership of companies listed on the Karachi Stock Exchange and suggested that 22 families, which he named, controlled two-thirds of the nation's industrial assets. Though he ignored the small- to medium-sized firms that had played a large role in Pakistan's economic growth during the decade, his underlying thesis that the rich had gotten much richer and the poor much poorer during the 1960s struck a responsive chord. From this speech the expression "22 families" entered the political lexicon, shorthand for the income concentration and economic exploitation upon which the economy was built. Zulfikar Bhutto bolstered his populist appeal with frequent blistering verbal attacks against the industrialist families. Haq's speech helped set in motion the thinking and action that led to the nationalization of heavy industries that would occur on January 1, 1972.

general elections would be held in October 1970. However, since the Constitution of 1962 had been voided, there was no legal basis for holding an election.

Talks were held with political figures in April and July 1969 to determine a way to proceed. Most opposition politicians favored a return to the constitution of 1956, believing that it had been illegally abrogated. However, the Awami League opposed this solution, as they did not feel East Pakistan was treated fairly under the Constitution of 1956. Yahya Khan appointed a commission to develop a new plan for a constitution, which was presented in March 1970. Known as the Legal Framework Order 1970, its highlights included the dissolution of the One Unit arrangement in West Pakistan and a restoration of direct balloting in place of parity, which would give the more populous East Pakistan greater representation. Though representatives who won seats in the election were to draft the constitution, the document was to be based on principles defined by the Legal Framework Order.

East Pakistan

Ayub Khan's departure did little to quell the unrest in East Pakistan. The constitution of 1956 had been accepted in the East Wing in the belief that the federal government would take genuine steps to end the economic and political disparities between the two wings. The constitution of 1962 had been forced on the East Wing under Ayub Khan's martial law that prevailed at the time. But as Ayub Khan's power weakened, Bengalis became more restive and vocal.

In an effort to assure fairness in the economic planning process, the economic planning commission developing the Fourth Five-Year Plan established parallel panels of economic experts, one from East Pakistan and one from West Pakistan. Each was to study changes in the nation's economy during the preceding five years and recommend policies and tactics in response. The economists from East Pakistan presented evidence of a widening disparity, requiring profound shifts in policy to reverse the trend. The West Pakistan panel's data indicated the disparity between East and West was quickly evaporating and would be greatly reduced if not eliminated without intervention by the mid-1980s. The opposing views were not reconciled before the draft of the five-year plan was presented in the spring of 1970. But the issue of regional disparity would soon become moot.

As the National Assembly's 1970 elections approached, the Awami League Party presented a six-point program aimed at restoring democracy and advancing East Pakistan's position. It called for a restoration of a parliamentary form of government and for limiting the federal government's role to defense and foreign affairs. It also called for economic and legal reforms to erase the disparities between East and West Pakistan, and for East Pakistan, which had no military force of its own, to have a militia or paramilitary force.

General Elections

No general elections had been held in Pakistan since 1947. The government faced the challenge of registering all eligible voters and preparing for nationwide balloting. Campaigning began on January 1, 1970. When registration was completed in March, 56,941,500 people were on the voter rolls, 31,211,220 of them from East Pakistan, and 25,730,280 from West Pakistan. A total of 1,579 candidates from 24 political parties ran for the 300 National Assembly seats. The Awami League and Zulfikar Bhutto's Pakistan People's Party drew the most public support as the campaign intensified. The Awami League campaigned on its six-point program, while the PPP represented socialistic ideals under the banner of "Rotti, Kapra aur Makan" (Food, Clothing, and Shelter). Bhutto also called for a 1,000-year war against India. Religious parties such as Jamaat-i-Islami, or Islamic Party, campaigned on a platform of greater Islamization for the country, while leftist parties promoted regional and socialist agendas.

Elections for the National Assembly were scheduled for October 5, and for provincial assemblies, October 19. However, due to floods and cyclones in East Pakistan, elections had to be rescheduled and were not completed until January 17, 1971. When the election results were tabulated, the Awami League, led by Mujibur Rahman, won a stunning victory and emerged as Pakistan's major political power, winning 160 of the National Assembly's 300 seats. The Awami League also won 288 of the 300 seats in the East Pakistan assembly, though it won no seats in any of West Pakistan's four provincial assemblies. The PPP won 81 of the 138 seats in the National Assembly reserved for West Pakistan, making it the dominant power in that wing.

Civil War

With a clear majority in the National Assembly, the Awami League was entitled to form the government. But Zulfikar Bhutto refused to permit Mujibur Rahman to become prime minister, or to accept Mujibur

Rahman's Six Points. Bhutto also refused to take part in scheduled meetings in the National Assembly to frame a new constitution. Finally, in an effort to find a solution, Mujibur Rahman and Bhutto, along with Yahya Khan, met in Dhaka on March 3, 1971. They failed to find common ground. Mujibur Rahman immediately mounted a noncooperation movement. The action paralyzed the government in the east. Public transportation was brought to a halt, and factories and businesses closed. Citizens withheld taxes. The Awami League established a shadow government to take the place of the state's administrative apparatus. A provisional Awami League army, the Mukti Bahini, incited public protest and violence.

The floods that had devastated Bengal and caused the postponement of elections in the East Wing brought worldwide attention to the impoverished and backward region and helped foster the view in the international community that East Pakistan had suffered from the indifference and rapacious policies of West Pakistan.

Seeking to defuse the growing crisis, General Yahya Khan announced the National Assembly would convene in Dhaka, East Pakistan, in March. In answer, Mujibur Rahman called for an immediate end to martial law and a transfer of power to newly elected representatives before the assembly convened as well as other demands. The demands led to the postponement of the meeting of the National Assembly. In its place the Awami League called for a Resistance Day to take place on March 23, the Republic Day of Pakistan.

Yahya Khan traveled to Dhaka during this period, ostensibly to negotiate a resolution to the crisis with Mujibur Rahman and West Pakistani political leaders, but making no real effort to reach a political settlement with the East Pakistani leadership. By then the excesses committed by the military against East Pakistani citizens under martial law had poisoned the atmosphere for a peaceful resolution. Without proclaiming the negotiations fruitless, Yahya Khan left Dhaka secretly on March 25, leaving orders for the armed forces to launch an offensive to restore order as soon as he arrived back in Karachi. That night Pakistani forces launched Operation Searchlight, a rampage through the East Wing. Thousands were killed, and Mujibur Rahman was arrested and taken to West Pakistan. The next day, March 26, an Awami League official announced that the East Wing was claiming independence under the name Bangladesh. This is now the nation's Independence Day. Awami League militants took up arms, and on March 27 Yahya Khan sent in troops to put down the revolution. Hundreds of thousands of Bangladeshis were killed as a result of the conflict, and some 10 million refugees fled to the neighboring Indian state of West Bengal.

In response to the refugee crisis India invaded the former East Pakistan to engage the Pakistani armed forces on November 21, 1971. Members of the Mukti Bahini allied themselves with the Indian forces against the Pakistani troops. Yahya Khan failed to appreciate the vigor with which India would try to take advantage of the instability, a weakness that contributed to his lackadaisical attitude toward finding a political solution to the crisis. Even before their full-scale invasion, Indian troops trained the Mukti Bahini and launched guerrilla raids into East Pakistan to take on Pakistani forces. Additionally, a military alliance treaty India concluded with the Soviet Union in August 1971 gave the Indian armed forces greater power.

Pakistan's army found itself in an unwinnable conflict from the beginning, but Yahya Khan made no effort to seek relief from the UN Security Council. Indian troops were advancing on Dhaka, but the Pakistani army had no defensive plan in place. The conflict spread to Kashmir, where Indian and Pakistani troops crossed the cease-fire line, and into West Pakistan itself as Indian troops invaded Punjab and Sind. With the situation deteriorating daily, on December 6, 1971, Yahya Khan resigned and appointed a civilian government. Nurul Amin, a prominent politician from Bengal and opponent of the Awami League, was named prime minister (r. Dec. 1971).

Later that December Bengali freedom fighters aided by Indian forces entered Dhaka, surrounding the main Pakistani forces under the command of General Amir Abdullah Khan Niazi (1915–2004). While it was later determined the Pakistan army could have held out for at least two weeks, General Niazi chose to surrender. On December 17 a formal offer of surrender was agreed upon by the United Nations. Some 45,000 troops from West Pakistan and a similar number of civilians from the west were taken as prisoners of war. The majority of the killings of civilians by the Mukti Bahini occurred after the army's surrender. So did a wave of discontent in what remained of Pakistan over the miscalculations and mismanagement of the civil war by its leaders.

10

BETWEEN EAST AND WEST
(1971–1988)

he simultaneous loss of its East Wing and the defeat in its war with India was a devastating blow to Pakistan, leaving many citizens stunned and angry. The presidency of Zulfikar Ali Bhutto, leader of the Pakistan People's Party (PPP), which replaced the discredited Yahya Khan regime, promised a peaceful, progressive period. But corruption charges and scandal ultimately led to widespread unrest, opening the door to another period of military rule. General Zia ul-Haq seized power in the name of restoring public order, suspended promised elections, and set the country on an Islamic course. It was during this period that the Soviet Union invaded Afghanistan. Pakistan became a key ally of the United States in a massive covert program to raise and equip an army of Islamic fighters to battle the Soviet forces. The ties forged between Pakistan's intelligence apparatus and the mujahideen would have important consequences as the specter of global terrorism arose at the end of the century. The lives of the leaders during this turbulent period came to violent ends. Bhutto's ended with his hanging in 1977 after a show trial. Zia ul-Haq was killed in a plane crash in 1987, an accident whose cause was never determined.

Zulfikar Bhutto's Regime

Zulfikar Bhutto was at the United Nations to speak to the Security Council about the crisis in Bengal when Yahya Khan resigned on December 6, 1971. He returned to Pakistan on December 18 and on December 20 was named president (r. 1971–77) as well as the civilian chief martial law administrator.

With its East Wing gone, the rationale for Pakistan's existence—a homeland for the subcontinent's Muslims—seemed hollow. Pakistan had lost more than half of its population—70 million people—and more than 54,000 square miles of its territory. While those in Bangladesh rejoiced at their independence, Pakistanis in the West Wing reacted in shock and anger, venting their rage at the armed forces and the government. In one of his first official acts, Bhutto addressed the nation and vowed to rebuild Pakistan and restore its pride.

War Investigation

The same week he was named president, Bhutto convened a commission to determine the causes of the military and political disaster Pakistan had suffered in Bengal, placing the chief justice of the Supreme Court, Hamoodur Rahman (served 1968–85), as head of the fact-finding body. More than 200 officials were interviewed, but the report, issued in July 1972, was classified and not made public. By this time Bhutto had been able to sway the public to accept recent events and welcome Bangladesh. At a mammoth public meeting in Karachi in February 1972 he sought approval for releasing Mujibur Rahman, still in jail for agitating for now-realized Bengali independence, from prison.

In 1974 the investigation was reopened and a supplemental report issued, though this too remained classified for more than 25 years. In 2000 a copy of the initial and supplemental report appeared in the Indian press, and, with its contents unveiled, Pakistan authorized publication. The long-suppressed report included accounts of atrocities against West Pakistanis committed by militants from the Awami League, as well as by Bengali members of Pakistan's armed forces against West Wing officers. When news of these atrocities reached West Pakistani troops during the war, they responded by committing atrocities of their own against Bengali officers and soldiers as well as civilian Bengalis and Hindus. The report also found the army guilty of mass killings of intellectuals and professionals and of the rape of large numbers of East Pakistani women. It recommended that the military officers deemed responsible for dereliction of duty be tried publicly.

The report concluded the military defeat was the result of systemic failures of political as well as military processes. A lack of courage among senior army commanders was identified as a key reason for the Pakistani army's defeat. So too were the effects of martial law, which had corrupted the military by allowing officers to neglect military duties in favor of acquiring wealth and property under its cloak.

The number of casualties of the war is unknown, but it has been estimated at least 300,000—the majority of them Hindus, whom West Pakistanis believed were principally behind the independence movement—died in the conflict.

The Simla Agreement

In the immediate aftermath of the war, India held some 93,000 Pakistani troops and civilians as prisoners of war. To win their release, Bhutto met Indian prime minister Indira Gandhi (r. 1966–77, 1980–84) at Simla, in northern India, in late June 1972 and agreed to recognize Bangladesh. India dropped plans to try some 200 soldiers accused of war crimes. The parties signed the Simla Agreement in early July, pledging to use peaceful means to settle differences between the two nations in the future. Both countries also agreed to pull back their troops in Jammu and Kashmir to their respective sides of the internationally recognized border and withdraw from other occupied territories seized in the war. India relinquished more than 5,000 square miles of Pakistani territory it held, and Pakistan relinquished about 70 square miles of Indian territory under its control. The agreement also stipulated the countries resume economic and diplomatic relations. Almost two years later, on February 22, 1974, Pakistan formally recognized Bangladesh, announced at the Islamic Conference in Lahore with the leaders of Islamic nations in attendance.

Bhutto's Policies

Though he had championed restoration of democracy, Bhutto initially retained martial law. In March 1972 Bhutto gained effective control over the military by putting officers loyal to him in command of the army and air force. He pushed through an interim constitution that gave him expanded powers. He initially allowed formation of non-PPP-led governments in the areas of NWFP and Baluchistan, but within a few months dismissed these local governments, alleging foreign powers held undue influence over them. He also banned the National Awami Party, the primary voice of the political opposition.

Bhutto set the nation on a more economically socialist and politically nonaligned course. In an attempt to break up the concentration of wealth symbolized in the expression "22 families" in early 1972 Bhutto nationalized 10 heavy industries, including steel, chemicals, and cement. In March he unveiled large-scale land reforms. Since 1959 landholdings had been restricted to 500 acres for irrigated land and 1,000 acres for nonirrigated land. To further break up large estates and make more land available to peasants, the Bhutto government limited ownership of agricultural land to a maximum of 150 acres for irrigated and 300 acres for nonirrigated land. Rights of tenant farmers were also strengthened.

On the foreign-policy front Bhutto terminated Pakistan's membership in the Commonwealth of Nations and SEATO and recognized the Communist nations of East Germany, North Korea, and North Vietnam. Soon after taking office, he commenced a tour of 20 countries. The display of solidarity with international leaders bolstered the spirit of Pakistanis devastated by the civil war.

Bhutto pursued a policy of bilateralism, maintaining good relations with all nations by eschewing alliances with any. The policy's purpose was to facilitate relations with the three competing major powers: China, the Soviet Union, and the United States. Early in 1972 he visited China and the Soviet Union; the United States, concerned about his policies of nationalization of private industries, was less welcoming to Bhutto when he visited in September 1973.

Now that Bengal was no longer part of Pakistan, Islamabad's standing as the nation's capital was unquestioned. When Bhutto summoned the members of the National Assembly to session in the spring of 1972, they met in Islamabad in a building borrowed from the State Bank of Pakistan. It was here that the constitution of 1973, the nation's third, was created and voted into law.

Unrest in Baluchistan

Baluchistan, with its tradition of independence and aspirations for autonomy, was inspired by the birth of Bangladesh. The Baluchi tribes, spread across Central Asia, had been separated by international borders in the 19th century when boundaries between Iran, Afghanistan, and British India were established, disrupting their nomadic life and culture. A large portion of Pakistan's mineral and energy resources were located in Baluchistan, but the local population, among the poorest in Pakistan, benefited little from the wealth of natural resources. The Baluchi were unhappy with the growing number of miners, traders, and settlers, mostly from Punjab, migrating to Baluchistan to explore these resources. The frustration and anger erupted in an insurgency in 1973 led by the Baluch People's Liberation Organization. Many of the most committed nationalists had communist leanings and considered seeking protection from the Soviet Union to guarantee the security of the independent Baluchistan they envisioned. The core of the insurgency was small, but as the conflict wore on, the appeal of its message grew.

Pakistan's government and military were still reeling from the loss of Bangladesh. The officer corps was in disarray and the troops ill-equipped, and the political leadership unsure of its direction.

Afghanistan was a close ally of India, and India was ruled by the resolute and implacable Indira Gandhi. Bhutto and others were concerned the Baluchi nationalists might receive support from the Afghan, Indian, or Soviet governments.

The shah of Iran, Mohammad Reza Pahlavi (r. 1941–79), eager to keep the insurgency from spreading to Baluchis in Iran, reportedly promised that should India give them assistance, the Iranian army would battle alongside Pakistani troops in Baluchistan. With the pledge of help from Iran, Bhutto used harsh methods to suppress the insurrection. The Pakistan army waged full-scale warfare against the insurgents, deploying Huey-Cobra helicopter gunships supplied and flown by the Iranians.

Bhutto gained public support for the war. Punjabis, who were targets of the insurgents' hostility, backed Bhutto. The threat of loss of another major piece of the nation, so soon after the loss of the East Wing, also helped solidify public backing. Western governments feared an independent Baluchistan allied with Moscow would give the Soviet Union its long-sought warm-water port, Baluchistan's port of Gwadar. The Soviet Union, which saw Bhutto as a friendly leader, did not want to alienate a potentially important client state. Afghanistan seemed eager to normalize relations with Pakistan and so refrained from supporting the Baluchi cause. And India did not want to see further fragmentation of the subcontinent and the instability that could accompany it. Bhutto's harsh methods ultimately quelled the opposition. Many involved in the movement sought sanctuary in Afghanistan and the Soviet Union as well as in the United Kingdom and France. But the insurrection did not end until 1977, after Bhutto had been removed from office. The regime of General Muhammad Zia ul-Haq, which deposed Bhutto's, used economic inducements to win the hearts and minds of the Baluchis and tamp down secessionist aspirations.

The Constitution of 1973

Bhutto oversaw the drafting of the nation's third constitution, accomplished with the cooperation of opposition parties, and was able to reach consensus on the fractious issues of provincial autonomy, Islam's place in government, and the nature of the federal government. The constitution declared the nation to be a federal republic; it continued to be known as the Islamic Republic of Pakistan. In place of the One Unit system that had been adopted in part to mollify East Pakistan, the nation was to have four provinces: Punjab, Sind, NWFP, and

Baluchistan. Islam was declared the state religion. The government would be a bicameral parliamentary system consisting of the National Assembly and the Senate. Members of these bodies would choose the president, who would serve a five-year term and be limited to two terms. The president would appoint a governor for each province and also appoint the attorney general, supreme and high court judges, and the chief election commissioner. The prime minister would appoint federal ministers from among members of Parliament. The constitution guaranteed citizens fundamental rights of life, liberty, equality, freedom of speech, and freedom of association. Unlike the previous constitution, which gave the president absolute power, this version made the prime minister the key power. It placed the military under civilian authority in an effort to prevent coups, which had previously brought military rulers to the presidency.

The constitution of 1973 was also more Islamic in nature than the two previous constitutions had been. It created an Islamic advisory council, the Council of Islamic Ideology, to ensure all laws were in keeping with the tenets of Islam. as had the constitution of 1962. However, it also mandated the government take further steps to promote Islam. These included making the teaching of the Qur'an compulsory in schools; making the government responsible for organizing the collection of *zakat,* or charitable donations, which Islam requires; and making the state responsible for preventing gambling and prostitution, which the religion forbids.

The constitution took effect on August 14, 1973, Pakistan's 26th anniversary. The passage of the new constitution was followed by elections in the legislative bodies for president, prime minister, and other key leadership posts. Bhutto resigned as president, and members of the National Assembly and the Senate elected him prime minister. He was sworn into office on August 14, 1973. Fazal Ilahi Chaudhry was elected president (r. 1973–78). Fazal Ilahi Chaudhry wielded no real power, as the constitution vested almost all authority in the prime minister.

Growing Repression

Pakistan appeared to be back on a democratic course. But Bhutto continued to use the powers of his office to undermine and battle the opposition on any disagreement. Amendments to the constitution adopted during his rule reflected the changing tenor of the Bhutto regime. The first recognized Bangladesh, following an accord on mutual recognition reached between the countries in early 1974; formal diplomatic relations would not be established until two years later. A second amendment was passed to win favor from religious parties. That amendment was adopted when a battle over the Ahmadiyya movement resurfaced in the fall of 1974. Seeking to bolster his credentials with the religious establishment, Bhutto issued a resolution passed by the National Assembly proclaiming the Ahmadiyya to be a non-Muslim sect. Legislation was later adopted that made it illegal for Ahmadiyya to call themselves Muslims or use Muslim terminology in reference to their faith. They were not, for example, allowed to call their place of worship a mosque. A third amendment adopted limited the rights of detainees, and a fourth, in 1976, curtailed the rights of political opponents of the ruling party as Bhutto's rule became increasingly autocratic.

Reluctant to use the military in his politics of repression, given the armed forces' history of coups, Bhutto created the Federal Security Force (FSF), a paramilitary police corps. Drawing on retired military officers and senior police personnel, the force worked closely with the staff of the prime minister. At first deployed to maintain law and order in situations beyond the capabilities of the police, in time the security force was used for gathering political intelligence and allegedly disrupting the activities of political opposition groups.

A Socialist Economy

For all the efforts of Ayub Khan's economic development plans in the early 1960s, by the end of his regime real wages had declined, poverty increased, and income was concentrated in the hands of a burgeoning industrial elite. At the time Bhutto took office, Pakistan was operating at a deficit, importing far more than it exported. The loss of East Pakistan added to the challenge facing the country's economy. To redress Pakistan's international trade imbalance, Bhutto's government devalued the rupee by more than half—58 percent—in relation to the U.S. dollar soon after coming to power. Pakistani goods became cheaper on the international market, and imported goods cost more. But devaluation also made paying off debts to international banks more expensive, and it stimulated inflation.

Zulfikar Bhutto's economic policies reflected his populist platform, an approach he called "Islamic socialism." More socialist than Islamic, it included land and labor reform initiatives, nationalization of industries and major business sectors, and efforts to alleviate economic inequities and improve social services. But draping the economic policy under the mantle of Islam minimized attacks from rightists who objected to socialism. Moreover, the message was malleable: Islam could be

208

stressed to religious constituencies, socialism to industrial workers, and land reform to Sind's rural lower classes. Bhutto also saw the policy as similar to those practiced in Algeria, Egypt, Iraq, and Syria, which he admired. Bhutto's blend helped win support across a spectrum of classes and interest groups.

Carrying through on his nationalization agenda, in 1972 the government took control of more than 31 large companies in 10 basic industries: iron and steel, basic metals, heavy engineering, motor vehicle assembly and manufacture, tractor assembly and manufacture, heavy and basic chemicals, petrochemicals, cement and public utilities. The nationalization was undertaken in part to reduce the hold Pakistan's 22 wealthiest families, who controlled these industries, had on the country's economy and political power. Banks were also nationalized, as were 32 life insurance companies. Credit policies for small farmers and small businesses and entrepreneurs were eased.

That same year Bhutto lowered the maximum limit on individual ownership of land from about 500 irrigated to 150 irrigated acres,

Zulfikar Bhutto nationalized heavy industries and other large companies in Pakistan, such as this oil refinery in Karachi. (Courtesy Pakistan Tourism Development Corporation)

and from about 1,000 to 300 unirrigated acres. However, loopholes enabled many landowners, including the Bhutto family, among the largest landowners in Sind, to retain their lands. Laws governing the landlord-tenant relationship were amended to prevent evictions and outlaw free labor. The rights of workers and trade unions were strengthened.

After the government nationalized industrial facilities such as this one in Taxila, many required significant public investment, which created a drag on the economy. (Courtesy Pakistan Tourism Development Corporation)

Bhutto also introduced educational reforms, making education through high school free and providing allowances to unemployed college graduates. He also mandated admission quotas to public universities, ensuring that students from rural areas had access to college degrees.

Higher oil prices following OPEC's 1973 oil embargo, along with natural disasters including floods and an earthquake, also impacted the economy during Bhutto's rule. The floods affected crops and boosted prices, and in response the cotton and rice export trade were nationalized. Flour-, rice-, and cotton-processing businesses were nationalized in 1976.

Owing to nationalization, the role of the public sector in the economy increased dramatically. In 1972 the public sector contributed 3 percent to the nation's output. By 1976 the figure rose to 13 percent, and a full 20 percent of nonagricultural output. The costs of nationalization, which included large investments in acquired industries and businesses, financed with international loans, quickly became a drag on the economy. By 1974 Pakistan was unable to make its debt payments on the loans, commencing ongoing payment rescheduling efforts by Pakistan over the next several years. This basic restructuring also caused widespread economic dislocation. Many left the country to look for work in the Middle East, Europe, and the United States. Remittances sent back to Pakistan from these émigrés helped bolster the country's economy during the Bhutto years.

The government experienced perennial budget deficits during Bhutto's rule. To finance them, money was printed, adding to inflationary pressures. The economic results of nationalization and of the investments made in formerly private enterprises are difficult to determine. In some cases investments made in these industries, for example in fertilizer and cement production, during the Bhutto regime did not begin to pay off until Zia ul-Haq's regime.

Overall the economy under his stewardship was characterized by stagnation. Industrial output increased only 2.1 percent annually, and agricultural output 2.3 percent annually during Bhutto's years in power.

The Elections of 1977

As Bhutto's rule continued, his authoritarian manner and efforts to suppress political opposition eroded public support. Charges of corruption and mismanagement grew, fueled by the country's imploding economy and rising level of inflation. Bhutto was also held responsible by some for having caused the crisis that led to the loss of East Pakistan. By 1977 the middle class was disillusioned with the Bhutto regime. General elections were scheduled to be held in the latter half of 1977, but in January Bhutto announced the dates for the election would be moved up. A week later, the chief election commissioner announced that all nominations for the National Assembly and the provincial assemblies had to be filed by January 19 and 22, respectively. Bhutto expected the opposition would be unprepared, and, indeed, the accelerated timetable hampered the ability of the opposition to field candidates as well as to register them. Bhutto immediately plunged into campaigning, allying himself not only with the disadvantaged, who had been the core strength of the PPP, but also with feudal lords. To bolster his support among the commoners, Bhutto announced new land reforms.

Rather than battle Bhutto and his party individually, nine opposition parties united under the banner of the Pakistan National Alliance (PNA). They campaigned on an anti-Bhutto platform, charging him with corruption and mismanagement while simultaneously claiming the Qur'an, the Muslim holy book, as their political as well as spiritual inspiration. The PNA generated surprisingly large support during the campaign. The political establishment, which was increasingly unpopular, displayed overt anti-PNA bias, enhancing the party's appeal among large numbers of voters. Public PNA rallies drew immense crowds. But in the elections for the National Assembly, held on March 7, Bhutto's PPP took the majority of seats and the PNA won only 36, a surprisingly poor showing given the crowds the PNA had drawn during the campaign. The PNA protested, claiming widespread election fraud and intimidation, and demanded new elections to be held under the supervision of the armed forces. The PNA also boycotted the provincial assembly elections. The resounding victory of the PPP in these elections—in some areas winning more votes than there were voters—bolstered the charges of corruption leveled by the PPP's opponents.

Bhutto rejected demands for new elections, and in response the PNA called for nationwide strikes and protests, which had the support of religious and business groups. Bhutto met the opposition with defiance. PNA leaders were jailed and martial law was declared in Karachi, Lahore, and Hyderabad, while major cities throughout the country were put under curfew. In May and June battles between PNA supporters and government security forces became particularly violent. Bhutto's repressive tactics failed to end the standoff. He shifted to a more conciliatory tone and had some of the PNA's leaders released from jail, initiating negotiations with them in June. Bhutto offered to hold new elections in November and promised the PNA five ministerial positions for their party until then. But the PNA demanded half of all cabinet positions and that elections be held before mid-August. Bhutto finally agreed to meet almost all the PNA's terms, but before formalizing the agreement he left Pakistan for a tour of Saudi Arabia, Libya, the United Arab Emirates, Kuwait, and Iran. His opponents viewed the trip as a delaying tactic.

Zia ul-Haq's Coup d'État

The army was called in to restore order in major cities. With the impasse threatening to incite anarchy across the country, on July 5, 1977, General Muhammad Zia ul-Haq (1924–88) arrested Bhutto and members of his cabinet and imposed martial law. The constitution was suspended and all legislative bodies dissolved. It was the country's third military coup.

Muhammad Zia ul-Haq was born to a middle-class family in East Punjab in 1924. Schooled in India and a veteran of the British Indian Army, where he attended officer-training school, he chose to join the Pakistani army upon partition. He later trained in the United States and, while working his way up to the rank of lieutenant general, developed a reputation as a professional soldier with little interest in politics. Furthermore, he had little affinity with most other high-level officers, many of whom came from northern areas of Pakistan, which had been favored recruiting grounds for the British. Given the history of military interference with civilian rule, Bhutto had been cognizant of the potential threat represented by the armed forces and had chosen Zia ul-Haq as army chief of staff in part because of his background.

General Zia ul-Haq seized power from Zulfikar Bhutto in a military coup in July of 1977, becoming Pakistan's leader under martial law. (Courtesy Pakistan Tourism Development Corporation)

Zia initially kept an appearance of civilian rule. The constitution

213

was suspended rather than abrogated. Zia announced that elections, overseen by the military, would be held within 90 days under "Operation Fairplay," but this pledge went unfulfilled. He disbanded the FSF, Bhutto's security force, and established a committee to investigate irregularities in the election.

Bhutto's End

Zulfikar Bhutto was released from detention on July 29, 1977, little less than a month after his arrest. Though removed from office, Bhutto was initially allowed to remain in politics. He embarked on a series of political rallies across Pakistan and proclaimed that those responsible for the military takeover would face legal consequences once he was restored to power. The constitution of 1973 made a coup d'état a capital offense punishable by death, and Bhutto left no doubt of his intention to seek such redress. Thus, the military was reluctant to allow him the chance to regain power.

The committee investigating the election irregularities reported finding a document in Bhutto's home, prepared in 1976, that it described as a blueprint for election fraud. Entitled "A Model Election Plan," it became known as the "Larkana Plan." The chief election commissioner later blamed the PPP candidates for using the power of their offices to circumvent election laws.

In early September 1977 Bhutto was rearrested and, though briefly released, was eventually brought to trial on charges that included conspiracy to murder a political opponent. The director-general of the FSF, Masood Mahmood (served ca. 1972–77) was implicated in the murder and pleaded guilty. His deposition formed the bulk of the case against Bhutto. The trial began in October and lasted into the new year. Much of the evidence presented seemed questionable and the witnesses for the prosecution unreliable. Nonetheless, in March 1978 the Lahore high court found Bhutto guilty and sentenced him to death. An appeal was rejected by the Supreme Court in early 1979, and on April 4 Bhutto was hanged in Rawalpindi's central jail.

By the time of his execution Bhutto had ceased to be a factor in Pakistani politics. In February 1978 political leaders had gathered for a conference to discuss restoration of civilian rule and democracy. But Zia had no intention of giving up his rule. In September, as Bhutto faced trial, Zia had taken the title of president (r. 1978–88) and made the martial law administrator of each province its governor. He was the nation's sixth president, and the third to assume the office in the aftermath of staging a military coup. In early 1979 Zia disbanded political parties and disenfranchised some politicians.

While Bhutto had been vanquished, his party, the PPP, had not. Bhutto's oldest child, Benazir Bhutto (1953–2007), became its leader. Zia and his regime set out to neutralize the party's power and to restructure the political process to ensure the PPP's impotence. From 1979 to 1985 Zia engaged in numerous maneuvers to achieve this objective, from strategic alliances with PPP opponents to cancellation of elections.

Zia's rule was marked by economic growth in the private sector and the growing influence of Islamic parties on the government. Responsibility for the economy was turned over to Ghulam Ishaq Khan (1915–2006). Pakistan had been without a coherent economic strategy since the early 1970s. The five-year plan in place at that time was shelved, made irrelevant after East Pakistan's secession. Zulfikar Bhutto's restructuring of the economy was conducted without a road map. It was not until July 1, 1978, that the next and Fifth Five-Year Plan (1978–83) was instituted, one year into Zia ul-Haq's imposition of martial law. The plan's stated goal was improving the reach and quality of social services. With the budget stretched by investments in the public sector, the new plan curtailed industrial and infrastructure expansion, focusing its spending on works in progress. However, development funds were also earmarked for agricultural projects, including investments in water resources and loans and subsidies for farmers. Economic planners were counting on a healthy return on investment. During the first five years of the 1970s Pakistan's GDP had increased 4.1 percent annually. The fifth plan called for a 7.0 percent annual growth in GDP, fueled by a projected 10 percent annual increase in industrial growth and 6 percent increase in agricultural output. The plan also provided a blueprint and timetable for bringing the economic and financial sectors of the country in line with Islamic principles.

Relations with the United States improved during Zia's rule as well. The Iranian Revolution had brought a virulently anti-U.S. Shi'i regime to power in Tehran, and the United States needed friends in the region. Pakistan, dominated by Sunnis, also saw a threat across the border in Iran. The Soviet invasion of Afghanistan in December 1979 was another catalyst for the suddenly strong relationship.

Pakistan and Islam

Since the republic's inception, the role of Islam in the government had been hotly debated. Pakistan was founded as a parliamentary democracy, with Islam as the state religion, although the constitution allowed freedom of religion to the members of other faiths. Jinnah, the father of the nation, wanted separation from the subcontinent's Hindu majority not because he thought Pakistan should be a theocracy but because he saw it as a refuge where Muslims could be free to pursue their religion as they wished. Zia, however, tried to bolster the influence of Islamic parties and the ulama on government and society. With the tacit support of the United States, which sought to undermine the Soviet regime in Afghanistan, he encouraged the formation and activities of militant extremist groups.

In his first speech to the nation, Zia pledged the government would work to create a true Islamic society. A federal sharia council, or religious law court, was created to determine cases based on the teachings of the Qur'an and the Sunna, the book of traditions of the Prophet's sayings and deeds from which much of Islamic law is derived. A sharia council was appointed to bring the state's legal statutes into alignment with Islamic doctrine. To address the Islamic prohibition against charging or paying interest, or *riba*, a system of profit-and-loss sharing was instituted on January 1, 1980, whereby account holders would share in their banks' profits and losses. Efforts to enforce the Islamic tenets of praying five times each day were adopted, and public eating and drinking during the holy month of Ramadan was outlawed.

The general also introduced the Islamic *hadood* into Pakistani law, which deals with the drinking and manufacturing of alcohol, theft, adultery, false accusations of adultery, and highway robbery. The Hadood Ordinance passed into law by Zia in February 1979 stipulated that punishments for crimes would be consistent with those called for under traditional Islamic jurisprudence, including floggings, amputations, and death by stoning. Women were particularly vulnerable under the third ordinance, as a woman who became pregnant as the result of rape could be charged with adultery. Furthermore, a woman's testimony was deemed only half as reliable as that of a man. Thus, the testimony of two women was required to rebut the testimony of one man under the revised legal code.

Islamic scholars were retained to devise laws pertaining to financing and the economy that would incorporate Islamic principles. The Zakat and Ushr Ordinance that resulted was adopted in June 1980. *Zakat,* or alms for the poor, would be deducted at the rate of 2.5 percent per year from all Muslims' bank accounts holding more than 3,000 rupees. For those who held land or cultivated crops, *ushr* in cash or crops would be levied at 10 percent of the land's yield. *Zakat* committees were established to oversee the distribution of the collected funds.

In 1986 the penalty for blasphemy against the prophet Muhammad was raised from life in prison to death. Islamic studies and Arabic became compulsory courses for many degree programs. The media was directed to present the news in Arabic on both television and radio, and female announcers were required to cover their heads. In the armed forces, religious teachers were elevated to the rank of commissioned officers.

However, the country's citizens began to chafe and protest at the increasing Islamization of their nation, and Zia had to stop short of adopting sharia as the law of the land; with their limited jurisdiction the sharia courts had primarily affected Muslim personal law and religious issues. Yet with the Soviet invasion of Afghanistan, Islam was seen as being threatened by infidel forces just across the border, giving added power to the general's call for governing Pakistan on Islamic ideals.

Nuclear Program

In May 1974 India became a nuclear power when it detonated a nuclear device underground with an estimated yield of 15 kilotons. Although India claimed that it did not have plans for nuclear weapons, the development was profoundly disturbing to Pakistan. After India's nuclear test, Pakistan proposed to India that South Asia be declared a nuclear weapons–free zone, but India declined. As the minister of power, fuel, and natural resources, Zulfikar Bhutto instituted a nuclear weapons development program in response.

Pakistan had had a research reactor in operation at Parr, in Rawalpindi, since 1965, and its nuclear ambitions—or at least consideration of its options—preceded Bhutto's tenure. When the United Nation's Treaty on the Non-Proliferation of Nuclear Weapons, created to staunch the spread of nuclear weapons, was completed in 1968, Pakistan declined to become a signatory, as did India and China.

Pakistan was the beneficiary of aid from the United States through the United States's Foreign Assistance Act of 1961. In an effort to put pressure on Pakistan to stop its nuclear weapons program, the U.S. Congress passed the first of several amendments to the act that prohibited assistance to countries for weapons development. The Symington Amendment, passed in 1976, banned assistance to any country trafficking in nuclear-enrichment technology outside of international controls. In 1979 Pakistan was found in violation of the Symington Amendment by U.S. president Jimmy Carter (r. 1977–81) for clandestinely building a uranium-enrichment plant. U.S. assistance was cut off. The sanctions had little impact in stopping the program. A 1983 U.S. government assessment concluded there was unambiguous evidence that Pakistan was actively pursuing a nuclear weapons capability. The U.S. Congress passed the Pressler Amendment in 1985, requiring that before Pakistan could receive aid, the president had to certify annually that Pakistan had no nuclear device. However, the president was given the power to waive sanctions when such action was perceived to be in the nation's interest. In fact, soon after assistance to Pakistan was cut off in 1979, regional events would prove to Pakistan that the United States could quickly change its priorities and policies.

Soviet Invasion of Afghanistan

In late December 1979 Leonid Brezhnev (r. 1964–82), general secretary of the Communist Party of the Soviet Union and the country's de facto leader, ordered Soviet forces to invade Afghanistan in support of the Soviet-allied regime of Hafizullah Amin (r. Sept.–Dec. 1979), whose government was under attack from tribal resistance groups. The invasion was supposed to be a quick surgical operation aimed at securing Kabul, the Afghan capital, and primary communication lines linking the country and the Soviet Union. But the Soviets wanted an even more compliant leader and on December 28 had Amin assassinated. Babrak Karmal (r. 1979–86), a Soviet protégé and puppet, was installed as president.

In response to the invasion President Carter canceled U.S. participation in the 1980 Summer Olympics, held in Moscow; put the SALT (Strategic Arms Limitation Talks) II missile treaty on hold; and reduced contracted shipments of grain to the Soviet Union. However, caught up in the Iranian hostage crisis, he was unable to take more decisive steps. Six months prior Carter had signed a secret directive authorizing assistance to the rebels fighting the Communist government in Afghanistan. After the Soviet invasion the United States encouraged Muslim countries around the world to help with propaganda and covert aid against the Soviets in Afghanistan. The goal was to harness the religious fervor of Muslims who viewed the battle as a holy war against invading infidels.

Pakistan became a major ally of the United States as money and matériel were routed through Pakistan to support the mujahideen, or holy warriors, who were organized to battle the infidel invaders. Pakistan, for its support of U.S. efforts, received most-favored-nation trading status. At the same time some 4 million Afghan war refugees fled into Baluchistan and the NWFP. Pakistan's primary intelligence agency, the Directorate for Inter-Service Intelligence (ISI), served as liaison between the Pakistani and U.S. governments and the mujahideen. Founded in 1948, the ISI's role was expanded under Ayub Khan's rule in the 1950s, when agents were employed in monitoring opposition politicians and supporting the country's martial-law rule.

In 1988 U.S. president Ronald Reagan (r. 1981–89), elected in November 1980, waived the aid sanctions imposed on Pakistan under the Symington Amendment. The assistance from the United States helped Pakistan's economy, removing the financial problems that had beset earlier regimes. The Pakistani army was also able to modernize with a $3.2 billion military-assistance package and U.S.-supplied weapons and training.

Training camps established in Pakistan and Afghanistan trained as many as 100,000 Muslims from dozens of countries. These mujahideen turned Afghanistan into what became known as the Soviet Union's Vietnam, leaving 15,000 Soviets dead and 37,000 wounded by 1989. More than 1 million Afghans died in the war, and 5 million became refugees. After a decade the Soviet Union could no longer afford to continue its losing war in Afghanistan. Negotiations for a withdrawal were conducted under General Zia's auspices, and the agreement ending the conflict, the Geneva Accords, was signed on April 14, 1988. The Soviets withdrew in 1989, leaving behind a shaky Communist regime barely in control of Kabul. When the government in Kabul fell in April 1992, it was regarded by the mujahideen as a grand victory for Islam, and by the West as a major defeat for communism.

But the impact of the war continued to reverberate across Pakistan. Pakistan was beset by the drug trafficking and gunrunning that had helped fund the resistance to the Soviet occupation. Meanwhile, the freedom fighters in Afghanistan turned on each other, transforming the country into a lawless land. Ultimately the Taliban, Islamic fundamentalists, gained control of the country, making it a haven for militant Islamists.

Effects of the War in Baluchistan and NWFP

The influx of Afghan refugees across the border into Baluchistan and NWFP added another destabilizing element to an already volatile territory. Both regions had joined Pakistan for the promise of economic benefit and in the name of Muslim solidarity but had come to feel shortchanged by the arrangement. One source of disaffection in Baluchistan was the inequitable sharing of revenues and benefits from the province's natural resources. Natural gas, for example, discovered in the province in 1953, was fueling cities in Punjab by 1964. But at the time of the Soviet invasion, there was still no pipeline to the Baluchi capital, Quetta, and it would not reach the city until 1986—brought in to supply a military garrison. Moreover, the federal government had long stressed the need for national unity over ethnic identity, and both Baluchis and Pashtun, with their strong cultural roots and tradition of independence, felt the brunt of this policy.

With more than 40 percent of Pakistan's land but only 5 percent of its population, most of them rural poor, the government saw little need to placate Baluchistan's population. The Baluchis represent a plurality but not majority of its inhabitants; Baluchis compose 45 percent, and Pashtun 38 percent, with the rest of the population of mixed or indeterminate ancestry. Though their plurality may be small, Baluchis regard themselves as the dominant power in the province. In NWFP, the Pashtun also agitated for more autonomy, with some calling for an independent Pashtun nation. Ongoing negligence of the provinces by Islamabad fueled the discontent.

The local population supported the war, however, and believed in the jihad against the Soviets. The ISI, Pakistan's intelligence agency, served as the conduit for the support to the mujahideen paid for by the CIA and Saudi Arabia, the two primary underwriters of the war against the Soviets. Though Zia ul-Haq, who endorsed and approved the anti-Soviet jihad, was head of the armed forces, he left direction of the Afghanistan campaign to the ISI. The ISI established camps where mujahideen volunteers trained, and the agency handled all logistical elements of funneling material to the Muslim warlords on the front lines. During this period the ISI, which had been discredited for intelligence lapses during Bangladesh's war of independence, regained its stature and power.

But the war against the Soviets in Afghanistan exacerbated conflicts between the Baluchis and Pashtun. Since the 1980s, more than 2 million Afghan refugees, most of them Pashtun, resettled in Pakistan, one-quarter of them in Baluchistan. The tide of Afghans fleeing over the border into Baluchistan led to charges by Baluchis that they were becoming minorities in their own homeland. Concurrently, with the Pashtun population swelled in the NWFP by the refugees, calls for Pashtun autonomy in the region became louder.

Ethnic tensions continued to build in Baluchistan. In October 1992 clashes between Baluchis and Pashtun erupted, sparked by the creation of

12 new wards in the municipality of Quetta. The Pashtun saw the change as an effort to reduce their representation and aid Baluchis in winning local elections. Baluchi disaffection with the federal government continued as well. In 1998 three Baluchis hijacked a Pakistan International Airlines (PIA) aircraft to draw attention to what they claimed was the discrimination of Baluchis by Pakistan and to protest what they believed were planned tests of nuclear weapons in Baluchistan.

Restoration of Civilian Rule

In 1980, with the National Assembly dissolved, Zia created a Majlis-i-Shoora, a council of handpicked advisers, to provide counsel and an appearance of communal rule. The council included intellectuals, religious scholars, and professionals. Still, calls rose for an end to martial law and elections. In February 1981 the Movement for Restoration of Democracy (MRD) was founded. In March the government established a provisional constitution to replace the constitution of 1973, which had been abrogated by the martial law imposed at the time of Zia's coup.

General Zia sought a way to restore civilian rule while retaining the presidency. Under the Referendum Order of 1984 Zia scheduled a vote on the country's future through which he sought backdoor approval for his continued rule. The referendum asked voters if they approved of the Islamization process Zia had initiated and if they wanted an orderly transfer of power to elected representatives. Zia considered a yes answer to be the equivalent of a vote for his retention as president for five years. The referendum was held on December 19, 1984. Though boycotted by the MRD, General Zia claimed the results validated his continuing rule as president. He then announced that elections for national and provincial assemblies would be held in February 1985, although candidates would run as individuals, not as representatives of any political party.

While the MRD boycotted the elections, the public voted in large numbers. Since many known political opponents were off the ballot because of their boycott, many obscure representatives were elected. This gave the elections a veneer of democracy without Zia having to contend with established opponents in the newly elected national and provincial assemblies.

Following the election Zia nominated Muhammad Khan Junejo (r. 1985–88) as prime minister. Junejo lifted martial law and restored

221

the constitution after extensive amendments were adopted at the behest of Zia that gave the prime minister little maneuvering room. Whereas the constitution of 1973 had vested most of the power in the office of the prime minister, Zia's constitutional changes greatly changed the power equation, elevating the president's position on a par with that of the prime minister. In November 1985 the Senate adopted the Eighth Amendment to the constitution. It gave the president the right to nominate the prime minister, provincial governors, and judges of the supreme and high court. The amendment allowed the president to call referenda on national issues, establish the legislative agenda, and order the prime minister to seek a vote of confidence from the National Assembly. Article 58 2(b), gave the president the right to dissolve the National Assembly at his sole discretion. Thus the government went from a parliamentary to a federal system.

SOUTH ASIAN ASSOCIATION FOR REGIONAL COOPERATION (SAARC)

In 1980 the president of Bangladesh, Ziaur Rahman (r. 1977–81), proposed creating a regional alliance in South Asia to promote greater cooperation among member states and regional peace, stability, and economic development. Representatives of regional states met in 1983 to consider the idea more thoroughly and decided to proceed. In December 1985 the South Asian Association for Regional Cooperation (SAARC) was launched. The seven member states were Pakistan, India, Bangladesh, Bhutan, Maldives, Nepal, and Sri Lanka. Members pledged that all action would be endorsed unanimously. Since then the summit conferences have provided a venue for leaders of these nations to discuss issues on social, economic, cultural, and other policies. A permanent secretariat's office is maintained in Kathmandu, Nepal. Though it has fostered improved regional relations, it has proven less successful as a forum for resolving difficult bilateral regional issues, such as resolution of the Kashmiri conflict. India has consistently declined to endorse calls for using the SAARC for this purpose, as proposed by Pakistan, Bangladesh, and Nepal. As unanimity is required for actions, without India's approval the proposal cannot advance.

Zia's supporters claimed that previous political deadlocks had made the imposition of martial law imperative. Bestowing the power to dissolve the assembly upon the president would ensure such deadlocks would never end in a military takeover again, because the president could now simply dismiss the assembly in the event of such a crisis.

Junejo, despite his diluted power, fulfilled his promises, returning basic freedoms to Pakistanis. In December 1985 Junejo unveiled an ambitious five-point program to set the government and society on a more progressive and egalitarian course. The objectives included economic reforms, social justice, ending corruption, and cutting illiteracy in half. Under the initiative, in rural areas roads were built and villages received electricity.

Unafraid to antagonize powerful interests, Junejo pursued a foreign policy developed with input from leaders across the spectrum of Pakistani politics. After martial law was lifted, generals who had grown accustomed to luxurious perks found their large staff cars replaced by small vehicles. In April 1988, at Ojheri Camp military base near Islamabad, an explosion at a weapons storage facility sent rockets raining down on the city, killing hundreds of civilians. Junejo attempted to investigate the incident, which further inflamed military leaders. He was returning from a visit to South Korea on May 29, 1988, when President Zia dismissed Junejo, his government, and the national and provincial assemblies, using Article 58 2(b) of the constitution to justify his action. Zia claimed a breakdown in law and order had left the government unable to conduct business. General Zia installed a caretaker government and promised elections in 90 days.

Zia's Death

On August 17, 1988, Zia, along with his military secretary, Najib Ahmed; ISI director Akhtar Abdur Rahman; the leadership of the army and other Pakistani officials; as well as the U.S. ambassador to Pakistan, Arnold Raphel (served 1987–88), went to Bhawalpur in Punjab to view a demonstration of tank maneuvers. On the return flight to Islamabad, the C-130 military transport they were aboard crashed shortly after takeoff, killing all 30 people on the aircraft. The cause of the crash was never identified, but suggestions of sabotage were raised. The report of the official inquiry was never released.

Political leaders gathered in Islamabad to determine how to deal with succession. The constitution stipulated that in the event of death, incapacitation, resignation, or removal of the president, the chairman of the Senate, a position held by Ghulam Ishaq Khan (1915–2006), was to take the position until a new president was elected. Military and civilian leaders agreed to proceed as constitutionally mandated. Thus Ishaq Khan assumed the presidency on August 17, 1988, an office he would hold until July 1993.

11

CIVILIAN RULE RESTORED (1988–1999)

General Zia ul-Haq's unexpected death in 1988 brought about a return to civilian rule in Pakistan. Over the next decade a series of leaders struggled to establish firm control over the government. Two rivals came to dominate the political landscape during this period: Benazir Bhutto (1953–2007), daughter of the executed former prime minister, and Nawaz Sharif (b. 1949). Bhutto became the first woman to lead a modern Muslim nation. But her rule, as her father's had been, was marred by charges of corruption, and she was dismissed from office, only to rise once more as prime minister before suffering another tumble from power. Sharif, scion of one of Pakistan's wealthiest families, whose power base was among the landless lower class, also lost and regained his office. Under his leadership the Pakistan Muslim League, the 1962 successor to the disbanded Muslim League, reemerged as a powerful political party. But political infighting again began to immobilize the machinery of state. Fearing another military takeover Sharif attempted to forestall a coup, but, instead, his efforts accelerated it. Once again Pakistan came under martial law and a general's rule, this time in the person of General Pervez Musharraf (b. 1943). Also during this period the still-unsettled Kashmir question again brought Pakistan and India to the brink of war, only this time the presence of nuclear weapons escalated the stakes in the standoff between the countries.

Benazir Bhutto's First Government

On August 17, 1988, Ghulam Ishaq Khan, former chairman of the Senate, succeeded General Zia ul-Haq and became interim president, as stipulated by the constitution. Ishaq Khan established an emergency council of advisers and directed general elections be held in November 1988.

PREPARING FOR DESTINY

The following excerpts from Benazir Bhutto's 1989 autobiography, *Daughter of Destiny*, reveal Bhutto's hopes and fears during the final years of the Zia regime. As Pakistan moved toward elections scheduled for November 1988, a nervous Zia announced a new law that called for nonparty elections. The law was to have been implemented too late for the opposition to challenge it in court. But Zia and 30 others, including the U.S. ambassador to Pakistan and an American general, died in a plane crash while returning to Islamabad from a military base in eastern Pakistan.

I felt confidant as 1987 dawned. . . . [A]fter the long ban on political activities, we were building the PPP as a political institution. Launching a membership drive, we enrolled a million members in four months, a remarkable figure for Pakistan, where the literacy rates are so low. We held party elections in the Punjab—an unheard of phenomenon in the subcontinent—in which over four hundred thousand members voted. We opened a dialogue with the opponents of the Muslim League in the Parliament and continued to highlight the human rights violations of the regime. . . .

On May 29, 1988, General Zia abruptly dissolved Parliament, dismissed his own handpicked Prime Minister, and called for elections. I was at a meeting . . . with party members from Larkana when the startling message was passed to me. "You must be mistaken," I said to the party official who had sent me the note. "General Zia avoids elections. He doesn't hold them.". . .

Regardless, the mood throughout the country was ebullient. Zia's own constitution called for elections within ninety days of the dissolution of the government, and to many it seemed that victory was within reach. . . . "No one can stop the PPP now," said one supporter after another. . . .

On June 15th, Zia announced the installation of Shariah, or Islamic law, as the supreme law of the land. . . . Many thought that the timing of Zia's latest exploitation of Islam was directed at me. The Urdu press was speculating that he could use the interpretation of the law by Islamic bigots to try to prevent me, a woman, from standing for election.

Source: Benazir Bhutto, *Daughter of Destiny*, New York and London: Simon and Schuster, 1989.

Benazir Bhutto, the daughter of former prime minister Zulfikar Bhutto, who had taken over the leadership of the Pakistan People's Party (PPP) after her father's execution in 1979, returned from exile when martial law was lifted in 1986.

After a decade of authoritarian military rule, the return of a Bhutto to Pakistan's political landscape helped energize the democracy movement. Benazir Bhutto was born in Karachi and educated at Radcliffe College in the United States and Oxford University in England. She returned to Pakistan in June 1977 with the intention of entering the foreign service. Two weeks later General Zia ul-Haq staged his coup and arrested Prime Minister Zulfikar Bhutto. Benazir Bhutto spent the next 18 months in and out of house arrest. The execution of her father in 1979 served only to intensify her efforts to coordinate opposition to Zia's regime. In the summer of 1981 she was imprisoned for five months under solitary confinement in Sind. She was released in 1984 and went into exile in London. Her return to Pakistan in 1986 was greeted by a welcoming crowd of hundreds of thousands in Lahore. She began organizing the opposition and calling on Zia to resign and hold national elections.

Had Zia not perished it is possible that the elections he had scheduled would have been canceled or the state apparatus would have been marshaled to ensure his electoral victory. But without him the 1988 election campaign proceeded as planned. The PPP remained unaligned and independent of other political parties. In the November elections the PPP won a majority in Sind, but no party gained a majority in any other province. Nonetheless, the PPP was the only party to have a significant following in all four provinces. Moreover, it was the largest party in the National Assembly, with 94 seats, one of them occupied by newly elected Benazir Bhutto.

Under the Revival of the Constitution of 1973 Order enacted by Zia, the president could appoint any member of the National Assembly as prime minister. With the backing of both the PPP and the Islami Jamhuri Itehad (IJI, or Islamic Democratic Alliance), a coalition of nine parties formed that year to oppose the PPP in elections, Ghulam Ishaq Khan won the legislative election for president on December 13, 1988. Following tradition as well as privilege, Ishaq Khan chose Benazir Bhutto, leader of the dominant party, to form a new government and serve as prime minister.

In order to form a government, Bhutto had to jettison the PPP's non-aligned stance and forge a coalition with the Muhajir Qaumi Mahaz (MQM, or Muhajir National Movement), which represented the *muhajir* (refugees from India following partition) community and several other parties. The MQM agreed to back the PPP at both the national

Benazir Bhutto became the first woman to head a modern Islamic nation when she was sworn in as Pakistan's prime minister on December 2, 1988. (Courtesy Pakistan Tourism Development Corporation)

and the provincial assemblies. Both parties pledged equal protection to all people of Sind, important to the *muhajirs* as they often felt discriminated against by native Sindis.

In her first address to the nation as prime minister, Bhutto presented her vision of a Pakistan that was forward-thinking and democratic but guided by Islamic principles. She announced the release of political prisoners, restoration of press freedoms, and the implementation of stalled educational and healthcare reforms. The ban on student unions and trade unions was lifted. She promised increased provincial autonomy, greater rights for women, and better relations with the United States, Russia, and China. Improved relations with India were pursued in December 1988 at the fourth SAARC Summit Conference, where the path was cleared for the acceptance of three peace agreements between Pakistan and India.

Bhutto's Foreign Policy

The end of the Soviet occupation of Afghanistan, which occurred in the last days of Zia's rule, signaled a change in Pakistan's foreign relations. The Geneva Accords, which ended the war, were signed in April 1988, and the following month Soviet forces began their withdrawal. Border skirmishes continued as mujahideen attacks went on, some staged from Pakistan. But Pakistan had lost its strategic importance in the cold war. Without the cold war, whose end was marked by the collapse of the Berlin Wall in November 1989, the economic and military blandishments both sides had offered Pakistan and other emerging countries had come to an end.

Benazir Bhutto had been a persistent critic of Zia's alliance with the United States and had denounced him for allowing Pakistan to be used as a base for the mujahideen. But after taking office, she attempted to strengthen the country's alliance with the United States. Like her father, Benazir Bhutto was an indefatigable traveler, making frequent trips to meet with heads of state around the world. In June 1989 Bhutto visited the United States to allay fears of Pakistan's nuclear capabilities. She told the administration that Pakistan had no nuclear weapons, but defended her nation's right to pursue its nuclear program. In an address to a joint session of Congress she proclaimed Pakistan's willingness to make a pact with India declaring the subcontinent a nuclear-free zone. Bhutto tried to ease tensions with India while seeking solutions to the disputes—primarily Kashmir—that had bedeviled relations since the birth of the two nations. In 1989 Rajiv Gandhi (r. 1984–89), India's prime minister, visited Bhutto in Islamabad. In talks Bhutto reiterated Pakistan's willingness to make the region a nuclear-free zone, a proposal Gandhi declined to consider.

Bhutto succeeded in gaining readmission to the Commonwealth in 1989, making Pakistan eligible for trading privileges with other dominions, which the country desperately needed. Previous efforts to rejoin had been blocked by India on the grounds that Pakistan was not a democracy, as it was under military rule. With a civilian again in charge of the nation, that objection was voided.

Bhutto's Domestic Policy

Bhutto championed a Western secularist, socialist agenda, eschewing the pro-Islamic policies of the Zia regime. Women's social and health issues were staples of her campaigns. However, her stated policies were rarely translated into action. No legislation to improve welfare services for women was proposed. Campaign promises to repeal Hudood and Zina ordinances, which called for punishments such as amputations for theft and stoning for adultery, went unfulfilled. To be sure, Bhutto faced significant obstacles in advancing any legislative agenda.

229

Much of the decision making remained in the hands of the military and the intelligence agencies, where Zia had placed it. Bhutto was reluctant to challenge these powers, since the military had time and again demonstrated readiness to take over the government when threatened. Perhaps she was fearful as well—the army, after all, was the institution responsible for the execution of her father.

She had also inherited many political enemies of her father's, and Pakistani politics remained as focused on personal power and gamesmanship as on advancing the national interest. A major PPP adversary was Nawaz Sharif, leader of the PML and chief minister of Punjab, the most populous province. The PML and PPP were natural enemies; PPP founder Zulfikar Bhutto had nationalized industries to break the power of Pakistan's wealthiest families, and one of those families was Nawaz Sharif's. Moreover, Nawaz Sharif was a protégé of Zia, the military ruler who had Zulfikar Bhutto hanged. Benazir Bhutto spent an inordinate amount of time and effort trying to oust Nawaz Sharif from his post in the Punjab. Another problem Bhutto faced was in the person of President Ghulam Ishaq Khan, with whom she clashed repeatedly, especially over military and judicial appointments.

Just as significant, Bhutto was unable to parlay the electoral success of the PPP coalition and her own popularity into creating a cohesive domestic policy for Pakistan. Bhutto's alliance with the MQM, while putting the PPP over the top in the national elections, proved an obstacle when it came to parliamentary action. Furthermore, her alliance with the rival political bloc weakened her credibility within the PPP (though it never threatened her leadership of the party), especially among the Sindi nationalists who had been among her strongest supporters. One of Bhutto's notable shortcomings during this and her second administration as prime minister was her failure to follow through on her announced campaign initiatives to improve women's health care and other social issues concerning women. In fact, "the PPP government's performance was lacklustre, with not a single new piece of legislation being passed or even introduced, apart from two annual budgets" (Jacques 2000, 170).

Another, but no less important, domestic issue where Bhutto floundered regarded Islam. Like her father, Benazir Bhutto was a secularist who, as an opposition leader, had denounced Zia's move toward Islamization of Pakistan. As prime minister she altered this stance for political expediency but discovered that other groups and leaders were farther ahead than she was in this approach. Nevertheless, her hard-line stance in early 1990 regarding the ongoing Kashmir dispute with India gained her credibility with the religious party Jamaat-i-Islami.

Despite these problems Bhutto's first term as prime minister was not completely ineffectual. During her 20 months in power, she ended a ban on unions in Pakistan and, as part of her program to modernize Pakistan, she pushed for rural electrification. She also attempted to encourage private investment in the Pakistani economy.

However, her efforts were hampered by the ethnic violence that pervaded Sind and would ultimately cause the MQM to remove itself from the ruling coalition, paralyzing Pakistan's Parliament and further destabilizing Bhutto's domestic program.

The Political Landscape of Sind

Following partition in 1947 Urdu-speaking Muslims from India, called *muhajir,* "migrant," in Urdu, settled in Sind's urban centers of Karachi, Hyderabad, and Sukkar. Concurrently, many Hindus left for India. The shift profoundly changed the dynamics of Sind's economy and politics. *Muhajirs* were generally nationalists, believing in the ideal of a united Islamic country, and opposed ethnic identification. Primarily middle class and better educated than native-born Pakistanis, *muhajirs* came to dominate the Civil Service of Pakistan (CSP) and formed a powerful administrative class. With *muhajir* support, efforts were made to adopt Urdu as Pakistan's national language as a way to unify the country and forge a national identity. But Sindis, whose language is called Sindi, felt their culture threatened, and when Urdu was made a compulsory subject in primary schools in 1962, Sindis called a strike in response, one of the first large-scale manifestations of Sindi-*muhajir* conflict.

During Ayub Khan's reign the Punjabi-Pashtun-dominated military took increasing charge of the state bureaucracy, reducing *muhajir* control over the CSP. The move of the capital from Karachi, the center of *muhajir* power, to Islamabad also diminished the émigrés' influence.

Sindis saw Zulfikar Bhutto, scion of a Sindi family of feudal landowners, as empowering Sindi nationalism and were core PPP supporters. The *muhajir,* on the other hand, rightly viewed Zulfikar Bhutto as an adversary. He made the study of Sindi compulsory in school, provoking language riots in 1972 as Sindi and *muhajirs* battled over the compulsory instruction. In the 1973 constitution Bhutto also introduced a quota system reserving 1.4 percent of posts in the central administration for rural Sindis. At the time, *muhajirs* held 35.5 percent of the civil service posts, although they constituted only 8 percent of the population. Bhutto also instituted a quota policy mandating that 60 percent of state jobs be reserved for rural residents and 40 percent for urban residents and a similar quota for admissions to state-owned universities. These quotas were enacted to improve the lot of rural populations, which represented the majority of Sindis. Bhutto also reformed the CSP, further reducing *muhajir* power. More language riots erupted in 1972 after the Sind assembly made Sindi the province's official language, while Urdu was adopted as the official language in Baluchistan, NWFP, and Punjab.

In 1978 growing feelings of *muhajir* disenfranchisement led Altaf Hussain (b. 1963) to form the All Pakistan Muhajir Student Organization (APMSO). The group quickly won converts from Islami Jamiat-e-Talaba (UT), the student wing of Jamaat-i-Islami, making the *muhajir* movement an adversary of the UT from its inception. The two groups clashed on college campuses in the early 1980s during Zia's rule. Following the Soviet invasion of Afghanistan in 1979, Pashtun refugees settled in Karachi. Many went into transportation and moneylending businesses and into housing, a market previously controlled by Punjabis and *muhajirs,* leading to tensions between Pashtuns and their *muhajir* tenants. In the mid-1980s Pashtun-owned minibuses, called the yellow devils, were causing an average of two deaths per day. In 1985 a Pashtun bus driver in Karachi ran a red light and plowed into a group of students from Sir Syed College. The accident triggered a protest by *muhajir* student activists, which was joined by *muhajir* renters and soon erupted into pitched battles called the transportation riots, between *muhajirs* and Pashtuns. In their aftermath, the Pashtuns formed an alliance with the Punjabis, with whom they already had dealings through their arms trade with the Punjabi-dominated military.

Muhajir ethnic consciousness overcame its nationalist impulses in 1984 with the rise of the Muhajir Qaumi Movement (MQM), now officially known as Muttahida Qaumi Movement, or United National Movement, which had its origin in APMSO. MQM quickly gained power in the urban centers of Sind, winning the mayorships of Karachi and Hyderabad in 1988. Government efforts to weaken the party led to its splintering into two factions: the main party, MQM(A), led by Altaf Hussain, and an offshoot, the MQM(H), for *Haqiqi* (or "truth") faction, which appealed to religious fundamentalists and was under the influence of the Pakistani government. Fighting between the two factions and with police and security agencies has claimed many lives in Karachi.

In the 1988 elections the MQM allied with the PPP, now headed by Benazir Bhutto, and emerged as the third-largest party in the National Assembly. To win their support, Bhutto had pledged to protect and safeguard the interests of all the people of Sind, regardless of language, religion, or origin of birth, as well as to stamp out violence and to support the rule of law. But tensions between the Sindis, the PPP's traditional base, and MQM supporters continued. In October 1988 hundreds of Sindis were killed during a protest in Hyderabad, for which the *muhajir* were blamed, triggering ethnic riots between the communities. In August 1989 MQM officially ended its alliance with the PPP, claiming the ruling party had failed to live up to its agreements. From May of that year to the following June, hundreds more died in ethnic violence between the two groups.

President Ishaq Khan Dissolves the Government

Bhutto was eager to reinstate the constitution of 1973, voiding the 1985 Zia amendments that allowed the president to dismiss the government and dissolve legislative assemblies, and to return the country to a parliamentary form of government. It would also assure she could not be dismissed from office. Failing to gain sufficient support, she soon dropped the effort. On August 6, 1990, President Ghulam Ishaq Khan, invoking the Eighth Amendment of 1985 and Article 58 2(b), dismissed the Bhutto government, alleging corruption and incompetence; dissolved the National Assembly; and declared a state of emergency. One of the nation's best-known journalists wrote at the time, "The scenario presented has become depressingly familiar—like repeat performances of a B grade movie. A well-rehearsed procedure is carried out, even the words used by the person in high authority to justify his action are paraphrases of what has been heard before, including the charges of corruption and ineptness leveled against the targeted incumbents . . ." (Khan 1998, 466).

Ghulam Mustafa Jatoi, leader of the Combined Opposition Parties, a second coalition party opposed to the PPP, was named caretaker prime minister (r. Aug.–Nov. 1990) after the dismissal of Benazir Bhutto's government. A native of Sind and one of Pakistan's largest landowners, Jatoi had been a PPP veteran and was in the first cabinet of Benazir Bhutto's father. But he was removed as head of the PPP in Sind upon Benazir Bhutto's return in 1986 and left the party. The partisanship behind selecting a member of the opposition rather than a member from the leading party magnified the sting of Ishaq Khan's action. Ishaq Khan soon dissolved the provincial assemblies as well and scheduled new elections for October 1990. Benazir Bhutto's husband, Asif Ali Zardari (b. 1956), was arrested on charges of blackmail and imprisoned for more than two years.

Mustafa Jatoi was also in charge of the accountability proceedings aimed at investigating and bringing to justice members of the national government accused of corruption and malfeasance. Bhutto was charged and testified before the accountability tribunals, but she remained free to conduct her political activities.

1990 Elections

Nawaz Sharif campaigned on a platform of conservative government and ending corruption. The elections for national and provincial assemblies were held on October 24 and 27, respectively. The caretaker government, chosen for its partisanship, took an active role in assisting the Islamic Democratic Alliance (IJI) in winning the elections. His Pakistan Muslim League (PML) had the backing of the IJI as well as the MQM. Evidence exists that the ISI, the state intelligence agency, engineered the IJI's initial support for Sharif during the 1990 election. During his second term as prime minister he was to lose the support of the IJI after he took a more secular course during his second term as prime minister. Despite widespread complaints of election irregularities, outside observers declared the 1990 election generally fair. More than 40 deaths were linked to election violence.

About 45 percent of the 47 million registered voters cast ballots. In the National Assembly 217 seats, 10 of which were held by non-Muslims and 20 of which were reserved for women, were to be chosen by the elected members. The principal parties were the Pakistan Democratic Alliance (PDA), dominated by the PPP, and the IJI, dominated by the PML. The PDA campaigned on the issue of the illegal dismissal of the government. The IJI stressed the incompetence of the Bhutto government as well as the corruption charges against it. The IJI trounced the PPP-led alliance, taking 105 seats to the PDA's 45 seats. The MQM won 15 seats, while the Awami National Party (ANP) and Assembly of Islamic Clergy (JUI) split a dozen seats between them. Independents and others took 30 seats.

Benazir Bhutto continued her opposition efforts during Sharif's rule, including attempts to mount large-scale antigovernment protests. In 1992 Sharif banned her from the nation's capital and had her confined to Karachi though she was not placed under house arrest.

Nawaz Sharif's First Government

On November 1, 1990, Mian Muhammad Nawaz Sharif, finance minister under General Zia and chief minister of Punjab under Bhutto,

Nawaz Sharif, a protégé of Zia ul-Haq and foe of Benazir Bhutto, became prime minister of Pakistan for the first time on November 1, 1990. In this photo he addresses Parliament during his first term. (Courtesy Pakistan Tourism Development Corporation)

became prime minister for the first time (r. 1990–93, 1997–99). He was a native of Lahore and scion of one of Pakistan's most prominent families.

In his first address to the nation he promised a comprehensive national reconstruction program and to increase the pace of industrialization. His leadership, after that of Bhutto and Jatoi, whose families were rooted in the rural aristocracy, represented the ascending importance and power of the industrial class. Identifying unemployment as the nation's primary problem, Nawaz Sharif saw industrialization as the cure.

Nawaz Sharif was a political moderate, but he was also a religious conservative and a Zia protégé, comfortable returning the country to a more Islamic course. And from a political and pragmatic perspective, his coalition included the Islamist JUI party, whose support was needed to maintain the coalition. Sharif's backing for a conservative religious agenda would cement their allegiance. In May 1991 his government passed the Shariat Bill—the bill that Zia had tried but failed to push through the National Assembly in 1985—which made the Qur'an and the Sunna the law of the land provided that "the present political system . . . and the existing system of Government, shall not be challenged" and provided that "the right of the non-Muslims guaranteed by or under the Constitution" shall not be infringed upon (Enforcement of Shari'ah Act, 1991, Act X of 1991, Section 3). The act was unpopular with both secularists and fundamentalists, the former fearing that Pakistan was becoming a theocracy, the latter angry that the law did not go far enough. Although a government group whose task it was to assist Islamization recommended several immediate steps, the act was never enforced. For example, in November 1991 the nation's supreme religious court, the Federal Shariat Court, declared a score of federal and provincial laws repugnant to Islam and therefore void, including one pertaining to the payment of interest. However, bans on interest on all loans would have been an impediment to Nawaz Sharif's industrialization plans. The ruling was appealed and never implemented.

Sharif's Economic Policy

A conservative industrialist whose family "owned the biggest industrial empire in the country" (Bennett Jones 2002, 231), Sharif supported an economic policy focused on restoring to the private sector industries that had been nationalized by Zulfikar Bhutto. This was as much personal as it was domestic policy to increase tax revenue: In 1972 Zulfikar Bhutto had nationalized the Sharif family's Ittefaq Foundary. (The company was denationalized in 1979, around the time Nawaz Sharif was beginning his political career.) Sharif also went farther than Benazir Bhutto in enticing foreign investment by opening Pakistan's stock market to foreign capital, and foreign exchange restrictions were loosened during this time. (However, in his second government Sharif inexplicably reversed this trend when he voided contracts signed between foreign power companies and the Bhutto government.) Having no ties to the landowning aristocracy, Sharif also undertook targeted land reform efforts in Sind, where land was distributed to the poor. He also "had a penchant for costly projects of questionable economic value" (Kux 2001, 44). Large development projects, such as the Ghazi Barotha Hydro Power Project on the Indus River in Punjab, the Gwadar Miniport in Baluchistan, and, in his second government, a superhighway connecting Lahore and Islamabad, were commissioned. Perhaps Sharif's most controversial economic program involved the distribution of "tens of thousands of taxis" to towns and villages. Technically, the government subsidized the purchase of the imported taxis by young men with the agreement that these "loans" would be repaid, but well into the Musharraf regime few of the loans had been paid off.

Sharif's economic policies placed him in good standing with the World Bank and the International Monetary Fund (IMF). The latter especially played a role in Pakistan's economic life during the 1990s, as the country, under changing leadership, struggled to remain solvent. However, IMF assistance was contingent upon debt reduction by Pakistan. Pakistan's national debt impeded Sharif's economic policies, and this was compounded by the suspension of the United States's military and economic assistance program (in response to Pakistan's nuclear-weapons program), and the end of the Soviet-Afghan War. Because of the fear of a Soviet threat on its border, Pakistan was able to garner foreign aid amounting to as much as 2.7 percent of its gross national product, equal to $10 per capita in 1990. Within seven years the per capita amount had fallen to half that amount (Kux, 2001, 44). Exacerbating Pakistan's dire economic situation during this time was a decline in worker remittances from the Persian Gulf.

The damage to the economy done by the unpaid taxi loans actually paled in comparison to the unpaid loans of various Pakistani politicians, including Sharif himself. These unpaid loans contributed to the destabilization of Pakistan's banking system so that by the late 1990s it was on the verge of collapse.

Foreign Policy and Kalashnikov Culture

In foreign affairs Nawaz Sharif strengthened relations with Central Asia's Muslim republics that had formed in the wake of the Soviet Union's collapse in 1991. Pakistan also joined the international coalition to drive Iraq out of Kuwait during the Gulf War (1990–91), although the largest religious party in the IJI coalition, the Jamaat-i-Islami (JI, or Islamic Assembly), opposed the policy, as a defeat of Iraq would strengthen the Shi'i regime in Iran.

Across the border to the west, Afghanistan was disintegrating into chaos. After the Soviet withdrawal in 1989 and the fall of the Communist government in 1992, warring factions carved the nation into fiefdoms, and law and order broke down. Nawaz Sharif attempted to broker a peace among the competing factions with the Islamabad Accord, negotiated under his direction, but the violence continued. The lawlessness spread into Pakistan. Fueled by ethnic and political rivalries and easy access to weapons, crime and terrorism in the country grew rampant. Pakistanis labeled this outbreak of violence "the Kalashnikov culture," after the ubiquitous Soviet-made automatic weapon that made the carnage possible.

BANK OF CREDIT AND COMMERCE INTERNATIONAL (BCCI)

Prime Minister Zulfikar Bhutto nationalized Pakistan's privately owned banks in 1974. However, foreign banks could still operate in the country. One of the most important was BCCI, the Bank of Credit and Commerce International. Though chartered in Luxembourg, BCCI had three major branches in Pakistan and was founded by a well-connected Pakistani banker, Agha Hasan Abedi (1922–95). Prime Minister Nawaz Sharif's family business was a major borrower. In 1991, the year that banking was opened to Pakistan's private sector under the government's economic liberalization program, the BCCI collapsed in what was called the biggest bank fraud in history, estimated to have involved losses of between $10 billion and $17 billion. A U.S. Senate report completed in 1992 concluded BCCI was "a fundamentally corrupt criminal enterprise" (Kerry and Brown, 1992, 1). In addition to fraud, money laundering, and bribery, the report also charged the bank with "support of terrorism, arms trafficking, and the sale of nuclear technologies; management of prostitution; the commission and facilitation of income tax evasion, smuggling, and illegal immigration; illicit purchases of banks and real estate; and a panoply of financial crimes limited only by the imagination of its officers and customers" (ibid., 1). The Pakistani branches were conduits for significant parts of these activities. BCCI received additional attention in the United States for two reasons: The bank was found to have secretly acquired 25 percent ownership of a large U.S. bank, First American, without regulatory approval, violating U.S. law; and it was found that the Central Intelligence Agency (CIA) had been aware for several years of BCCI's activities, but had not informed other agencies, prompting speculation that the spy agency itself may have been among those taking advantage of the bank's lax controls and illegal practices. Most of the financial losses had mundane roots: poor business practices and bad lending decisions. In the years since, most lost funds were recovered through forfeitures, fines, and settlements.

The roots of the violence lay in the cultural heritage of the Pashtun, for whom carrying a gun has long been a tradition born of necessity. Defense of tribal lands, banditry, blood feuds, and pursuit of *badal,* or revenge, all required firearms. The availability of weapons increased dramatically in the aftermath of the Soviet invasion. Black market Soviet weapons and guns intended for the mujahideen swept into Pakistan. So did heroin. Afghan warlords, who managed the fight against the Soviets, financed arms purchases in part by the trafficking of heroin, refined from Afghanistan's abundant opium crop at hundreds of small labs. A culture of smuggling and drug trafficking grew. Arms were also needed to protect the heroin.

The Pakistani towns of Sakhkot, which had a gun market boasting more than 200 gun dealers, and Darra Adam Khel, 25 miles south of Sakhkot, where townspeople craft working imitations of almost any handgun or rifle, became symbols of the Kalashnikov culture.

Pakistan had virtually no drug culture prior to the Afghan war. The number of heroin addicts went from fewer than 10,000 to 12,000 in 1979 to more than 500,000 by the mid-1980s and as many as 3 million to 4 million by 1999. Many refugees from the war resettled in urban areas of Pakistan, particularly in Karachi. The cycle of guns, addiction, and violence took root here too. By the late 1980s, Karachi and Hyderabad were being compared to Beirut for their level of violence.

Adding to the problem of violence is the police force, whose members are typically regarded as corrupt and ineffective. Those who want justice seem compelled to seek it for themselves, and taking the law into one's own hands rarely carries consequences from law enforcement agencies.

In an effort to stem the chaos the Sharif government ordered citizens to turn in weapons, with little success. To deal quickly with those sowing the mayhem the legislature passed the Twelfth Amendment, which allowed for the quick establishment of trial courts to dispense summary justice.

Pakistan's legislative bodies mirrored the chaos. Dissension grew rife in the IJI coalition, particularly within the Pakistan Muslim League, the IJI's largest party. The right-of-center and religious parties comprising the coalition had been united in their opposition to the PPP, but with their primary adversary defeated, their unity splintered. Relations between Nawaz Sharif and President Ishaq Khan were also souring. In 1993 the prime minister and president began trying to oust each other through behind-the-scenes maneuvering.

As he had once before, on April 19, 1993, President Ishaq Kahn invoked the Eighth Amendment, dismissed Nawaz Sharif and his government for corruption, and dissolved the National Assembly. Ishaq Khan named Balakh Sher Khan Mazari (r. April–May, 1993), head of a clan of landowners, as the caretaker prime minister. General elections were scheduled for July 1993. However, in May the Supreme Court overturned the presidential order ousting the government, and Nawaz

LAW ENFORCEMENT

The basic structure of Pakistan's police force was defined in Article 23 of the Indian Police Act of 1861. The police were responsible for preventing crime and detecting and arresting criminals, executing orders and warrants, and gathering and reporting information concerning public order. Other than revisions to the act dating from 1888 and the adoption of the Police Rules of 1934, the document still defines the role of Pakistan's police. The mission or approach changed little after partition. Each of the four provinces has its own police force, and traditionally there has been little integration of their operations. The senior positions are staffed by members of the Police Service of Pakistan, an organization similar to the Civil Service of Pakistan. Members are relatively well paid and have a greater degree of power than other civil servants; therefore, it is often the first choice of high-ranking students seeking entry to government service.

Each provincial force is headed by an inspector general, aided by a deputy inspector general and an assistant inspector general. They oversee the work of a division, or range, which coordinates police activity within areas of each province. Most police work is conducted at the district level, under the direction of a superintendent, and at the subdistrict level, headed by an assistant or deputy superintendent. The great majority of police personnel are assigned to subdistrict stations. The lowest rank is constable, then, in ascending order, head constable, assistant subinspector, subinspector, sergeant, and inspector. Larger cities have their own police forces, but these are under the direction of the provincial police forces. Police in Pakistan are generally unarmed. They frequently use a *lathi,* a five-foot wooden staff, for crowd control, used to hold back throngs or as a club. Traditionally provincial police were almost exclusively male. Under Benazir Bhutto women were inducted into the police force as part of a campaign for equal rights for women.

Sharif was reinstated as prime minister. He and the president remained at odds, bringing the government to a standstill.

Benazir Bhutto's Second Government

In July 1993, after two weeks of negotiations, both Nawaz Sharif and Ishaq Khan resigned their positions, and the national and provincial assemblies were dissolved once again. Moeenuddin Ahmad Qureshi (r. July–Oct. 1993), a senior World Bank official, was named caretaker prime minister, and Wasim Sajjad (r. July–Nov. 1993), Senate chairman, the caretaker president. Though he served only a few months, Moeenuddin Qureshi undertook important reforms. Without concern that he would be voted out of office, he made tough decisions that would have been difficult for an ambitious politician. Qureshi devalued the currency, cut farm subsidies, slashed public sector expenditures, and eliminated 15 ministries. He also raised the prices of critical items, including wheat, gasoline, and electricity. Qureshi also published the names of individuals with unpaid loans from state banks totaling some $2 billion; the list included many prominent politicians. Those who failed to repay their debts were barred from running for office in the upcoming October 1993 elections.

Bhutto's Return

New national and provincial elections were held October 6–7, 1993. The PPP campaigned on the platform of an "Agenda for Change," focused on improvements of social services. The MQM boycotted the election. Turnout was low, with only about 40 percent of those eligible voting. The Pakistan Muslim League (PML) led by Nawaz Sharif won 72 seats. The PPP won a plurality, with 86 seats in the National Assembly, but failed to win a majority. Yet the party did well in all four provinces. Bhutto, through a coalition with minor parties and independents, achieved a majority, earning the right to form a new government. In November, the national and provincial assemblies elected as president Farooq Ahmed Khan Leghari (r. 1993–97), a young PPP party loyalist. Hailing from a family of hereditary chiefs of the prominent Leghari tribe, Leghari began his career in the civil service after earning a degree from England's Oxford University. His service as government appointee and elected official was interrupted by four years in prison during the martial-law years after 1983. In his first address as president, Leghari pledged to revoke the Eighth Amendment, which had previously been used to dissolve governments at presidential whim. He also supported weakening the power of religious courts and expanding women's rights. With the prime minister and president from the same party, many hoped the continual warring between these offices would end. But Leghari was soon embroiled in scandal and controversy, dooming his push for reforms.

Bhutto and the opposition, particularly the MQM, continued to be at loggerheads. In the fall of 1994 Nawaz Sharif embarked on a "train march," traveling by rail from Karachi to Peshawar to dramatize their opposition to the Bhutto government. The "march" drew massive crowds along the route in a display of the agitational and confrontational tactics that characterized both Pakistani politics and these two bitter rivals. In September a general strike was declared, and Nawaz Sharif called for another demonstration of resistance in October. Bhutto arrested several opposition leaders who took part in the protests, drawing widespread condemnation.

Relationship with the United States

Throughout the late 1980s Pakistani officials made statements indicating the country had achieved a nuclear capability, as intelligence reports continued to describe advances in its weapons program. Since 1990 the United States had been withholding delivery of 28 F-16 fighter jets Pakistan had ordered—and paid for at a cost of $1.2 billion—under the terms of the Pressler Amendment, enacted by the U.S. Congress in 1985. The amendment required that before the president could authorize foreign aid to Pakistan, he had to certify that the country was not developing and did not possess nuclear weapons. President Ronald Reagan had waived the requirement, as allowed by the law, in 1988, when Pakistan's assistance in the U.S. fight against the Soviet occupation of Afghanistan seemed crucial. However, the Soviets had withdrawn in 1989, and in 1990 President George H. W. Bush (r. 1989–93) did not certify Pakistan as a nuclear-free nation, thereby triggering an aid embargo. At the time, Pakistan was the third largest recipient of U.S. military assistance—after Israel and Egypt. In 1986 the United States and Pakistan had agreed on a $4 billion economic development and security assistance program that Pakistan would receive, paid out from 1988 to 1993. Pakistan was in the midst of an ambitious program to refurbish its armed forces, looking across the border at its bigger, nuclear-armed enemy, India. In addition to depriving Pakistan of material it needed to have a credible defensive force, the Pressler Amendment targeted only Pakistan, though other nations were known to have nuclear weapons programs that violated the terms of the UN nuclear nonproliferation treaty. Moreover, India had started the nuclear arms race and had escaped all penalties of the Symington and Pressler amendments. Relations between Pakistan and the United States deteriorated sharply from 1990 through 1993, as issues of weapons development, terrorism, and narcotics caused a growing rift between Islamabad and Washington. In 1992 the United States almost declared Pakistan a state sponsor of terrorism, primarily due to its support for Kashmiri militants. In the summer of 1993 the United States placed more sanctions on Pakistan, charging it with receiving prohibited missile technology from China.

In late 1993 U.S. president Bill Clinton (r. 1993–2001) proposed revising the Pressler Amendment, citing the unequal treatment of Pakistan and India over their respective nuclear programs. But Clinton faced strong objections from legislators and withdrew his proposal in early 1994. A few months later his administration proposed a one-time sale of F16s, contingent upon Pakistan pledging to cap the production of weapons-grade uranium. This proposal paralleled a liberalization of Pakistan's economy to a more market-based system, which the United States was eager to encourage. In January 1995, the thawing relationship between the two nations was underscored by a visit to Pakistan by U.S. defense secretary William Perry (r. 1994–97). Following the visit, Perry proclaimed that the Pressler Amendment had failed in its objective to halt Pakistan's nuclear program and had actually been counterproductive. Benazir Bhutto traveled to Washington, D.C., in April, and in early 1996 the Brown Amendment was passed, which removed nonmilitary aid from the purview of the Pressler Amendment and gave the president a onetime waiver to permit the release of the military equipment embargoed since 1990. President Clinton authorized the release of some $368 million in military equipment. Though the F-16s were not among the approved items, Clinton pledged to reimburse Pakistan for the money it had already paid for the jets. Meanwhile, Pakistan continued to make progress in its nuclear program.

A visit to Pakistan by First Lady Hillary Rodham Clinton and her daughter, Chelsea, in 1995 helped project to the world an image of Pakistan as a modern, progressive country. Bhutto's visit to the United States the previous year had already helped raise the country's visibility. International investment in Pakistan increased.

Bhutto's Central Asia Policy

Benazir Bhutto continued to pursue the country's long-standing policy of seeking influence and power in Afghanistan to balance the threat felt from India. During her first term as prime minister, training camps for mujahideen had remained open, and Pakistan had issued visas for thousands of militants from more than 20 countries traveling to the camps. The goal, many observers believed, was to maintain an army of jihadists who could be deployed to wage proxy wars against Pakistan's rivals in Kashmir and Central Asia.

Bhutto had accompanied her father to Simla when he signed the agreement with India in 1972 that ended the war triggered by East Pakistan's declaration of independence and laid down the blueprint for future peaceful relations between the two signatories. But it was evident Bhutto intended to keep a force of militants available to use as a weapon against India in Kashmir.

When Bhutto was reelected for a second term as prime minister in 1993, she was eager to encourage trade with Pakistan's neighbors in Central Asia. As part of that initiative she backed a pipeline running from Turkmenistan through southern Afghanistan to Pakistan, proposed by an Argentinean oil company, rather than a rival route championed by U.S. oil company Unocal. However, the region had become less stable in the aftermath of the war against the Soviets, even as the Taliban began to emerge as a power in Afghanistan in 1993. Rather than support a wider peace process in Afghanistan, Bhutto backed the Taliban, who she saw as a force that would provide security to protect the proposed pipeline and give stability to their country.

Her policy was influenced by the ISI, whose stature had risen during the Soviet occupation. After the Soviet withdrawal from Afghanistan, the ISI sought to extend Pakistan's regional control across Afghanistan and the Central Asian republics. The ISI began funding the Taliban ("students"), a Pashtun Islamic student movement in Kandahar. Using bribery, guerrilla tactics, and military support, the ISI helped install the Taliban as rulers in Kabul in 1996 and eventually extend its control over 95 percent of the country.

During the same time that the Bhutto government backed the Taliban in Afghanistan, the Jamiat Ulema-i-Islam (JUI), a strict religious party, began to gain power in Pakistan: Bhutto welcomed the party into her ruling coalition. Meanwhile the proxy war in Kashmir was heating up, again with government support. Thus, it was under Bhutto, and with her encouragement, that the Taliban rose to power in Afghanistan and the power of religious fundamentalists grew in Pakistan. Bhutto would come to regret these decisions. In a 1998 address Bhutto said that these policies had created a strategic threat to Pakistan and led to Islamic militancy, suicide bombings, weaponization of the population, the drug trade, and increased poverty and unemployment. And in an interview with the Council on Foreign Relations a few months before her death in 2007, Bhutto said, "I remember when the Taliban first came up in neighboring Afghanistan. Many of us, including our friends from the U.S.,

DEOBAND AND BARELWI SECTS

Avariety of schools of Islamic thought, or sects, exist among Sunni Muslims on the subcontinent. In Pakistan, Deoband and Barelwi are the two primary sects. Deoband is a town 100 miles (160 km) north of Delhi. A madrasa established there in 1867 became the headquarters for virulently anti-British Muslims who believed Western influence was corrupting Islam and who swore allegiance to religion over state. This became the model for other madrasas established throughout Pakistan after independence. Deoband is often linked to the spread of religious extremism, most notably as a seedbed for the Taliban in Afghanistan. To some degree this influence is real, as students, or *talibs,* from these Deoband madrasas provided the grassroots strength that gave birth to the Taliban in 1996. However, the authority inherent in the name Deoband is invoked to legitimize all kinds of Islamic conservatism; it is estimated some 15 percent of Pakistan's Sunni Muslims consider themselves part of the Deoband movement.

The Bareiwi sect, to which some 60 percent of Pakistan's Sunnis belong, was founded by a Sufi scholar, Mullah Ahmad Raza Khan (1856–1921), in the town of Barelwi in northern India. He is not related to the military and religious leader Sayyid Ahmad Barelwi (1786–1831). Ahmad Raza Khan taught that Islam is compatible with the subcontinent's earlier religions, and Barelwis are apt to pray to holy men, or *pirs,* both living and dead. This practice is an abomination to orthodox Sunni Muslims, though Shi'i Muslims engage in similar rites.

---

initially thought they would bring peace to that war-torn country. And that was a critical, fatal mistake we made. If I had to do things again, that's certainly not a decision that I would have taken" (Bhutto 2007).

Internal Feuds

Internal feuds had long been part of the Bhutto family legacy. Zulfikar Bhutto had feuded with family members as he rose to power. and his children followed in his footsteps. After Zulfikar's death, Benazir fought with her mother, Begum Nusrat Bhutto (b. 1929), for control of the PPP. Nusrat favored Benazir's brother, Mir Murtaza (1954–96), as heir to the Bhutto political mantle. Murtaza, meanwhile, went into exile in Kabul, Damascus, and Libya, and formed a militant breakaway PPP faction called al-Zulfikar Organization. From beyond Pakistan's borders he accused Benazir of betraying their father's ideals. Murtaza also strongly opposed Benazir's husband Ali Zardari's involvement with the PPP, due to concerns about corruption.

Murtaza's supporters had been implicated in violence, including the hijacking of a Pakistan International Airline aircraft as a display of protest against the Zia regime, responsible for executing Murtaza's father and their political leader.

In the 1993 election Mir Murtaza had won a seat as an anti-Bhutto candidate. When he returned from Damascus after years of exile, he was jailed on the longstanding terrorism charge. Benazir Bhutto also removed her mother from leadership in the PPP. The internecine conflict was perceived as another blot on Benazir Bhutto's image. In September 1996 Mir Murtaza Bhutto was killed in a police ambush in Karachi with six companions. None of the police involved in the killing were arrested, and some were subsequently promoted. A judicial review of the killings concluded it could not have occurred without the approval from the highest levels of government.

Throughout the first half of the 1990s relations between Bhutto and Leghari deteriorated. Despite earlier pledges to revoke the Eighth Amendment, Leghari instead invoked it. On November 5, 1996, Leghari

Benazir Bhutto's policies were widely criticized and provoked large opposition rallies, such as the protest in this photo. (AP Photo/K. M. Choudary)

dismissed the Benazir Bhutto government, alleging crimes including corruption, mismanagement, and murder. The National Assembly was also dissolved. Bhutto's husband, Asif Ali Zardari (b. 1956), who held the cabinet post of investment minister, was accused of taking bribes, receiving kickbacks on government contracts, and sponsoring extrajudicial killings in Karachi. Bhutto labeled the charges politically motivated and went into voluntary exile. She and her husband were tried in absentia in 1999 and convicted. In 2001 the Supreme Court ordered a retrial. She was tried in a separate trial in absentia and convicted and sentenced to three years in prison. Facing arrest and incarceration if she returned to Pakistan, Bhutto remained in exile through the middle of the first decade of the new century. After Bhutto's dismissal, Malik Meraj Khalid (r. 1996–97), rector of the International Islamic University, was named caretaker prime minister. In the February 1997 elections the Pakistan Muslim League (PML) won a two-thirds majority in the National Assembly and Nawaz Sharif was reelected prime minister (r. 1997–99).

Nawaz Sharif's Second Government

Ever since the passage of the Eighth Amendment in 1985 during Zia ul-Haq's regime, it had played havoc with Pakistan's political stability. During his second term in office Sharif made overturning the Eighth Amendment a priority, and in April 1997, with the support of all the political parties, the Thirteenth Amendment to the constitution was adopted by the National Assembly. It gave the prime minister authority to repeal Article 58 (2)(b), the Eighth Amendment article that allowed the president to dismiss the prime minister and the National Assembly, thus restoring the original powers of the prime minister and returning the presidency to its ceremonial role. The Thirteenth Amendment also transferred the power to appoint the three chiefs of the armed forces and provincial governors from the president to the prime minister.

Nawaz Sharif also attempted to rein in the political practice of switching parties and alliances that had over the past few decades stalled progress and encouraged corruption. Because the parties and prime ministers depended on shaky coalitions to provide them with the majorities they needed to rule, politicians could threaten to abandon their party and shift their support to rival politicians. This was mostly done to win favors or gather power, rather than to promote the public's agenda. Ministry posts, bank loans, and other benefits had been extracted by politicians as a price for continued party loyalty or for switching allegiances. Attempting to redress the problem, Nawaz Sharif introduced the Anti-Defection Bill, which the Senate and National Assembly passed overwhelmingly in July as the Fourth Amendment.

Growing Repression

However, Sharif's support for the Thirteenth and Fourteenth amendments was accompanied by an increasingly autocratic political style, and thus many saw the amendments as part of his attempt to stifle opposition to his rule. Sharif arrested journalists who wrote critical articles about him, including respected figures Majam Sethi and Hussain Haqqani, and turned tax investigators on the editors who published their work. When the Supreme Court presided over a corruption case in which Nawaz Sharif was a defendant in 1997, his supporters attacked the court building, forcing proceedings to be suspended. No longer concerned about dismissal from his position, Nawaz Sharif let his relationship with President Leghari, his primary political foe, deteriorate. The chief justice of Pakistan, Syed Sajjad Ali Shah (served 1994–97), had become embroiled in judicial disagreements with the Sharif government, and Leghari threw his support behind Ali Shah. Sharif had party enforcers storm the Supreme Court in November and remove Chief Justice Ali Shah from office. Unable to dislodge him by dissolving the government, as he had with Benazir Bhutto, President Leghari resigned on December 2, 1997.

The new president would be indirectly elected by the two houses of Parliament, the National Assembly and the Senate, along with the four provincial assemblies. On December 31, 1997, the PML candidate, Muhammad Rafiq Tarar, a senator and former Supreme Court judge, was elected to replace Leghari, having beaten the PPP and Jamiat Ulema-i-Islam candidates by a 10-to-1 margin. The nation's ninth president, Tarar (r. 1998–2001) took office on January 1, 1998.

Nuclear Tests and the Economy

Early in May 1998 India's new government under Prime Minister Atul Bihari Vajpayee (r. May–June 1996, 1998–2004), leader of the Hindu Bharatiya Janata Party (BJP), tested a nuclear device, thereby confirming that it possessed nuclear weapons. Two weeks later, on May 28, Pakistan conducted its own tests of five nuclear devices, with a reported yield of up to 40 kilotons, at a nuclear test facility at Chaghi, in Baluchistan. On the same day the Sharif government proclaimed an emergency, suspending basic rights and freezing all foreign-currency accounts in Pakistani banks. The nuclear tests brought international condemnation, but Pakistan claimed it needed the weapons for self-defense against India. The United Nations passed a unanimous resolution calling on both Pakistan and India to end their nuclear weapons programs, and UN secretary-general Kofi Annan (r. 1997–2007) urged both countries to sign the Comprehensive Test Ban Treaty. Pakistan expressed willingness to sign the treaty if India did the same, but India declined. In June 1998, Pakistan declared a moratorium on future testing and India made a similar declaration.

By the time of the 1998 nuclear tests, Pakistan's nuclear program (both military and domestic) had been functioning for more than two decades with assistance from the United Kingdom, the Netherlands, the Federal Republic of Germany (West Germany), France, and China. The United States's response to Pakistan's nuclear program during this period swung between cutting off foreign aid to reinstituting assistance. Following Pakistan's nuclear tests of late May and early June 1998, the United States reimposed sanctions (excluding humanitarian assistance), which had been eased in 1995, against Pakistan. The U.S. sanctions included a "ban on financing from the Trade and Development Agency, Overseas Private Investment Corporation, and the Export-Import Bank, restrictions on U.S. exports of high-technology products, opposition to loans from international financial institutions, and a ban on U.S. bank loans to the government of Pakistan." Japan joined the United States, freezing most of its development aid to Pakistan and withdrawing support for new loans for Pakistan in international bodies (Peterson Institute, 2007).

The nuclear tests temporarily bolstered Prime Minister Sharif's popularity among Pakistanis, despite the fact that the effects of the sanctions on Pakistan's economy were felt immediately and that he had earlier declared a state of emergency curtailing human rights. Nevertheless, Pakistan's fragile economy, buffeted since the beginning of the 1990s, faced potential collapse. The Sharif government had to negotiate bank loans in July 1998 to cover the budgetary shortfall caused by the sanctions, while increasing the price of nondiesel gasoline. That same month Standard and Poor's downgraded Pakistan's rating, predicting imminent bankruptcy.

Although some of the restrictions against Pakistan were eased by the end of the year and in early 1999, Nawaz Sharif's hold on power grew ever more precarious. The poor economic situation was but one factor. Since the death of Zia, the military had been an ever-present threat to Pakistan's feeble democracy. Furthermore, "Sharif had to look over his other shoulder . . . at the militant Islamists who were a powerful force in Pakistan" (Talbott 2004, 107). The latter were given support by the neighboring Taliban in Afghanistan, even as a cash-strapped Pakistan provided financial aid to the Taliban government in 1998. Sharif exacerbated Islamists' fears (and conservative concerns) when he canceled the traditional Friday holidays. But the failure of his economic program during a period of worldwide economic growth and, especially, his attempt to exert control over the military would ultimately lead to his undoing.

After the army chief of staff, Jehangir Karamat, suggested that the military leadership be given a role in the National Security Council of Pakistan, Sharif forced his resignation in early October. Karamat had warned that Pakistan was facing grave problems, namely, an economy that was on the brink of collapse. He said Pakistan "could not afford the destabilizing effects of polarization, vendettas, and insecurity-expedient policies" (quoted in Abbas 2004, 166). He was replaced by General Pervez Musharraf (b. 1943).

To strengthen his hold on power, Nawaz Sharif oversaw passage of the 15th Amendment of the constitution in the National Assembly in late October. Once passed by the Senate, it would have made sharia the supreme law of Pakistan and given the prime minister the unfettered right to rule by degree in the name of Islamic law. But unsure of the level of support in the Senate, where a two-thirds majority was needed for passage, Nawaz Sharif never brought the legislation for a vote within the 90 days required for ratification.

The Kargil Conflict

After the two countries tested nuclear devices, tensions between India and Pakistan steadily increased. In February 1999 Sharif and Vajpayee attempted to de-escalate the situation. Vajpayee traveled to Lahore by bus and was met by Sharif at the Wagah border crossing on the Grand Trunk Road. The two leaders issued the Lahore Declaration, defining the measures the countries would each take to stabilize relations. The religious party Jamaat-i-Islami, a partner in Sharif's coalition government, opposed the visit, but all other political groups welcomed the effort to promote peace between Pakistan and India. However, Kashmir remained a flashpoint between Pakistan and India, ever threatening to plunge the two countries back into war. India had refused to hold the plebiscite mandated by a UN Security Council resolution in 1948, and Muslim Kashmiri fighters, supported by Pakistan, continued their battle against Indian occupation forces. The fighters infiltrated Indian-controlled Kashmir and attacked symbols of Indian rule, including army posts and police stations. In response the Indian army established border posts along the Line of Control to combat the attacks. Because of the high altitude of these posts—from about 12,000 to more than 15,000 feet (4,000–5,200 m)—troops were withdrawn during the winter.

In April 1999, before Indian troops returned to their high-altitude garrisons, Kashmiri guerrillas captured posts along mountain ridges near the Indian-occupied towns of Kargil and Drass. From their positions the guerrillas launched artillery fire on National Highway 1, which runs north from Kashmir's capital, Srinagar. Pakistan denied any knowledge of or support for the guerrilla action. But India claimed identification taken from slain guerrillas revealed they were members of Pakistan's Northern Light Infantry, a paramilitary force under Pakistan's control. Beginning in May Indian forces counterattacked in what was to become the first land war in history between two declared nuclear powers. Two of its aircraft strayed into Pakistani territory, one of which was shot down. The potential for a nuclear confrontation caused worldwide concern. As the fighting continued from May into July, and the Pakistani forces were slowly pushed back, U.S. president Clinton helped persuade Pakistan to use its influence with the guerrillas to stop fighting. Bowing to international pressure, Sharif withdrew all Pakistani troops from Indian-held territory to the Line of Control. The guerrillas left the captured territory by August 1999. The withdrawal of Pakistani forces further increased Sharif's unpopularity at home.

The Coup against Sharif

The object of increasingly unflattering media coverage, Nawaz Sharif attempted to intimidate the press. In May 1999 Nawaz Sharif's secret police invaded the home of a leading journalist and critic of the regime, Najam Sethi, and assaulted and kidnapped him. An international protest forced Sharif to release the journalist. Signs of public disenchantment with the entire political process grew. In the four national elections held from 1988 to 1997, voter turnout had dropped progressively, from 43 percent in 1988 to 35 percent by 1997.

The military remained the one state institution Nawaz Sharif had not brought under his control. Karamat's departure in late 1998 had provoked great resentment in the military, placing Nawaz Sharif in a vulnerable position. As mass opposition rallies were staged against his government, Sharif, worried about the potential for a coup, planned to replace Musharraf, a veteran of both the 1965 and 1971 wars with India, with a more compliant official. On October 12, 1999, General Musharraf was on a commercial flight to Karachi, returning from a visit to Colombo, Sri Lanka, one of 198 passengers. According to a police report filed by a colonel in the army, Nawaz Sharif ordered the Civil Aviation Authority to deny the flight permission to land anywhere in Pakistan. This became known as the "Plane Conspiracy" case. Simultaneously, Nawaz Sharif announced he was appointing the director of the ISI, Pakistan's intelligence service, as the military's new chief of staff. The military refused to recognize the appointment and took over Karachi airport, allowing Musharraf's flight to land with only minutes of fuel left onboard. Once on the ground, General Musharraf ordered the military to take control of the government, claiming the turmoil and uncertainty gripping the nation necessitated the action. Musharraf proclaimed himself the chief executive of Pakistan. The Thirteenth Amendment had proven insufficient to protect democracy, however flawed the democratic system may have been. Although Musharraf did not declare martial law, as had been done in previous military takeovers, Pakistan was once more under military rule.

12

A RETURN TO THE WORLD STAGE (1999–2008)

General Pervez Musharraf's 1999 coup demonstrated that constitutional safeguards could not protect the civilian government from military takeover. Musharraf, who took the title of chief executive at the time of the coup, later removed President Muhammad Rafiq Tarar from office and installed himself as president.

From the time of the takeover Musharraf faced international pressure to restore democracy. But priorities changed in the wake of the attacks of September 11, 2001, in the United States. Across Pakistan's border in Afghanistan the ruling Taliban were shielding the putative architect of the 9/11 attacks, Osama bin Laden (b. 1957). Pakistan, which had helped foment radical and militant Islam, as had the United States during the Soviet occupation of Afghanistan, was once more the linchpin in a global struggle. Musharraf gained economic and military assistance in exchange for Pakistan's partnership in the U.S.-led War on Terror. But Musharraf faced bitter opposition to the alliance from Pakistanis who did not want to see fellow Muslims branded as enemies or terrorists. Meanwhile, violence wrought by Sunni and Shi'i religious extremists fanned divisions within Pakistan's Muslim community. Yet there were hopeful signs for the nation's future as well. Relations between Pakistan and India eased, and progress on the Kashmir issue was made.

However, Musharraf's autocratic style led to wide dissatisfaction across the political spectrum. In 2007, in an effort to shore up support after eight years in power, he announced elections would be held; he allowed former prime ministers Benazir Bhutto and Nawaz Sharif, both exiles, to return and stand for election. Bhutto was assassinated soon after returning to Pakistan, but her party won the elections held in February 2008. With a coalition civilian government leading them, the citizens of Pakistan once more attempted to create a working democratic state respectful of both cultural traditions and individual freedom.

Musharraf's Coup d'État

On October 12, 1999, after Prime Minister Nawaz Sharif tried to bar General Musharraf's commercial flight from landing in Pakistan, Musharraf staged a coup and took control of the government. He took immediate steps to consolidate his power: Nawaz Sharif; his brother Shabaz Sharif, the former chief minister of Punjab (r. 1997–99); and five other officials were arrested. They were charged with hijacking, kidnapping, and attempted murder, as the plane was running low on fuel and the refusal to allow it to land endangered the lives of all onboard. The coup was criticized by the international community for short-circuiting the democratic process; the United States stressed the need to restore civilian rule as quickly as possible.

In the aftermath of the October coup, police and paramilitary and military personnel detained scores of leaders and activists of opposition political parties, according to Human Rights Watch. The arrests were made under laws governing sedition and the maintenance of public order. Figures including Rama Sanaullah Khan, from the Punjab provincial assembly, and PML leaders Kulsoom Nawaz. Mamnoon Hussain, Shah Mohammad Shah, and Haleem Siddiqui were among those arrested and in some cases beaten and tortured.

The case against Nawaz Sharif was brought before an antiterrorism court in Karachi. Found guilty of corruption, hijacking, tax evasion, embezzlement, and terrorism he was sentenced to several terms of life imprisonment. He was pardoned in 2000 and exiled on condition that he forfeit property worth some 500

General Pervez Musharraf seized power from Nawaz Sharif in a military coup in October 1999, becoming Pakistan's ruler under martial law. (Courtesy Pakistan Tourism Development Corporation)

million rupees (about $8 million) and not seek public office for 21 years. He moved to Saudi Arabia.

The Musharraf camp took the absence of large street protests against Nawaz Sharif's deportation as an indication that average Pakistanis had become disengaged from politics. Soon after the deportation, the U.S. assistant secretary of state for South and Central Asian Affairs, Christina Rocca (served 2001–06), visited Pakistan. Although she expressed concern about the police crackdown on Nawaz Sharif's political party, she reaffirmed U.S. support for General Musharraf's rule.

On May 12, 2000, the Supreme Court ruled that Musharraf's coup was valid. Though the court found the takeover represented a constitutional deviation, the judges found military intervention had been undertaken as a necessity, the only way to bring about economic reforms and halt corruption. The court directed Musharraf to hold general elections by October 2002.

Economic Reforms

Musharraf had come to power promising economic reforms and effective steps against corruption. The bar for economic growth was not set high for Musharraf. During the 1990s the growth rate in national income had dropped to less than 4 percent annually from more than 6 percent annually in the 1980s, due to government mismanagement and the economic sanctions imposed in response to Pakistan's nuclear-weapons program. Industrial growth rates dropped almost by half, from 8.2 percent to 4.8 percent annually during the decade. The percentage of households living in absolute poverty increased from 21.4 percent in 1990–91 to 40 percent in 2000–01. Corruption had brought the gears of government to near standstill.

Musharraf made economic development an early priority. He courted international financial institutions such as the World Bank and the IMF. Loans were used to invest in communications, energy, water supply, and railway infrastructure and highways and ports. For the first three years of his rule the economy remained stagnant before per capita income began to rise. The economy was kept from expanding too rapidly by following the IMF's model of economic stabilization.

Efforts at Religious Reform

Musharraf was a secular Muslim and a modernist. In an interview shortly after the coup his father Syed Musharraf-ud-Din, a career diplomat, was asked if Pervez prayed five times a day. "If the father doesn't, I don't see why the son should," he answered (quoted from Jones 2002, 19). In his first major policy address, in October 1999, Pervez Musharraf issued a challenge to demagogues exploiting religion. "Islam teaches tolerance not hatred; universal brotherhood and not enmity; peace and not violence; progress and not bigotry. I have great respect for the Ulema and expect them to come forth and present Islam in its true light. I urge them to curb elements which are exploiting religion for vested interests and bring a bad name to our faith" (Musharraf 1999). But his efforts to curtail religious extremism had little effect. Musharraf tried to reform the antiblasphemy law, which declared that speaking against the prophet Muhammad or desecrating the Qur'an a capital crime. The law was open to abuse, for any disgruntled individual could accuse someone of blasphemy, and by law the accused would be imprisoned before an investigation occurred. Musharraf sought to have the law amended to require a preliminary investigation before an arrest. In a sign of how strong the influence of the religious conservatives had become, in May 2000 Musharraf announced an end to his effort to reform the law. Religious parties had threatened demonstrations and a general strike.

Likewise, efforts to disarm the public were announced with great fanfare. Musharraf announced a ban on the public display of weapons in February 2001, but the law went unenforced. At rallies religious leaders were still protected by gun-toting bodyguards who went unchallenged by government or military authorities.

Government Reforms

On June 20, 2001, Musharraf removed Rafiq Tarar as president under the provisional constitutional order, which dissolved the already suspended Senate, and the national and provincial assemblies. Musharraf took the title of president for himself.

In August he introduced the Local Government System. The stated purpose was to give individuals at the grassroots level more say in local government. The system restructured governance by transferring authority previously exercised by provincial administrators down to the district and local level. The system was intended to create more responsive local governments and to decentralize the state's administrative power. Meanwhile, with Musharraf serving as both president and army chief of staff in combination with the crackdowns on opposition parties, political power became more centralized at the apex of the government.

The system created a three-tier structure consisting of the union, or local council; the *tehsil* council; and the district, or *zilla* council. The country would be divided into 105 *zillas,* or districts. Each *zilla* would be subdivided into *tehsils,* corresponding roughly to large counties, and *tehsils* themselves would consist of local, or union jurisdictions. Citizens would gain control through representatives they elected to these councils.

Harking back to the Basic Democracies System of Ayub Khan, representatives would be chosen in direct, nonparty elections; the representatives in turn would vote for provincial and national assembly members. One-third of the seats were reserved for women. The voting age was lowered from 21 to 18 years of age.

Foreign Policy and the Events of September 11

During his first two years in power Musharraf sought to bolster his image and support within Pakistan by taking the traditional position regarding India and expressing support for the Taliban in Afghanistan. The former position upheld his popularity with his main base of support, the military, while the latter placed him in good standing with the Islamists. He also had to reposition himself with the West, which was dismayed at yet another military coup in Pakistan.

His policy toward India was marked by tacit support of the Kashmir uprising—as army chief of staff under Prime Minister Sharif he had been responsible for the 1999 Kargil invasion. That the insurgency had ties to the Taliban seemingly caused Pakistan to play a proxy role in the province for its neighbor. In fact, "before 11 September he [Musharraf] had consistently supported Mullah Mohammed Omar's Kandahar regime. This was not because he sympathized with the Taliban's interpretation of Islam ... but because he believed the Taliban served Pakistan's regional interests" (Bennett Jones 2002, 2). Under Musharraf Pakistan not only supported the Kashmir uprising but infiltrated manpower into the region. The overall effect of this for Musharraf was to placate his Islamist critics.

Yet, in July 2001 Musharraf met with Indian prime minister Atal Behari Vajpayee (r. 1996, 1998–2004) at Agra, India, to pursue a settlement on the Kashmir issue. At the Agra Summit the leaders also discussed reducing the risk of nuclear confrontation, closer commercial ties, and freeing of prisoners of war. But a solution to the Kashmir dispute continued to elude the leaders, and the meetings collapsed. Nonetheless, the two expressed the need to forge a peaceful relationship, rejecting the venom of the past, and tensions between the two nations were eased by the meetings. However, on December 13, 2001, the relationship took a turn for the worse. Pakistani terrorists disguised as tourists planned to attack the Indian parliament and hold the legislators hostage until they agreed to settle the Kashmir dispute. But security stopped their explosives-laden car from entering the compound; the terrorists were killed in an ensuing gunfight. The Pakistani government denied involvement, but in reaction Vajpayee ordered the Indian army to deploy on Pakistan's border, and the Indian navy sailed within striking distance of Karachi. Pakistan's ambassador to the United Nations threatened a nuclear response to an attack. The United States, eager to diffuse the crisis, broke into the Indian navy's communication system and sent a false message instructing the four warships to withdraw from the harbor (Sud, n.p.). Meanwhile, U.S. officials pressured the Indian government to pull back its forces from the border.

During 2000 and the first half of 2001 Musharraf's policy toward the United States focused on getting the sanctions lifted or, at the very least, the money returned that Pakistan had already paid for the undelivered fighter jets while employing his regional strategy. He managed to score a coup when President Bill Clinton came to Pakistan for a brief visit in March 2000 (and spoke for 15 minutes on Pakistani television), which caused anxiety in New Delhi—exactly what Musharraf had wanted. Clinton not only urged Musharraf to reinstate the democratic institutions of Pakistan's government, he also pushed for a settlement of the Kashmir conflict and assistance with getting the Taliban to turn over Osama bin Laden, whom the United States held responsible for two attacks against U.S. embassies in 1998. Of these three points, the only one Musharraf agreed to was the one in which he had no power to effect the outcome. He promised to intervene with the Taliban on behalf of U.S. interests, but as he later admitted in his memoirs, "After the Taliban came to power, we lost much of the leverage we had with them" (Musharraf 2006, 203). Musharraf simply rebuffed Clinton, who, as a lame-duck president, had little leverage during his final months in office.

In June 2001 the Bush administration reiterated the same three points to Pakistani foreign minister Abdul Sattar during his visit to Washington, D.C. Islamabad noted that Washington was prepared to take a tougher stance if these points were not acted upon, but the events of September 11 altered the dynamic of the region and once again brought Pakistan into a close alliance with the United States.

Within hours of the attacks the U.S. government concluded that they probably had been planned by Osama bin Laden in Afghanistan, where he had been given sanctuary by the Taliban. Any military reprisal would require Pakistan's cooperation.

Until the events of September 11 Musharraf had continued the Central Asia policy of his predecessors. He supported the Taliban government in Afghanistan, seeking stability in the region, improved access to Central Asia, and an ally in Kashmir against India. And since most Taliban were Pashtuns, they had a kinship with Pakistan's population along the border, which fostered friendly relations between the two nations. However, on September 12 Pakistani diplomats were given a choice by the U.S. government, delivered by U.S. deputy secretary of state Richard Armitage (served 2001–06): Pakistan could either support the Taliban, or it could support the United States. General Musharraf chose to join the United States in its War on Terror. He knew his decision would face opposition from fundamentalist elements who supported the Taliban and opposed the United States for its stanch support for Israel and perceived anti-Islamic agenda. But Musharraf was a pragmatist and realist. Pakistan could not withstand the economic and military pressure and power of the United States if he refused to accede to its demands. Conversely, if he agreed, Pakistan stood to gain substantial benefits in terms of economic and military assistance, as well as power and prestige on the world stage.

On September 14 Musharraf informed the army command of his decision. Musharraf reassigned some pro-Taliban senior army officers and retired others. In the immediate aftermath of the attacks. Pakistan assisted in unsuccessful negotiations aimed at persuading the Taliban to turn over or deport bin Laden. On September 19 Musharraf spoke to the nation in a televised address and explained his decision to the citizens. He said that only a small, vocal minority opposed his decision. But Pakistan was already awash in anti-American feelings. Though Musharraf gained the stature of an international statesman for joining the War on Terror, at home demonstrations against Musharraf and the United States were staged in Quetta, Karachi, Islamabad, Peshawar, and other cities.

In a matter of days after the attacks, the United States was permitted to use four air bases in Pakistan for support, rather than offensive, operations. Pakistan also allowed use of its airspace for overflights of military aircraft engaged in combat operations. In return Pakistan received some $600 million per year in aid, and $3 billion in loans was forgiven. The United States and coalition partners launched Operation Enduring Freedom to invade Afghanistan, remove the Taliban from power, and capture Osama bin Laden. Within two months the operation had driven the Taliban from power, though bin Laden eluded capture. In the aftermath of the U.S. campaign bin Laden was believed to have fled to Waziristan, in Pakistan's tribal areas. The U.S. war in Afghanistan caused another refugee crisis for Pakistan, as tens of thousands seeking safety fled over the Pakistan border.

Now fully vested in the situation in Pakistan, U.S. secretary of state Colin Powell (served 2001–06) traveled there in January 2002, following the crisis caused by the attempted terrorist attack on India's parliament. Powell made all future military and economic assistance contingent upon Pakistan divulging the location of its nuclear weapons, which Pakistan reluctantly agreed to do. U.S. and British firms built a command and control system to ensure that the nuclear weapons were secured. Pakistan also agreed to de-mate its nuclear core from the trigger mechanism and store the two separately, as was the practice in India and other nuclear powers. As a reward the United States provided Pakistan with an additional $1.2 billion in economic aid, and additional military equipment to aid the search for Osama bin Laden. The United States also used the crisis provoked by the attack on India's parliament to demand that Pakistan crack down on the rogue nuclear scientist Abdul Qadeer (A. Q.) Khan (b. 1936), regarded as the father of Pakistan's nuclear weapons program. Pakistan placed him under house arrest. A subsequent U.S. investigation discovered that a network created by Khan and the Pakistani military had funneled nuclear weapons technology to Iran, Libya, and North Korea. The investigation also revealed that Pakistan's nuclear weapon was an exact copy of a U.S. nuclear weapon from the 1980s. The United States suspected China as the source of the design, and, concerned that its own nuclear program had been compromised, the government overhauled security at nuclear weapons installations.

Nuclear Proliferation

In September 2004 the United Nations' International Atomic Energy Agency reported that as early as 1995 Pakistan was providing Iran with the designs for sophisticated centrifuges capable of making bomb-grade nuclear fuel. In November a CIA report said the arms-trafficking network led by A. Q. Khan provided Iran's nuclear program with significant assistance, including the designs for advanced and efficient weapons components. George Tenet (served 1997–2004), the former director of the Central Intelligence Agency, described Khan as being "at least as dangerous as Osama bin Laden" because of his role in providing nuclear technology to other countries (Rabman, B., 2). Khan remains in Pakistan, where he was pardoned in 2003 by Musharraf. In September 2005 Musharraf stated that after two years of interrogations, investigators had been unable to learn if Khan had passed along designs for a Chinese nuclear weapon to North Korea and Iran. However, he said Khan had likely exported about a dozen centrifuges to North Korea to produce nuclear weapons.

Referendum on Musharraf

Seeking more legitimacy for his continued rule, Musharraf scheduled a referendum on his presidency for April 2002. The sole question on the referendum was "For the survival of the local government system, establishment of democracy, continuity of reforms, end to sectarianism and extremism, and to fulfill the vision of Quaid-i-Azam [the "Great Leader," referring to Pakistan's founder, Muhammad Ali Jinnah], would you like to elect President General Pervez Musharraf as President of Pakistan for five years?"

However, the constitution mandated the president be elected by members of the Senate and the national and provincial assemblies—which had been suspended in June 2001—making the referendum illegal in the view of many, including the Alliance for the Restoration of Democracy (ARD), a coalition of 15 political parties headed by the Pakistan People's Party (PPP) and the Pakistan Muslim League (PML). The ARD, formed in the aftermath of Musharraf's 1999 coup, urged voters to boycott the election and organized demonstrations against it. However, an attempt by the opposition to halt the referendum was rejected by the Supreme Court. After the vote the government claimed that about 70 percent of the 78 million eligible voters had participated in the referendum and that 98 percent had voted in favor of an extension of Musharraf's presidency, but according to Human Rights Watch by most accounts the vote was rigged and the numbers grossly inflated (Human Rights Watch 2002). In preparation for the October 2002 general election Musharraf issued the Legal Framework Order of 2002 in August. Its stated purpose was to give the president the power to make laws as necessary to facilitate the general elections. Yet it also gave the president the power to dismiss the prime minister and dissolve Parliament, much as the Eighth Amendment to the constitution had before it was rescinded. Opposition parties viewed the framework order as illegal and unconstitutional and refused to recognize Musharraf's dual roles as head of the military and head of state. As the election approached, the Islamic parties, which had formed a coalition called the Muttahida Majlis-e-Amal (MMA, or United Council of Action), tried to exploit the public's unhappiness with Pakistan's support for the U.S.-led War on Terror. Up until the October 2002 election the combined results for all religious parties together had never exceeded 7 percent of the vote; in the October election the MMA drew unexpectedly large support, becoming the third largest party in the national parliament. The coalition also won an absolute majority in the provincial assembly of NWFP, and formed the largest party in the provincial assembly in Baluchistan. Despite the impressive gains of the MMA, no political party won an absolute majority. The party that Musharraf had endorsed, the Pakistan Muslim League Quaid-e-Azam (PML-Q), won a plurality with 34.5 percent of the vote, and the PPP came in second with 23.7 percent. In November Parliament and provincial assemblies elected Zafarullah Khan Jamali (r. 2002–04) of the PML-Q as prime minister, and Musharraf gave up the title of chief executive. Jamali affirmed Pakistan's support for the War on Tenor.

Musharraf's War on Terror

Though the government threw its support behind the War on Terror, Pakistan remained a haven for terrorist activity, as it had been well before 9/11. The madrasas run by fundamentalist clerics inculcated youngsters with lessons in jihad and anti-Western attitudes. In 1993 a Pakistani had come to the United States and murdered two CIA employees and wounded three others in an attack outside of CIA headquarters in Virginia. That same year Ramzi Yousef (b. 1967) traveled to the United States and helped orchestrate the first bombing of the World Trade Center in New York, where six died and some 1,000 were injured. He fled to Southeast Asia where he conducted a bombing in Cebu City in the Philippines and aboard a Philippine airliner, which killed one passenger, and was arrested in Islamabad in 1995 while planning to carry out simultaneous bombings of 11 U.S. airliners. Two U.S. diplomats were shot to death by militants in Karachi in 1995, and two years later four U.S. businessmen were shot to death by militants in that same city. In the post-9/11 world the threat was exemplified by the abduction and subsequent beheading in Pakistan of a U.S. reporter for the *Wall Street Journal,* Daniel Pearl (1963–2002), in February 2002. Three of the four suspected principals in the 2005 terrorist bombings in London that killed 55 had visited Pakistan the previous year.

In March 2003 Khalid Shaikh Mohammed (b. ca. 1964), the former head of al-Qaeda operations, linked to both Ramzi Yousef and the

MOST WANTED TERRORISTS

Rs 1 CRORE
MATI-UR-REHMAN
Alias Samad
District: Multan

Rs 2 CRORE
AMJAD HUSSAIN
Alias Amjad Farooqi
District: Faisalabad

Rs 2 CRORE
ABU FARAJ AL LIBBI
Alias Dr. Taufeeq
Country Libya

Rs 50 LAKH
MANSOOR
Alias Chota Ibrahim
District: Karachi

Rs 50 LAKH
QARI EHSAN
Alias Shahid
District: Bahawalpur

Rs 50 LAKH
OMAR AQDAS
Alias Sohail
District: Shiekhupura

ABOVE INDIVIDUALS ARE WANTED FOR ACTS OF TERRORISM. GOVERNMENT OF PAKISTAN OFFERS CASH REWARD TO PERSON GIVING INFORMATION LEADING TO THEIR ARREST. IDENTIFICATION OF THE INFORMER WOULD BE KEPT SECRET.

TELEPHONE NUMBERS (UAN) 080034567 (TOLL FREE)
080076543

E-MAIL:
helpus_555@hotmail.com
helpus_555@yahoo.co.uk

GOVERNMENT OF PAKISTAN

Islamic terrorism became a growing threat in Pakistan at the beginning of the 21st century. This Islamabad newspaper advertisement from 2004 shows the nation's six most wanted terrorists. (AP Photo/AP Images)

Daniel Pearl murder, was arrested in Pakistan. Five army officers with possible ties to Mohammed were put in military detention as part of the investigation. The links between the military and terrorists and religious extremists aroused concern about the loyalties of the armed forces. Musharraf himself survived assassination attempts and planned attacks, several of which involved members of the military officer corps. In December 2003 he survived two attacks while traveling by car, and other planned attacks were reportedly uncovered and stopped.

Despite these assassination attempts Musharraf stayed the course. He was rewarded for his efforts with economic and military assistance from the United States, including an end to U.S. economic sanctions, an increase in foreign aid, and the waiver or payment rescheduling of more than one-third of Pakistan's external debt. Direct foreign investment increased after 9/11 as well. Cash inflows enabled the government to balance its books, increase economic growth, and procure weapons. Internal revenue collection also improved, reducing deficits. Inflation, which had been running in double digits, declined. But some reforms were complicated by the events of 9/11. Almost half of Pakistan's GNP and most of its export earnings come from the agricultural sector, controlled by a few thousand feudal families. In February 2000 the government had announced plans for a massive land-reform program to end feudalism and the power of landed families. That October the government had issued a report calling for rapid land redistribution to empower landless peasants. But no action was taken at the time, and after Musharraf allied Pakistan with the West—an unpopular decision among many Pakistanis—he needed all the support he could get, and could not afford to antagonize the powerful feudal families. At the same time, many U.S. officials continued to doubt Musharraf's commitment to the War on Terror. In 2003 Musharraf dispatched some 70,000 to 80,000 troops to NWFP, FATA, and Baluchistan. Trained to battle Indian troops on open plains, the troops were poorly prepared and equipped for mountain warfare and sustained heavy initial casualties. Tribal leaders were paid to end the fighting. After the U.S. elections in November 2003, the Bush administration gave Pakistan another $1 billion in military aid, including P-3C Orion surveillance aircraft, Phalanx weapons systems for naval ships, and 2,000 Tow antitank missiles. The CIA opened clandestine bases in Pakistan in late 2003 to search for bin Laden, but claimed its operations were hampered by the oversight and policies of Pakistan. Pakistani officials claimed supervision was needed for the Americans' safety, as they were unpopular and immediately identifiable. Whatever the level of cooperation, the Musharraf government was reluctant to flaunt its support for the United States because of hostility to the United States in the tribal areas and among Islamic militants. The Pakistani government had long been resented in the region for both its interference and its neglect.

Since the October 2002 elections the dispute over the validity of the Legal Framework Order (LFO) of 2002 had remained unresolved, leading to a legislative stalemate. In December 2003 Musharraf was able to gain the support of the MMA, the alliance of religious parties, in part by tempering his support for secularization initiatives such as efforts to roll back Hudood laws that the MMA wanted to keep in place. And in the run-up to the general elections of 2002, Musharraf created arbitrary educational qualifications for holding public office to disqualify members of moderate parties, while recognizing degrees from madrasas, so fundamentalist candidates could run unimpeded. With the MMA in Musharraf's legislative camp, he now had the two-thirds majority required to adopt the LFO. Prosperity helped dampen dissent. Spurred by the end of the United States's foreign-aid embargo, Pakistan's GDP had increased by 6.4 percent in 2003/4, well above the target 5.3 percent. That December, by legislative vote, the Legal Framework Order of 2002 became the Seventeenth Amendment of the constitution. Musharraf promised to relinquish on January 1, 2004, some of the authority and powers he had exercised since the coup, and he agreed to give up his military position on December 31, 2004. In return Musharraf received a vote of confidence from Parliament and the four provincial assemblies, and his five-year term ending in 2007 was endorsed. However, the opposition boycotted the vote, though they did not try to block the confidence vote itself from taking place. The Seventeenth Amendment also indemnified Musharraf for any actions undertaken since the coup of October 12, 1999.

With this new endorsement in hand Musharraf continued to crack down on militants. In June 2004 Pakistani troops attacked suspected al-Qaeda hideouts and a training facility in a tribal region near the town of Shakai in South Waziristan. Tension had grown in South Waziristan in the preceding month as authorities pressured tribesmen to evict hundreds of Central Asian, Arab, and Afghan militants, many of whom moved there from Afghanistan after the fall of the Taliban regime in late 2001. The militants refused to surrender and register with authorities despite a government offer of amnesty allowing them to settle in Pakistan if they renounced terrorism. The army eventually deployed 25,000 troops in South Waziristan.

Meanwhile, the international community accused Pakistan of continuing to harbor and finance Afghani Islamic militants. In August

2004, President Musharraf vowed that Pakistan would not allow Islamic militants from Afghanistan and now living in Pakistan to disrupt elections in Afghanistan. But diplomats familiar with the border region claimed Pakistan had been training, funding, and organizing such elements. Diplomats said militant training operations in Baluchistan were so extensive that it was not possible for the ISI to be ignorant of the activity. In September and October Pakistani air and ground forces attacked several suspected training bases in NWFP and tribal areas near the Afghan border. Hundreds of militants, soldiers, and civilians were reportedly killed.

Political Repression

Whatever lip service the Musharraf regime paid to restoring democracy, its actions served to stifle dissent. In 2003 Pakistani officials arrested Javed Hashmi (b. 1948), a leader of the Alliance for the Restoration of Democracy and provisional head of the PML. Accused of urging army officers to rebel against General Musharraf, Hashmi was sentenced to seven years in prison. In April 2004 he was sentenced to 23 years in prison on sedition charges after a closed trial. In May Shahbaz Sharif, former chief minister of Punjab and brother of former prime minister Nawaz Sharif, was deported upon his arrival in Pakistan following three years in exile. Hundreds of PML followers were reportedly arrested. The Supreme Court had ruled in April that Shahbaz Sharif had the right to return to defend himself in court against charges that included extrajudicial killings—executions carried out by police, state agents, or other authorities without permission of courts or legal authority—while in office. But the government claimed a secret agreement prevented family members of the deposed prime minister from returning for a decade. Shahbaz Sharif maintained no such agreement existed. At the time of his arrival in Lahore, cellular phone service was blocked throughout the city.

Prime Minister Zafarullah Khan Jamali resigned on June 26, 2004, without offering an explanation. Chaudhry Shujaat Hussain of the PML-Q was appointed caretaker prime minister (r. June–Aug. 2004) until Parliament chose Shaukat Aziz, the minister of finance who had supervised the recent economic recovery, as prime minister (r. 2004–07).

In November 2004 Asif Ali Zardari, the husband of former prime minister Benazir Bhutto, who had been in jail for eight years awaiting trial on murder and corruption charges, was released on bail. Zardari criticized Musharraf and called for free elections. He was rearrested in late December while preparing to fly to Islamabad to address a political rally. At the same time hundreds of armed police officers set up barricades to prevent members of Ms. Bhutto's political party from going to the airport or attending the rally. After word of Zardari's arrest spread, supporters clashed with the police, smashing windows as the police fired tear gas and carried out baton charges. Zardari's arrest came days after General Musharraf confirmed in a Pakistani TV interview that he was withdrawing his promise to step down as army chief and become the country's civilian president by the end of 2004. He said that for the sake of the country's stability he would continue to hold both posts, which gave him sweeping powers, until elections scheduled for 2007.

In December 2004 U.S. president George W. Bush (r. 2001–09) praised General Musharraf after meeting him in Washington, D.C., calling him a crucial ally in the War on Terror and a force for democracy in Pakistan. American support helped encourage Musharraf to deal with domestic opposition as he chose. With the leaders of the two main opposition parties in exile—Nawaz Sharif in Saudi Arabia and Benazir Bhutto in London—his chief critics had been neutralized.

Factional and Religious Violence

Political, sectarian, and criminal violence increased throughout Pakistan during the Musharraf years, a tragedy exemplified by the assassination of former prime minister Benazir Bhutto in December 2007. During 2007, an average of one suicide bomb per week was detonated in Pakistan. The violence was caused in part by a lack of state authority combined with the power of local insurrectionist groups. In 2007 violence associated with terrorist activities was estimated to have cost the lives of more than 1,500 civilians, and almost 600 security personnel and 1,500 insurgents. This was more than double the total of the previous year, and a remarkable increase over the 189 total such fatalities recorded in 2003. Not surprisingly, the problem of violence associated with terrorism was worse in areas where insurrectionists and the government forces mobilized to counteract them were most active.

Sectarian violence also increased markedly in 2007. In a total of 341 acts of such violence, more than 440 people were killed, and 630 were injured. The previous year saw only 38 such incidents, resulting in 201 deaths and 349 injuries. The problem is hardly Pakistan's alone. More than 80 percent of the suicide bombers in Afghanistan are recruited and trained in Pakistan.

Federally Administered Tribal Areas (FATA)

More than 100,000 Pakistani soldiers are deployed in FATA to fight the Taliban, al-Qaeda and other militant groups. More than 1,680 persons were killed here as a result of this battle during 2007, making this the second most violent subnational geographic unit in South Asia after Sri Lanka's Northern Province. Though primarily affecting North and South Waziristan and Kurram, the violence also is felt in the other four agencies—Bajaur, Mohmand, Khyber, and Orakzai. In September 2006 the government signed a peace agreement with tribal leaders in North Waziristan. This dismayed many who counted on Musharraf to take a strong hand against Islamic militants. Violence flared again after the July 2007 siege of the Lal Mosque, or Red Mosque, in Islamabad. A hotbed of Islamic militancy, clerics had been inciting students to stage antigovernment actions and engage in Islamic vigilantism, trying to force the public to obey sharia, or Islamic religious laws. The clerics' refusal to surrender to authorities led to the eight-day siege of the mosque by the army. The army's assault on the mosque resulted in 87 reported deaths. The public for the most part did not support the extremists' position, and relatively little public demonstrations of anger were staged in the aftermath in most of the country. However, violence surged in the tribal regions, and the 10-month old cease-fire agreements with tribal leaders broke down.

In August militants in the tribal areas captured 242 soldiers from the Pakistani army. The government freed two dozen incarcerated militants to win the soldiers' release. But alarmed at the growing lawlessness and loss of control over the region, in November 2007 the army began a large operation against militants in the Swat Valley. In January the army commenced a major military offensive in South Waziristan. However, in early February 2008 the Pakistani government and the Taliban agreed to a cease-fire. Again, those looking for decisive action against the militants—an approach many Pakistanis opposed, seeing it as a U.S.-driven policy—were disappointed.

NWFP

NWFP has become a major battleground for Islamic insurrectionists. In 2007 this conflict claimed the lives of at least 1,190 people, compared to a total of 163 deaths due to such activity recorded in 2006. Twenty-two of the province's 24 districts harbor various levels of militant activity. The NWFP is now regarded by terrorism experts as the heart of Islamic militant mobilization in the Pakistan-Afghanistan

region. This is all the more noteworthy as NWFP traditionally had a strong federal presence, unlike the largely ungoverned FATA. The process of radicalization increased markedly since the Islamist alliance, the Muttahida Majlis-e-Amal, won an absolute majority in the provincial assembly in 2002 after Musharraf reportedly rigged the election in their favor. The trajectory of violence in NWFP is especially troubling to experts, who note that past experience in South Asia has shown that once antistate violence reaches a critical threshold it is difficult to contain or reverse.

Baluchistan

While Islamic extremists have increased their activities in recent years in Baluchistan, the majority of the unrest in the province is linked to the Baluchi nationalist movement, and there is no evidence of cooperation between Baluchis and either Pashtun Islamist militants, the Taliban, or al-Qaeda.

A revival of nationalism in Baluchistan emerged in the new century spearheaded by the Baluch Liberation Organization, a group possibly linked to the Baluch People's Liberation Organization; the latter had led the uprising under Zulfikar Bhutto, who brutally suppressed the rebellion. The disparity between the poor economic state of the province and the wealth it produced for the rest of the nation helped fuel the unrest. So did the lack of royalty payments to the province or its tribes for gas extracted from their land. In December 2004 nationalists staged several attacks that claimed dozens of lives across the province. Forces of the Frontier Corps, a paramilitary patrol, were also attacked. The Baluch Liberation Army (BLA) claimed credit for most of the attacks.

The BLA established guerrilla training camps for Baluch militants; even the government, loathe to show signs of vulnerability, admitted the existence of at least 15 such facilities, each reportedly with 300 to 500 recruits. The government pursued a policy of isolating and containing the nationalists in Baluchistan, though Musharraf indicated he was willing to take stronger measures. "Don't push us," he said in a warning to the BLA and their supporters, "This is not the 1970s, and this time you won't even know what has hit you" (Rahman, 2004, 1).

Musharraf was referring to a previous Baluch insurgency that occurred in the aftermath of the loss of East Pakistan. The nation was now much more militarily powerful. But Musharraf did not have the popularity or support in Punjab and Sind that had allowed Bhutto to use his harsh tactics in Baluchistan. In addition, the involvement of military officers in attempts on Musharraf's life indicated a lack of complete support within the armed forces. And the army was engaged in battling foreign fighters in South Waziristan—Arabs, Uzbeks, Chechens, and others—complicating any potential campaign in Baluchistan. Moreover, Baluchistan contains the gas fields and mineral deposits upon which much of the country and the economy depend; military action and insurgent strikes against economic targets could cripple the nation.

The government was also constructing a new seaport in Baluchistan, Gwadar Port, begun under Nawaz Sharif. It was planned as an adjunct to Pakistan's sole international seaport, Karachi, which had dominated as well as constrained the country's maritime trade. The government relied on imported labor to construct the facility and other projects, another sore point with Baluchis, who demanded more jobs for local residents.

As of 2007 all 30 districts of Baluchistan were affected by either tribal insurgency or Islamist extremism or both. The tribal insurgency, driven by Baluchi nationalism, accounted for most of the violence. All told, as many as 1,170 people were killed in Baluchistan as a result of this activity from 2004 to 2008.

In 2006 government forces killed Akbar Khan Bugti, a Baluchi insurrectionist leader, one of at least 450 people killed in the province that year as a result of militant activity. In 2007 the level of nationalist violence declined, as some leaders left the country or were effectively neutralized by government action, and the death toll attributed to such violence declined to about 245. Yet despite the decline in deaths, sabotage and bombings of gas pipelines, railway tracks, power transmission lines, bridges, communication infrastructure, and military and government facilities were widespread.

Traditionally, the government observed "A" and "B" areas of Baluchistan, the former under the jurisdiction of Pakistani police, the latter where police do not operate. A community-based "Levies" force kept order in these latter areas, as they had for centuries. An experiment beginning in 2004 to reduce violence by allowing the police into "B" areas has been a failure, as crime in these areas has grown dramatically in the aftermath of the shift in law-enforcement strategy.

Sunni-Shi'i Violence

Between 1990 and 2005 some 1,200 people died in clashes between Sunni and Shi'i extremist groups in Pakistan. Sunnis make up 77 percent of the country's population and Shi'is 20 percent. The roots of the current violence can be traced back to the regime of Zia ul-Haq. A Sunni, Zia had Zulfikar Bhutto, a Shi'i whom he deposed, executed. Many Shi'is viewed Zia's efforts to enhance the role of Islam in Pakistan as a "Sunnification" of the country, as the laws were based on Sunni interpretations of Islamic strictures. The Shi'i revolution in Iran that brought Ruhollah Khomeini (1902–89) to power in 1979 had already inspired the radicalization of some Shi'is in the region. As the conflict between the two sects intensified, Shi'is and Sunnis formed political parties and militia groups. Meanwhile, the Taliban, a Sunni group, provided training for militants dedicated to this internecine battle.

Two prominent Sunni figures were assassinated in 2003/4: Maulana Azam Tariq (b. 1962), a leading militant, in fall 2003, and Mufti Nizamuddin Shamzai, a pro-Taliban cleric, in May 2004. Shi'i militants were blamed for both killings. In May 2004 a suicide bombing in a Shi'i mosque led to a chain of violence that claimed more than 90 lives and 200 injuries. Police and members of the armed forces were implicated in some of the attacks.

Kashmir

It is estimated that the dispute in Kashmir has cost more than 50,000 lives since 1989, when the latest cycle of violence began, and the closing years of the first decade of the 21st century (HRWF 2007).

In another effort to resolve the dispute Foreign Secretary Riaz Khokhar (served 2002–05) went to Delhi in late June 2004 for two days of discussions with Indian prime minister Vajpayee. In a show of good faith before the meeting began, Vajpayee had declared a cease-fire on the Kashmir frontier, announced the reopening of cross-border road links, and pledged to maintain a freeze on nuclear testing. In February 2005 Pakistan and India agreed to establish a bus service between Srinagar and Muzaffarabad, the capitals of the Indian- and Pakistan-controlled portions of Kashmir, respectively. The highway between the two capitals had been more or less closed since 1947, when the subcontinent was partitioned to create Pakistan and India, separating tens of thousands of families.

The Kashmir bus-service agreement did not address the disputed Line of Control (LOC), which cuts through Kashmir. It allowed authorities on the two sides to issue an "entry permit" to passengers. India had earlier insisted on conventional passports and visas for those traveling across Kashmir, a practice that Pakistan rejected on the grounds that it would make the LOC a national border. In March 2005 a 220-foot-long bridge, now called the Peace Bridge, was rebuilt crossing the LOC near Salamabad in Indian-held Kashmir.

On April 7 the first crossing occurred. Thirty Pakistanis walked across from west to east to board buses for a reception in Salamabad before proceeding to Srinagar. About three hours later 19 Indians made the reverse crossing, east to west. They boarded buses bound for Muzaffarabad, the capital of Pakistan-controlled Kashmir. Continuing in the spirit of rapprochement, in April Musharraf and Indian prime minister Manmohan Singh (r. 2004–   ) met in New Delhi and pledged to increase trade and continue their peace efforts. Before beginning negotiations, the two watched the first hour of a cricket match between their national teams together. Improved relations would enable both countries to cut defense expenditures. In 2004 Pakistan had spent about $3.7 billion, or 25 percent of its budget, on defense.

On October 8, 2005, a 7.6-magnitude earthquake centered in Pakistan-controlled Kashmir struck the area, the worst natural disaster in the nation's history. By early November the government put the death toll at 79,000 in Pakistan. An estimated 1,400 died in Indian-controlled Kashmir, where more than 30,000 masonry buildings collapsed in Srinagar. At least 69,000 people were severely injured in the earthquake.

In the wake of the earthquake India and Pakistan agreed to open crossings through the Line of Control between the contested areas of

A MASSIVE EARTHQUAKE

On October 8, 2005, an earthquake registering 7.6 struck an isolated mountainous area in NWFP, Pakistan-controlled Kashmir, and a small corner of India. It was the worst earthquake in Pakistan in at least a century and the worst natural disaster to befall it since the nation's birth in 1947. At least 50,000 people died, and more than 75,000 were injured. As many as 550,000 families were left homeless by the disaster. The government had difficulty responding to the emergency due to damage to infrastructure, limited resources, and poorly coordinated relief efforts. The government's perceived failure undermined the legitimacy of Musharraf, who had come to power claiming only the military had the capability to run the government effectively. The slow and limited search and rescue efforts were exacerbated by the relatively weak response from the international community, which had already been overextended by the massive natural disasters that year, including the tsunami that swept the coast of the Indian Ocean and Hurricane Katrina, which devastated the Gulf Coast of the United States. In the aftermath of the quake India and Pakistan made gestures to demonstrate mutual concern. Rules governing access to the heavily militarized border areas were suspended, enabling the flow of supplies and assistance. Pakistan accepted aid from its long-time enemy, but refused the offer of helicopters unless Pakistani crews were allowed to operate them, a condition that India declined to accept.

Kashmir for the first time in decades. Phone links, which had been severed since the rebellion in the Indian-controlled area 16 years before, were also restored.

Musharraf's Tenuous Hold on Power

By 2005 Pakistan was receiving $700 million annually in bilateral assistance and $84 million monthly from the United States to underwrite its antiterrorist efforts, as well as $1.7 billion from international financial institutions, secured with the support of the United States. By 2006 foreign reserves had risen to $16 billion, though foreign debt rose to $40 billion. As of the following October, the eighth anniversary of Musharraf's coup, the economy had grown almost 50 percent, and income had risen by almost 25 percent. Throughout this eight-year period, GDP per capita increased at nearly twice the rate of growth of the population. Yet this did not greatly affect the prevalence of poverty. The lower classes did not see the benefits that the upper classes did, as the expansion came mainly from sectors that offered high returns to investors, such as real estate development and the modern service sector, neither of which provided much employment for the lower class. That same month the government was projecting a 7 percent to 8 percent annual increase in GDP over the next several years, though many economists took this to be overly optimistic.

Musharraf worked to make the country attractive to foreign investors. However, the lack of political stability slowed international investments, as did religious fundamentalism and its anticonsumerist ethos. Recent examples of foreign investment include U.S. tobacco company Altria's purchase of a domestic cigarette manufacturer and investments by consumer companies such as MacDonald's and PepsiCo and mobile telephone companies from the Middle East and China. However, such businesses do not offer the long-term economic stability that investments in more basic industries typically provide. Moreover, Pakistan's budget deficit continued growing, exports stagnated, and power shortages, artificial price controls, and inflation continued to plague the economy.

Pakistan's economic story has been characterized as "growth without development." Though per capita income increases of the last half-century have been respectable, the country was still behind on most social and political indicators of progress: education, health, sanitation, gender equality, fertility, corruption, political instability, violence, and democracy.

The Seventeenth Amendment to the constitution had stated that, after December 31, 2004, the offices of president and chief of army staff shall not be held concurrently by the same person. However, a month before Musharraf was to give up his military position, the Senate chairman, acting as president while Musharraf was out of the country, signed into law a bill allowing Musharraf to continue to hold both posts. While the Supreme Court was considering the question of whether his current tenure was legal, Musharraf suspended the chief justice of the Supreme Court, Iftikhar Mohammad Chaudhry, in March 2007 on charges of abuse of power and nepotism. The charges were widely viewed as an attack by Musharraf on the judge's increasingly independent rulings; the general was thought to have feared that Chaudhry would someday declare unconstitutional Musharraf's intention to be reelected as president while retaining his army position. The suspension sparked protests led by lawyers and increased calls for Musharraf's resignation.

Increasingly under pressure and isolated, Musharraf cast about for a way to retain power. To tamp down public discontent, Musharraf called for new elections. He suggested that Benazir Bhutto and Nawaz Sharif might be allowed to return to Pakistan and stand for office. In July news that Musharraf had met Benazir Bhutto in Abu Dhabi to discuss a possible power-sharing arrangement became public. The same month the Supreme Court reinstated Chief Justice Chaudhry, declaring his suspension illegal. In August, after the chief justice's return, the Supreme Court freed one of the country's most prominent opposition politicians, Javed Hashmi of the PML, whom Musharraf had jailed four years before for criticizing the military. In the same month it ruled Nawaz Sharif had an inalienable right to return to Pakistan. The Supreme Court was emerging as the only potential check on Musharraf's power besides the military itself. With political turmoil deepening, Musharraf hinted he might declare a state of emergency, as allowed under the constitution, should he deem the country's security threatened by war, external aggression, or internal disturbance beyond the authority of the provincial government's authority to control.

Nawaz Sharif returned in September but was promptly arrested, charged with corruption, and deported to Saudi Arabia. He was allowed to return to Pakistan in November but was forbidden from running for Parliament. But he threatened to lead mass protests if emergency rule was not lifted.

Bhutto, whose negotiations with Musharraf had failed, returned to Pakistan on October 18 and began campaigning. On the eve of her return a presidential ordinance had granted Bhutto and other opponents amnesty from all pending corruption cases in return for support for Musharraf's rule for another term.

Musharraf announced he would run for president in a separate election in October, pledging that if elected he would give up his position as army chief of staff. Opposition parties boycotted the election as unconstitutional. Musharraf was reelected to the presidency by parliamentary vote in the national and provincial assemblies. Opponents contested the constitutionality of the election and of Musharraf's dual roles. The result remained in limbo pending a Supreme Court ruling on the issues. Meanwhile, in late November 2007 Musharraf resigned as army chief of staff, appointing General Ashfaq Parvez Kayani to the position.

With the Supreme Court poised to rule on the constitutionality of the presidential election and Musharraf's rule, Musharraf declared a state of emergency on November 3, 2007, despite international protests. He claimed emergency rule was necessary to counter the Islamic militants in the tribal areas. He appointed a new Supreme Court; meanwhile, thousands of opposition-party activists, lawyers, and judges were arrested. The state of emergency was lifted in mid-December.

Benazir Bhutto returned from exile in October of 2007 to campaign for office and promote her party's candidates. Here she addresses a group of supporters during the campaign. She was assassinated in December while leaving a rally in Rawalpindi.

Bhutto had returned to London for a few days just before Musharraf declared emergency rule, then came back to Pakistan to resume her campaign. At the welcoming rally a bomb intended to assassinate her killed 140 people. Bhutto escaped injury and continued her political quest. She decried the emergency rule and the lack of decisive movement against Islamic militants, and was placed repeatedly under house arrest. The election was scheduled for January 2008.

On December 27, 2007, Bhutto was assassinated as she left a rally in Rawalpindi. At least three other candidates were murdered during the campaign. After her assassination, Musharraf announced elections would be pushed back until February 18. Bhutto's widower, Asif Ali Zardari, took control of the PPP, claiming he would act as caretaker until their son, Bilawal, finished college and could lead the party.

In a reversal of Musharraf's practice of encouraging military involvement in the government and politics, in January 2008 the new army chief of staff, General Ashfaq Parvez Kayani, ordered military officers to refrain from involvement in political affairs and the upcoming elections. In February he ordered them to withdraw from civil service positions.

National Elections of 2008

Tensions rose in the weeks leading up to the contest, as fears of election fraud, violence on the campaign trail, and voter intimidation grew. But the elections were relatively calm. The results were a resounding defeat for Musharraf and his party, the PML-Q, which won only 38 seats out of the 272 in the National Assembly. At least 10 of its ministers and senior leaders also lost their seats.

The MMA, the coalition of six religious parties, was also soundly defeated, winning just 5 seats. The PPP, headed by Zardari, won the most seats, and the PML, headed by Nawaz Sharif, came in second. Together the two parties gained 171 seats. Needing a two-thirds majority to change the constitution and weaken Musharraf's powers as president, the two parties began discussions on forming a coalition government.

The major issue dividing the two parties involved the reinstatement of the 60 dismissed judges, whose removal by Musharraf had been one of the lightning rods for opposition to his regime. Sharif and the PML sought the judges' immediate reinstatement. The PPP preferred to avoid a confrontation with Musharraf they felt an immediate reinstatement would likely provoke. Moreover, Chaudhry, the dismissed chief justice, had previously raised issues about the legality of the pardon Musharraf had granted Benazir Bhutto and Zardari for corruption and other charges, which had allowed them to return to Pakistan without facing arrest. The PPP's concern about Chaudhry's position on the pardon likely affected the party's position on the cashiered judges' reinstatement. The two parties were unable to reach an agreement on the issue and, in May, the PML withdrew from the cabinet, though at the time party officials said it would continue to support the coalition government. Though the PPP–PML partnership was unsuccessful, the brief alliance marked the first time Pakistan's two main parties joined to provide civilian rule.

One of the most immediate results of the election was a new policy toward Pakistani militants in the tribal areas and NWFP. Whereas Musharraf had sent in army troops in an effort to root out home grown and foreign militants (though his level of commitment to this effort was a subject of longstanding debate), the new government sought a truce with them. Opposition to Musharraf's military approach was widespread, in part because it was seen as an affront to Pakistani sovereignty, a policy set in Washington rather than Islamabad. In April 2008 the government began negotiations with leaders of Pashtun tribes that historically had controlled the areas where militants linked to al-Qaeda

Asif Ali Zardari (r.), widower of Benazir Bhutto, and former prime minister Nawaz Sharif hold a joint press conference in March 2008, after the PPP and PML election victories, to announce an agreement to form a coalition government. (AP Photo/Anjum Naveed)

operated. That same month the government announced a tentative accord with the militant groups. The agreement would require tribes to expel foreign militants, cease attacks and kidnappings, and allow the Frontier Corps, the government's local security force, freedom of movement in the region. It also called for an exchange of prisoners and the gradual withdrawal of Pakistani military forces from part of the tribal region in South Waziristan. But it held no promise of reining in militant activity. In June Baitullah Mehsud, leader of Tehrik-e-Taliban, a coalition of militant groups. who was himself accused of involvement in the assassination of Benazir Bhutto, vowed to continue mounting cross-border raids to fight against NATO forces in Afghanistan in support of the Taliban.

The United States continued trying to blunt the militant activity on its own. In May a house in the border region was destroyed by what was believed to be a missile fired from a drone aircraft operated by the United States. It was at least the third site known to be used by al-Qaeda operatives struck by missiles from drones. However, neither Pakistan nor the United States would confirm that such attacks took place. In July, U.S. president George W. Bush authorized military operations by U.S. ground forces in Pakistan without the approval of the Pakistani government. In September, Special Operations forces carried out the first publicly acknowledged ground raid in Pakistan. Attacks on suspected militant targets in Pakistan by U.S. drone aircraft also increased. Charges by Pakistanis and independent monitors that attacks by missiles fired from drone aircraft frequently killed civilians exacerbated anti-U.S. sentiment in the country. Violence wrought by militants in other areas of Pakistan also continued. In June a suicide car bomber attacked the Danish embassy in Islamabad, killing at least six people. The target was thought to be chosen because in February Danish newspapers had reprinted cartoons considered insulting to the prophet Muhammad.

The Pakistan government's degree of control over the ISI, and the ISI's involvement in attacks carried out by militants in Afghanistan also came to the fore at this time. U.S. and Afghan intelligence agencies concluded that ISI operatives were involved in a July bombing of the Indian embassy in Kabul that killed 58 people, as well as in a bombing that targeted Afghanistan's president, Hamid Karzai, in April.

When Pakistan's prime minister (from 2008–   ), Yousaf Raza Gilani, visited the United States in late July, administration officials pressed him to exert greater control over the ISI. Gilani publicly denied charges that the ISI assisted or colluded with Islamic militants. Yet on the eve of his visit, Pakistan issued a memorandum stating the ISI would henceforth report to the civilian officials in the Interior Ministry, rather than to the military. However, the following day, the government reversed the new policy, reportedly due to objections from the ISI, stating its announcement had been misinterpreted and that the government would simply improve its coordination with the ISI.

Meanwhile, in the wake of the bombing of India's embassy in Afghanistan and several cease-fire violations along the Line of Control in Kashmir, relations between India and Pakistan sank to their lowest level since the two countries came to the brink of war in 2003, according to statements by Indian officials.

Relations with the United States had also grown more strained due to unwavering American support for president Pervez Musharraf; U.S. officials viewed Musharraf as a more reliable foe of terrorism than coalition leaders Nawaz Sharif or Asif Ali Zardari, despite whatever lack of commitment to democracy Musharraf evinced while in office and despite the rejection of his government by Pakistani voters in the 2008 election.

Pakistan's fractious ruling coalition, widely seen as ineffectual in its first months in office, harnessed its fragile unity to move toward impeaching president Musharraf. Lacking support, Musharraf resigned in late August of 2008 rather than face impeachment. Shortly after his resignation the PML(N), which had already withdrawn from the cabinet over a dispute with the PPP about reinstatement of the Supreme Court justices the president had fired, left the coalition. The PML(N) wanted the justices reinstated; the PPP resisted restoring the justices, perhaps fearing they would overturn the amnesty for corruption charges the replacement justices granted Zardari.

Zardari was elected president of Pakistan in September and pledged to improve relations with Afghanistan. His administration also promised to eliminate the constitutional provision that allowed the president to dismiss Parliament. Whatever its intentions, Zardari's government faced significant challenges in bringing Pakistan the stability that has eluded the country for most of its history.

Looking Ahead

One of the most fundamental questions of Pakistan's future is whether it can exist as a democracy. Stable political institutions never had a chance to take root in the nation's first turbulent years. The country's political father, Mohammed Ali Jinnah, died only 13 months after the country's founding in 1947. His closest associate and political heir was assassinated four years later, setting a precedent for political upheaval that has afflicted Pakistan ever since.

Pakistan is united by history and religion and rightly wears its independence with pride. But there are strong countervailing trends, groups, and attitudes working against the integration of its myriad parts into a greater whole. Ethnic and sectarian violence and a congenital inability of political institutions to function for the benefit of those they represent are ongoing problems.

The battle between militant and more moderate strains of Islam will be a major factor in future government policy. What constitutes progress and equality to the latter group represents apostasy and damnation to the former. Is there a possibility that these divisions will plunge the country into civil war?

Relations with India have warmed, but Kashmir remains a flashpoint ever ready to push the two countries into war. In the past, progress on forging normal relations between the two countries has been easily undone by violence wrought by small groups opposed to any negotiated settlement that stops short of delivering all the concessions they seek. And with their nuclear arsenals, a crisis could quickly spiral out of control. Will both governments be more cautious about their rhetoric and actions now that they could end in a nuclear confrontation?

And how will Pakistan address the poverty and lack of education that still afflicts so many of its people, or the endemic corruption that has undermined faith in its governmental institutions? Can democracy of the model Pakistan has developed, even if free of military interference, rise to meet these challenges? Or will the repeated bouts of military rule lead to some more permanent form of autocracy?

And what will happen if and when the United States's emphasis on the War on Terror wanes, or the government refuses to take part in it? Can Pakistan meet its internal challenges without the support and assistance of the United States? And what if the tacit approval for authoritarianism the United States has long extended to a succession of regimes around the world ends, and assistance only comes at the price of meaningful democratic reforms?

Yet Pakistan has resources to retain its newfound position of importance, filled as it is with the energy and determination that are increasingly the currency of a flattened world.

APPENDIX 1
GLOSSARY

Ahmadiyya Muslim sect that moved from India to Pakistan after partition; deemed heretical by religious leaders

ajrak Local crafts such as pottery, carpets, leatherwork, sericulture, and embroidery

Aryans "Noble ones" in SANSKRIT. One of a large group of nomadic tribes from Central Asia that invaded and controlled what is now Pakistan from 2000 B.C.E. to 1000 B.C.E. before migrating to what is now India

Azad Kashmir "Free," or "liberated" Jammu and Kashmir; the portion of Jammu and Kashmir under Pakistani control

British Raj The period of British colonial rule over the Indian subcontinent, including what is now Pakistan, lasting from 1858 until independence was proclaimed in 1947

chaudhry A village storehouse for crops

dharma In early Buddhism, the truth of the world's nature, or elements of existence.

diarchy System of government in the subcontinent whereby some government departments were under native rule, while other, more powerful, agencies remained under British control

doab The land between two rivers. The Indus has five major tributaries, and thus Punjab has four *doabs*.

East Wing A synonym for the province of East Pakistan, which became an anachronism when the territory gained independence as the nation of Bangladesh in 1971

factory Trading posts established by the Dutch, Portuguese, British, and French along the coast of the subcontinent and in the East Indies

fiqh Jurisprudence; the study of SHARIA, or Islamic law

Five Pillars of Islam   Five practices that define the duties of the faithful Muslim: *shahada* (testimony of faith), *salat* (daily prayer), ZAKAT (almsgiving), *sawm* (fasting during Ramadan), and hajj (pilgrimage to Mecca)

hartal   A nonviolent general-protest strike in which businesses remain closed, and workers stay home

imam   The leader of congregational prayer. Among SUNNIS, it also denotes the spiritual leader of the Islamic community and is an honorific bestowed on eminent Islamic scholars. For the Shi'is, *imam* refers to the cousin of the prophet Muhammad, Ali, or any of his descendants seen as the divine, true leaders of the Islamic community

iqta   Arabic term for a terrirorial assignment given to an administrative officer (*iqtadar*). By the time of Akbar's reign the term had been replaced by the Persian JAGIR.

jagir   Land assigned to a military officer, who was also known as a *jagaridir.* Officers administered the land, and the income generated paid their expenses and salaries as well as those of their subordinates.

jihad   "Striving" in Arabic; refers to both the personal struggle for holiness and holy war against infidels

jirga   A council system of government. A *jajirga* is a village council, and a *loya jirga* is a council that advises a ruler.

jizya   A tax of protection levied on non-Muslims

kareze   An underground water conduit

karma   From Sanskrit, the accreted spirit of one's good and bad deeds, determining the quality of next life

kashmiriyat   A Kashmiri Muslim identity based on Sufi traditions native to Kashmir's Srinagar Valley

khalsa   State lands. Revenue from these lands went to the royal treasury. This is also the name of the Sikh movement's military arm, created in 1699.

khel   A clan council based on the JIRGA system

lathi   A five-foot wooden staff used by police for crowd control

Line of Control   De facto border dividing the Pakistani- and Indian-controlled areas of Jammu and Kashmir. It was established at the cease-fire line the two nations agreed on at the Simla Conference after the Indo-Pakistan War in 1971.

mansabdari The enlightened administrative system that included a policy of advancement based on ability rather than birth. The administrators were known as *mansabdars.*

muhajir Immigrant or descendant of immigrants from India who fled to Pakistan after partition in 1947

mujahideen Muslim holy warriors. Pakistan, the United States, and Saudi Arabia established an army of *mujahideen* to battle the Soviet Union in Afghanistan.

Mukti Bahini Bengali for "liberation force." The fighters who led attacks, against Pakistani forces during the civil war in 1971, leading to the sundering of Pakistan and the creation of Bangladesh.

nirvana An exalted state of bliss and understanding

One Unit The name given to the 1955 administrative unification of the four provinces of the WEST WING into West Pakistan

panchayat A local committee presided over by a Brahman priest that settled disputes between Buddhists and Hindus

paramountcy The legal principle according one authority's law primacy over another's should the laws conflict. Under this principle the British imposed the doctrine of lapse in India, depriving rulers of the right to choose a successor in the absence of a natural heir.

qadi An Islamic judge who settles disputes among Muslims according to SHARIA, or Islamic law

Qur'an The book of Allah's revelations as brought forth by Muhammad; literally, the "recitation"

Rajputs "Sons of kings" SANSKRIT. A name adopted by regional Hindu rulers in northern Punjab and Kashmir.

rupee (R or Re) Pakistan's national currency. One U.S. dollar is the equivalent of about 60 rupees. A rupee is subdivided into 100 *paisa.*

Sanskrit The written language of the Aryans

sati The Hindu practice of burning widows alive on their husband's funeral pyre

satrapy A province under the rule of Persia's Achaemenian Empire, as was the Indus Valley in the middle of the first millennium B.C.E.

sharia Islamic law. It is based on the Qur'an, the accepted words and deeds of the prophet Muhammad, and codified interpretation of them by Islamic judges in the centuries immediately following his death.

Shia The smaller of the two major branches of Islam. (SUNNI is the other.) The Shi'is recognize Ali, cousin of the prophet Muhammad, and his descendants as the divine, true leaders of the Islamic community. Ali's death at the orders of an early caliph begot the schism.

soosi Cotton cloth, historically an important product of the Indus region

Sunni The larger of the two main branches of Islam. The Sunni reject Shi'i belief in the divine right of Ali, cousin of the prophet Muhammad, and his descendants to lead the Islamic community. Sunnis gave their fealty to a line of caliphs whose rule was based on dynasty rather than divinity.

ulama; s. *alim* Muslim religious leaders

Vedas Sacred text of the Aryans. These texts developed when the Aryans settled in what is now Pakistan and are the basis of the Hindu religion.

West Wing Former synonym for present-day Pakistan before East Pakistan—the EAST WING—gained independence as Bangladesh in 1971

Yavana Sanskrit for "Greeks," most commonly applied to Greek subjects during the reign of Ashoka (272–31 B.C.E.), who relied on them at court

zakat Alms tax levied on Muslims based on wealth

zamindar A landlord, particularly one under the zamindar system established by the British in the late 18th century, in which former Mughal tax collectors were given the status of landlords

APPENDIX 2

BASIC FACTS ABOUT PAKISTAN

Official Name
Islamic Republic of Pakistan

Geography

Area	Total: 307,380 sq. miles (796,095 sq. km); does not include Pakistan-administered portions of Jammu (4,483 sq. miles; 11,639 sq. km) and Kashmir (28,000 sq. miles; 72,520 sq. km), whose possession is disputed by India. Pakistan is slightly smaller than twice the size of California.
Land borders	Iran, Afghanistan, China, India
Coastal borders	Arabian Sea, Indian Ocean
Elevations	Highest: K2 (Mt. Godwin-Austen), 28,250 feet (8,611 m)
	Lowest: Indian Ocean, sea level
Terrain	Flat Indus Plain in the east, Baluchistan Plateau in west, mountains in north and northwest

Government
Founded on August 14, 1947, Pakistan is a federal republic. The prime minister is head of the government and appoints the cabinet. The prime minister is selected by the National Assembly for a five-year term. The president is the chief of state and appoints the judges of the Supreme Court. The legal system is based on English common law, with provisions to accommodate Pakistan's status as an Islamic state. The constitution was adopted on April 12, 1973; suspended on July 5,

1977; restored with amendments on December 30, 1985; suspended on October 15, 1999; restored on December 31, 2002; and amended on December 31, 2003. The legislative branch is the bicameral Parliament consisting of the Senate (100 seats), whose members are indirectly elected by provincial assemblies to a four-year term, and the National Assembly (342 seats), whose members are elected by popular vote to a four-year term. All citizens 18 years of age or older are eligible to vote. Since its founding in 1947, civilian rule has alternated with periods of martial law resulting from military coups.

Political Divisions

Capital	Islamabad (Population: 955,629)
Other Cities	Karachi, Lahore, Rawalpindi, Multan, Hyderabad
Subdivisions	Four provinces: Baluchistan, Sind, Punjab, North-West Frontier Province. One territory: Federally Administered Tribal Areas; One capital territory: Islamabad Capital Territory. The Pakistani-administered portion of the disputed Jammu and Kashmir region consists of two administrative entities: Azad Kashmir and Northern Areas

People

Population	167,762,040 (July 2008 est.)
Growth Rate	1.805% (2008 est.)
Ethnic Groups	Punjabis (44.2%); Pashtuns, or Pathans (15.4%); Sindhis (14.1%); Baluchis (3.6%); other ethnic groups, include Siraikis, *muhajirs*, and Brahuis.
Languages	Punjabi (48%); Sindhi (12%); Siraiki a Punjabi variant (10%); Pashtu (8%); Urdu (official; 8%); Baluchi (3%); Hindko (2%); Brahui (1%); and English, the official and lingua franca of Pakistani elite and most government ministries, Burushaski, and other (8%)
Religions	Muslim (97%; Sunni, 77%; Shia, 20%), Hindu (1.6%), Christian (1.6%), Bahai, Sikh, and others (0.3%)
Literacy	(Ability to read and write at age 15) 49.9%: 63% for males, 36% for females (2005 est.)

Age Structure	0–14 years: 36.3% (male 31,316,803/female 29,567,622) 15–64 years: 59.4% (male 51,000,863/female 48,648,480) 65 years and over: 4.3% (male 3,409,246/female 3,819,026) (2008 est.)
Median Age	Total: 21.2 Male: 21 Female: 21.4 (2008 est.)
Birth Rate	26.93 births/1,000 population (2008 est.)
Death Rate	7.83 deaths/1,000 population (2008 est.)
Infant Mortality	Total: 66.95 deaths/1,000 live births Male: 67.05 deaths/1,000 live births Female: 66.85 deaths/1,000 live births (2008 est.)
Life Expectancy	Total Population: 64.13 Male: 63.07 Female: 65.24 (2008 est.)
Total Fertility Rate	3.58 children born/woman (2008 est.)

Economy

For much of its history Pakistan's economy has been hobbled by the lack of internal political disputes, low levels of foreign investment, government mismanagement, corruption, and the costs associated with its long-standing disputes with its neighbor India. In 2002 the economy began a recovery due to changes in government policies and the resumption of international lending. The Musharraf government continued a process of economic liberalization that began in the 1980s. Privatization of government-owned industries, deregulation of the private sector, and financial reforms have spurred growth internally. The alliance with the United States and its allies in the global war on terrorism has stimulated economic assistance from the United States and foreign investment. The government's development spending, which equaled about 2 percent of the GDP (gross domestic product) in the 1990s, grew to 4 percent in 2003. During the same period, industrial production achieved double-digit annual growth. Dependence on the agricultural sector declined. Foreign reserves reached record levels in 2004 due to strong exports and remittances from Pakistanis working abroad. The nation's unreported economic activity is estimated to account for as much as 30 percent of the economy.

Gross Domestic Product (GDP)	$446.1 billion purchasing power parity (2007 est.)
GDP real growth rate	6.3% (2008 est.)
GDP per capita	$2,600 purchasing power parity (2008 est.)
Natural Resources	
Arable Land	23.44%
Permanent Crops	0.84%
Other	74.72%
Irrigated Land	70,386.42 sq. miles (182,300 sq. km)
Economic Sectors	
Agriculture	19.6% of GDP
Industry	26.8% of GDP
Services	53.7% of GDP
Agriculture	Cotton, wheat, rice, sugarcane, fruits, vegetables, milk, beef, mutton, eggs
Industries	Textiles and apparel, food processing, pharmaceuticals, construction materials, paper products, fertilizer, shrimp
Services	
Major Exports	Apparel, bed linens, cotton cloth, yarn, rice, leather goods, sports goods, chemicals, manufactures, carpets and rugs
Labor Force	49.18 million (includes extensive export of labor, mostly to the Middle East, and use of child labor)
By Occupation (2008 est.)	
Agriculture	42%
Industry	20%
Services	38%

Environmental Issues

Water pollution from raw sewage, industrial waste, and agricultural runoff; limited natural fresh water resources; adequate access to potable water for a majority of the population; deforestation; soil erosion; desertification

Transnational Issues

Kashmir remains the site of the world's largest and most militarized territorial dispute, with portions under the de facto administration of

China (Aksai Chin), India (Jammu and Kashmir), and Pakistan (Azad Kashmir and Northern Areas). The UN Military Observer Group in India and Pakistan (UNMOGIP) has maintained a small group of peacekeepers along the Line of Control since 1949. India does not recognize Pakistan's ceding of historic Kashmir lands to China in 1964. In 2004 India and Pakistan instituted a cease-fire in Kashmir and in 2005 restored bus service across the highly militarized Line of Control.

Pakistan has taken its dispute on the impact of India's building of the Baglihar Dam on the Chenab River in Jammu and Kashmir to the World Bank for arbitration; in general the two states still dispute Indus River water sharing. To defuse tensions and prepare discussions on a maritime boundary, in 2004 India and Pakistan resurveyed a portion of the disputed Sir Creek estuary at the mouth of the Rann of Kutch. Pakistani maps continue to show the Junagadh claim in India's Gujarat State.

By 2005 Pakistan, with UN assistance, had repatriated 2.3 million Afghan refugees and had undertaken a census to count the remaining million or more, many of whom remain at their own choosing. Pakistan has sent troops into remote tribal areas to control the border with Afghanistan and stem organized terrorist or other illegal cross-border activities. Meetings with Afghan and Coalition allies have taken place regularly to resolve periodic claims of boundary encroachments.

Sources: CIA World Factbook, 2008; the Library of Congress Country Profile: Pakistan, 2005; and the government of Pakistan

Appendix 3

CHRONOLOGY

The Land and Its Early History

45 million years ago	Deccan Plateau landmass and Eurasia join together
11 million years ago	Migration of animals to the subcontinent ends
1.5–5 million years ago	Extinction of numerous prehistoric species in the subcontinent
3,000,000–500,000 B.C.E.	Pre–Stone Age humans inhabit the Soan River area
300,000–150,000 B.C.E.	Stone Age settlements established in the Indus region
ca. 10,000 B.C.E.	Last ice age ends; grazing animals populate the Indus region
ca. 6500–5000 B.C.E.	Agriculture established in the Indus region
ca. 4000 B.C.E.	Dravidians appear in the Indus region
ca. 2600–1800 B.C.E.	Indus Valley Civilization
ca. 2000–1500 B.C.E.	Aryans appear in the Indus region

Inroads of Armies and Ideas

ca. 1000 B.C.E.	Aryans migrate from the Indus to the Ganges Valley
ca. 623	Birth of Siddhartha Gautama, founder of Buddhism
517 B.C.E.	Scylax, from Persia, explores the Indus River Valley
ca. 514 B.C.E.	Darius annexes Sindh and Punjab to Persia's Achaemenian Empire
480 B.C.E.	Troops from the Indus satrapy join Xerxes' invasion of Greece

Late 5th century B.C.E.	Mahapadma Nanda founds the Nine Nandas dynasty
326 B.C.E.	Alexander the Great begins conquest of the Indus Valley
305 B.C.E.	Mauryan kingdom defeats Seleucus I Nicator, Alexander's successor, ending Greek rule in the Indus Valley
ca. 185 B.C.E.	Greco-Bactrians establish the Bactrian kingdom
ca. 50 B.C.E.	Scythians, nomads from Central Asia, invade the Indus Valley
78 C.E.	The Kushans found the Gandhara civilization
ca. 320–335 C.E.	Chandragupta I founds the Gupta empire
ca. 450 C.E.	White Huns invade the Indus Valley region
Late 6th century C.E.	Rajput kingdoms begin to appear in the Indus Valley region

The Coming of Islam

665	Arab forces conquer Kabul, seat of the Afghan empire
699–700	General Qatayba bin Muslim mounts military campaigns in the Indus Valley region
700–1000	Kabul, Peshawar, and Swat settled by Afghan tribes
710	Sindi pirates seize Muslim ships, provoking an Arab invasion
714	Arab forces conquer Sind, giving Islam a path (*bab-al Islam,* or door of Islam) to the subcontinent
751	Arabs defeat Chinese at the Battle of Talas in 751, gaining control of Kashmir
843	Brahman minister Kallar founds the Hindu Shahi dynasty, making his capital on the Indus River
871	Yaqub given rule of Persia and Sind by the caliph in Baghdad
903–999	Samanid rule over the Indus Valley region
1001	Mahmud of Ghazni conquers Peshawar
1059–1115	The golden age of the Ghaznavids in what is now northern Pakistan

1173	Ghurids begin conquest of Gekkar and Ghaznavid kingdoms
1192	Muslims establish the Delhi Sultanate after the Second Battle of Tarain
1241	The Mongols conquer Lahore
1397	Timur invades the subcontinent to conquer all Mongol lands for Islam
ca. 1500	Independent Muslim kingdoms established in Multan, Gujarat, Malwa, Sind, and Khandesh
1503	Vasco da Gama establishes the first Portuguese factory on the subcontinent

The Mughal Period

1525	Babur defeats Lodi forces at the First Battle of Panipat and takes Delhi
1527	Babur defeats the Rajputs, winning control of the northern subcontinent
1540	Sher Khan Sur takes control of Delhi; proclaims himself Sher Shah Suri
1555	The Portuguese sack and burn Thatta
1556	Akbar proclaimed emperor of Hindustan
1600	London merchants form the East India Company
1601	Akbar's last campaign of conquest ends; Mughals control most of the subcontinent
1605	Jehangir assumes rule of the Mughal Empire
1618	Jahangir gives British permission to build a factory in Surat
1685	Mughals defeat a British naval force at Chittagong
1734	Shah Waliullah mounts Muslim reform movement to counter Hindu influence

Trading Company Wars

1757	British defeat the Mughals at the Battle of Plassey, beginning British rule in the subcontinent
1758–61	Third Carnatic War, involving the British, French, and Marathas
1759	Shah Abdali drives the Marathas from the Punjab

late 18th century	British gain a political interest in present-day Pakistan to counter growing Afghan power
1799	British reoccupy their trading post at Karachi
1804	Anti-British Faraizi movement for Islamic reform established in Bengal
1830	Britain institutes reform measures
1843	British annex Sind, Hyderabad, and Khairpur
1845–49	Sikh wars; British annex Punjab; Kashmir sold to Dogra dynasty
1857–58	First War of Independence, also known as Indian Mutiny or Sepoy Rebellion

The Raj Era

1858	East India Company dissolved; rule of subcontinent under British Crown (the British Raj) begins; end of the Mughal Empire
1861	Indian Councils Act passed
1864	Revolt in Punjab suppressed
1869	Karachi becomes major port with the completion of the Suez Canal
1873–74	Famine in Bengal and Bihar
1875	Muhammadan Anglo-Oriental (M.A.O.) College founded in Aligarh; British establish frontier trading post at Quetta
1877	Queen Victoria proclaimed empress of India
1878	Vernacular Press Act and Arms Act passed
1879	Statutory Civil Service established
1885	Indian National Congress (INC) formed
1905	Partition of Bengal
1906	All India Muslim League founded

The Road to Independence

1909	Morley-Minto Reforms establish separate electorates for Muslims
1911	Partition of Bengal annulled
1914	Aga Khan resigns Muslim League presidency as the league hardens anti-British stance
1916	Indian National Congress–Muslim League Pact (Lucknow Pact) signed
1918	Muslim League endorses Khilafat Movement

1919	Jallianwala Bagh Massacre, or Tragedy: British kill 379 Muslim protestors in Amritsar; Montagu-Chelmsford Reforms adopted
1924	Muslim League calls for federation of autonomous provinces to protect Muslim majority status in Punjab, Bengal, and NWFP.
1928	The All Parties Conference is held; Muslim and Hindu political organizations meet to draft a constitution
1935	Government of India Act of 1935 becomes law; the backbone of civil law in Pakistan
1940	Muslim League adopts Lahore Resolution, also known as Pakistan Resolution, demanding a separate state for Muslims of subcontinent; "Two Nation Theory" articulated by Muhammad Ali Jinnah
1946	Muslim League observes "Direct Action Day"; widespread communal rioting spreads across the subcontinent
1947	British parliament calls for independence and partition of subcontinent; mass movements of population begin, resulting in 250,000 deaths and up to 24 million refugees

The Challenges of Independence

1947	Partition of subcontinent; Pakistan incorporates East Bengal (East Pakistan); Muhammad Ali Jinnah becomes the first governor; first Indo-Pakistan war over Kashmir
1948	Jinnah dies; Prime Minister Liaquat Ali Khan assumes leadership
1949	United Nations arranges cease-fire between India and Pakistan
1950	Liaquat-Nehru Pact with India aims to ease sectarian violence
1951	Liaquat Ali Khan assassinated; Khawaja Nazimuddin named prime minister; Awami League formed in Bengal
1952	Protests sweep East Pakistan, opposing the designation of Urdu as the national language

1953	Governor General Ghulan Muhammad dismisses prime minister and cabinet
1954	Pakistan becomes member of the Southeast Asian Treaty Organization (SEATO)
1955	"One Unit" plan establishes the four provinces of West Pakistan as a single administrative unit
1956	A constitution is adopted; Iskander Mirza named president; National Assembly proclaims both Urdu and Bengal state languages
1958	Mirza abrogates constitution; martial law declared; Muslim League dissolved

Military Rule

1958	General Mohammed Ayub Khan assumes presidency; Mirza sent into exile
1959	Basic Democracies Order, curbing political and social freedoms, adopted
1960	Indus Water Treaty with India signed
1961	Work begins on a new capital city, Islamabad
1962	Constitution of 1962 consolidates presidential authority
1965	Second Indo-Pakistan war over Kashmir
1969	Martial law declared; Ayub Khan resigns; General Agha Mohammed Yahya Khan assumes presidency
1970	"One Unit" plan abolished
1971	Civil war between East and West Pakistan; Bangladesh gains independence; President Yahya Khan resigns, succeeded by Zulfikar Bhutto

Between East and West

1971	Government investigation ordered into Pakistan's civil war military defeat
1972	Simla Agreement, concluded with India, adjusts Line of Control in Kashmir; Zulfikar Bhutto nationalizes heavy industry and institutes land reforms
1973	New constitution adopted
1974	Pakistan formally recognizes Bangladesh

1976	Pakistan and Bangladesh establish diplomatic relations
1977	Disputed general election results cause widespread rioting and protest; Army general Mohammed Zia ul-Haq proclaims martial law
1978	Zia assumes presidency
1979	Islamic penal code introduced; Zulfikar Bhutto executed; Benazir Bhutto, his daughter, is held briefly by authorities after his execution.
1983	President Zia announces that martial law will be lifted in 1985
1985	Non-Islamic banking abolished; general elections held for National Assembly
1986	New federal cabinet sworn into office; martial law lifted; Benazir Bhutto returns to Pakistan
1987	President Zia dismisses government, dissolves national and provincial assemblies, and orders new elections
1988	President Zia and top army officials die in an airplane crash; Ghulam Ishaq named acting president

Civilian Rule Restored

1988	National Assembly elections; Benazir Bhutto becomes prime minister; Soviets withdraw from Afghanistan; Kashmir insurgency begins
1990	Benazir Bhutto dismissed by President Ghulam Ishaq Khan; Nawaz Sharif becomes prime minister
1991	Collapse of Bank of Credit and Commerce International (BCCI)
1993	Sharif and Ishaq Khan resign
1994	Benazir Bhutto becomes the prime minister
1996	Benazir Bhutto dismissed; the Taliban come to power in Afghanistan
1997	Nawaz Sharif becomes prime minister
1998	Pakistan conducts first nuclear weapon test
1999	Kargil conflict in Kashmir; Benazir Bhutto and husband convicted of corruption; Nawaz Sharif dismissed from office and placed under house arrest by General Pervez Musharraf

A Return to the World Stage

October 12, 1999	General Pervez Musharraf takes charge of Pakistan's government in a military coup; Nawaz Sharif convicted of corruption
2000	Nawaz Sharif pardoned and deported; Supreme Court validates Musharraf's coup; Musharraf assumes presidency
February 2001	Public display of weapons is banned
July 2001	Musharraf and Indian prime minister Atal Behari Vajpayee meet at Agra Summit to address Kashmir issue
September 19, 2001	Musharraf informs the nation that Pakistan will support the U.S. War on Terror
December 13, 2001	Pakistani terrorists attempt to attack the Indian parliament
February 2002	*Wall Street Journal* reporter Daniel Pearl abducted and murdered in Pakistan
August 2002	Legal Framework Order of 2002 adopted
March 2003	Khalid Shaikh Mohammed, the former head of al-Qaeda operations and linked to both the Ramzi Yousef and the Daniel Pearl murders, arrested in Pakistan
June 2004	Pakistani troops attack suspected al-Qaeda hideouts in the tribal area
November 2004	Pakistani scientist A. Q. Khan identified as providing assistance to Iran's nuclear program
February 2005	Pakistan and India agree to allow travel between the capitals of disputed Kashmir
March 2005	United States agrees to sell F-16 fighter planes to Pakistan
April 2005	Limited travel between Pakistan- and Indian-controlled Kashmir inaugurated
October 2005	An earthquake in North-West Frontier Province and Pakistan controlled Kashmir kills more than 79,000 and leaves more than 3.3 million families homeless
June 2006	Political opponents protest Musharraf's plan to stage a reelection
August 2007	The Supreme Court rules Nawaz Sharif can return from exile

September 2007	Nawaz Sharif returns to Pakistan and is immediately sent back to exile
October 2007	Benazir Bhutto returns to Pakistan
November 2007	Musharraf suspends judges and declares a state of emergency
December 2007	Benazir Bhutto assassinated in Rawalpindi
February 2008	The PPP and PML parties trounce Musharraf's supporters in national elections
April 2008	The government begins negotiations aimed at reaching an accord with Islamic militants
May 2008	The PML withdraws from the cabinet, unable to reach agreement with the PPP on the reinstatement of Pakistan's ousted judges
July 2008	U.S. president George W. Bush authorizes U.S. forces to conduct ground operations inside Pakistan without Pakistani government approval
August 2008	Pervez Musharraf resigns presidency under threat of impeachment
August 2008	PML(N) withdraws from Pakistan's ruling coalition
September 2008	Asif Ali Zardari, widower of Benazir Bhutto, elected president of Pakistan

APPENDIX 4

BIBLIOGRAPHY

Abbott, Freeland. *Islam and Pakistan*. Ithaca, N.Y.: Cornell University Press, 1968.

Abdulla, Ahmed. *The Historical Background of Pakistan and Its People*. Karachi: Tanzeem Publishers, 1973.

Afzal, M. Rafique. *Pakistan: History & Politics, 1947–1971*. Karachi and New York: Oxford University Press, 2001.

Ahmad, Kazi S. *A Geography of Pakistan*. Karachi: Oxford University Press, 1972.

Ahmad, Mushtaq. *Government and Politics in Pakistan*. Karachi: Pakistan Publishing House, 1959.

Ahmed, Akbar. *Jinnah, Pakistan and Islamic Identity: The Search for Saladin*. London and New York: Routledge, 1997.

Ahsan, Aitzaz. *The Indus Saga and the Making of Pakistan*. Karachi and New York: Oxford University Press, 1996.

Ali, Chaudhri Muhammad. *The Emergence of Pakistan*. New York: Columbia University Press, 1967.

Baille, Alexander Francis. *Kurracheee, Past, Present and Future*. Karachi: Oxford University Press, 1997.

Baxter, Craig, ed. *Pakistan on the Brink: Politics, Economics, and Society*. Lanham, Md.: Lexington Books, 2004.

Baxter, Craig, ed. *Zia's Pakistan: Politics and Stability in a Frontline State*. Boulder, Colo.: Westview Press, 1985.

Bhutto, Benazir. "A Conversation with Benazir Bhutto." In Council on Foreign Relations, August 15, 2007. Available online. URL: www.cfr.org/publication/14041/conversation-with-benazir-bhutto.html. Accessed May 2, 2008.

Bishai, Wilson B. *Islamic History of the Middle East: Backgrounds, Development, and Fall of the Arab Empire*. Boston: Allyn and Bacon, 1968.

Bolitho, Hector. *Jinnah, Creator of Pakistan*. New York: Macmillan, 1954.

Burke, S. M. *Pakistan's Foreign Policy: An Historical Analysis.* Karachi and New York: Oxford University Press, 1990.

Burki, Shahid Javed. *Pakistan under Bhutto, 1971–1977.* New York: St. Martin's Press, 1980.

Burki, Shahid Javed. *Pakistan under the Military: Eleven Years of Zia ul-Haq.* Boulder, Colo.: Westview Press; Lahore: Pak Book, 1991.

Callard, Keith. *Pakistan: A Political Study.* New York: Macmillan, 1957.

Caroe, Olaf Kirkpatrick. *The Pathans, 550* B.C.–A.D. *1957.* Karachi: Oxford University Press, 1958.

Cavaliero, Roderick. *Strangers in the Land: The Rise and Decline of the British Indian Empire.* London and New York: I. B. Taudis, 2002.

Choudhury, G. W. *Pakistan: Transition from Military to Civilian Rule.* Buckhurst Hill, Essex, England: Scorpion, 1988.

Christophe, Jaffrelot, ed. *A History of Pakistan and Its Origins.* London: Anthem Press, 2002.

Cohen, Stephen. *The Pakistan Army.* Karachi and New York: Oxford University Press, 1998.

Cunningham, Joseph Davy. *A History of the Sikhs: From the Origin of the Nation to the Battles of the Sutlej.* London and New York: Oxford University Press, 1918.

Diodorus Siculus. 12 vols. Loeb Classical Library. Trans. C. H. Oldfather. New York: G.P. Putnam and Sons, 1933–1967.

Draper, Alfred. *Amritsar: The Massacre That Ended the Raj.* London: Cassell, 1981.

Dunlop, D. M. *Arab Civilization to* A.D. *1500.* London: Longman, 1971.

Edwardes, S. M. *Mughal Rule in India.* New Delhi: Atlantic Publishers and Distributors, 1995.

Erndl, Kathleen M. *Victory to the Mother: The Hindu Goddess of Northwest India in Myth, Ritual, and Symbol.* New York: Oxford University Press, 1993.

Fox, Richard Gabriel. *Lions of the Punjab: Culture in the Making.* Berkeley. Calif.: University of California Press, 1985.

Fredunbeg, Mirza K., trans. *The Chachnamah: An Ancient History of Sind, Giving the Hindu Period Down to the Arab Conquest.* Karachi: The Commissioner's Press, 1900.

Friedman, Thomas L. *Longitudes and Attitudes: Exploring the World After September 11.* New York: Farrar, Straus & Giroux, 2002.

Gankovsky, Yu V. *The Peoples of Pakistan: An Ethnic History.* Moscow: Nauka Publishing House, 1971.

Gascoigne, Bamber. *The Great Moghuls.* New York: Harper & Row, 1971.

Gauhar, Altaf. *Ayub Khan: Pakistan's First Military Ruler.* Oxford and New York: Oxford University Press, 1996.

George, Linda S. *The Golden Age of Islam.* New York: Benchmark Books, 1998.

Gibb, H. A. R. *Islam.* Oxford: Oxford University Press, 1949.

Gilmartin, David. *Empire and Islam: Punjab and the Making of Pakistan.* Berkeley, Calif.: University of California Press, 1988.

Godolphin, Frances Richard Borroum, ed. *The Greek Historians. The Complete and Unabridged Historical Works of Herodotus.* New York: Random House, 1942.

Grare, Frederic. *Pakistan and the Afghan Conflict, 1979–1985.* Karachi: Oxford University Press, 2003.

Guillaume, Alfred, trans. *The Life of Muhammad: A Translation of Ishaq's Sirat Rasul Allah.* London and New York: Oxford University Press, 1955.

Haig, Malcom Robert. *The Indus Delta Country, a memoir, chiefly on the ancient geography and history,* originally published 1894. Karachi: Indus Publications, 1972.

Hardy, Peter. *The Muslims of British India.* London: Cambridge University Press, 1972.

Hasan, Ibn. *The Central Structure of the Mughal Empire and Its Practical Working up to the Year 1657.* London: Oxford University Press, 1936.

Hitti, Philip K. *History of the Arabs from the Earliest Times to the Present.* London: Macmillan, 1953.

Hitti, Phillip K. *The Origins of the Islamic State. Being a translation . . . of the Kitab Futuh al-Buldan of al-Imam abu-l 'Abbas Ahmad ibn-Jabir al Baldhuri.* Vol. 1. New York: Columbia University, 1916. Reprint. New York: AMS Press, 1968.

Hodgson, Marshall G. S. *The Venture of Islam.* 3 vols. Chicago: University of Chicago Press, 1974.

Hourani, Albert. *A History of the Arab Peoples.* London: Faber, 1992.

Hunter, W. W. *The Indian Musalmans.* 3d ed. Delhi: Indological Book House, 1969.

Hussain, J. *A History of the Peoples of Pakistan: Towards Independence.* Karachi and New York: Oxford University Press, 1997.

Hussain, Rizwan. *Pakistan and the Emergence of Islamic Militancy in Afghanistan.* Aldershot, Hampshire, England: Ashgate, 2005.

Ibu Hisham, Abd al-Malik. *The Life of Muhammad: A Translation of Ishaq's Sirat rasul Allah.* London: Oxford University Press, 1955.

Ide, Arthur Frederick, and Jacob Ronald Auliff. *Jihad, Mujahideen, Taliban, Osama bin Laden, George W. Bush & Oil: A Study in the*

Evolution of Terrorism and Islam. Garland, Tex.: Tangelwuld Press, 2002.

Ikram, S. M. *Muslim Civilization in India.* New York: Columbia University Press, 1964.

Imran, Ali. *The Punjab under Imperialism, 1885–1947.* Princeton, N.J.: Princeton University Press, 1988.

Irvine, William. *Later Mughals.* New Delhi: M.C. Oriental Books Reprint Corp., 1971.

Jacques, Kathryn. *Bangladesh, India and Pakistan: International Relations and Regional Tensions in South Asia.* New York: St. Martin's Press, 2000.

Jaina, Ema. *The Aligarh Movement: Its Origin and Development, 1858–1906.* Agra: Sri Ram Mehra, 1965.

Jalal, Ayesha. *The Sole Spokesman: Jinnah, the Muslim League, and the Demand for Pakistan.* Cambridge and New York: Cambridge University Press, 1985.

Jones, Owen Bennett. *Pakistan: Eye of the Storm.* New Haven, Conn.: Yale University Press, 2002.

Kamra, Sukeshi. *Bearing Witness: Partition, Independence, End of the Raj.* Calgary: University of Calgary Press, 2002.

Kaur, Amarjit. *The Punjab Story.* New Delhi: Roli Books International, 1984.

Kennedy, Hugh, ed. *An Historical Atlas of Islam.* Leiden and Boston: Brill, 2002.

Kerry, John, and Hank Brown. *The BCCI Affair.* Report prepared for the Senate Committee on Foreign Relations, 102d Cong., 2d sess. 1992. Committee Print 102–140.

Khan, Ayub Mohammad. *Friends Not Masters: A Political Autobiography.* New York: Oxford University Press, 1967.

Khan, Mazhar Ali. *Pakistan, the Barren Years.* Oxford: Oxford University Press, 1998.

Khan, Mazhar Ali. *Pakistan, the First Twelve Years.* Oxford: Oxford University Press, 1996.

Khan, Muqeem Fazal. *The Story of the Pakistan Army.* Karachi: Oxford University Press, 1963.

Khan, Roedad. *Pakistan: A Dream Gone Sour.* Karachi and New York: Oxford University Press, 1997.

Khilnani, N. M. *British Power in the Punjab, 1839–1858.* New York: Asia Publishing House, 1972.

Kukreja, Veena, ed. *Pakistan: Democracy, Development, and Security Issues.* New Delhi and Thousand Oaks: Sage Publications, 2005.

Lal, Ruby. *Domesticity and Power in the Early Mughal World.* Cambridge: Cambridge University Press, 2005.

Lane-Poole, Stanley. Mediaeval India under Mohammedan Rule, A.D. 712–1764. New York: Kraus Reprint, 1970.

Lari, Subhail Zaheer. *A History of Sindh.* Karachi and New York: Oxford University Press, 1994.

Lelyveld, David. *Aligarh's First Generation: Muslim Solidarity in British India.* Princeton, N.J.: Princeton University Press, 1978.

Mahmood, Safdar. *Pakistan: Political Roots and Development, 1947–1999.* Karachi and Oxford: Oxford University Press, 2000.

Mahmud, S. F. *A Concise History of Indo-Pakistan.* Karachi and New York: Oxford University Press, 1988.

Majumdar, Ramesh C., H. C. Raychaudhuri, and Kalikinkar Datta. *An Advanced History of India.* New York: St. Martin's Press, 1967.

Malik, Hafeez, ed. *Pakistan: Founders' Aspirations and Today's Realities.* Oxford: Oxford University Press, 2001.

Malik, Zahir Uddin. *The Reign of Muhammad Shah, 1719–1748.* New York: Asia Publishing House, 1977.

Masson, Charles. *Narrative of Various Journeys in Balochistan, Afghanistan, the Panjab.* Karachi and New York: Oxford University Press, 1974–1977.

Minault, Gail. *The Khilafat Movement: Religious Symbolism and Political Mobilization in India.* New York: Columbia University Press, 1982.

Moore, R. J. *The Crisis of Indian Unity, 1917–1940.* Oxford: Clarendon Press, 1974.

Pervez Musharraf. "Address to the Nation, October 17, 1999." Available online. URL: www.pak.gov.pk/public/president-address-19-09-01.htm. Posted on September 19, 2001.

Niemeijer, A. C. *The Khilafat Movement in India, 1919–1924.* The Hague: Nijhoff, 1972.

Nightingale, Pamela. *Trade and Empire in Western India, 1784–1806.* Cambridge: Cambridge University Press, 1970.

Noman, Omar. *Pakistan: A Political and Economic History since 1947.* London and New York: Kegan Paul International, 1990.

O'Brien, Patrick K., ed. *Oxford Atlas of World History.* New York: Oxford University Press, 1999.

Paustian, Paul William. *Canal Irrigation in the Punjab.* New York: Columbia University Press, 1930.

Payne, Charles H. *A Short History of the Sikhs.* 2d ed. Punjab: Patiala Dept. of Language, 1970.

Rahman, B. "A.Q. Khan: The Ghost That Continues to Haunt." Paper 1196. South Asia Analysis Group. December 21, 2004.

Rapson, E. J., ed. *Cambridge History of India*. Vol. 1. Delhi: S. Chand, 1963–1968.

Raza, Rafi, ed. *Pakistan in Perspective, 1947–1997*. Karachi: Oxford University Press, 1997.

Reid, C. Lestock. *Commerce and Conquest: The Story of the Honourable East India Company*. London: C.J. Temple, 1947.

Richards, John F. *The Mughal Empire*. Cambridge and New York: Cambridge University Press, 1993.

Scarre, Christopher, ed. *Past Worlds: The Times Atlas of Archaeology*. Maplewood, N.J.: Hammond, 1988.

Schwartz, Stephen. *The Two Faces of Islam: The House of Sa'ud from Tradition to Terror*. New York: Doubleday, 2002.

Singh, Khushwant. *A History of the Sikhs*. Princeton, N.J.: Princeton University Press, 1963–1966.

Singhal, Damodar P. *Pakistan*. Englewood Cliffs, N.J.: Prentice Hall, 1972.

Smith, Vincent Arthur. *Akbar, the Great Mogul, 1542–1605*. Delhi: S. Chand, 1966.

Smith, Vincent Arthur. *Oxford History of India*. 3d ed. Oxford: Clarendon Press, 1958.

Spears, Thomas George Percival. *Twilight of the Mughuls: Studies in Late Mughul Delhi*. Karachi: Oxford University Press, 1973.

Stephens, Ian Melville. *Pakistan*. 3d ed. New York: F.A. Praeger, 1967.

Subrahmanyam, Sanjay. *Mughals and Franks: Explorations in Connected History*. New Delhi and New York: Oxford University Press, 2005.

Sud, Hari. "Pakistan: Why Is Musharraf Smiling These Days?" South Asia Analysis Group. Available online. URL: http://www.southasia analysis.org/papers12/paper1188.html. Accessed June 6, 2008.

Symonds, Richard. *The Making of Pakistan*. London: Faber and Faber, 1950.

Talbot, Ian. *Pakistan: A Modern History*. New York: St. Martin's Press, 1998.

Talbot, Ian, and Gurharpal Singh. *Region and Partition: Bengal, Punjab and the Partition of the Subcontinent*. Oxford and New York: Oxford University Press, 1999.

Thackston, Wheeler, ed. *Babur, Emperor of Hindustan, 1483–1530*. Washington, D.C.: Smithsonian Institution, 1996.

Thackston, Wheeler, ed. *Jahangir, Emperor of Hindustan, 1569–1627*. Washington, D.C.: Smithsonian Institution, 1999.

United Nations Statistic Division (STAT). *Women in Pakistan: A Country Profile—Statistical Profiles No. 8, 1997.* New York, 1997.

U.S. Congress. Senate. Hearing on Pakistan & India: Steps Toward Rapprochement. Committee on Foreign Relations. 108th Cong., 2d sess., 2004. Washington, D.C.: U.S. Government Printing Office, 2004.

Weeks, Richard. *Pakistan: Birth and Growth of a Muslim Nation.* Princeton, N.J.: Van Nostrand, 1964.

Weinbaum, Marvin G. *Pakistan and Afghanistan: Resistance and Reconstruction.* Boulder, Colo.: Westview Press, 1994.

Weiss, Anita M., ed. *Islamic Reassertion in Pakistan: The Application of Islamic Laws in a Modern State.* Syracuse, N.Y.: Syracuse University Press, 1986.

Wells, Ian. *Jinnah: Ambassador of Hindu-Muslim Politics.* London and New York: Seagull, 2005.

Wheeler, Richard S. *The Politics of Pakistan: A Constitutional Quest.* Ithaca, N.Y.: Cornell University Press, 1970.

Wilber, Donald Newton. *Pakistan: Its People, Its Society, Its Culture.* New Haven, Conn.: HRAF Press, 1964.

Wilbur, Marguerite Knowlton. *The East India Company and the British Empire in the Far East.* Stanford, Calif.: Stanford University Press, 1945.

Wolpert, Stanley. *Jinnah of Pakistan.* New York: Oxford University Press, 1984.

Wolpert, Stanley. *Zulfi Bhutto of Pakistan: His Life and Times.* New York: Oxford University Press, 1993.

Ziring, Lawrence. *The Ayub Khan Era: Politics in Pakistan, 1958–1969.* Syracuse, N.Y.: Syracuse University Press, 1971.

Ziring, Lawrence. *Pakistan in the Twentieth Century: A Political History.* Karachi and New York: Oxford University Press, 1997.

Appendix 5

Suggested Reading

The Land and Its Early History

Ahmad, Kazi S. *A Geography of Pakistan*. Karachi: Oxford University Press, 1972.

Gankovsky, Yu V. *The Peoples of Pakistan: An Ethnic History*. Moscow: Nauka Publishing House, 1971.

Hussain, J. *A History of the Peoples of Pakistan: Towards Independence*. Karachi and New York: Oxford University Press, 1997.

Mahmud, S. F. *A Concise History of Indo-Pakistan*. Karachi and New York: Oxford University Press, 1988.

Majumdar, Ramesh C., H. C. Raychaudhuri, and Kalikinkar Datta. *An Advanced History of India*. New York: St. Martin's Press, 1967.

Rapson, E. J., ed. *Cambridge History of India*. Vol. 1. Delhi: S. Chand, 1963–1968.

Scarre, Christopher, ed. *Past Worlds: The Times Atlas of Archaeology*. Maplewood, N.J.: Hammond, 1988.

Inroads of Armies and Ideas (500 B.C.E.–700 C.E.)

Caroe, Olaf Kirkpatrick. *The Pathans, 550 B.C.–A.D. 1957*. Karachi: Oxford University Press, 1958.

Gankovsky, Yu V. *The Peoples of Pakistan: An Ethnic History*. Moscow: Nauka Publishing House, 1971.

Mahmud, S. F. *A Concise History of Indo-Pakistan*. Karachi and New York: Oxford University Press, 1988.

O'Brien, Patrick K., ed. *Oxford Atlas of World History*. New York: Oxford University Press, 1999.

Smith, Vincent Arthur. *Oxford History of India*. 3d ed. Oxford: Clarendon Press, 1958.

The Coming of Islam (700–1526)

Abbott, Freeland. *Islam and Pakistan.* Ithaca, N.Y.: Cornell University Press, 1968.

Bishai, Wilson B. *Islamic History of the Middle East: Backgrounds, Development, and Fall of the Arab Empire.* Boston: Allyn and Bacon, 1968.

Dunlop, D. M. *Arab Civilization to AD 1500.* London: Longman, 1971.

Hussain, J. *A History of the Peoples of Pakistan: Towards Independence.* Karachi and New York: Oxford University Press, 1997.

Ikram, S. M. *Muslim Civilization in India.* New York: Columbia University Press, 1964.

The Mughal Period (1526–1748)

Edwardes, S. M. *Mughal Rule in India.* New Delhi: Atlantic Publishers and Distributors, 1995.

Gascoigne, Bamber. *The Great Moghuls.* New York: Harper & Row, 1971.

Richards, John F. *The Mughal Empire.* Cambridge and New York: Cambridge University Press, 1993.

Spears, Thomas George Percival. *Twilight of the Mughuls: Studies in Late Mughul Delhi.* Karachi: Oxford University Press, 1973.

Trading Company Wars (1748–1858)

Cavaliero, Roderick. *Strangers in the Land: The Rise and Decline of the British Indian Empire.* London and New York: I. B. Taudis, 2002.

Hardy, Peter. *The Muslims of British India.* London: Cambridge University Press, 1972.

Hussain, J. *A History of the Peoples of Pakistan: Towards Independence.* Karachi and New York: Oxford University Press, 1997.

Mahmud, S. F. *A Concise History of Indo-Pakistan.* Karachi and New York: Oxford University Press, 1988.

Wilbur, Marguerite Knowlton. *The East India Company and the British Empire in the Far East.* Stanford, Calif.: Stanford University Press, 1945.

The Raj Era (1858–1909)

Ahsan, Aitzaz. *The Indus Saga and the Making of Pakistan.* Karachi and New York: Oxford University Press, 1996.

Jaina, Ema. *The Aligarh Movement: Its Origin and Development, 1858–1906.* Agra: Sri Ram Mehra, 1965.

Kamra, Sukeshi. *Bearing Witness: Partition, Independence, End of the Raj.* Calgary: University of Calgary Press, 2002.

Mahmud, S. F. *A Concise History of Indo-Pakistan.* Karachi and New York: Oxford University Press, 1988.

Stephens, Ian Melville. *Pakistan.* 3d ed. New York: F.A. Praeger, 1967.

Symonds, Richard. *The Making of Pakistan.* London: Faber and Faber, 1950.

The Road to Independence (1909–1947)

Ali, Chaudhri Muhammad. *The Emergence of Pakistan.* New York: Columbia University Press, 1967.

Gilmartin, David. *Empire and Islam: Punjab and the Making of Pakistan.* Berkeley: University of California Press, 1988.

Hardy, Peter. *The Muslims of British India.* London: Cambridge University Press, 1972.

Jalal, Ayesha. *The Sole Spokesman: Jinnah, the Muslim League, and the Demand for Pakistan.* Cambridge and New York: Cambridge University Press, 1985.

Lelyveld, David. *Aligarh's First Generation: Muslim Solidarity in British India.* Princeton, N.J.: Princeton University Press, 1978.

Minault, Gail. *The Khilafat Movement: Religious Symbolism and Political Mobilization in India.* New York: Columbia University Press, 1982.

Moore, R. J. *The Crisis of Indian Unity, 1917–1940.* Oxford: Clarendon Press, 1974.

Wolpert, Stanley. *Jinnah of Pakistan.* New York: Oxford University Press, 1984.

The Challenges of Independence (1947–1958)

Afzal, M. Rafique. *Pakistan: History & Politics, 1947–1971.* Karachi and New York: Oxford University Press, 2001.

Ahmad, Mushtaq. *Government and Politics in Pakistan.* Karachi: Pakistan Publishing House, 1959.

Christophe, Jaffrelot, ed. *A History of Pakistan and Its Origins.* London: Anthem Press, 2002.

Hussain, J. *A History of the Peoples of Pakistan: Towards Independence.* Karachi and New York: Oxford University Press, 1997.

Mahmood, Safdar. *Pakistan: Political Roots and Development, 1947–1999.* Karachi and Oxford: Oxford University Press, 2000.

Wheeler, Richard S. *The Politics of Pakistan: A Constitutional Quest.* Ithaca, N.Y.: Cornell University Press, 1970.

Military Rule (1958–1971)

Christophe, Jaffrelot, ed. *A History of Pakistan and Its Origins.* London: Anthem Press, 2002.

Gauhar, Altaf. *Ayub Khan: Pakistan's First Military Ruler.* Oxford and New York: Oxford University Press, 1996.

Khan, Ayub Mohammad. *Friends Not Masters: A Political Autobiography.* New York: Oxford University Press, 1967.

Ziring, Lawrence. *The Ayub Khan Era: Politics in Pakistan, 1958–1969.* Syracuse, N.Y.: Syracuse University Press, 1971.

Between East and West (1971–1988)

Baxter, Craig, ed. *Zia's Pakistan: Politics and Stability in a Frontline State.* Boulder, Colo.: Westview Press, 1985.

Burki, Shahid Javed. *Pakistan under Bhutto, 1971–1977.* New York: St. Martin's Press, 1980.

Choudhury, G. W. *Pakistan: Transition from Military to Civilian Rule.* Buckhurst Hill, Essex, England: Scorpion, 1988.

Jacques, Kathryn. *Bangladesh, India and Pakistan: International Relations and Regional Tensions in South Asia.* New York: St. Martin's Press, 2000.

Noman, Omar. *Pakistan: A Political and Economic History since 1947.* London and New York: Kegan Paul International, 1990.

Civilian Rule Restored (1988–1999)

Kukreja, Veena, ed. *Pakistan: Democracy, Development, and Security Issues.* New Delhi and Thousand Oaks: Sage Publications, 2005.

Kux, Dennis. "Pakistan: Flawed Not Failed State." *Foreign Policy Association Headline Series* 332 (Summer 2001): 76.

Mahmood, Safdar. *Pakistan: Political Roots and Development, 1947–1999.* Karachi and Oxford: Oxford University Press, 2000.

Malik, Hafeez, ed. *Pakistan: Founders' Aspirations and Today's Realities.* Oxford: Oxford University Press, 2001.

Peterson Institute for International Economics. Case Studies in Sanctions and Terrorism: Case 79-2, U.S. v. Pakistan, 1979– : Nuclear Missile Proliferation, 2007. Available online. URL: http://www.iie.com/research/topics/sanctions/pakistan.cfm. Accessed May 3, 2008.

Raza, Rafi, ed. *Pakistan in Perspective, 1947–1997.* Karachi: Oxford University Press, 1997.

Talbot, Ian. *Pakistan: A Modern History.* New York: St. Martin's Press, 1998.

Talbott, Strobe. *Engaging India: Diplomacy, Democracy, and the Bomb.* Washington, D.C.: Brookings Institution Press, 2004.

A Return to the World Stage (1999–2008)

Friedman, Thomas L. *Longitudes and Attitudes: Exploring the World After September 11.* New York: Farrar, Straus & Giroux, 2002.

Hussain, Rizwan. *Pakistan and the Emergence of Islamic Militancy in Afghanistan.* Aldershot, Hampshire, England: Ashgate, 2005.

Ide, Arthur Frederick, and Jacob Ronald Auliff. *Jihad, Mujahideen, Taliban, Osama bin Laden, George W. Bush & Oil: A Study in the Evolution of Terrorism and Islam.* Garland, Tex.: Tangelwuld Press, 2002.

Jones, Owen Bennett. *Pakistan: Eye of the Storm.* New Haven, Conn.: Yale University Press, 2002.

Kukreja, Veena, ed. *Pakistan: Democracy, Development, and Security Issues.* New Delhi and Thousand Oaks: Sage Publications, 2005.

Musharraf, Pervez. *In the Line of Fire: A Memoir.* New York and London: Free Press, 2006.

INDEX

Boldface page numbers indicate primary discussion of a topic. Page numbers in *italic* indicate illustrations. The letters *c*, *g*, *m*, and *t* indicate chronology, glossary, maps, and tables, respectively.

A

Abbasids **49–51**, 60
Abd al-Malik ibn Marwan, Caliph 45
Abdullah Bhatti 83, 84
Abdur Rahman Khan 129, 132
Achaemenian Empire **24–25**
Adina Beg Khan 98
Ibn Adi, Suhuail 43
administration. *See also* civil service
  British 103, 119–120, 122, 123
  Mauryan empire 30
  Mughal Empire 67, 80
  post-independence 162
administrators, British. *See* governors, British
Afghanistan
  Anglo-Afghan wars 110–111, 128–129, 143–144
  Bactrian kingdom 31
  borders 2, 6, 132–133
  British in 110–111, 123
  civil war and guns 237–239
  Durrani Empire 98–99, 104
  Ghaznavid kingdom 53–55
  Ghurid kingdom 56
  Kushan empire 34
  militants from 265–266
  Mughal Empire 74
  Muslim immigration to 143
  Pakistan relations 163–164, 243, 258–259
  Pakistan's Inter-Service Intelligence operations in 219, 220, 279
  railways 124–125
  Russian expansion 127–128
  Soviet invasion 218–220, 228–229
  Timurids 69
  U.S. war in 259–260
Afghan tribes 45
  conversion to Islam 54
  entering Pakistan 61, 292c
  officers in Delhi Sultanate 61, 62
  Sher Shah Sur and 74
Afridi tribe 82, 133

Aga Khan III (Ismaili Muslim leader) 136, 140, 294c
Agra 73, 79, 86
agriculture. *See also* land tenure
  Baluchistan 12
  British taxes on 104
  government department of 125
  Mughal economics 79
  Neolithic history 14, 291c
  Punjab 8
  reforms in 133–134
  Sind 10
Ahmadiyyas **174–175**, 208, 282g
Ahmad Khan, Sir Sayyid **124**, 125, 130, 132
Ahmadnagar Sultanate 85, 86
Ahmad Shah Durrani 98, **99–100**
Ahmed Shah Abdali 93
Ahmedzai tribe 91
Aibak, Qutb-ud-Din 57
Akali Dal party 154
Akbar 74, 76, 77–**83**, 78, 293c
Akbar Khan 172
Ala Singh 99
Ala-ud-Din Khalji 62, 63
Ala-ud-Din Muhammad II 57, 60
Alexander the Great 10, 11, **25–29**, 26m, 292c
Ali ibn Abu Talib, Caliph 43
Ali, Liaquat. *See* Liaquat Ali Khan
Alliance for the Restoration of Democracy 261, 266
alliances
  Baghdad Pact 176–177
  SEATO 176, 205
All India Muslim League. *See* Muslim League
All Parties Conference 145
Al-Mamun, Caliph Abdullah 50
Amandpur 90
Amanullah Khan 144
ambassadors
  British to Mughal court 85
  Pakistani to UN 258
  Pakistani to U.S. 175, 178
  U.S. to Pakistan 223, 226

Amir Khusro 62–63
Amritsar 98, 107–108, 109
Anglo-Afghan War, Second **128–129**
Anglo-Afghan War, Third **143–144**
Anglo-Sikh Wars **111–112**
Ansari, Bayazid 82
Appolodidus 31
Arab conquests **42–48**, 44m, 292c
Arabian Sea 2
Arabic language 112, 124, 216
archaeological sites
  Dravidians 14–15
  Indus Valley 15–16, *16*
  Neolithic 14
  Paleolithic 13–14
  preservation of 134
  in Sind 10
architecture
  Indus Valley Civilization 15
  mausoleums 8
  Mughal Empire 77, 85
Arghun, Shah Beg 71
aristocrats and nobles
  under British 103, 112, 120, 122, 127
  Mughal Empire 71, 73, 81, 90
  Punjab rulers 106
arjak 282g
Arjan Dev, Guru 84
army. *See* military
army chief of staff 213, 250, 256, 267, 275, 276
arts
  Bactrian kingdom 31
  Delhi Sultanate 62
  Gandhara 31, 32, 34–35
  Gupta empire 36
  Indus Valley Civilization 16
  Lahore 56
  Mughal 8–9, 77, 83, 84
Aryans 12, **19–21**, 282g, 291c
Asaf Jah II 104
Ashoka (third king of the Mauryan empire in India) **30–31**
Assam 135, 158